The Culture of Calamity

THE CULTURE OF
Calamity

DISASTER AND THE
MAKING OF MODERN AMERICA

Kevin Rozario

THE UNIVERSITY OF CHICAGO PRESS

Chicago and London

KEVIN ROZARIO is assistant professor in the
American Studies Program at Smith College.

The University of Chicago Press, Chicago 60637
The University of Chicago Press, Ltd., London
© 2007 by Kevin Rozario
All rights reserved. Published 2007
Printed in the United States of America

16 15 14 13 12 11 10 09 08 07   1 2 3 4 5
ISBN-13: 978-0-226-72570-3 (cloth)
ISBN-10: 0-226-72570-7 (cloth)

Library of Congress Cataloging-in-Publication Data
Rozario, Kevin.
The culture of calamity : disaster and the making of modern America / Kevin Rozario.
p. cm.
Includes bibliographical references and index.
ISBN-13: 978-0-226-72570-3 (cloth : alk. paper)
ISBN-10: 0-226-72570-7 (cloth : alk. paper)
1. Disasters—United States—History. 2. Disasters—Social aspects—United States—
History. 3. Disasters—United States—Psychological aspects—History. 4. National
characteristics, American. 5. United States—Civilization. 6. United States—Social
conditions. 7. United States—History—Anecdotes.   I. Title.
E179.R9 2007
973—dc22
2006034202

Contents

Acknowledgments

This project has occasioned many jokes of the "your book must be a real disaster" variety. It would have been much more of a disaster without the advice and guidance of many friends, colleagues, and teachers. And it might not have appeared at all without generous support from educational institutions and foundations.

I would like to thank the National Endowment for the Humanities, the Picker Foundation at Smith College, the Chace Foundation, the Andrew Mellon Foundation, the Enders Foundation at Wellesley College, and the Sterling Foundation at Yale University for awarding me fellowships that funded key research trips and "writing vacations." I am also grateful to Smith College for the generous sabbatical policy that gave me the time to complete the manuscript, as well as for the liberal provision of funds to pay for research assistance, conference appearances, and visits to key archives. This project has taken me to many libraries. I am particularly grateful for the help offered by librarians at the Chicago Historical Society, the Newberry Library in Chicago, the San Francisco Public Library, the Bancroft Library at UC Berkeley, the California Historical Society, the American Antiquarian Society in Worcester, Massachusetts, the Houghton Library at Harvard University, the Sterling, Mudd, and Beinecke Libraries at Yale University, the Sophia Smith Collection at Smith College, the Johnstown Flood Museum in Johnstown, Pennsylvania, and the Aspinock Historical Society in Putnam, Connecticut (where local historian Bob Miller took me on a tour of Putnam and spent several hours answering questions about the great flood of 1955). Thanks also to Elizabeth Guertin and Molly Shea, excellent research assistants at Wellesley and Smith who tracked down key documents and images for this book.

One of my oldest and deepest debts is to Iain Smith, mentor and friend since my days as a student at the University of Warwick, who, through his teaching and his example, first filled me with the ambition to become a scholar. He and William Dusinberre, my undergraduate academic adviser, helped me develop the academic skills and contacts that carried me to graduate school, where this book first sprang to life as a PhD thesis in the history department at Yale University. My dissertation committee was at once supportive, exacting, and inspiring. My committee chair, William J. Cronon, provided early encouragement for an ambitious project. Both through his example as a superb innovator and stylist and through his careful readings of my work, he encouraged me to ask big questions, to seek sweeping syntheses, and to write with verve and vividness. Jon Butler provided the encouragement that led me to believe that I might make a career as an academic. Ann Fabian encouraged me to go cultural, convincing me of the possibilities of a broad interdisciplinary study of disasters. And Jean-Christophe Agnew offered a valuable commentary on my introduction.

It was my good fortune to share an apartment in New Haven with two friends who turned out to be excellent historians and perceptive critics. Todd DePastino read my earliest drafts and helped me to clarify my arguments and stay focused on my main themes. A vigorous critic and an elegant writer, he helped me discipline my thinking whenever I rambled too far from my subject; the finished product is much tighter as a result. Lane Hall-Witt has been a font of penetrating questions and ideas, many of which I have borrowed and remodeled here. His trenchant and imaginative written commentaries on various chapters have been brilliant essays in their own right. This is a much more philosophical work because of his interventions and promptings. Many thanks also to Louis Warren for heightening my appreciation of the power of scholarship to speak to the concerns of our time.

At Smith College I have benefited from the counsel and wisdom of many friends and colleagues, especially from two directors of the American Studies program, Dan Horowitz and Rick Millington. Dan, a prizewinning mentor, shepherded me through my early scholarly career and carefully read and commented wisely on nearly all of the manuscript. Rick also has been both an extremely supportive senior colleague and friend and a highly perceptive reader who has helped me to understand my "own" work so much better. The American Studies program is a

remarkably congenial space within which to think and write; the friend-
ship, support, and scholarly example of my colleagues have encouraged
me to range across disciplinary borders and to trespass into fields of
knowledge outside of my primary area of expertise in search of a broad
synthesis of the American experience. I particularly want to thank the
members of my faculty cohort in the program—Floyd Cheung, Alex
Keller, Marc Steinberg, Michael Thurston, Steve Waksman, and Frazer
Ward—and my coteachers of the introductory course for our major:
Rosetta Cohen, Alice Hearst, and Helen Lefkowitz Horowitz.

Writing this book has imposed upon me an alternating pattern of
withdrawal into isolated contemplation and association with other
scholars. I am grateful for the many opportunities I have had to present
work in progress over the past decade. I learned much from audiences
at MIT (especially from my hosts Larry Vale and Thomas Campanella),
the Center for 21st Century Studies in Milwaukee, Middlebury College, Oberlin College, Wellesley College, and Amherst College. I am
also grateful to audiences and copanelists for feedback at the American
Studies Association in Houston, the Marxism 2000 Conference at the
University of Massachusetts at Amherst, a meeting of the Five College
History Group at Amherst College, the Historiographic Currents Conference at the University of West Virginia, the Futures of American
Studies Institute at Dartmouth College, the International Narrative
Conference at the University of Florida in Gainesville, and the confer-
ence of the Popular Culture Association in Worcester, Massachusetts.
One other public space that deserves mention is Northampton Coffee,
the stimulating and inviting venue in which a good deal of the book was
written.

Thanks also to Steven Biel, who included an earlier version of chapter 2 in his collection *American Disasters* (New York: New York University Press, 2002) under the title "What Comes Down Must Go Up: Why
Disasters Have Been Good for American Capitalism."

I feel very fortunate to have had the opportunity to work with the editorial staff at the University of Chicago Press. I could not imagine a better
editor than Doug Mitchell; he grasped and enthusiastically supported my
project from the moment I pitched it to him. Tim McGovern and Ruth
Goring worked tirelessly and skillfully, turning a manuscript into a book.
John Raymond was an extraordinarily thorough and efficient copyeditor.
The outside reviewers provided valuable recommendations about the argument and presentation of the book. Max Page, in particular, offered
an especially detailed and searching critique that helped me identify the
book's core concerns and saved me from some intellectual overreaching.

It is to my family that I owe the deepest debt of all. My mother, Moya; my father, Rex; my sister, Michelle; and my stepfather, Derek, all supported me and kept me grounded as I navigated my way through the surpassing strangeness of an academic career. They gave me the confidence, courage, and cash that enabled me to embark on this project; their disbelief that it could take so long to write a book also pushed me to declare this work finished and send it off to publishers. They were ably assisted in bringing this book to a close by my two daughters, Anya and Amara, who demanded (and deserved) so much of my time that further procrastination was no longer an option. I first saw a sonogram of Anya, my eldest, shortly before the attacks of September 11, 2001, and the events of that day and the ensuing "age of terrorism" have cast a long shadow over this book. My sense of the vulnerability of my daughters, as well as the opportunities the modern world presents them, has kept me mindful that my book is no mere play of words but involved in the stuff of life itself. In closing, I would like to thank my wife and life-partner, Ambreen Hai. Not only has she been my closest friend and companion, she brought her formidable literary and philosophical skills to close critical readings of my chapters. I dedicate this book to her, and to my family, with love.

Introduction

Only a catastrophe gets our attention. We want them, we need them, we depend
on them, as long as they happen somewhere else.
    DON DELILLO, *White Noise*

In his remarkable 1985 novel *White Noise*, Don DeLillo stages a primal
scene of the electronic age. A postnuclear family—two adults and an
assortment of children from previous marriages, an endearingly dys-
functional Brady Bunch—is gathered together on a Friday night, eating
Chinese takeout, watching TV. All eyes are riveted on the screen, taking in image after image of "floods, earthquakes, mud slides, erupting
volcanoes."[1] The scene is familiar enough, but there is something arresting about the enthusiasm of these media consumers for all things
catastrophic: "Every disaster made us wish for more, for something
bigger, grander, more sweeping." So narrates Professor Jack Gladney,
matter-of-factly describing his family's response to the evening's entertainment. But the experience weighs on him, and by the next day he
is looking to his university colleagues for explanations. "Why is it," he
asks, "that decent, well-meaning and responsible people find themselves
intrigued by catastrophe when they see it on television?"

This is a good question. If the content of movies, video games, and
network news reports is any indication, we live in a culture of calamity. It
sometimes seems that we can't turn on our televisions without encountering dramatic images of destruction: a hurricane battering a southern

1

resort; a sea of fire engulfing a national forest; a great river breaking through its levees and rolling over the surrounding countryside; a tower of glass and steel bursting into flames and crumbling to the city streets below. Why are these images ubiquitous? What makes disasters so fascinating, so thrilling, so involving? *White Noise*, to the extent that it is a story about a disaster, "an airborne toxic event," is a symptom of the culture of calamity. It also offers a diagnosis. Troubled by the inevitability of death, haunted by postnuclear anxieties about impending technological and environmental annihilation, the novel presents our interest in disasters as an expression of existential anxiety, as an entirely natural response to the prospect of personal and collective obliteration. More remarkable, however, are those passages that attend to the claims of culture, insisting on the intensified attraction of images of calamity in a mass media society. "Only a catastrophe gets our attention," Gladney is assured by a professor of popular culture, Alfonse Stompanato. "We want them, we need them, we depend on them." This is an extraordinary assertion, but one that deserves to be taken seriously. DeLillo properly places disasters at the center of contemporary fields of desire, gesturing at a theory of attention for the postmodern age. Of course, it is necessary to be precise about the subject of Stompanato's statement. Who, exactly, needs disasters? In one sense everybody, or nearly everybody. The culture of calamity reveals a general psychological addiction to images and stories of disaster in our society, though this varies in significant ways across registers of class, gender, and race. There is also a decisive structural or ideological component to the American dependency on disasters. After all, dominant political and economic systems have long relied for their authority and legitimacy on the presence or threat of calamities and other crises. We must consider the development of both of these forms of dependency if we are to fathom the power and place of calamity in American culture.

In this book I offer an analytical history that traces and analyzes the evolution of American ways of managing and imagining disasters between the seventeenth century and the present. I take notice of the political, economic, and environmental dimensions of this story even as I endeavor to track down the cultural meanings that Americans have attached to natural disasters (fires, floods, hurricanes) and to sudden catastrophes that share many properties with natural disasters (nuclear hazards, terrorist attacks). Seeking to detail changing responses to calamity, I have consulted relief records, legislative transcripts, economic data, private papers, newspapers, letters, memoirs, diaries, sermons, philosophical treatises, poems, novels, photographs, movies, and television footage. The sheer volume and intensity of this material (collected in local and national archives across the country) convinces me that disasters have been, and continue to be, occasions for extraordinary cultural production. Disasters have made history. It is clear from this documentation that critics working at that uncommonly productive junction of Marxist and postmodern theory (David Harvey, Marshall Berman, Edward Soja, Frederic Jameson, Michel Foucault, to name a few) are not the only ones who have grasped the peculiar prominence and resonance of disasters in the world that capitalism has made.[2] It is our lot, our predicament, and possibly our fortune to possess a crisis-oriented imagination.

My own research persuades me that disasters, and discourses of disaster, have played a long and influential role in the construction of American identities, power relations, economic systems, and environmental practices. It is conventional, and by no means inappropriate, to think of disasters in strictly negative terms, but calamities have also often presented opportunities. The most potent philosophies of the last two centuries have insisted that improvement or "progress" unavoidably moves through catastrophic rhythms of destruction and reconstruction, ruin and renewal. Just recall Hegel's "slaughterbench" of history, Marx's annihilating forces of capital, Darwin's murderous conflicts of evolution, or the capitalist processes of industrial innovation that economist Joseph Schumpeter famously described as a "perennial gale of creative destruction."[3] Given this, it may be less of a surprise to discover that Americans, especially those in positions of power and influence, have often viewed disasters as sources of moral, political, and economic renewal. A strong case can be made that ideological commitments to economic growth and material improvement have emerged out of encounters with calamity. Indeed, I have come to wonder whether dominant American ideas of progress would even be imaginable without disasters. Certainly, a close analysis of the extraordinary capacity for turning disasters into "blessings," for seeing silver linings in adversity, helps to explain how so many Americans have managed not only to sustain but to construct a faith in progress while coping with the wars, social disorders, and boom-and-bust cycles that have characterized modern life. Whether we can go so far as to claim that modern America has emerged from its emergencies and calamities and the responses they have provoked, these undeniably hold a key to understanding the twentieth- and twenty-first-century world.

It is tempting, when considering why calamities dominate our television screens, to single out the role of the news and entertainment industries. A good deal of recent Continental philosophy and critical theory, after all, insists that technology and the electronic mass media have radically transformed our senses, changing what we notice about the world and how we feel about what we see. This notion is amply explored in *White Noise*. Stompanato, whose orphic pronouncements are given a respectful hearing in the novel, explains popular interest in disasters as a "natural" response to "brain fade," the craving of the benumbed and media sated for "an occasional catastrophe to break up the incessant bombardment of information" (66). In a world of too much information, only extreme events seemingly have the power to cut through the white noise, to grab and to hold us. This, he says, is why we watch. His explanation has a self-consciously postmodern flavor, presenting calamities as mere spectacles noteworthy for the emotional and aesthetic impressions they make rather than for any moral significance or meaning they might possess. And it is a powerful case.

This denatured understanding of the spectacular character of "events" has transformed cultural criticism over the past generation, with weighty implications for disaster studies. In the same year that *White Noise* appeared, Neil Postman published *Amusing Ourselves to Death*, a gloomy philosophical jeremiad on the decline of morality and reason in the new media age. Adapting and revising Marshall McLuhan's famous formulation "the medium is the message," he argued that it was an intrinsic property of electronic visual media to convert all experience into entertainment, vacating incidents and events of complexity, depth, and history.[4] According to his analysis, death and destruction, like sex and violence and anything else for that matter, now appeared on television only as amusing or distracting images; this, indeed, was the inevitable fate of all representations enhanced by stirring music, voiceovers, and dramatic editing techniques and inserted into a data flow that blurred distinctions and transitions between dramas, sitcoms, commercials, and news reports.[5] Disasters, in this interpretation, were extreme cases, evidence that even the most horrifying events were bound to end up as spectacles.

So one answer to Gladney's question—what makes televised calamities so entertaining—might be this: the visual media turns *all* events into entertainment. And, as DeLillo suggests, such instruction, or programming, reaches deep into the psyche. When an actual disaster strikes in his novel in the form of an "airborne toxic event" it stirs much the same feelings in the fleeing Gladney family as the earlier televised disasters. Viewing the "black billowing cloud" through the windshield of their car, Gladney records their strange fascination: "We weren't sure how to react. It was a terrible thing to see, so close, . . . But it was also spectacular" (127). His metaphors, his entire frame of reference, become inevitably cinematic: "The whole thing was amazing. They seemed to be spotlighting the cloud for us as if it were part of a sound-and-light show, a bit of mood-setting mist drifting across a high battlement where a king had been slain" (128). Disasters are captivating in part, then, to the extent that they mimic and evoke popular Hollywood movies. And, as DeLillo infers, they must therefore be in some way desirable. Elsewhere, he has made this point directly; in the novel *End Zone*, his protagonist admits unhappily to a "thrill almost sensual" when reading about mass destruction and carnage.[6] This reaction prompts feelings of guilt, but DeLillo avoids lazy analysis of the sort that dismisses the public's appetite for (spectacles of) destruction as a predictable manifestation of the degraded taste of a population raised on trashy movies and television shows. On the contrary, he requires us to recognize that disasters in the media age have accrued an erotic dimension, that they have become the stuff of fantasies, and that this tells us something profound about the conditions of life in a postmodern world.[7] He pays insufficient attention to the market logics and ideological considerations that prompt media corporations to push images of violence and destruction, even as he overlooks the obvious point that in a corporate mass culture "the people" rarely get the programming they want.[8] But we do have to consider the delights of destruction. It is not simply a matter of mass media turning disaster into entertainment; there is something intrinsically fascinating about spectacles of calamity.

How do we account for this fascination? Two intriguing explanations that deserve mention, even though they receive only cursory attention in this book, are those proposed by evolutionary psychologists and psychoanalytic philosophers. The former maintain that humans are adapted to pay special attention to anything unusual or threatening that happens across our line of vision, responding with heightened physical and emotional arousal to potentially dangerous situations—this is the adrenaline rush that prepares us to fight or for flight. Some of the most interesting work in this field has charted how feelings of fear turn to exhilaration when an anticipated threat passes or turns out to be illusory. So appealing is this rush, according to psychologist Michael Apter, that most people actively seek out what he calls "the dangerous edge" in pursuit of the thrills that perilous encounters can elicit. Although these encounters would surely trigger a feeling of panic in the absence of controls, they can be relied on to generate a sense of enjoyment when a "protective frame"—a physical or psychological distancing mechanism—is in place. Amusement park rides or suspense movies, for example, trick us into a pleasure response by involving us emotionally in (simulated) harrowing events while shielding us from actual risks.[9] This is essentially what

Stompanato has in mind when he says we take pleasure in spectacles of disaster, so long as they are "somewhere else."

Many psychoanalytic critics agree that media-borne disasters exert a natural attraction, but they tend to view this as a matter of longing rather than adaptive behavior. Exemplary here is Slavoj Žižek's analysis of the cultural impact of the destruction of New York's World Trade Center on September 11, 2001. As he points out, images of this calamity, like the terrorist attack itself, were "obviously libidinally invested."[10] Similar scenes had played out repeatedly in blockbuster movies from *Independence Day* to *Die Hard*, lending substance to the idea that catastrophes had become objects of popular fantasy; hence his superb observation that "in a way, America got what it fantasized about, and that was the biggest surprise."[11] Why should comfortable Americans fantasize about calamity? Žižek's answer to this question is highly complex, applying a technical Lacanian understanding of the circuits connecting instincts, dreams, and desires that cannot be reproduced here with any adequacy. Suffice to say, he insists that the frisson provoked by spectacles of destruction owes a great deal to the power of such images to conjure up the tumultuous drives, the desires for sensual gratification and acts of violence, that are repressed when we are socialized into adulthood.[12] Calamities, in his vocabulary, offer us a glimpse of "the real." Of course, it is always perilous to try to make definitive statements about the workings of the unconscious, but, if Freud's depiction of the id as "a chaos, a cauldron of seething excitement" has any validity, it seems at least plausible that spectacles of destruction should exert a compelling hold over our imaginations, speaking to our yearnings for a life less ordered.[13] This is all highly speculative, and we should be spending as much time thinking about how the social world shapes unconscious desires as investigating how the unconscious shapes the social world.

Social conditions and experiences have somehow become sedimented into our fantasies. It is no surprise that we dream of catastrophes because we live in a catastrophic world. Spectacles of calamity command our attention because they present an occasion for processing, intellectually and emotionally, the experience of living in a world of systematic ruin and renewal, destruction and reconstruction, where technological and environmental disasters always loom.[14]

The fact that anxieties and desires fuel an appetite for spectacles of destruction is especially significant precisely because disasters now so thoroughly present themselves to us as spectacles. The annihilation of the twin towers was famously described by eyewitnesses, television commentators, and viewers across the country in terms of its filmic qualities:

it was, in the parlance of the day, "like a movie." Even as sophisticated an observer as John Updike, watching from a distance, could not resist televisual references when he described his reaction:

> From the viewpoint of a tenth-floor apartment in Brooklyn Heights, where I happened to be visiting some kin, the destruction of the World Trade Center twin towers had the false intimacy of television, on a day of perfect reception. . . . As we watched the second tower burst into ballooning flame . . . there persisted the notion that, as on television, this was not quite real; it could be fixed; the technocracy the towers symbolized would find a way to put out the fire and reverse the damage.[15]

Involuntarily reimagining his window frame as a television screen, he found himself in a position of passivity, waiting for the situation to correct itself (or be corrected by the powers that be). So rendered, this looks like a textbook postmodern experience, substantiating the contention that in a world bereft of historical bearings even the most awful events inevitably offer themselves up as pure spectacles. But of course this was hardly the entirety of Updike's response. As soon as the enormity of the event sunk in, as soon as he started to fathom the extent of the carnage, he and his wife, by his account, "clung to each other as if we ourselves were falling." A few days later, he spoke of his shock about this "horror of horrors" to a BBC News reporter: "To actually be seeing it not a mile away was very moving, disturbing, unsettling. It's like the bottom fell out of your own existence somehow."[16]

This discharge of feeling led to deeds. Being a writer, Updike wrote, trying to wrench meaning out of the event. And, not too surprisingly for a man with a fondness for quoting existentialist theologian Paul Tillich, he was soon at work on a short story reflecting on the religious implications of this shattering event.[17] Updike was hardly exceptional in his energetic response to September 11. Even those who witnessed the event only through its representations were moved to act, whether agitating for political reforms, taking part in patriotic rallies, or participating in one of the biggest fund-raising campaigns in U.S. history in support of the victims and their families. This spectacle of destruction, in other words, like most of the disasters covered in this book, was a galvanizing force. It was an aesthetic display, but hardly an anesthetizing one. Although spectacles have the capacity to numb, to distance viewers from events, leaving them adrift on a raft of sensations, they also have extraordinary power to command attention, to focus energies, to make us feel alive, and to involve us in the world around us.[18] Whether this is the right sort of involvement is a matter to which I will return, as is the issue of what problems get overlooked or neglected in the society of the spectacle. What is clear, however, is that more attention needs to be paid to the activating aspects of calamity.

One of DeLillo's achievements in *White Noise*, a text that maps out recent (middle-class) responses to disaster as richly as any work of fiction I know, lies precisely in his ability to grasp the mingled hope and dread, distaste and delight, involvement and distance so characteristic of responses to disaster in our time. *White Noise* properly treats calamities as events that make things happen. And it is alert to the continuing imprint of established values and outlooks. One of the most powerful is a residual romanticism that continues to have a profound influence on our understanding of the good life, and which reserves a privileged place for adversity. Gladney's sardonic fourteen-year-old son Heinrich, for example, bursts suddenly to life as his family encounters the "airborne toxic event." He is "steeped happily in disaster," "practically giddy," his voice betraying "a craving for terrible things" (123). Buoyed by a new sense of confidence, a new awareness that life is real and intense, he suddenly finds himself surrounded by other refugees at the evacuation center, grown men and women who warm to his spirit and his aura of authority. The calamity, in other words, is his proving ground ("Let him bloom, if that's what he's doing," says his father, "in the name of mischance, dread, and random disaster"); it is here that he is transformed from spectator to actor, intoxicated by a powerful sense of self ("Was it possible that out of the turmoil and surge of this dreadful event he would learn to make his way in the world?") (131). Like romantic philosophers and poets, Heinrich embraces calamity, thrilled to discover that the imperiled life is the life most fully lived. And he is by no means the only person thus roused by the crisis. His "spirited enjoyment" is fully matched by the spiritual exhilaration of the godly. Jehovah's Witnesses, for example, are in their element, passing out tracts and assuring all who will listen that the Day of Judgment is at hand: "Wars, famines, earthquakes, volcanic eruptions. It's all beginning to jell." Disasters, here too, are welcomed, because they make things happen. They matter. At the same time they seem to simplify an otherwise intolerably complicated world, seemingly revealing dualisms of good and evil or right and wrong that are so hard to identify in the ordinary run of events.[19] Thus disaster presents a chance to overcome some of the inertia that inhibits decisive action.

Without a cultural history we cannot begin to fathom the powerful hold of these customary reactions on the contemporary imagination of calamity. Nor can we grasp how and why the conditions of modernity might play such an important, possibly paramount, role in the story I tell here. For all the surface cynicism, for all the irony, *White Noise* is also thoroughly susceptible to the fraying modern dream of a world without disaster, the prospect of a future in which technology might be harnessed to protect us from the harms of nature and the hazards of science itself. Despite his suspicion of the motives of politicians and experts and his sneaking disillusionment with the ways of the modern world, Jack Gladney, for example, takes heart from the presence of bureaucrats, technicians, and soldiers, gladly submitting to their commands and ministrations. "They seem to have things under control" is a thought, or wish, that brings assurance and satisfaction (147).

Even as disasters have become entertaining spectacles, they have also laid the cultural groundwork for the expansion of a powerful national security apparatus. This suggests a widespread longing for protection from calamity, and underscores the extent to which the current political system depends on disasters to justify exercises of power in an era of supposed fiscal restraint and deregulation, as well as the degree to which laws and institutions are organized around the avoidance and mitigation of disaster—risk management. In the novel, to be sure, disaster officials assume a rather outlandish appearance in the guise of Advanced Disaster Management, a private consulting firm that "interfaces" with state governments to simulate evacuations in preparation for disasters. The inevitable joke is that the organization ends up treating a real toxic spill as a statistical deviation: "The insertion curve isn't as smooth as we would like. There's a probability excess. Plus which we don't have our victims laid out where we'd want them if this was an actual simulation" (139). This passage reads like a literary gloss on Jean Baudrillard's well-known and provocative assertion that in postmodern society life is actually *"organised according to a script for a disaster film."*[20] Still, DeLillo has identified one of the most important developments of our time, the morphing of a national security state into what might better be described as a disaster-security state in which official and semiofficial agencies have come to wield extraordinary power—all in the name of disaster prevention and relief. This, the novel suggests, is an age in which disasters are always happening, or always about to happen, and in which emergency management, however disconcerting and preposterous, is necessary and unavoidable.

The Catastrophic Logic of Modernity

The sky of modernity has seen several stars in the ascendant: the sable sun of melancholy and ennui, disaster's pale moon, the red sun of joy.

HENRI LEFEBVRE, *Introduction to Modernity*, 1962

9

DeLillo alludes, then, to one of the abiding, and defining, contradictions of our time: that we live in a society infatuated with, and entertained by, spectacles of calamity that is nevertheless willing to sacrifice all sorts of civil liberties in exchange for government and corporate protection against those same calamities. Postmodern theorists have not been inattentive to this conundrum. Baudrillard, for example, has insisted that the culture of hyperreality and the culture of security are two sides of the same coin.[21] Fredric Jameson, delineating the relationship in more detail, examines the free-floating terrors and exhilarations ("intensities") that supposedly constitute the primary affect of extreme images in a society that no longer has a sense of history or a proper understanding of causes and consequences, of origins and outcomes. He argues that a pervasive sense of cultural disorientation accounts both for the thrill of spectacles—the intoxicating appeal of spectacular images—as well as frantic demands for safety measures in a world that appears, thanks to relentless mass media coverage, to be permanently imperiled by random violence and calamities.[22]

The logic here is persuasive as far as it goes, but it does not explain the singular magnetism of disasters. This, I submit, can only be understood if we take into account what I call the catastrophic logic of modernity: a tag that grasps modernization as a quest to make the world more secure (modernity as anti-disaster) through development patterns that move through cycles of ruin and renewal, bust and boom, destruction and construction, producing as their collateral damage myriad social conflicts as well as technological and environmental hazards (modernity as disaster). Notice that the concept of catastrophe, as invoked here, retrieves from the *Oxford English Dictionary* an older, largely forgotten, definition of the word as that which "overturns"—for good and ill; it thus refers both to modernity's dizzying transformative promise and to its most acute dangers.

This, as I am fully aware, is a condensed and abstract formulation, one that I will endeavor to substantiate, but it does allow me to state my premise here that any convincing account of the culture of calamity must take notice of the rhymes and rhythms of modern (capitalist) development. A history of disasters must double as an inquiry into the modern and postmodern conditions. This is an easier claim to assert than to demonstrate, of course, and some of my observations must remain in the realm of the speculative, the impossible to prove. Although it might thus be safer "simply" to stick to the story, recovering what the documentary record has to say about changing social, intellectual, and emotional responses to disaster, there is enough in the archives to reassure me that the conceptual leaps I make here are sound, and indeed that any history of disaster that fails to take into account contexts of modernization and capitalist development is doomed to leave its data cold and inert, bereft of interpretive force and significance.

Before we can even begin we need a more precise grasp of key words like *modernity* and *disaster*. As it turns out, even disaster, ostensibly the most transparent of these terms, is not easy to pin down. For a start, it has become conventional to deploy three words—*disaster, calamity*, and *catastrophe*—to describe terrible misfortunes, but each possesses a slightly different shade of meaning. Calamity once referred primarily to the state of an individual afflicted by misfortune (as in Calamity Jane) rather than the misfortune itself. Although these variations are not insignificant, such linguistic niceties will not detain us here; I will follow customary practice by using the three terms interchangeably. This, however, does not resolve all matters of terminology. It is maddeningly difficult to get a fix even on the word *disaster* because its connotations have changed so much over time and across space. Then again, this definitional instability can be turned to the historian's advantage. Each alteration in the word's meaning bears witness to the evolving ideas about nature and society that I am seeking to track here.

The strict astrological definition of disaster originates in the "premodern" conviction that all incidents were directed by the heavens: "dis-aster" means "ill-starred," or, in the translation preferred by the *Oxford English Dictionary*, "an unfavorable aspect of a star or planet." This belief in the supernatural sources of calamity, absorbed increasingly into a Judeo-Christian worldview that emphasized the divine origins of calamity, flourished in Europe and North America in the colonial period and struck such deep roots into the culture that even today many Americans impulsively conceive of disasters as acts of God. Over the past three or four centuries, however, amid scientific, industrial, and political revolutions, the word *disaster* has been largely evacuated of its otherworldly connotations, coming to refer primarily to "natural" or "man-made" misfortunes. This outlook, prefigured in Shakespeare's *King Lear* where Edmund rails against those fools who would make guilty of their disasters the sun, the moon, and the stars, prepares the way for a distinctively modern understanding that pulls disasters into the orbit of the state—with government agencies assuming primary responsibility for relief, management, and prevention by the twentieth century. These days, Americans are more likely to consult federal documents rather than sermons for a working definition of disasters. The tautological classification favored in the Disaster Relief Act of 1950 seems to be simply a statement of fact: " 'Major disaster' means any flood, drought, fire, hurricane, earthquake, storm,

11

or other catastrophe in any part of the United States which, in the determination of the President, is or threatens to be of sufficient severity and magnitude to warrant disaster assistance by the Federal Government."[23] And certainly the disasters covered in this book are mostly of the major floods, fires, and earthquakes variety, events that gripped the public imagination, challenging and transforming ideas of nature, religion, social organization, and public policy, while inspiring intense deliberation about the meaning of America and of life itself. By the end of the twentieth century, however, distinctions between natural and man-made disasters had become blurred once again, and "other catastrophes" such as technological perils and terrorist attacks have increasingly captured the cultural and social space hitherto occupied by natural disasters. Indeed, in Hollywood disaster movies, where appearances matter more than substance, a calamity increasingly refers to any incident involving the spectacular destruction of buildings and bodies.

These changing definitions, in their own way, bear witness to, and tell the story of, the evolving relationship between "modernity" and catastrophe. And, as the sociologist Kai T. Erikson reminds us, these meanings are not as innocent as they may seem. On the contrary, definitions serve specific political agendas. He has sought to steer scholars away from a taxonomical classification of disasters (one that emphasizes unexpected property damage or loss of life) to one that emphasizes psychological effects. He suggests that we define a disaster as an event that produces widespread "traumatic reactions." He does so to encourage us to think of chronic social problems such as poverty and homelessness as disastrous, thereby to capture for the victims of these hardships the interest, sympathy, and material support customarily extended to victims of "natural disasters."[24] But why did the victims of sudden disasters come to occupy such a privileged position in the first place? That is one of the questions I set out to explore. And it suggests that an answer is to be found in the special relationship between catastrophe and the conditions of modernity.

Modernity is an extraordinarily difficult concept to pin down. For most people today, the word still stands vaguely for the recent or the contemporary, as opposed to, say, the premodern or ancient or times past; to "modernize" is to bring something up to date. Cultural critics by contrast have sought to assure us that modernity is a bygone age, one that has been eclipsed by a postmodern epoch that may itself already be passing. The concept of postmodernism is a useful one, but I propose to retain the concept of modernity as my primary point of reference and organizing principle because I believe it offers the most useful framework for investigating the conditions out of which the culture of calamity emerged.[25] In so doing, I am not arguing that there has been any singular or universal experience of modernity. Given the vast disparity in circumstances endured by the powerful and powerless, the documented and undocumented, the first world and the third world, and so forth, there is something to be said for thinking about modernity as a plural rather than singular condition—as "modernities."[26] As long as we acknowledge this, however, modernity retains considerable power as an analytical and structural category that speaks to processes and developments that have remade the entire globe over the past few centuries.

I understand modernity broadly as a project originating in the social and cultural conditions of seventeenth- and eighteenth-century Europe.[27] At the heart of this venture is the determination to apply instrumental reason to the task of making human life on earth safer and more predictable, an endeavor that has entailed an ongoing effort to control, or at least manage, nature. This quest for security, one that shows no signs of abating, provides a crucial context for my investigation into the politics and poetics of disaster. When we think about modernization as a struggle to prevail against adversity, we can begin to appreciate why disasters have been a central preoccupation (arguably *the* central preoccupation) of the modern project. The French intellectual Henri Lefebvre once demonstrated that the concept of modernity was articulated by thinkers who sought to investigate and come to terms with the "shadows" of the modern world, with "multiple crises, ever more frequent and profound, inextricable contradictions and confusions, dramas and catastrophes."[28]

The modern project was not born of abstract principles but rather out of engagement (actual and imaginative) with the perils and ordeals of everyday life. I will sketch out a preliminary argument about the relationship between disaster and modernity through an examination of responses to one particular calamity, the Lisbon earthquake of 1755, long identified by European historians as a watershed event dividing the premodern from the modern age. Inquisition-era Portugal may seem like an odd place to launch a study of New World disasters, but it fits my purposes well, driving home the point that the "American" outlooks and practices traced in this book are neither local nor entirely exceptional. Nor are they recent in origin. On the contrary, they arise from social and economic developments that have long been transnational, developments that are increasingly global in scope. At the same time, of course, a comparative dimension enables us to better appreciate what is truly distinctive about the American culture of calamity. Thus it is that a study of the making of modern America begins in Europe in the Age of Empire.

Certainly, this case study substantiates the general point that catastrophes generate an extraordinary amount of cultural production, and it underlines the vital contribution of disasters to modern thought and activity. This event is particularly noteworthy because it was here that the three interwoven strands of modernity that most interest me were first articulated with any great fluency and influence: (1) modernity as a "rational" and scientific endeavor to improve life on earth; (2) modernity as a dynamic system of spatial reorganization and capital accumulation (creative destruction); and (3) modernism as a romantic structure of feeling that values "natural" and sensational events (like disasters) as antidotes to the alienating effects of urbanization, bureaucracy, and industrialism, but which paradoxically enables modern endeavors to subject the natural and social world to human administration.

The Lisbon earthquake was one of epic proportions. Portugal's capital was shaken to its foundations on the morning of November 1, 1755. As described by an American merchant on his return to Boston, the ground started to shudder at about ten in the morning, to devastating effect: "Every Building rolled and jostled like a Ship at Sea; which put in Ruins almost every House, Church, and Publick Building, with an incredible Slaughter of the Inhabitants."[29] The timing could not have been worse. It was All Saints' Day and the churches were full. Thousands upon thousands of lighted candles spilled to the floor and fires broke out everywhere, sweeping quickly through the ruins, and incinerating countless unfortunate souls trapped under the wreckage. To add to the horror, the Tagus River abruptly rose twenty feet, swamping low-lying areas of the town and drowning many inhabitants but failing to extinguish fires that would continue to burn for five more days. This biblical catalog of afflictions—earthquake, fire, and flood—added up to a calamity that stunned the Western world, killing fifteen thousand people (reports at the time mistakenly put the number closer to fifty thousand) and destroying seventeen thousand of the city's twenty thousand homes.[30]

These shocking events directly inspired Voltaire's philosophical view of modernity as a project to bring order to the world. The celebrated Enlightenment philosopher was deeply affected by news of the cataclysm. His response was characteristic of a man of reason, science, and sympathy. He threw himself into a weeklong frenzy of passionate and compassionate literary creativity, the product of which was one his most enduring verses, *Poème sur le désastre de Lisbonne*. This "sermon," rehearsing an argument that he would revisit four years later in his masterpiece, *Candide*, amounted to a withering attack on those dominant beliefs and attitudes of his day that, in his view, blocked the "improvements" that

FIG 1. Copper engraving of the Lisbon earthquake of 1755: "View of Lisbon with very rough water in the foreground (probably the Tagus River), caused by the earthquake" (France, 1755). Reprinted courtesy of the National Information Service for Earthquake Engineering, University of California, Berkeley.

could avert future catastrophes. The poem announced a modern point of view by assailing two forms of cosmic fatalism, one optimistic ("whatever is, is right"), the other pessimistic (whatever is, is wrong: fallen and sinful man deserves to be punished by calamities). Most of Voltaire's contemporaries took it for granted that the catastrophe was literally an act of God.[31] In Lisbon, the prominent Jesuit Gabriel Malagrida argued forcefully that repentance should take priority over reconstruction, urging residents to put down their tools and "retreat" from the world for six days to reflect on their sins and thereby win back God's favor.[32] Elsewhere, prominent evangelical Protestants such as George Whitefield and John Wesley interpreted the earthquake as a divine judgment against popery.[33] Voltaire thought that both of these religious positions stood in the way of a properly rational or sympathetic response to disaster.

Quite as objectionable to him was the optimistic theology so beloved by the philosophers of his day with their blithe assurances that this was the best of all possible worlds. The most widely read proponent of this view, the poet Alexander Pope, had explicitly addressed the problem of catastrophes in his influential 1733 *Essay on Man*, asking: "But errs not Nature from this gracious end . . . / When earthquakes swallow, or when tempests sweep / Towns to one grave, whole nations to the deep?" To which question he had responded with an emphatic denial: "'No ('tis reply'd), the first Almighty Cause / Acts not by partial, but by general laws.'"[34] Voltaire was incensed by this sort of "optimism"; the Lisbon tragedy confirmed the moral bankruptcy of all forms of fatalism.[35]

> Those savants erred who claim, "All's for the best."
> Approach and view this carnage . . .
> In answer to the frail, half-uttered cry,
> The smoking ashes, will you make reply,
> "God, in His bounty, urged by a just cause,
> Herein exhibits His eternal laws"?
> Seeing these stacks of victims, will you state,
> "Vengeance is God's; they have deserved their fate"?[36]

Voltaire established his status as a forward-looking man through his own commitment to reason and to sympathy for the victims. Optimistic philosophers and Augustinian theologians had never been particularly concerned with the thoughts or feelings of individuals; their scale was cosmic, focused on the momentous movements of providence rather than the fleeting hurts of ordinary men and women. And this is exactly what upset Voltaire, the foremost advocate of an emerging culture of compassion that would profoundly influence the way people not only thought but felt about natural disasters.[37] Voltaire insisted that the only truly ethical response to any calamity was to act, to treat the wounds of sufferers, and to rebuild the ruins.[38] The Lisbon earthquake had convinced him that God did not govern events on earth and that unmanaged nature tended to catastrophe. It was therefore incumbent upon humans to penetrate the mysteries of the natural world and to figure out how to subdue it more completely. The point was not to philosophize but rather, as he concluded in *Candide*, to cultivate ("we must go and work in the garden"), "working" nature until it could be made to work for us.[39] Reason, science, and sympathy: these were the central ingredients of an incipient modern project that looms over the history of disasters.

But there is a second component of modernity that Voltaire missed because he was so eager to speak on behalf of the victims. Answering claims that the Lisbon catastrophe had benefits that compensated for its costs, he was magnificently facetious. Could any survivor, he asked, really be expected to be consoled by the fact that "the heirs of those who have perished will increase their fortune; masons will earn money by rebuilding the houses; beasts will feed on the carcasses buried under the ruins."[40] Surely not. But the disaster did make some extraordinary improvements possible, ones that Voltaire himself would have appreciated. In *Candide* he rebuked the Portuguese for responding to the calamity with absurd rituals instead of actions: "When the earthquake had subsided after destroying three-quarters of Lisbon, the authorities of that country could find no surer means of avoiding total ruin than by giving the people a magnificent *auto-da-fé*."[41] This made for fine polemic, but as a statement of fact it was far from the truth. Most prominent clergymen contributed energetically to rebuilding the city, and the restoration of Lisbon would eventually be acknowledged as a model of Enlightenment ambition and achievement.

Already in 1755, there were signs that a major calamity was full of possibility for a mercantile (protocapitalist) economy, providing opportunities for urban development, capital accumulation, and political reform. The key actor, besides the economic factor, in this drama was the "enlightened absolutist" Sebastiao José de Carvalho, known to history as the marquis of Pombal. He took full advantage of the calamity to modernize his country and to consolidate his personal authority. Although he officially held a position as secretary of state for foreign affairs, he acquitted himself with such poise in the aftermath of the earthquake that Dom José I gave him full command of the relief and restoration of his imperial seat. Largely uninterested in theology, Pombal devoted himself to such practical matters as restoring order, feeding the homeless, and turning ruins into dwellings. He ruled through hastily written decrees. To forestall the outbreak and spread of disease, he arranged for the disposal of human and animal corpses at sea. To punish and deter looters, he erected seven large gallows in the main public square—soon to be adorned with thirty-four cadavers. To prevent the flight of laborers, and the removal of stolen property, he set soldiers at the city gates. To feed the hungry, he opened public granaries, meat markets, and soup kitchens, confiscating or controlling the price of the most urgent provisions. To clear lots for new buildings, he compelled all "idlers" (anyone without a regular job) to remove the rubble under military direction. A detailed social history written from the perspective of ordinary men and women would undoubtedly reveal dissatisfaction with the peremptory methods of the state, recording how the poor worked outside the system to attend to their own needs, but the relief was by and large efficiently organized: the population did not starve, and within six months the homeless could find shelter in thousands of new wooden structures that had been erected in the aftermath of the earthquake.

Pombal's ambitions, however, extended well beyond mere recovery; he was a true modernist to the extent that he seized on the disaster as an opportunity for urban development and commercial expansion. Employing the absolute power of the monarchy and the dwindling but still fabulous riches of empire, Pombal built a magnificent new metropolis, and he overhauled the economic and political structure of his country. Outlawing unauthorized construction in central Lisbon, Pombal appointed military engineers to develop a coherent blueprint for the city, and within months hills were flattened, a confusion of narrow alleyways had given way to a grid of wide thoroughfares, and a system of sewers had appeared beneath the streets. New buildings were safer and more uniform in appearance, constructed out of standardized building materials and built around flexible, earthquake-proof frames designed to move with the shaking of the earth.[42] The resulting city was much better suited to the pursuit of commerce and the government of empire than its gilded predecessor had been.

Few had expected such a happy outcome. After the earthquake, talk in merchant circles had been of inevitable business failures, irreparable financial damage, and decline. And the material and economic costs were huge: foreign merchants lost an estimated £12 million in assets, with local inhabitants losing a great deal more.[43] Nevertheless, Pombal succeeded in turning one of the worst natural disasters in European history into an occasion for modernization.[44] The lesson was clear, and it was one that would resonate down through the centuries: in a commercial economy, crisis and catastrophe could be instruments of improvement—for some, if not for all.

Disaster and destruction were necessary mechanisms of modernization; but according to a third distinctively modern perspective, modernity itself—urbanization, commerce, bureaucracy—was unavoidably establishing conditions for future calamities. Or so Jean-Jacques Rousseau asserted. As far as Voltaire was concerned, Rousseau was stuck in the past, believing that all events were directed by a presiding deity, but there is much that is distinctly modern about Rousseau's response to the earthquake. In a private communication to Voltaire (later published as the "Letter on Providence"), he expressed resentment at the older man's attempts to deprive him of the consolations of providence. He admitted that nature was not always benevolent for individual humans (whose bodies were destined to perish and become worm food), but he continued to insist on the benevolence of God and to reiterate Leibniz's argument that nature was organized for the good of the whole. Accordingly, he insisted on the general benefits of earthquakes. The Lisbon disaster was appalling, no doubt, but God was not to be blamed. Voltaire had reacted to the slaughter by asking why, if earthquakes were necessary, God did not ensure they only happened in deserts where they could do no harm. Rousseau, always more interested in cultural criticism than theological controversy, supplied the obvious rejoinder: earthquakes did happen in deserts, but they caused no comparable damage there because the local "savages" were scattered across the land and therefore endangered neither by "the fall of housetops, nor the conflagration of houses." The problem, in other words, was not earthquakes but reckless urbanization: "nature did not construct twenty thousand houses of six and seven stories," he pointed out, and "if the inhabitants of this great city had been more equally spread out and more lightly lodged, the damage would have been much less, and perhaps of no account." Nature, it seemed, was deadly only to those who neglected to heed its ways. "Should it be said," he concluded sarcastically, "that the order of the world ought to change according to our whims, that nature ought to be subjugated to our laws, and that in order to interdict an earthquake in some place, we have only to build a city there?"[45] Civilization, in short, was less a cure for disaster than a cause, and one of the greatest dangers posed by calamities was the opportunity they presented for further urban and economic development, for political centralization, and for the establishment of an administered society. It is opinions such as these that led Allan Bloom to conclude of Rousseau that he "gave antimodernity its most modern expression and thereby ushered in extreme modernity"—by which he meant that Rousseau had penetrated to the core of modernity's own contradictions, discovering limits to human control and social progress and anticipating the skepticism that would characterize the postmodern view that we have examined in *White Noise*.[46] But this antimodernism, as we shall see, has turned out to be more congenial to modern development than Rousseau could possibly have imagined.

Rousseau, famously, placed a high value on sentiments and the imagination. Curiously, he was outraged by Voltaire's determination to inflame sympathy for victims, emotionally violated by vivid descriptions of the dead and dying. But many kindred spirits who came after him would find in the horrors and thrills of calamity a revitalizing antidote to a civilization they agreed was insipid, regimented, de-natured, and overly comfortable. His preoccupation with the emotional impact of disasters, in other words, was symptomatic of a new romantic structure of feeling that has left a deep imprint on the modern consciousness, helping to generate an enthusiasm for the media-generated spectacles of destruction that sustains our consumer society.[47]

Taking these three sets of responses together we arrive at a schematic understanding of modernity that complements Lefebvre's poetic astral trilogy: "the sable sun of melancholy and ennui, disaster's pale moon, the red sun of joy." We find extravagant modern hopes for the happy and secure world that could be achieved by pitting science and reason against calamity. We find catastrophe as the projected and feared outcome of modernity. And we find a world-weariness to which exciting images of calamity would seem to promise at least temporary release.

By now many of the connections that I am seeking to establish between disaster and modernity should be apparent, as should the fact that this relationship has global implications. Resilience in the face of disasters is by no means an exclusively American phenomenon. On the contrary, since 1800, it has proven to be "a nearly universal fact of urban settlement around the globe."[48] Cities on every continent have recovered quickly from devastating fires, floods, earthquakes, storms, and wars. Indeed, massive destruction has been seized upon as an opportunity for urban and political renewal in contexts as varied as post–World War II Europe, Deng Xiaoping's China, and Meiji Restoration Japan. But a comparative perspective makes it clear that there have been significant disparities in the ways different societies and cultures have managed and imagined disasters in the modern age. And what has most distinguished American responses to destruction over the past three centuries or so is a widespread conviction, born of beliefs and experience, that calamities are instruments of progress. In place of stoic resolve, many Americans (and certainly dominant American ideologies) embrace disasters as a means of escaping from the present into a better future.

American Disasters, American Dreams

This optimistic view of disasters was apparent even in 1755. The physical effects of the Lisbon earthquake were reportedly felt in the New World within eight hours, when a tidal wave sweeping westward submerged coastal areas in the Caribbean. North Americans did not learn about the Iberian calamity until a ship arrived in Boston from Europe several weeks afterward.[49] Earthquakes were already much on the minds of New Englanders because powerful tremors had jolted the region just days before. Although there were no casualties and damage was limited, people throughout Massachusetts expended an extraordinary amount of time and energy trying to figure out what their ordeal meant and how best to respond.[50] What is remarkable is how many commentators insisted on an optimistic interpretation of both earthquakes, resolutely searching for blessings in a manner that I am arguing is characteristic of a distinctively American way of disaster that continues to influence our outlooks today.

20

FIG 2. Woodcut of the Massachusetts earthquake of November 18, 1755: "Wooden build-ings shaken and damaged; church steeples leaning. People outside in panic. Image used to illustrate a religious tract" (Boston, eighteenth century). Reprinted courtesy of the National Information Service for Earthquake Engineering, University of California, Berkeley.

There were several sources of optimism here, drawing upon compet-ing and increasingly overlapping providential, evangelical, and millennial religious teachings. Charles Chauncy, the prominent pastor of Boston's First Church, for example, struck a cheery note, insisting that calami-ties were best viewed as "great instruments of providence" designed to promote the spiritual growth of humankind. He paid lip service to the notion that the earth was a fallen dominion, with the transgressions of Adam and Eve having "so changed the whole external constitution of nature, as that, instead of tending to render the earth a paradisaick one, it conspires to make it a place of vanity and sorrow, suffering and death." But he recast this as an opportunity: "The *final cause* . . . of God's *curs-ing the earth*, and fitting it for the production of so much evil, in the course of providence," he concluded reassuringly, "might be the *good* of mankind."[51] Apparent misfortune, in other words, was to be under-stood as a blessing that could be measured in increments of moral and spiritual development. Amid the growing influence of evangelicalism in the middle years of the eighteenth century, rival preachers seized on di-sasters specifically as spurs to personal spiritual awakening, while a third and relatively new apocalyptic theology cast the 1755 earthquakes as the convulsions prophesied in the Book of Revelation.[52] Natural disasters took on heightened significance as omens and vehicles of an impending millennium that assumed an increasingly nationalistic guise toward the end of the century as catastrophes were absorbed into a powerful narrative about America's glorious destiny.

What is striking about these otherworldy religious outlooks is how neatly they mapped onto emergent ideologies of material progress, whereby the "good" performed by calamities was understood in explicitly social and environmental terms. For example, John Winthrop, professor of mathematics and natural philosophy at Harvard University and a descendant of his namesake, the founder of the Massachusetts Bay Colony, took advantage of the popular interest spurred by the New England and Lisbon earthquakes to produce one of the most influential manifestos for the scientific method to appear in colonial America. His profound faith that God had designed nature for the benefit of humankind led him to assume that even earthquakes *had* to be sources more of good than of evil, and in this case that meant appreciating them as mechanisms for producing a congenial (resource-rich and pleasing) natural environment. After finding out about the Lisbon calamity he could hardly deny that natural processes could cause extreme suffering, but he blamed this on human mismanagement. Not unlike Rousseau, he argued that earthquakes were only hazardous because people had failed to build safe dwellings. Lisbon, he insisted, was not a victim of tremors so much as of shoddy construction: buildings had been too tall, they had been poorly designed, and, consisting largely of clay bricks, they had been unacceptably fragile. "Had *Boston* been built in that manner," he argued, "probably at this day it would have been little better than a heap of ruins."[53] Winthrop, in short, exemplified an influential branch of American Enlightenment thought that deemed the natural world to be benevolent, designed by the Creator to provide for the material needs of man.[54] Even fires, floods, and earthquakes were agents of beneficial natural processes; all people had to do was figure out how to manage nature properly so as to liberate its progressive energies.

This was exactly the premise that had led Winthrop's correspondent Benjamin Franklin to found the pioneering Union Fire Company in Philadelphia in 1736 as well as the colonies' first successful fire insurance company a couple of years before the 1755 earthquakes.[55] These initiatives anticipated two of the most important strands of the modern American approach to disaster: the administration of the social and natural world and the establishment of mechanisms to manage risk in such a way as to liberate the propulsive energies of an economy built on creative destruction. One of my goals in this book is to explain the origins of these ways of imagining and managing disaster as well as to trace and examine the implications.

These optimistic approaches to calamity culminated in the mid-twentieth century with such measures as the Disaster Relief Act of 1950, a key building block of an emerging national security state that promised a more orderly, rational society—a world safe from natural and man-made disasters—even as it was designed to support a dynamic capitalist economic system. Mine, however, is not a triumphal narrative. It is not a celebration of the human spirit or the glory of American institutions, though there is plenty of heroism here and much to marvel at in the accomplishments of public and private disaster-response agencies. Indeed, one of my concerns is to challenge and complicate the assumption, which has been promoted and shared by many previous studies, that federal emergency management was the natural and inevitable outcome of an Enlightenment project to control nature and minimize human suffering. In fact, modern disaster programs and philosophies have been largely improvised in the face of actual calamities and owe as much to social and political conflicts as to dispassionate (or compassionate) deliberation, let alone to any abstract crusade for mastery over the natural world. Disasters have been laboratories for social reform. They have allowed American leaders to introduce extraordinary, and sometimes severe, policies in the name of necessity—dynamiting private property, executing looters without trial, subsidizing housing, instituting price controls, administering compulsory vaccinations, and generally expanding the powers of government in ways that helped to redraw the boundaries of public and private jurisdiction. Many American institutions and organizations were created specifically to offer protection from disasters, not only fire departments and the Red Cross but the police and the National Guard. And disasters also contributed to the construction of an economic and urban infrastructure that was well suited to the requirements of business. The result has been a dynamic system oscillating between imperatives of order (managing nature and society) and abandon (liberating the creative and destructive energies of a corporate capitalist economy). Indeed, since the early 1970s there has been a massive expansion of the disaster-security state amid sweeping economic deregulation, two processes that have proven to been oddly compatible in the aftermath of the terrorist attacks of September 11, 2001.[56] The point is that this complex arrangement has not simply emerged out of the logics of our time; it is also a fulfillment of the history that I describe and analyze in this book.

The Shape of Things to Come

Previous academic studies of disasters have tended to be limited in temporal or geographic scope, from Carl Smith's fine work on late nineteenth-century urban disorders in Chicago to John M. Barry's magisterial narrative history of the Mississippi flood of 1927 to Mike Davis's chilling account of the social and environmental devastations wrought by late capitalism in Southern California.[57] Ted Steinberg's *Acts of God* is more capacious, offering a valuable history of disasters that emphasizes environmental and social consequences.[58] What distinguishes my work is its attempt to deliver a history that insists on intimate connections between calamity and modern American economic, political, and cultural developments. This book, accordingly, offers a history, albeit a selective one, that tracks major changes in ways of managing and imagining disasters between the seventeenth century and the present. But if the book traces a sweeping chronological arc, each chapter also offers a discrete essay, focusing in turn on such topics as religion, the catastrophic logics of capital, mass media sensationalism, the disaster-security state, and the postmodern culture of calamity.

In chapter 1 I return to the seventeenth and eighteenth centuries to emphasize the importance of theology and American social and environmental conditions in creating a durable faith in the "blessings of disaster," according to which ruptures and crises were grasped by elites as opportunities for political and economic renovation. I establish a background for my investigation into modern responses to disaster, revealing the deep and enduring imprint of religion on the American imagination of disaster and delineating the structures of faith and feeling that bound catastrophe, apocalyptic thinking, and ideologies of progress in a singular narrative.

After this preamble, we move directly to the industrial era. Although my primary concern here is to analyze broad trends, I pay especially close attention to one illuminating case study, the San Francisco earthquake and fire of 1906. To ground my larger claims about the catastrophic logic of modernity in the complex conditions of lived experience, I offer a brief narrative of this disaster. My central analytical concern in chapter 2 is to examine the strange and intimate relationship between calamity and capitalism, explaining how belief in the blessings of disaster came to frame and energize (ambivalent) modern commitments to constant economic expansion and unending urban renewal.

In chapter 3 I examine the appearance in the United States of a broad-based cultural fascination with spectacles of chaos. Although Americans have devoted enormous resources to subduing nature and curbing misery over the last hundred and fifty years, in the same period, it seems, they have developed a "love" of disasters. In 1906, a significant number of comfortable men and women, recoiling from the banality of "overcivilized" lives, were already insisting that they would not have missed the excitement and thrills of the San Francisco earthquake for the world. In this chapter I reveal the contribution of this emergent "culture of calamity" to the formation of a consumer imagination that feeds on images of destruction.

In chapter 4 I examine the rise of what I call a disaster-security state in the mid-twentieth century, an age marked by extraordinary faith in modern science and social organization as well as by nagging cold war anxieties about civil defense and global nuclear annihilation. The chapter examines the origins of the Disaster Relief Act of 1950, a legislative innovation that laid the groundwork for the construction of a system of federal emergency management. It explores the implications of this nationalization of the politics of disaster via a discussion of political responses to the 1955 hurricanes in the Northeast, America's first "billion dollar disaster." Noting that the 1950s was also marked by an unprecedented craze for disaster movies, I propose that there is an integral connection between the rise of the national security state and the emergence of a cinematic imagination of calamity.

In chapter 5 I seek to tie these complex cross-cutting themes together through an analysis of cultural and political responses to the destruction of New York's World Trade Center on September 11, 2001. Examining responses by the commercial news media, evangelical Christians, and political and economic actors, I argue that we have decisively entered an age dominated by a postmodern culture of calamity. I suggest that the longstanding faith in disaster as an instrument of progress is breaking down in the United States but that disaster still remains a rare opportunity for political experimentation. Significantly, most of these innovations have served the interests of multinational corporations. I ponder what effects this is likely to have on the future management of calamities as well as the administration of society in an age of "permanent disaster."

A brief epilogue considers the greatest natural disaster in American history, 2005's Hurricane Katrina. I examine the resurgence of concern with issues of race, class, and environmental sustainability in a world dominated by a national security state and a deregulated economy. I ask whether responses to Hurricane Katrina mark a fulfillment of, or a retreat from, the new regime of disaster politics established after 9/11.

The Catastrophe of History

A Klee painting named "Angelus Novus" shows an angel looking as though he is about to move away from something he is fixedly contemplating. His eyes are staring, his mouth is open, his wings are spread. This is how one pictures the angel of history. His face is turned toward the past. Where we perceive a chain of events, he sees one single catastrophe which keeps piling wreckage upon wreckage and hurls it in front of his feet. The angel would like to stay, awaken the dead, and make whole what has been smashed. But a storm is blowing from Paradise; it has got caught in his wings with such violence that the angel can no longer close them. This storm irresistibly propels him into the future to which his back is turned, while the pile of debris before him grows skyward. The storm is what we call progress.

WALTER BENJAMIN, "Theses on the Philosophy of History"

An overarching concern of this book is to explain how and why Americans came to view disasters as agents of economic, political, and moral progress, and to show how these responses have enabled the quest for endless development and economic expansion that has shaped and defined our world. This outlook has always had its critics—one thinks of Henry Adams and his nihilistic conviction that the universe was governed by, or rather abandoned to, chaos, or Henry James and his gloomy "imagination of disaster," born of his sense that life was "ferocious and sinister."[59] Meanwhile, large numbers of ordinary Americans have remained fatalistic about misfortune and adversity. Nevertheless, dominant beliefs (and myths) have consistently cast catastrophes as instruments of personal and national renewal. Why is this? What are the implications? I hope to answer these questions and in the process to suggest why calamities have occupied such a prominent place in the modern and postmodern imaginations.

So let us return to Gladney's question. By now it should be clear that asking why so many ordinary people find spectacles of calamity entertaining is not an idle or esoteric question: it helps us examine and come to terms with the catastrophic logic of modernity itself; it reveals the endlessly destructive and reconstructive social and economic forces that have shaped American experiences over the past two centuries; it measures the cultural reverberations of the age of hypercapitalism and allows us to take seriously Walter Benjamin's complex and ironic recasting of modernity, "the golden age," as "catastrophe."[60] This, for him, takes two principal forms. One is the dispiriting surrender of the consumer age to commodities and to "the sadistic craving for innovation."[61] The culture of calamity, with its endless parade of new-but-always-the-same disaster footage, underlines his point all too aptly. Perhaps even more significant is the sheer destructiveness of capitalism and its relentless assault on the environment, on the vulnerable members of society, on life itself. Benjamin, appropriately enough, devoted the last of his seminal radio broadcasts for youth in January 1933 to the Mississippi flood of 1927. He insisted that this calamity was not simply a "natural" disaster but one created by the demands of capitalism and the rulings of a compliant bourgeois state.[62] This insistent yoking of the natural and the social, of the disastrous event and disastrous modern logics, offers an exemplary starting point for this book.

But while Benjamin properly identified the costs, he finally paid insufficient attention to the vibrancy and creativity and humanity of the modern world. For an account that better captures the catastrophic logic of modernity, as I am establishing the concept here, we do better to turn to a playwright who is deeply influenced by Benjamin but who is willing to "risk . . . an excess of optimism," a gesture properly identified as an "American trait."[63] In his extraordinary play *Angels in America*, Tony Kushner gives artistic shape and mythic resonance to the culture of calamity. Whatever else this capacious play is about it offers a profound meditation on life as movement, and movement as creative destruction.

To convey this point, Kushner devises a fable, one that is thoroughly immersed in American apocalyptic and progressive traditions. In the beginning, the universe was a place of constancy and order (though sustained by the ceaseless and tediously repetitive copulation of Angels). But then God created human beings: "In making people God apparently set in motion a potential in the design for change, for random event, for movement forward" (175). Restlessness, then, is a defining human quality, but Kushner switches insistently from the universal and theological to the specific in order to keep our attention fixed on the particulars of the modern: "Migration. Science. Forward Motion" (176). The play compels us to feel "human progress" as a destructive force. Here, significantly, disaster-stricken San Francisco supplies the image and principle through which catastrophic modernity can be grasped. Human motion and commotion produces tremors in heaven (described as "a city Much Like San Francisco)," and these persistent "heavenquakes" turn paradise into a place of ruin (176): "Heaven looks mostly like San Francisco after the Great 1906 Quake. It has a deserted, derelict feel to it, rubble is strewn everywhere" (252).

But this is not an entirely negative outcome. There are two crucial twists here. The first is that destruction is recognized to be seductive. It is precisely on the day of the San Francisco earthquake, April 18, 1906,

27

FIG 3. A still depicting heaven from the 2003 HBO movie of Tony Kushner's play *Angels in America*, directed by Mike Nichols. Reproduced by permission of HBO Films.

that God abandons heaven and his dull and dutiful angels in search of adventure, "In Mortifying imitation of" human beings (177). Change entails destruction, and this is never portrayed as anything other than devastating in its physical and psychic effects—figured especially in the AIDS epidemic. But catastrophe also has its attractions. A second twist is that destruction is accepted as an unavoidable and indeed constructive element. Once God leaves them the Angels are left to witness the ongoing destruction and misery on earth, awaiting the end of time. Unlike Benjamin's angel of history they are not entirely powerless to intervene. In an eerie symbolic prefiguring of the disaster-security state, they establish a "permanent emergency council." Their chief initiative, however, is to persuade humans (represented by "The Prophet" Prior Walter, a gay man dying of AIDS) to "Stop Moving," to appreciate "Stasis" (178–79).

This option is refused; stasis is equated with death rather than peace. Despite his sickness, his agony, his decay, Prior insists on life: "We can't just stop. We're not rocks—progress, migration, motion is . . . modernity" (263–64). "Modernity" here is finally embraced not as the best of all possible worlds but as "life" in all its complex, shattering, tragic, ennobling glory. It is a superbly nuanced rendering. There is no Reaganite "morning-in-America" myopia here. The costs of modernity are squarely confronted: the social disintegration, the environmental devastation, the endemic alienation, the class conflicts, the culture wars. The AIDS epidemic looms over the play and stands for all of the threats that modern technology and capitalist social organization pose to human survival. Indeed, Kushner is nicely particular, rather than theological, about the problems of our time. In the end, the source of danger here is not the nature

28

of "man" but specific social expressions: racism, homophobia, hunger for power. And perhaps this is why Kushner can take a more optimistic view of modernity than Benjamin: he clings to "a belief in the effectiveness of activism and the possibility of progress" even as he is thoroughly susceptible to the apocalyptic anxieties of the age ("Afterword," 286). What makes Kushner's work so intriguing is the self-awareness with which the play yields to the lure of the catastrophic, the way it acknowledges adversity as the process that makes imagination and creativity possible, even as he demands a more humane management of the processes of creative destruction. This is why he can describe *Angels in America* as "essentially a comedy, in that issues are resolved, mostly peaceably; growth takes place and loss is, to a certain degree, countenanced." But, as the playwright properly insists, "it's not farce; all this happens only through a terrific amount of struggle, and the stakes are high."[64]

Kushner's play raises questions that I try to answer in this book. Why is he impelled to tell the story of American progress through an apocalyptic fantasy that seeks its profoundest truths in the chaos of disaster? Why search for the meaning of life, and modern life in particular, in the unavoidable and troubled dialectic that binds creation and destruction? The cultural critic Fredric Jameson, invoking Henri Lefebvre, once wrote that all history progresses "by way of catastrophe and disaster."[65] It is a compelling formulation, though we might also keep in mind the derision of Henry Perowne, the protagonist of Ian McEwan's novel *Saturday*, for the fashionable negativism of contemporary academics: "The young lecturers there like to dramatise life as a sequence of calamities. It's their style, their way of being clever. It wouldn't be cool or professional to count the eradication of smallpox as part of the modern condition. Or the recent spread of democracies." The passage has a satirical flavor—and Perowne's sunny assessment of modernity is not spared gentle lampooning. But there is surely some truth here. After the events of September 11, 2001, I certainly feel the tug of McEwan's account of the blessings of modern Western life: "But if the present dispensation is wiped out now, the future will look back on us as gods, certainly in this city, lucky gods blessed by supermarket cornucopias, torrents of accessible information, warm clothes that weigh nothing, extended life spans, wondrous machines."[66] Whether such a society can endure, or whether it is doomed to collapse under the weight of its contradictions and injustices, remains to be seen. It is important, however, to think dialectically here, to consider both the creative and destructive qualities of a modern life that is, like Shakespeare's Romeo, "wedded to calamity." What we should surely wish, of course, is to avoid Romeo's fate.

1

The People of Calamity

CATASTROPHIC OPTIMISM IN EARLY AMERICA

There is something astonishing in the American courage for an observer who comes from Europe: although mostly symbolized in the early pioneers it is present today in the large majority of people. A person may have experienced a tragedy, a destructive fate, the breakdown of convictions, even guilt and momentary despair: he feels neither destroyed nor meaningless nor condemned nor without hope. When the Roman Stoic experienced the same catastrophes he took them with the courage of resignation. The typical American, after he has lost the foundations of his existence, works for new foundations. This is true of the individual and it is true of the nation as a whole. One can make experiments because an experimental failure does not mean discouragement. The productive process in which one is a participant naturally includes risks, failures, catastrophes. But they do not undermine courage.

PAUL TILLICH, *The Courage to Be*, 1952

In 1950, as the pathbreaking Disaster Relief Act was making its way quietly through Congress and launching the era of federal emergency management in the United States, the prominent theologian Paul Tillich presented a series of lectures at Yale University that would cause a popular sensation when they appeared two years later as *The Courage to Be*. If the act was an expression of confidence in the power of the modern state to contain natural disasters, Tillich was more interested in seeking solace in what he characterized as an "age of anxiety." He sought encouragement in a world devastated by two world wars and haunted by the prospect of global nuclear annihilation. Despite his well-known disdain for a conformist American society that seemed all too eager to sacrifice civil liberties for the sake of a doubtful national security agenda, he took unexpected comfort from his experiences in the United States, his adopted homeland since fleeing Nazi Germany in the 1930s. Americans, it seemed to him, possessed an exceptional "courage" that spared them from the existential anguish afflicting many Europeans in those years. This courage, in his view, was the centerpiece of a crisis-oriented mode of consciousness that had enabled Americans to navigate the challenges of the modern world with unusual ease; it was an extraordinary psychological resource that enabled adjustment to a dynamic economic and social order that treated "risks, failures, and catastrophes" as unavoidable side effects of development. This courage, he explained, was not a matter of "simple optimism" but was rather the product of a way of being in the world that remained buoyant, in one of his favorite elliptical phrases, "in-spite-of" (106, 172).

The best evidence for American resilience, in other words, was to be found in the way people dealt with adversity, especially in their intuitive sense that there was an intimate relationship between "catastrophe" and "progress." This phenomenon is one of the starting points for my own study. Tillich, of course, was primarily interested in theological and existential questions. He acknowledged that any account of American courage required attention to social processes and material conditions, but he was most concerned with matters of the mind and heart, with self-actualization and the achievement through grace of a union with God. Thus he could minimize, in his analysis of the characteristically American "democratic conformism," such "merely contributing factors as a frontier situation, the need to amalgamate many nationalities, the long isolation from active world politics, the influence of Puritanism and so on."[1] But it is precisely these sorts of factors that most interest me as I examine the crucial contribution of catastrophes to the making of modern America.

Disasters (real and imagined) have from the first days of settlement played a vital role in shaping American religious beliefs and practices, political and economic systems, social relations, environmental outlooks, and identities. Despite the profound heartbreak, misery, anxiety, and terror occasioned by calamities, European colonists converted a troubled sense of themselves as a people of calamity into a comforting sense of themselves as a people of progress. They did so by imagining disasters as "blessings," as instruments of religious salvation, moral reformation, and (ultimately) material improvement. So profound was this expectation that for many the very idea of "progress" became unimaginable in the absence of catastrophes.

I begin this chapter in the 1630s, because we must look to the beliefs and conditions of the colonial period if we are to understand the origins and contours of our own culture of calamity. Many of the idioms or clichés that occur most readily to us today when we seek words to describe calamities (acts of God, judgments, trials, blessings in disguise, and so forth) accrued their popular meanings and resonances in the seventeenth and eighteenth centuries. These are not dead metaphors; such phrases and the histories behind them continue to influence how we understand and respond to fires, floods, earthquakes, epidemics, and attacks. Most of the chapter focuses on New England. It does so not because New Englanders were representative colonists (how could they be when they so doggedly resisted the pronounced fatalism that dominated religious and natural thought in Virginia and Maryland?), nor because the Northeast was especially susceptible to natural calamities (on the contrary, the South and West were much more prone to hurricanes, earthquakes, and droughts), but because it was in New England that many of the most enduring American myths of disaster and progress were devised.[2]

I grant a prominent role in this narrative to the Puritans. Tillich would have found this perplexing. Like most intellectuals of his day, he understood Puritanism as a source of debilitating "guilt" that had shackled American creativity and vitality. As we shall see, however, these death- and disaster-obsessed New Englanders played a decisive role in casting calamities as blessings and turning them into instruments of renewal. What follows, it should be noted, is by no means a comprehensive treatment of disasters in early America. On the contrary, I seek in this chapter to establish a proposition: that colonial experiences of calamity (born of an unsettling but productive collision of religious beliefs and material conditions) established practical and emotional responses that provided a frame for modern responses to disaster. I endeavor to explain why disasters were so significant for the settlers, and how, over the seventeenth and eighteenth centuries, a series of providential, evangelical, and apocalyptic teachings encouraged a view of disasters as "corrections," as opportunities for personal and collective improvement. Paying particular attention to the Boston fire of 1676, I follow the intellectual maneuvers that enabled the prominent divine Increase Mather to assert the benefits of urban destruction. We also see the emergence of an expectation that disaster could contribute to urban and economic expansion, an early expression of the concept of creative destruction that would come to govern capitalist views of development over the following centuries.

I also pay close attention to the politics of disaster. The imaginative link forged between calamity and progress unleashed energies that would propel the colonies and the early republic through phases of extraordinary productivity and expansion. But it was also an integral part of an ongoing project of class formation, implicated in the construction of a distinctively "bourgeois" idea of progress that Tillich would condemn for its inattention to issues of social justice and environmental sustainability. What is clear is that the imagination of disaster traced in this chapter was by no means universal; it was tied to an ideology of personal and social development that tended to serve the interests of the powerful at the expense of the powerless. It is certainly noteworthy that few poor and subjugated inhabitants viewed disasters as blessings. For them an enduring fatalism forestalled fantasies of progress. Disaster remained a symptom and symbol of all that was most miserable about the American experience. At the same time, it may also be true, as the writer Albert Murray argued in the 1950s, that the most viable and appealing "American" form of courage originated not among elites but among the most oppressed, especially among African Americans, whose characteristic cultural expressions, in his view, demanded "affirmation in the face of adversity" and "improvisation in situations of disruption and discontinuity" without succumbing to sentimentality or false optimism.[3] This was an existential worldview, an imagination of disaster, that came much closer to meeting Tillich's criteria for artistry and grace under pressure than did the dominant progressive worldview Tillich (mis)took to be most typically American.

The theologian's ambivalence is worth pausing over here. Although Tillich found much to admire in American dynamism and future-mindedness, he tended to find the American way of life shallow, alienating, and unjust, overly committed to material production without any consideration of ultimate ends or higher purposes.[4] It certainly is worth taking the measure of such criticisms. It is also worth following Tillich in demanding for religion a central role in the story of America. Only by beginning in the seventeenth and eighteenth centuries can we appreciate the long shadow that religious ideas have cast over American ways of imagining and managing disasters.

An American Earthquake: New England, 1638

Moving of th'earth brings harmes and feares,
Men reckon what it did and meant
    JOHN DONNE, "A Valediction: Forbidding Mourning," 1611

"It came," William Bradford later recalled, "with a rumbling noyse, or low murmure, like unto remoate thunder." And it shook the earth with such violence that "platters, dishes, and such like things" rattled on shelves and crashed to the floor, while men and women caught out of doors found that they "could not stand without catching hould of the posts and pails that stood next them."[5] Such was the "great and fearfull earthquake" of 1638, a convulsion that rocked New England on a balmy June afternoon, tossing ships upon the sea and shaking Indian villages deep in the interior, far beyond the frontiers of European settlement. According to the chronicle of Edward Johnson, these shocks caused "diverse men to cast downe their working-tooles, and run with gastly terrified looks, to the next company they could meet withall."[6] This was hardly the first time that Bradford had confronted nature's harms in the New World: the Pilgrim governor and his followers had endured blizzards, storms, and even a "mighty" hurricane since disembarking from the *Mayflower* in 1620. But this was exactly the sort of event guaranteed to provoke colonists to acts of interpretation, as they sought to make sense of, and come to terms with, an apparently endless series of calamities.

Famously describing North America as a "hideous and desolate wilderness," Bradford organized his history of the settlement around a series of encounters with disasters.[7] Although this was to some extent an understandable response to conditions in the New World, this literary strategy was primarily dictated by a religious worldview that granted extraordinary significance to catastrophes. To be sure, New England was not an easy place for the colonists to build a comfortable and secure life. At first, most enjoyed only the slightest margin of security against hunger and destitution, and settlers all along the eastern seaboard were victim to high death rates from disease and hunger as they attempted to adapt to their new surroundings.[8] Although many travelers expressed wonderment about the abundance of land, animals, fish, and trees, even the most ardent enthusiasts could not conceal the fact that North America was often a threatening and violent place for English men and women.[9] The only abundance that many colonists knew was measured in famines, crop failures, earthquakes, fires, and "hostile" Indians.

North America seemed to the English a land of extremes, constantly battered by natural forces unknown in the Old World. The frigid temperatures of what is now called the Little Ice Age made winter living an ongoing ordeal, especially in New England.[10] "They that know the winters of that country," Bradford shivered, "know them to be sharp and violent, and subject to cruel and fierce storms."[11] Europeans did not even have words to describe the frequent hurricanes and blizzards.[12] Experiencing such tempests in a land so far from home was unsettling for the settlers and disposed them to take nature's furies very seriously. In such a context, calamities loomed large not only as material hazards but as symbols of the perils that confronted the pioneers of a forbidding land. Bradford, applying Peter Martyr's account of the Spanish conquest of the Americas to describe the experience of the first Pilgrims, concluded "that with their miseries they opened a way to these new lands, and after these storms, with what ease other men came to inhabit in them, in respect of the calamities that these men suffered, so as they seem to go to a bride feast where all things are provided."[13]

The settlers may have encountered adversities aplenty in America, but Bradford exaggerated the tribulations of the early colonists.[14] Their life was hard but by no means unremittingly miserable. Indians had long since cleared land for crops and villages along the Atlantic coast, significantly easing European settlement, particularly in those locations deserted by Indian communities decimated by the pathogens brought over by pioneers from the Old World.[15] The Pilgrims, for example, established their colony on a site recently abandoned by Wampanoags after a smallpox epidemic.[16] Although immense labor would be required to transform this densely forested region into the sort of landscape favored by the English, it is important not to overstate the strangeness or hostility of the North American environment.[17] Indeed, as historian Alfred Crosby has shown, the Atlantic region turned out to be remarkably hospitable for European settlement. The vagaries of ecological history and a (relatively) temperate climate ensured the successful reproduction and multiplication of Old World peoples, plants, and animals.[18] Even the notoriously cold winters of New England ensured the decimation of dangerous pathogens, making that region an uncommonly healthy environment for Europeans, certainly in comparison to the deserts of the Southwest or the swamps of the Mississippi Delta. The colonists of the Northeast did suffer natural disasters, but these were never on such a scale as to threaten the survival of their communities or to retard the larger enterprise of colonization. They were spared the massive earthquakes and storms that repeatedly devastated the Caribbean and South America.

And yet many New Englanders insisted on portraying themselves as dwellers in a land of disaster. "Nature," Ralph Waldo Emerson observed in 1836, "always wears the colors of the spirit." For "a man laboring under calamity," he explained, "the heat of his own fire hath sadness in it."[19] His Puritan forebears certainly supposed they labored under calamity and projected this belief onto their environment. What is curious is that this preoccupation with calamity did not produce unmixed "sadness." Instead, a combination of religious faith and social experiences prompted leading New Englanders to view their land of disaster as a land of opportunity. Indeed they prepared the way for Emerson's own later conviction that disasters were blessings.

New Englanders treated fires, floods, storms, earthquakes, famines, epidemics, and wars as matters of rare significance that had to be surmounted as well as explained. When Bradford set out to comprehend the earthquake of 1638, he mingled naturalistic and religious understandings. Like other seventeenth-century Europeans, he possessed only the most rudimentary scientific understanding of earthquakes, but he was predisposed to describe the event in physical terms.[20] He wrote his *History of Plymouth Plantation* in the plain style favored by post-Reformation writers, describing in detail the lives of the Pilgrims and the land they inhabited, paying close attention to natural developments and historical incidents. He was as familiar as other colonists, the vast majority of whom were farmers, with seasonal cycles and the crucial role of moisture, sunshine, and rich soils in producing rich harvests; he knew that in the natural order of things one reaped what one sowed. And he wondered about the material effects of the earthquake, noting that in subsequent years summers became cooler and frostier, decimating corn harvests; but he was not confident enough in his knowledge of natural processes to insist on a connection: "whether [the earthquake] was any cause, I leave to naturallists to judge." There is no evidence that any naturalist investigated this hypothesis. The aristocratic physician and scientist John Josselyn, who traveled through New England a few weeks after the tremors, seems to have been more interested in studying the possible contribution of earthquakes to the formation of the region's White Mountains.[21] But both Bradford and Josselyn did share a belief that the cycles of nature were mostly predictable and would have agreed with Harvard president Urian Oakes's observation in 1677 that "to assert the contrary" was "to say that Causes are no Causes, and to speak a flat Contradiction."[22] In the seventeenth century, however, an earthquake was never simply a geological event, and no naturalist would have the last word explaining it.

Bradford lived in an enchanted universe where invisible spirits influenced events in the seen world. Although he believed that cause and effect usually prevailed, like his contemporaries he took it for granted that witches, devils, or God could alter the course of nature at any moment. In fact, when nature went awry, such an intervention was presumed to have happened, and it became extraordinarily important to understand what it meant. To explain what Edward Johnson called "opposition in nature," settler communities drew on a variety of cultural resources, consulting astrological almanacs, mulling over folktales, and even exploring the darker arts of magic and witchcraft for answers. Like the Indians with whom they traded, mingled, and fought, and like the Africans they brought over as slaves, Europeans habitually scanned the natural world for signs of supernatural favor or disfavor.²³ Just as Caribbean peoples had named the fierce tempests that frequently wracked their islands *huru-cans*, or evil spirits, Europeans often blamed storms on witches, devilry, and magic.

Indians, Africans, and Europeans in North America routinely appealed to the invisible world to alter the course of nature, to bring rain or to calm a storm. During the war of 1675, for example, Indian shamans claimed that they had successfully conjured up a hurricane that hurled itself at Boston.²⁴ The English were quite as convinced of the power of ritual and charms to shape the weather. For example, as Edward Johnson recounted, one ship's crew in 1634 "made a strange construction of the sore storme they met withal, saying, their ship was bewitched, and therefore made use of the common Charme ignorant people use, nailing two red hot horse-shoos to their maine mast." Johnson's scornful report reveals the continuing importance of folk beliefs even as it announces the growing intolerance of Puritan leaders for the occult arts and other ungodly superstitions. In his view, the Lord Christ alone commanded the "Winds and Seas," but few clergymen could entirely resist the idea that evil forces were able to conjure up disasters.²⁵ Even in the eighteenth century, the educated clergyman Cotton Mather suspected that witches, working on behalf of Satan, brewed up earthquakes, plagues, and tempests.²⁶ But these suspicions were mostly quelled by, or absorbed into, a providential theology that was the primary filter through which calamities were perceived in the seventeenth century.

In his 1757 essay "The Natural History of Religion," the philosopher David Hume attributed the continuing appeal and influence of Christianity to its power to make sense of death, destruction, and adversity. What was especially striking to him was the determination of Christian divines "to display the advantages of affliction."²⁷ This was certainly true of North American divines. According to the providential outlook shared by settlers throughout the colonies, no natural event could happen without God's consent: a butterfly could not fly, a rainbow could not shimmer, a blade of grass could not grow. God, however, was closest when nature was at its most violent.²⁸ "So powerfull is the mighty hand of the Lord," Bradford explained after the 1638 earthquake, "as to make both the earth and sea to shake, and the mountaines to tremble before him, when he pleases." Bradford was hesitant about claiming any certain knowledge about what these events meant, summoning a variety of likely explanations. Following biblical tradition, he characterized the earth as a place of

harsh and unforgiving exile, attributing the existence of pain and affliction in the world to Adam and Eve's expulsion from paradise.[29] He also
gestured at an Augustinian view of afflictions as divine punishments for
specific sins and transgressions.[30] And he linked this to a Calvinist understanding of misfortunes as trials sent to test and invigorate the piety of a
chosen people.[31] These last two notions could have reinforced the pessimism that informed the theology of the Fall, but they turned out instead
to be building blocks of a theory of disasters as blessings.

"Fatherly Corrections": The Covenant of Calamity

As good Calvinists, Puritans formally accepted that God was unfathom-
able and unknowable. This might well have discouraged them from daring to read the mind of God (as manifested in the Bible and the Book
of Nature) had they not possessed an extraordinarily valuable key for
deciphering the meaning of worldly events: the covenant. According to
the dominant theological economy of punishment and reward, God was
expected to heap material blessings on those who obeyed his laws and
to shower calamities on those who violated them. After all, in such oft-
invoked passages as 2 Chronicles 7:14 God had promised to care for the
elect: "If my people, which are called by my name, shall humble themselves, and pray, and seek my face, and turn from their wicked ways; then
will I hear from heaven, and will forgive their sin, and will heal their
land."[32] The rewards for godliness were great, but so too were the penal-
ties for disobedience. As John Winthrop explained in 1630, "the price of
the breache of such a Covenant" was high: in such a case the Lord would
surely "break out in wrathe against us."[33]

This covenant theology conferred on Christians an extraordinary, if
not entirely dependable, power over their environment. If sins spurred
God to send storms and earthquakes, repentance was a means for restoring harmony to the natural world. Of course, there was nothing auto-
matic about this relationship. God was not bound to heed the petitions
of his people. Nevertheless, the covenant did give Puritans in particular
a sense of psychic control over their environment.[34] Although they were
famously hostile to traditional Christian holy days, like many heirs of
the Reformation they believed the most appropriate response to collective misfortunes was to observe fast days, attending long church services,
dressing plainly, and avoiding work or play as if it were the Sabbath.[35]
Like prayer, the fast day was an important ritual for performing communal repentance and beseeching God to spare a wayward people from
calamity.[36]

Although an affliction was always a punishment for some offense in this scheme, it was also evidence of God's overruling mercy and justice. Starting from the Calvinist premise that human sins were always great enough to justify the total obliteration of all individuals, any lesser punishment was a great kindness best appreciated as an instrument of moral reformation to keep a chosen people on the path to salvation. Therefore, the appropriate response to misfortune, as Pilgrim pastor John Robinson explained in 1628, was "to thank God, that makes afflictions bittersweets, by turning deserved curses into fatherly corrections to us."[37] So close was the assumed connection between calamity and divine concern that some pious souls became unnerved when things went too well. The English archbishop James Ussher, an Anglican much respected by Cotton Mather, had worried about the absence of calamities during his youth in the first years of the seventeenth century, fearing that this meant that God had abandoned him.[38]

Calamities had long inspired not only moral reformation but also the cultivation of conscience; indeed, they were necessary foils against which Puritan selves were fashioned. In the *Institutes of the Christian Religion* (1536), John Calvin had taught that "true and sound wisdom, consists of two parts: the knowledge of God and of ourselves."[39] Disasters were updates from God on the state of men's souls and, as such, were supreme occasions for learning about providence and human nature. Puritans judged themselves to a considerable degree in terms of their predisposition to misfortune: they were afflicted because they were sinners, and when they were afflicted it was their duty to identify and root out wickedness within. This, of course, was no easy task. As Calvinists they believed they were steeped in sin and that misfortune was unavoidable. This truth could provoke resentment, as when Boston magistrate Samuel Sewall became exasperated with God for making him "a person that might be a fit subject of a calamity"—for making him, in short, a being so imperfect that he was doomed to sin and to suffer "difficulties and perplexing miseries."[40] But Sewall never doubted that it was his duty to judge the state of his soul according to his susceptibility to affliction. These exercises in self-examination and self-recrimination nurtured his conscience, and this produced in him a strong, if conflicted, sense of himself as a person with a complex and meaningful interior life.[41] The imagination of disaster, in other words, had a part to play in the formation of American individualism. But the early colonists tended to pay most attention to the communal implications of misfortunes.

Calamities had special resonance in the New World. John Winthrop, for example, hoped that God would shelter a devout commonwealth from severe misfortunes as well as the "generall calamity" that God was surely destined to wreak upon a sinful world.[42] At the same time, biblical precedent suggested that a godly people might well experience more than their fair share of hardships.[43] This was a compelling idea for these religious colonists. As Edward Johnson observed:

> As the Lord surrounded his chosen Israel with dangers deepe to make his miraculous deliverance famous throughout, and to the end of the World, so here behold the Lord Christ, having egged a small handfull of his people forthe in a forlorne Wildernesse, stripping them naked from all humane helps, plunging them in a gulph of miseries, that they may swim for their lives through the Ocean of his Mercies, and land themselves in the armes of his compassion.[44]

Johnson did not speak for all settlers, but he was typical of the first generation of Puritans, who tended to focus on the purifying rather than the punitive aspect of calamities.

Disasters, by this reasoning, were the unique burden of a chosen people, proof of the calling of the American colonists, evidence of "the Lords Special Controversie with this Land."[45] Augustine had insisted that the outcome of a calamity depended on the holiness or otherwise of sufferers: "The same violence of affliction proveth, purifieth, and melteth the good, and condemneth, wasteth, and casteth out the bad."[46] Increase Mather updated this observation and applied it to his own people:

> The dealings of God with our Nation . . . and with the Nations of the World, is very different: for other Nations may sin and do wickedly, and God doth not punish them, untill they have filled up the Measure of their sins, and then he utterly destroyeth them; but if our Nation forsake the God of their Fathers never so little, God presently cometh upon us with one Judgement or other, that so he may prevent our destruction.[47]

As we shall see, over the following century this sort of thinking would help to shape an evangelical tradition that would have an extraordinary and enduring influence on American religion. And disasters would figure centrally here. Whereas seventeenth-century Puritans had rarely deviated from the view that calamities were temporal punishments with little bearing on any individual's prospects for salvation, in the 1670s this began to change. By the eighteenth century, Increase Mather's son, Cotton, came to believe that disasters could be relied on to provoke the emotional states necessary to precipitate a religious revival.[48] Although he appreciated the role of study and quiet contemplation in promoting Christian behaviors, he believed that it was only in a state of agitation, only in the presence of misfortune, that most people could grasp the necessity for moral reformation or conversion. "In deadly *Dangers*," he determined, "the *Conscience* comes to operate."[49] And this was a step toward salvation.

In his view, disasters were welcome aids to the cultivation of faith. On the evening of October 29, 1727, an earthquake rumbled through Boston. By the next morning, the Old North Church was full to bursting, and Cotton Mather could not have been more pleased. He had called a special service to reflect on the shocks, and townspeople had responded with uncommon zeal. In truth, it had not been a particularly impressive earthquake. The vibrations caused only minor damage and no lives were lost. Certainly, there were no horrifying scenes to compare with the carnage of the smallpox epidemic that had visited Boston a few years earlier. And yet the fear and curiosity of New Englanders had been aroused, and Mather found this heartening. Whereas settlers had responded to the earthquake of 1638 with impromptu prayers, their descendants now turned to formal institutions for instruction and reassurance: churches would fill with new converts, fast days would be observed, and a revival would ensue.[50] Cotton Mather took the opportunity to berate church members who had fallen into the habit of drowsing during his sermons, an impertinence he characteristically denounced as "an affront to Heaven." He was pleased to see that the earthquake had jolted the good people of Boston out of their slumbers. "I see none *Asleep* at this Time," he crowed, gladdened that God should involve himself in "the Awaking of . . . Drowsy Sleepers."[51] Indeed, he dared to hope that the fears produced by the calamity might precipitate a more general awakening. He was not entirely disappointed. Seventy-one new members joined his church in the months after the earthquake, and other New England churches enjoyed similar gains. Many of these new converts, like Jeremiah Eaton of the Lynn End church, admitted that it was the earthquake that had led them to God: "I desire to bless God for ye awakening Considerations which I have had by his late providence ye Earth-quake wch made me have quick Apprehensions of my own Sins and guilt."[52]

This wave of conversions foreshadowed and, by some accounts, precipitated the revivals of the Great Awakening that would spread rapidly through the colonies in the next two decades. "More than any other event," according to historian Harry Stout, "the Great Earthquake convinced ministers of the potential for mass revival."[53] Over the 1720s, many Protestants on both sides of the Atlantic had come to agree that preachers had to reach the heart as well as the minds of men and women if they were to promote Christian faith in a world of modern distractions.[54] Evangelicals from Jonathan Edwards to George Whitefield maintained that the best way to serve religion was to inflame emotions rather than appeal to cool reason, though they understood that the wrong sort of enthusiasm could obstruct God's end.[55] Although he accepted the conventional premise that disasters were divine afflictions, Edwards in particular was less interested in their punitive dimensions than in their contributions to spiritual development. He portrayed calamities as gifts from God, and he characterized God as a "prudent husbandman" who sought to cultivate the souls of his people in order to prepare them to receive his grace: "He doth as it were plow and mellow the hard ground, and breaks the hard clods and evens their roughness to fit them to receive the seed and to bring forth good fruit."[56] And Edwards went further. Disasters, in his view, promised not only to facilitate individual awakening but also to bring about the Second Coming of Christ.

Millennialism proved to be quite as potent a legacy of colonial religious thought as evangelicalism. And here disasters acquired additional significance as portents of the apocalypse. "It is indeed the *Faithfulness of our God unto us*," as Cotton Mather explained, "that we should find the *Earth* more full of *Thorns* and *Briars* than ever, just before he fetches us from *Earth* to *Heaven;* that so we may go away the more willingly, the more easily, and with less Convulsion, at his calling for us."[57] Drawing on Revelation 16:18, Mather claimed biblical authority for his assertion that afflictions would accumulate as the Day of Reckoning approached. Indeed, he was convinced that the earthquake of 1727 was a "Praemonition" of the apocalypse. Interestingly, he did not dwell on this notion in his sermons for fear of being "much mocked" by his neighbors, and indeed it would take time before millennialism would achieve respectability.

But by the end of the eighteenth century a significant number of ministers and congregations began to hail disasters as welcome evidence that the thousand-year rule of Christ was nigh.[58] The orthodox Augustinian view maintained that the apocalypse was supposed to be heralded by a series of awesome calamities, after which a great conflagration (the Day of Doom) would destroy the earth and its wicked inhabitants, sparing only the elect, who would at that moment ascend to their heavenly paradise. This was similar to the influential late-twentieth-century belief in the Rapture, which also looked to earthquakes and floods and fires as signs of an apocalypse, expecting that the born-again would be raised to heaven and thus escape the tribulations and the rule of the Antichrist that would precede the Battle of Armageddon, the victory of heaven's armies and the establishment of the Kingdom of Christ on earth. Mather also expected disasters to multiply on the eve of the Second Coming, but he was convinced that a thousand years of peace and prosperity would precede the tribulations and the ascension of the elect.

This laid the foundation for thinkers such as Jonathan Edwards to suspect that the millennium would happen in North America, and it added a powerful historical and nationalist dimension to popular understandings of the blessings of disaster.[59] Edwards, for one, routinely scanned contemporary events for evidence of the final defeat of the Antichrist and the imminent arrival of Christ's thousand-year rule on earth.[60] If Rome was Babylon, then any misfortune that befell the "popish powers" of France and Spain could be greeted as evidence of Satan's declining influence on earth. Misfortune could arrive through natural or military means. Edwards was quite as gladdened by the losses suffered by the Spanish after the Lima earthquake of 1746, when "all the ships in the harbor were dashed in pieces as it were in a Moment, by the immediate Hand of God," as he was by the "almost miraculous taking of Cape-Breton" by British forces in 1745.[61]

But it was the happy conclusion of the French and Indian War in 1763 that really began to convince religious leaders that the millennium was at hand—and perhaps in North America itself.[62] As Britain displaced France as the primary threat to American liberty and virtue during the 1760s, patriotic ministers revived old jeremiad formulas to justify resistance to the new oppressor. In the 1770s, Americans were more preoccupied with military disasters than with natural ones, but all afflictions could be interpreted to demonstrate God's support for (or opposition to) the patriots' cause. If it was true, as the Reverend John Joachim Zubly contended during the political crisis of the 1760s, that "national sins" brought on "national calamities," then repentance and moral reformation became suddenly necessary for national salvation.[63] On the other hand, the logic of salvation and millennialism taught that it was at the moment of greatest calamity that God usually intervened to deliver his people from their sufferings. Trials were necessary to purify the saints so that they could become worthy to inherit the earth, and calamities now portended the achievement of an earthly paradise in America. This, above all, explained the paradoxical title of Connecticut pastor Ebenezer Baldwin's 1775 sermon: "The Duty of Rejoicing Under Calamities and Afflictions."

Whether emphasizing the role of disasters as purifying trials, corrective afflictions, or apocalyptic portents, religious doctrine in the colonial period created ample cultural space for an appreciation of fires, floods, and earthquakes as blessings. The exact meaning of calamity and the exact benefits, however, were matters of considerable disagreement. These disputes were driven as much by competing opinions about proper social organization and economic development as they were by ideas about the designs of God or the workings of nature.

"The Blasting Rebukes of Providence": Boston, 1676

To begin to understand the colonial politics of disaster, and the relationship between social and religious outlooks, let us look more closely at one important event: the Boston fire of 1676. On November 27, at about five in the morning, a drowsy young apprentice fell asleep during the fulfillment of his early morning duties, leaving a candle unattended. When he awoke, the room around him was burning. The house quickly succumbed, and in short order the building next door was ablaze. A hard-blowing wind propelled the flames through the north end of the town, destroying about fifty homes, stores, and warehouses before a heavy downpour finally brought an end to the conflagration.[64] There were no human casualties. Indeed, the disaster was modest by later standards, but it nevertheless acquired considerable cultural significance because of the way it spoke to the social and religious preoccupations of the community.

At this fluid historical moment there was considerable uncertainty about what calamities meant. This mattered because calamities were presumed to be unusually meaningful—speaking directly to God's designs and purposes. And the stakes were unusually high because New England was embroiled in a particularly brutal conflict (King Philip's War of 1675–76); Indian attacks seemed to be threatening the very existence of the colony. Given the religious and intellectual beliefs of the time, any attempt to make sense of the Boston fire was thus also an intervention in larger theological and social debates. It was nothing less than an attempt to describe, or perhaps to manufacture a sense of, reality.

Most colonists had a complex and multifaceted understanding of disasters. In his well-known book on the Indian war, published a few months after the August cessation of hostilities, the prominent Ipswich minister William Hubbard broke off from a lengthy chronicle of military misfortunes and deaths ("Calamities and Troubles" of another sort) to offer the following account of the fire:

> It pleased God to alarm the town of *Boston*, and in them the whole Country, by a sad Fire, accidentally kindled by the Carelessness of an Apprentice that sat up too late over Night, as was conceived; which began an Hour

before Day, continuing three or four, in which Time it burned down to the Ground forty six Dwelling Houses, besides other Buildings, together with a Meeting-house of considerable Bigness: some Mercy was observed mixt with the Judgment: for if a great Rain had not continued all the Time, (the Roofs and Walls of their ordinary Buildings consisting of such combustible Matter) that the whole end of the Town had at that Time been consumed.[65]

For Hubbard, the fire was both an accident *and* a divine affliction caused by the negligence of a boy who was acting (unwittingly) as an agent of the Lord's designs. If the rain was a manifestation of God's "mercy," it was strongly implied that the calamity could have been avoided if houses had been built out of less "combustible matter." Hubbard, in other words, married naturalism and supernaturalism. Significantly, he refused to specify the sins that had brought about this "judgment," a reticence that marked him as a religious moderate in a society that was falling under the spell of his rival, Increase Mather, a man who was making a career out of naming sins and sinners.[66]

More than any other colonial figure, Mather demonstrated how important control over the interpretation of disasters was to the exercise of power.[67] During King Philip's War, many ordinary New Englanders began to take prophecies of doom seriously for the first time. Although the English suffered many fewer casualties than the Indians, they still lost between six and eight hundred lives and endured the destruction of twelve hundred houses and about half of their towns.[68] A year of skirmishes seemed to have set the colonial enterprise back by decades. William Hubbard explained the war as one of the inevitable calamities that fallen man could be expected to undergo, even as he characterized the struggle as one between virtuous New Englanders and devilish Indians who were sent to try them.[69] With survival hanging in the balance, however, settlers became more attentive to ministers who claimed to know exactly what the troubles meant and how to end them. Mather was particularly confident in his analysis, preaching that the war was a punishment for the sins of the settlers and that moral and religious reformation would bring about the victory they craved.[70] Historian David D. Hall has explained that the war "intensified" the politics of calamity, with competing groups pressing social agendas under the guise of their attempts to interpret this and other misfortunes.[71]

By 1676, the young Mather was establishing himself as New England's Jeremiah. He had finally found his most durable themes: the failure of second-generation Puritans to live up to the pious standards of their fathers, the inevitable calamities that would follow, and the need for moral and spiritual reformation to forestall future punishments. Scouring the Bible for portents and comparing the Puritans to the Israelites, he found plenty of cause for both alarm and reassurance. "The wayes of God are ever-lasting," he declared, "wherefore he brings the same Judgements upon his People now as in the dayes of old, in case there be the same trans-gressions: if then we would know why Droughts, Blastings, &c. have been upon our Land, let us search the Scriptures, and see for what sins those Judgements have befallen God's Israel of old."[72] In 1674, Mather published two jeremiads as *The Day of Trouble Is Near*, warning that New England was soon to be engulfed by the "Calamity of War" unless set-tlers abandoned sinful pursuits.[73] When his prophecy seemed to come true, his personal authority and influence increased enormously.[74] Al-though military commissioners continued to emphasize the importance of strategy and weaponry as the best way to win the war, the General Court bowed to Mather's demands to ban a host of "Provoking Evils," including the sale of alcohol and the wearing of long hair by men, in the hope of winning back God's favor and thereby improving their chances of victory.[75] Interpreting disasters, here as elsewhere, led directly to the policing of personal and social behaviors.

In the weeks immediately preceding the 1676 fire, Mather had been hammering home from his North End pulpit his conviction that the set-tlers had so thoroughly immersed themselves in wickedness that addi-tional calamities were surely imminent. He was not entirely convincing. Even his wife apparently thought this was "only a phansy in my head, and would not be persuaded."[76] When the inferno came, however, he had a powerful explanatory framework in place to make sense of it.

But he was in for a surprise, because his own home and church (the "Meeting-house of considerable Bigness" described in Hubbard's ac-count) were among the first structures to perish. In his public utterances, Mather claimed vindication for his prophetic abilities; privately, though, he admitted to being shaken. During the war, he had been struck by the preservation of churches from the general destruction and took this as an indication that piety could be a dependable shield against misfortune.[77] Now he found himself among those most afflicted. On the day after the fire, he wrestled with this vexing matter in his diary. He was willing to allow that he was being punished for his own sins, but he was clearly hurt that he should be singled out for suffering: "Is Judgt begun at ye House of God! Must it begin with me? And is this all? Shall ye cup pass away from me so?"[78] In a letter to his brother-in-law, John Cotton, he wondered if his own "unfaithfullness" had not been "a special cause of the desolation."

47

He acknowledged his own limitations as a minister: "I see plainly that I am so farr from being able to keep judgement off from others, that I cannot keep off from my owne House."[79] Although Mather was always eager to present an assured public face to his community, rarely admitting to doubts, his letters and diaries reveal the intense anxieties and uncertainties with which he struggled.[80] And yet he felt compelled to insist on and identify the blessings of affliction.

After the fire, he thanked God (and his angels) for ensuring that he had had a sleepless night, ensuring that he would become aware of the fire before the alarm was sounded and thus have time to save his family and some of his most treasured possessions. And these mercies extended to matters of the spirit. Accordingly, he praised the "tender hearted and loving Father" for his religious instruction, for sending a calamity to "correct me with so much gentleness, notwithstanding all my unworthy walkings before him." The fire, by his account, was a mild rebuke to inspire the people of New England to acts of moral and spiritual reformation that alone would make them worthy of salvation. After all, it was well known that the Lord sent calamities to test the "sincerity and fidelity" of the elect, leading them into "the Furnace of Affliction" so that "they may be purged and sanctified, and become vessels meet for their Masters use."[81]

Believing that calamities were opportunities, the most influential American interpreter of disasters in the seventeenth century was remarkably positive in his response to adversity, always searching for silver linings.[82] But there were no grounds for complacency. As Mather warned, it was necessary to reform quickly "lest greater Fires be kindled, and more Candlesticks be removed out of their places, and then it be too late to prevent those evils which as yet may possibly be diverted."[83]

Significantly, Increase Mather appealed both to his education and to his virtue to justify his exclusive authority as an interpreter of disasters. He viewed himself as an educated man who was able to draw on his scientific knowledge to explain the workings of nature. Over the following decade he embraced a version of Newtonian science that convinced him that the natural world was fundamentally regular in its operation.[84] Significantly, the more convinced that Mather and other thinkers were about the basic orderliness of nature, the more fascinating they found extraordinary events such as comets, earthquakes, hurricanes, and fires. This led him to share a widespread preoccupation with calamities as wonders that inspired passionate scientific inquiry.[85] Although Mather, for example, was endorsing study of nature's laws as one way to read the mind of God by the 1680s, he was increasingly convinced that God spoke only through ruptures rather than regularities.[86] Mather offered his most sustained attempt to explain the meaning of disasters eight years after the Boston fire in his book *Remarkable Providences*. He viewed his book as an exemplary application of the scientific method. But Mather also insisted that "special providences" were often sacred utterances.[87] He insisted that the natural language of God was complex and ambiguous and that only the most righteous people could possibly hope to decode it. "I have ever thought it unwarrantable," he wrote in 1682, "for men, not acted by an extraordinary spirit, to make particular and positive determinations concerning the Judgements (or Persons eminently concerned therein) by such Prodigie menaced."[88]

He allowed that it was tempting to suppose that any affliction was a judgment on a sinner, but he made a point of reminding readers of the story of Job, an instance when a good man had suffered. He could think of many occasions when the virtuous had suffered calamity (he was surely thinking also of his own misfortunes in the fire of 1676) and could only conclude: "We may not judge of men meerly by outward accidents which befal them in this world, since all things happen alike unto all, and no man knoweth either love or hatred by all that is before them. We have seen amongst ourselves that the Lords faithful servants have sometimes been the subjects of very dismal dispensations."[89] His concern here was to deflect the accusations of Papists and Quakers who were inclined to interpret local afflictions as evidence of God's disfavor with Protestants and Puritans.[90] Certainly, he himself showed no restraint in his efforts to politicize disaster. He devoted ten gruesome pages of his book to an enumeration of "the blasting rebukes of Providence" against Quakers and several more on the proper afflictions of profaners and drunkards.[91]

Disasters contributed crucially to an expansion in the power of the constituted authorities. In the seventeenth century, municipal powers tended to be vague, and many towns were weak in defending public against private interests.[92] This was true even in Boston. It was the experience and continuing threat of conflagrations that provided occasions for exceptional interference by the authorities in the lives of townsmen and women. Town records suggest that fire prevention was one of the principal spurs to municipal activism in Boston. After a fire killed three children in 1653, homeowners were required by town ordinances to keep on hand ladders and twelve-foot poles with a "large swob on the end of it, to rech the rofe of his house to quench fire," so as to make it easier to put out flames as they spread from roof to roof.[93] A 1670 law ordered every household to keep a container of water available for throwing on fires, and it threatened delinquents with a penalty of five shillings.[94] The city also regularly fined people for possession of faulty or filthy chimneys, on the grounds that this was the principal cause of fires.[95] Cotton Mather himself was fined in 1708 for possessing a dirty chimney.[96]

The Puritans are well known for their activist governments and for their commitment to sacrificing private rights for the sake of the public interest, but this tendency to centralization was most apparent during and immediately after calamities. A Massachusetts law of 1658 decreed that those convicted of arson could be executed, and in 1679 a supposedly lenient General Court exiled ten individuals who were "under vehement suspicion of attempting to burn the town of Boston."[97] In the 1650s, Boston officials followed English precedents and passed laws that gave them the authority to tear down any private house during a fire in the hope that this would deprive any advancing flame of fuel.[98] In the first decades of settlement, dwellings tended to be flimsy, and it was easy enough to pull thatched roofs down with hooks. But by 1676 there were enough brick structures to require explosives, and townspeople used powder to blow up five buildings, though rain probably did more to end the fire than demolition.[99] Disaster and concentrations of state power tended to go hand in hand, and as we shall see, this was not a happy prospect for all inhabitants in the colonies.

The Material Blessings of Disaster

One of the more remarkable benefits of disaster, according to the official pronouncements of ministers, was their propensity for destroying material possessions. Edward Johnson suspected that a "longing lust for gain" was responsible for a sudden increase in the scale and incidence of droughts and fires in the second half of the seventeenth century. After 1650, in his view, a once-protective God had "let in the King of Terror among his new-planted Churches," showering "his people" with calamities to "awaken, rouze up, and quicken them with the rod of his power." Johnson's response was heartfelt: "Lord stay thy hand, and stop my earthly mind, / Thy Word, not world, shall be our sole delight."[100] Increase Mather felt much the same way about the fire of 1676. To be sure, he regretted the "great misery" that had "lamentably impoverished" members of his congregation, and he was pained by the loss of his own home and most of his furniture, clothes, and winter provisions, but he hoped this calamity might offer a corrective to the materialism of his age.[101] According to Mather, an "inordinate Affection to the World" was one of the more egregious sins responsible for the fire.[102] Several months before the blaze, with Bostonians devoting themselves ever more unashamedly to commerce and self-advancement, he had excoriated his countrymen for their base pursuits: "*Land! Land!*" he lamented, "hath been the Idol of many in *New England.*" And the results had been shocking: "They that profess themselves Christians have foresaken Churches, and Ordinances, and all for land and elbow-room enough in the World."[103]

This was one of the Puritan dilemmas. On the one hand, a high premium was placed on property and prosperity as guarantors of social order, and thus it was both a social and a religious duty to rebuild homes and plantations in the aftermath of calamities. Moreover, it was expected that within the providential order of things the industrious and saintly would prosper. On the other hand, it was never acceptable for church folk to become preoccupied with the pursuit of earthly riches. And herein lay the problem. As Mather's son Cotton explained, "*Religion* brought forth *Prosperity*" but "the *Enchantments* of this World" always threatened to make the Puritans "forget *their Errand into the Wilderness.*"[104] In such a context, as Mather and Hubbard for that matter agreed, the destroying flame provided an overdue reminder of the transience of worldly goods.[105] The destruction of property could theoretically be counted among the blessings of the calamity.

In practice, however, Puritans clearly found it easier to assert than truly feel this benefit. It would be quite improper to understate the anguish and misery that accompanied personal and collective misfortune. As Ann Bradstreet's famous poem, written on the occasion of the burning of her house in 1666, attested, rhetorical pieties about the vanity of earthly goods only partly salved the pain caused by the loss of her dearest possessions.[106] Moreover, it never occurred to Increase Mather to stand by in 1676 and watch the punishing flames devour his property. On the contrary, he devoted his efforts to salvaging as many things as he could and was delighted that he was able to save not only precious books but such mundane comforts as linen and bedding. Even this most pious of Puritans was hardly otherworldly. He did not think that prayer alone could stop a fire. And when piety and expediency clashed, he chose expediency. For example, in his sermons he repeatedly counted Sabbath breaking among the sins most likely to provoke a disaster, but when a blaze broke out on a Sunday he insisted a concerted human response was appropriate: "If an House is on Fire, on the Sabbath Day, all Hands may go to work to Quench it, because the Necessity is Present *and Certain.*"[107]

Looking back on the fires that swept through Boston over the seventeenth century, Cotton Mather wondered, "That such a *Combustible heap* of Contiguous Houses yet stands, . . . may be called A *Standing Miracle.*" The town had been afflicted so often that he could think of no better way to describe it than as a *"City of Destruction:* Or I will rather say, *A City of Salvation."* To explain the miracle of repeated deliverance, he gave credit not to the town's watchmen or to its firefighting practices but to the *"watchful Protection"* of God.[108] But Bostonians did not leave their security to God alone. On the contrary, the Puritan quest to build an orderly, godly society in the wilderness gave them all the religious sanction they needed to prevent conflagrations and to rebuild demolished settlements. In 1702, Mather was struck by the fact that the ruins left behind by earlier fires had "mostly and quickly been Rebuilt."[109]

Calamities prompted efforts to build safer homes and towns, thus becoming material as well as spiritual blessings. Increase Mather's North Church was among the first structures to be restored after the fire of 1676; the new structure was larger, more substantial, and more imposing than its burned-out predecessor.[110] And this was not the only upgrade. The fire turned out to be a welcome occasion for household and citywide improvements. Of course, town authorities did not require a calamity to build and repair roads, maintain streets, and promote development at the taxpayer's expense, but crises like the 1676 fire facilitated increased government activism.[111] Boston's founders had not built for expansion, and by the 1670s an influx of refugees from King Philip's War had accelerated the transformation of this New England village on the hill into an increasingly congested seaport of forty-five hundred inhabitants. After the fire, the Boston Court of Assistants seized the opportunity to widen and straighten downtown streets. First, they prohibited reconstruction in the burned district except with the express "advice and order of the selectmen," and then they passed a law to widen the thoroughfare later known as Hanover Street to an almost uniform width of twenty-two feet, which helped to speed up the flow of traffic and stimulate business in this rapidly commercializing port city. The Massachusetts General Court approved this initiative, overriding the objections of one recalcitrant property owner, ruling that he should "have proportionable satisfaction tendered him for so much of his land that is taken and staked out to the street."[112] The General Court increased the width of thoroughfares after further fires in 1690 and 1691, and after yet another fire in 1711 it raised public money for widening highways again. Although city funds were so scarce that New Englanders had to depend on private money to build many roads and bridges, these initiatives helped ensure that by 1720 Boston boasted the best system of paved highways in North America. This would not have been possible without the endless series of fires. Nor would it have been possible without discriminatory laws approved in 1707 and 1708 that empowered officials to force "Negroes and mulat-toes" to work on these projects for free.[113]

Frequent fires also led to building codes that helped produce safer and more solid buildings. The threat of such blazes had led to prohibitions against wooden chimneys and thatched roofs in Boston as early as 1631.[114] And a fire in 1679 had finally prodded the Massachusetts General Court into passing the first comprehensive building law for the town. It required homes to be built from stone or brick and roofs to be composed of slate or tiles and provided for fines of twice the value of the structure for lawbreakers.[115] The law was comprehensive enough, but it was incompletely enforced until another fire in 1691 convinced the General Court to forbid exemptions. By the eighteenth century such regulations finally began to bite, and brick buildings became more common in Boston, especially after a great fire in 1711 destroyed the center of the town, presenting an opportunity to rebuild much of the old downtown with impressive brick buildings, including an elegant new First Church and the Boston Town House.[116]

Disasters played a crucial role in the shaping and reshaping of urban space in colonial America. But even the most optimistic and energetic colonists were sometimes stymied in their attempts to turn calamities into blessings by the absence of sufficient economic capacity and infrastructure. No town was more hindered by calamities than Charleston, South Carolina. A series of hurricanes, earthquakes, and fires seriously retarded the development and expansion of the town in the years before 1720, and slowed it thereafter.[117] Bostonians also could not take improvements for granted. Very few individuals had access to reliable forms of insurance, though there were some mutual aid societies, and individual merchants had access to the policies offered by European companies that had begun at the end of the seventeenth century to adapt more traditional forms of marine insurance to provide some protection against losses from fire.[118] In the absence of insurance, dependable relief, or easy credit, disasters caused at least as much ruin as renewal. But probably more damaging was the scarcity of relief and credit for the victims of fires.

Models of Christian Charity

Very few people in Boston or America generally had access to any sort of fire insurance before the Revolution, so victims had to depend on loans, savings, charitable donations, tax exemptions, and poor relief. The Mathers were able to buy a new house to replace the one that burned in

1676 with money Increase's wife Maria inherited from her mother.[119] But few were so well provided for. According to the system of poor relief that the colonists had brought with them from England, it was the responsibility of parishes to support the destitute with funds raised from taxes.[120] To cover the unexpected costs of famines and fires, parishes were expected to raise and disburse money from property taxes.[121] Even though American towns were able to provide for most orphans, widows, and disabled men in the seventeenth century, exceptional events were apt to place intolerable burdens on town treasuries.[122] When refugees poured into Boston in 1675 and 1676, fleeing the devastations of King Philip's War, the town fathers petitioned the General Court to relieve them of permanent responsibility for the unfortunates.[123] On other occasions, the town was more generous, for example, selling some land in 1644 to compensate a resident for "his late greate losse through the hand of Gods Providence by fire," but public funds were rarely sufficient to meet the needs of sufferers in the wake of general calamities.[124]

The most common form of government relief in colonial New England was the temporary reduction or cancellation of taxes.[125] This form of support became sufficiently established over the eighteenth century for the victims of yet another fire in Boston to be positively outraged when the Massachusetts General Court refused requests for such relief in 1760. But it was always an erratic form of assistance, and it was of little help to those who lost everything in a blaze. In the second half of the eighteenth century, provincial governments began to step into the breach with outright gifts.[126] The Massachusetts legislature, for example, gave £3,000 to the sufferers of the 1760 fire, and the legislatures of New York and Pennsylvania quickly followed suit in providing gifts to disaster victims. But the most important sources of aid were the private sums raised by churches, merchants, and ordinary men and women from cities as far afield as New York and London.[127] Indeed, charity was the primary source of disaster aid throughout the colonial period.

Fire relief was more haphazardly organized in America than in England. With the decline of the guilds and monasteries that had traditionally assumed most of the burden of charitable enterprises in the Old Country, the monarchy had become increasingly involved in philanthropy during the sixteenth century. The Crown was motivated to this action by a desire to avert social unrest amid ongoing and widespread enclosures and evictions, revealing a close connection between disaster relief, social control, and the disturbances of modern economic organization that would remain operative in the New World.[128] American colonists borrowed many of their approaches to disaster relief from the Old Country, but their distance from Crown and Parliament required them to develop distinctive relief and reconstruction practices. When a calamity struck, it remained a local responsibility, certainly until the middle of the eighteenth century. Disaster victims could not depend on any reliable disaster relief. As late as 1760, a fire that destroyed 174 homes and 175 shops in Boston at a cost of £53,000 caused such severe economic hardship and political instability that one historian has identified this calamity as an important source of revolutionary resentment.[129] Such circumstances ensured that disasters would be occasions for tremendous class anxiety and, in most cases, authoritarianism.

If anywhere, New England should have been an unusually comforting place to become suddenly destitute. Although the Protestant settlers did not view good works as a way to achieve salvation, they certainly did insist that the elect would naturally display their saintliness through their generosity and care of strangers. For Puritans, charity was a profound moral and religious obligation, as important for the spiritual development of the giver as for the material sustenance of the recipient. Moreover, it was a primary means of dispelling potential sources of misery and disorder, as was clear from the famous sermon "A Model of Christian Charity" delivered by John Winthrop aboard the *Arabella* in 1630. A stable and virtuous society, in his view, was one that provided for the unfortunate. Charity was a constant obligation, but relief was most urgently required to alleviate the distress of any "community of perills."[130] To be sure, this was not based on any expectation of the innocence of disaster victims—after all, everyone was a sinner and disasters were divine judgments—but such sufferers, especially when local and known, did seem to be more deserving than vagrants and the poor who always carried a taint of idleness and immorality.[131]

Compassion and social control became even more closely intertwined as the proper response to eighteenth-century disasters. After the Boston fire of 1711, Cotton Mather was adamant that townsmen should "show Pitty to them, who have Lost their Houses," browbeating more fortunate residents to donate food, clothing, and shelter to the homeless: "O Let us Do all we can for them."[132] But he was motivated, at least in part, by the desire to contain the chaos that threatened if ever a large group of people was to be suddenly without means of support. Amid a market revolution that was destabilizing eighteenth-century New England society, propertied citizens such as Mather were demonstrably anxious about the disintegrating effects of natural disasters. The population of Boston surpassed twelve thousand in 1720, and this commercial city began to experience urban problems such as unemployment, destitution, and riotousness. The increasing numbers of paupers, immigrants, and slaves were widely believed to be the cause of a steep rise in crimes against property.[133] And during a calamity, even the compassionate Mather was inclined to endorse repressive measures to combat looting and other criminal or rebellious acts. Looting, of course, was not a new problem. Somebody had stolen money from the pile of goods salvaged by Cotton Mather and his father from the fire of 1676.[134] But in the context of the eighteenth century, such acts seemed to constitute an especially sinister threat to order.

Although ministers like Mather only rarely acknowledged social differences among their readers and listeners in their writings or sermons, race and class played an absolutely central role in shaping legal and political responses to disasters. As far as most European settlers were concerned, the forces of chaos wore black and red faces. Eighteenth-century laws designed to avert looting and unrest were openly discriminatory. Under normal circumstances, slaves could not travel without a pass and had to abide by curfews that prohibited their presence on Boston Common after dark, but when a fire broke out, blacks and Indians were not allowed on the streets at all.[135] Growing fears that servants and other lowly groups were going to rise up and burn the town down ensured that slaves or Indians were treated with extreme suspicion during any conflagration.

To be sure, there was no incident to match New York's "great Negro plot of 1741" for hysteria or drama. As New York was the second largest slave-owning city in America (after Charleston), with two thousand blacks out of a population of eleven thousand, it is perhaps understandable that anxieties about slave rebellion ran high there. Town authorities hanged seventeen blacks (and four whites) and incinerated thirteen more at the stake as punishment for an alleged conspiracy to torch the city—a "mad panic" later described by Theodore Roosevelt as "the darkest page" in the annals of New York City.[136]

Boston's nonwhite population was substantially smaller than that of New York, but even here the number of slaves was growing, and conflagrations fanned fears of rebellion. Boston authorities ordered the public whipping of several blacks after fires in 1721 and 1723 on suspicion of incendiarism, with the intention of deterring future arson attacks.[137] Whatever Cotton Mather might have wished or claimed, when calamities struck, Bostonians relied on power and violence rather than civic feeling, religious virtue, or conscience to keep the peace. Unsurprisingly, in such circumstances the poor were rather less likely than affluent citizens to think of disasters as blessings.

Indeed, there is every indication that the poor remained thoroughly fatalistic about the calamities throughout the colonial period and beyond.

The growing slave population, for example, certainly had little reason to believe that any great happiness or comfort was likely in this world. And white skins did not preserve the European immigrants who came over as indentured servants from miseries. After enduring horrendous ocean voyages marked by deprivation, disease, and storms, and years of oppressive servitude, few imagined the world as being designed for their happiness.[138] Understandably, many slaves, free blacks, and immigrants continued to turn to magic and other occult practices for a sense of control over their chaotic universe rather than to the teachings of science or institutional religion, which insisted on the fundamental orderliness and dependability of the universe.[139] And if most ordinary Americans continued to accept a providential understanding of calamities well into the nineteenth century, this usually translated into a mood of resignation before God's mysterious purposes.[140] Divine afflictions were to be endured, and even if they could be supposed to be blessings in disguise, few of the humbler sort had any reason to expect to profit in the here and now. This fatalism or pessimism, as we shall see, inspired a religious outlook that paid quite as much attention to disaster as did the dominant apocalyptic and evangelical traditions.

New Madrid, 1812

The persistence of fatalistic, and occasionally revolutionary, popular attitudes can be seen in responses to "the greatest outburst of seismic energy in American history."[141] Here we witness the reach and limits of a progressive view of calamities. An earthquake struck New Madrid in the Missouri Territory (and in present-day Missouri) early in the morning of December 16, 1811, the first of two thousand shocks that would convulse the Mississippi valley region for five months, leveling towns, tearing down forests, opening chasms in the earth, causing the ground to explode, whipping up whirlpools, causing extensive flooding, creating expansive new lakes, compelling the Mississippi River to run backward, and abruptly extinguishing as many as a thousand lives.[142] Shocks were felt as far away as Canada and Mexico. Most survivors and commentators treated the tumult as the judgment of an angry God. The Territorial Assembly of Missouri, for example, declared the tremors to be among "the Catalogue of miseries and afflictions, with which it has pleased the Supreme being of the Universe, to visit the Inhabitants of this earth," and evangelicals of all types, but especially Baptists and Methodists, flocked to the region to harvest "Earth-Quake Christians," provoking a dramatic religious revival among the shaken inhabitants.[143] But what is striking is

FIG 4. Sketch made in 1851 of the New Madrid earthquake of 1811–12: "Cabins shaken and damaged. People outside in a panic" (near New Madrid, Missouri). Reproduced by permission of the State Historical Society of Missouri, Columbia.

the subversive and destabilizing impact of the calamity, especially among dispossessed peoples such as the Indians who still greatly outnumbered white Americans along the banks of the Mississippi in this period.

The earthquake occurred at a critical moment for the Indians of the Mississippi valley. The Cherokee, for example, were in a state of crisis after two decades of white incursions, land losses, military defeats, famines, epidemics, and cultural transformations that were dividing the community into adversarial groups of traditionalists and those who favored acculturation. In the early years of contact between the Northeastern tribes and the Europeans, it had been common for Indian leaders to blame "calamities" on deviations from ancestral religious practices and rituals.[144] In 1811, many Indians on the American frontier were once again giving a respectful hearing to prophets who ascribed their troubles to the abandonment of traditional ways. What made the teachings of these prophets so compelling was the promise of redemption for those who rededicated themselves to worship of the Great Spirit, and the prospect that if they did so the Provider would send a host of calamities (from hailstorms to eclipses) to wipe out the white intruders, replenish the earth with game animals, and restore a lost Indian world.[145]

This was not so much a millennialism inspired by hope as it was a chiliasm of despair. It was into this spiritual ferment that the Shawnee leader Tecumseh stepped in a last-ditch bid to recruit the tribes of the South to join his confederation for a final war of resistance against the encroaching Americans. His forces had already been routed at Tippecanoe while he was traveling, but according to a white captive he was magnificent in his attempts to use the earthquakes to win support for his cause. "The Great Spirit is angry with our enemies," he assured the Osage in 1812. "He speaks in thunder, and the earth swallows up villages, and drinks up the Mississippi. The great waters will cover their lowlands; their corn cannot grow; and the Great Spirit will sweep those who escape to the hills from the earth with his terrible breath."[146] This sentiment was infectious. Even many members of the peaceful and "civilized" Cherokee reportedly responded to the quakes by acting in what one federal agent described as "a remarkable manner," reviving "religious dances of ancient origin" so as to "appease the Anger of the Great Spirit."[147]

Although there was little doubt that some divine force was speaking through the earthquakes, there was no consensus as to its nature or purpose. Traditional religious beliefs mingled with eschatological expectations that owed a great deal to Christian teachings. Indian and European (as well as African) worldviews were reshaping each other along the frontier in these years. Moravian missionaries had been living among the Cherokee for a decade, and although they harvested few converts they did succeed in winning some respect for their beliefs. According to transcripts of their conversations with Indians about the origins and implications of the convulsions, some of the Cherokee blamed sorcerers, others attributed the calamity to the Great Spirit, and still others, sounding rather like Cotton Mather, thought that they were witnessing the approach of the apocalypse as prophesied in the Bible. Chief Charles Hicks was concerned to see that "fear and terror [had] spread through the whole Nation," but he thought this was only to be expected. "How else could it be?" he asked. "Do not these belong to the signs which are to come to pass before the [last] great day?" For their part, the Moravians seem to have been largely noncommittal in their replies, explaining that earthquakes were often entirely natural (without divine meaning), that they were sometimes punishments intended "to discipline people," but agreeing that God had indeed "destined one day on which He will judge all people, will reward each one according to his works. At that time the earth will be consumed by fire, etc." Whereas Tecumseh had called upon the Indians to return to their old ways and to take up arms against the Americans, the Moravians countered that the real lesson was that Indians should "do away with the service to sin and listen to his voice," becoming pious, industrious, and honest.[148]

What is important about this event is that it reveals both the standard attempt of Americans to exploit disaster for expansive bourgeois agendas and the degree of resistance these agendas provoked among those groups that opposed the dominant forms of American development. What we also see is a disaster that utterly failed to become a material blessing—even though it inspired the nation's first federal Disaster Relief Act. Having recently appropriated $50,000 to help Venezuelans recover from an earthquake that had killed twenty thousand people in Caracas, Congress came under pressure to respond with similar generosity to homegrown victims. Because Missouri was still a territory, the federal government was authorized to offer support that would have been deemed unconstitutional for states. The people of New Madrid, for example, found themselves legally entitled to exchange ruined lands for up to one square mile of unclaimed land anywhere else in the Missouri Territory. Unfortunately, the management of the act proved to be disastrous. News of the law reached speculators long before it reached victims, and profiteers descended on the region, buying up properties from locals who, believing they had no other options, were all too willing to sell for a pittance. Some opportunists thus grew rich off the calamity, though a profusion of counterfeit claims and counterclaims ensured that many involved in transactions were tied up in litigation for years afterward.[149]

The earthquake, then, had a devastating impact on New Madrid. When Col. George Morgan had founded the town in 1789, he imagined a metropolis that would dominate western trade by virtue of its commanding position overlooking the Mississippi River.[150] But such imperial dreams finally faded when most of the town subsided as a result of the tremors. Floods washed away the ruins in the spring of 1812, and in time the entire site would succumb to the westward drift of the great river. This calamity did not provide opportunities for improvement or expansion. Most of New Madrid County's three thousand residents fled to the countryside or deserted the region altogether after the most intense earthquake of all struck at the beginning of February. The population failed to reach pre-earthquake levels again for over two decades, and this in an age of dramatic westward migration and settlement.

And yet even the great 1812 earthquake would find itself absorbed into a narrative about the progressive contributions of calamity. In 1846, the British geologist Charles Lyell arrived in New Madrid to examine the physical effects of the tremors. By now the town was nothing more than a "rude" village, lacking even an inn, and dwellings were still slipping one by one into the westward-shifting river. The famous naturalist was visiting the area hoping to compile further evidence for his argument that earthquakes (like floods and volcanoes and other disruptive events) were essentially benign, contributing over the millennia to the rise and fall of mountains, the ebb and flow of rivers, and the achievement by the planet of a steady state: "This cause, so often the source of death and terror to the inhabitants of the globe, which visits, in succession, every zone, and fills the earth with monuments of ruin and disorder, is, nevertheless, a conservative principle in the highest degree, and, above all others, essential to the stability of the system."[151] The conservative Englishman, in other words, sought to convince scientists and the public that disasters were mechanisms through which the planet achieved a happy equilibrium, a theory that became known as uniformitarianism. He claimed that the 1812 earthquake provided physical evidence for his claims.[152] New Madrid thus had a small role to play in one of the great scientific controversies of the nineteenth century, which pitted Lyell against a school of thought that dismissed his theories out of hand. These "catastrophists" countered that the principal source of planetary evolution was major calamities on the scale of Noah's flood.[153] What the two sides shared, of course, was the conviction that natural convulsions were instruments of beneficial global transformations. What really distinguished most catastrophists was their faith that these transformations were not cyclical but progressive, and that they served a benign providential plan.

Lyell's most eminent rival was the Swiss geologist Louis Agassiz, who was voyaging from Europe to take up residence in the United States, even as the Englishman trekked through the swamps of Missouri. With the help of an endorsement from Lyell, he was soon to be appointed to a position at Harvard from which he would preside over the American scientific community until his death in 1873. Buoyed by his Congregationalist religious beliefs, Agassiz, sounding very much like Jonathan Edwards on occasion, insisted throughout his life that God had devised periodic events such as ice ages to ensure the development of a planet suitable for human habitation.[154] In the nineteenth century, however, it was the influential geologist Clarence King who most unequivocally absorbed into geology

dominant American assumptions about the interdependence of catastrophe and progress. The day would come, he claimed, when all would
grasp that

> He who brought to bear that mysterious energy we call life upon prime-
> val matter bestowed at the same time a power of development by change,
> arranging that the interaction of energy and matter which make up envi-
> ronment should, from time to time, burst in upon the current of life and
> sweep it onward and upward to ever higher and better manifestations. . . .
> Moments of great catastrophe, thus translated into the language of life,
> become moments of creation, when out of plastic organisms something
> newer and nobler is called into being.[155]

His conclusion was stirring and as vivid an expression of the principle of
creative destruction as nineteenth-century science would muster. Back
in New Madrid, such optimistic assumptions were rather less likely to
be voiced, but even here Lyell was amused to come across a trapper who
assured him that the earthquake was "a blessing to the country" because
it had created vast expanses of swampland in which fur-bearing animals
were now visibly thriving.[156]

New Madrid failed to profit from the commercial revolution that
was launched by the very first steamboat voyage down the Mississippi
River, a journey that was undertaken even as tectonic shock waves pulsed
through the region. The crew of the *New Orleans* arrived in the town just
three days after the first major tremors only to find it largely abandoned,
but the safe return of the vessel to the port city after which it was named
announced the opening of western markets in the age of steam. The
industrial era, of course, would bring a whole new range of calamities.
In 1814, the *New Orleans* became the first steamboat to sink on the great
waterway, and it was by no means the last. Indeed, 30 percent of the
powered boats that traveled on the Mississippi in the first half of the
nineteenth century were lost to collisions, fires, and explosions. More
than one hundred boats and one thousand lives would be lost in the
1830s alone.[157] By 1844, New York diarist Philip Hone would observe
with some dismay, "I never open a newspaper that does not contain
some account of disasters and loss of life on railroads. They do a retail
business in human slaughter, whilst the wholesale trade is carried on (especially on the Western waters) by the steamboats. This world is going
on too fast."[158] Speed, however, was intrinsic to modernity, and so were
technological accidents. And, ultimately, comfortable people like Hone

were willing to accept this as the price of progress.[159] Disasters would not only persist but become more devastating in the industrial period. And persisting alongside them was the conviction that calamities were opportunities, that catastrophes were nothing less than instruments of progress.

The Wild Road of Providence

Disasters exerted a decisive influence on the social and political formations of early American settlements. The urgent demand for protection against fires, in particular, provided occasions for comprehensive state and municipal regulations, legitimating the expansion of government powers and the erosion of private property rights throughout the colonial period. Reading through Boston city records, it can appear as if local courts and governments convened primarily to pass laws recruiting individuals for an ongoing war against calamity: town residents were required by law to keep buckets of water by their doors for use in times of fire; they could be fined for possessing dirty (and combustible) chimneys; they could be prohibited from building homes with inflammable (but affordable) timber rather than more expensive "fire-proof" materials like brick or stone; and many had no legal standing to resist authorities who decided to blow up their homes if this was deemed the best way to stop the advance of a conflagration. In short, disasters facilitated government activism and tipped the legal and political balance away from individual rights to a public interest defined in security terms.

Political and religious elites seized on calamities to consolidate their authority over expanding and fragmenting colonial societies. Much has been written about the use of disaster sermons (or jeremiads) by ministers such as Increase Mather to unsettle, motivate, and reform their congregations. Sacvan Bercovitch, for example, has brilliantly revealed the role of these sermons in establishing crisis as an American norm, shaping a society that valued movement over stasis and progress over stability.[160] Disaster sermons did not follow a strict script, but they generally served a particular ideological function, affirming the hegemony of elites and calling upon all classes to embrace recognizably "bourgeois" values of piety, discipline, and industriousness. Because ministers were so skillful at exploiting the fears stirred up by calamities to bully congregations to cultivate habits of self-discipline and hard work, disasters may well have promoted productivity. Indeed, on occasion, unexpected destruction proved to be an immediate boon, providing the opportunity for urban reforms and structural improvements (from wider streets to safer buildings) that facilitated commercial development. Of course, as the fate of New Madrid after the 1812 earthquakes attested, such material benefits could not be taken for granted. In the days before fire insurance and the production of capitalist surpluses, it often took years for householders or communities to recover from the devastations of war, arson, or natural disasters. Over time, however, experience taught ministers and laypersons to conflate the spiritual and material benefits of disaster, to the point where many took it for granted that calamity would bring moral reformation, an invigorated work ethic, and prosperity.[161]

The intellectual journey of Ralph Waldo Emerson from Jeremiah to cosmic optimist follows, in compressed form, the narrative arc that I have sought to trace in this chapter. In March 1828, in his role as a Unitarian minister, Emerson delivered a Fast Day sermon at Divinity Hall explaining that he saw no reason why such "awful calamities as the earthquake of Lisbon should not be punishments & monitions." In classic jeremiad mode, he insisted that further judgments could be forestalled only by praying for mercy and deliverance and by fasting and bowing "humbly in sorrow & penitence."[162] By the time New York City suffered its terrible fire of 1835, he was at work on his transcendentalist manifesto *Nature*, the American book that mostly famously converted God from a punitive father figure into a benign spirit. Like Rousseau, he was now satisfied that nature was a source of "steady and prodigal provision" and that natural laws were so designed that humans could learn to live comfortably in nature.[163] And calamities? On the eve of the Civil War, he attempted to address head on the problem of affliction. In his searching essay "Fate," he admitted that the harms inflicted by a natural disaster such as the Lisbon earthquake (that "killed men like flies") left no room for any view of Nature as a "sentimentalist." "Providence has a wild, rough, incalculable road to its end," he allowed, and it was futile "to try to whitewash its huge, mixed instrumentalities, or to dress up that terrific benefactor in a clean shirt and white neckcloth of a student in divinity." But having conceded so much, Emerson was unwilling or unable to go further. Fire and water could burn and drown, but they were also necessary for the sustenance of life: "Every jet of chaos which threatens to exterminate us is convertible by intellect into some wholesome force." And so he concluded with what was by now a classic American statement that "every calamity" was "a spur and valuable hint."[164]

Given that this book begins with the seventeenth century, the religious origins of a durable American faith in the "blessings of disaster," one that presented ruptures as opportunities for spiritual and later material renewal, should now be clear. Over the ensuing 250 years, belief in the creative properties of destruction would frame and energize capitalist commitments to constant economic expansion and unending urban renewal. The religious genealogy is significant. By the modern age, American expectations about the blessings of ruination (of the dependence of progress on affliction) would rest as much on faith as on calculation.

Interlude

THE SAN FRANCISCO EARTHQUAKE AND FIRE OF 1906

"Sunlight was coming out of the early morning mist. The city was almost noiseless. Occasionally a newspaper wagon clattered up the street or a milk wagon rumbled along." That's how one journalist remembered the scene. He had been standing at the corner of Market Street, waiting for a streetcar with some co-workers after a late shift at the *San Francisco Examiner*. It was twelve minutes past five on the morning of Wednesday, April 18, 1906. Most San Franciscans were at home sleeping, and the streets were all but empty. The tired men shared a joke and as their laughter trailed away, they became aware of a low rumbling sound. Suddenly the earth began to shudder and the correspondent was thrown to the ground. He recalled watching "the big buildings in what looked like a crazy dance. Then it seemed as though my head were split with the roar that crashed into my ears. Big buildings were crumbling as one might crush a biscuit in one's hand. Great gray clouds of dust shot up with flying timbers, and storms of masonry rained into the street. Wild, high jangles of smashing glass cut a sharp note into the frightful roaring."[1] The great San Francisco earthquake had begun.

Most people awoke to scenes of chaos. From their shaking beds they looked out at swaying walls, jumping furniture, tumbling ornaments, and falling masonry. Finally, after what seemed an eternity—actually less than a minute—the shaking stopped. Dazed survivors spilled out into the streets to recover their senses. In many parts of the city, people cast eyes over buckled streets, dipped sidewalks, shattered chimneys, and even collapsed buildings. The damage was particularly severe in the working-class neighborhoods south of Market Street, where casualties were trapped under the debris of fallen hotels and homes. The situation was better in the area north of Market, but even in this affluent commercial district buildings built over reclaimed marshland had sustained damage. In the east, the walls of the city hall, only just completed after nearly thirty years of construction, were spread across the surrounding court-yard. Nevertheless, few doubted that the city had escaped lightly. The great majority of buildings were still standing, even the controversial new skyscrapers that had been reshaping the skyline since the 1890s.

Aftershocks kept San Franciscans off balance throughout the day, but, for the most part, people were in remarkably high spirits. Many thousands of men and women streamed downtown to report for work, inspect property, search for friends and family, or simply take in the spectacle. Picking a path through the ruins, Bishop Nichols was struck by the frenetic activity around him:

> Sidewalks were thronged with people treading over the shattered glass from show windows,—the wares of which were in many places open to the public,—over the debris from fallen walls, cornices, etc., vehicles of all sorts were cluttering up the streets, soldiers, policemen, rushing ambulances, all mingling in the mass and making the semblance of greater confusion from the very shoutings and gallopings to try to evolve order.[2]

Most were reassured when soldiers started taking up positions on street corners. Everything seemed to be under control, but things were going to get a lot worse before they would get any better.

About fifty fires had broken out across the city—started variously by crumpled chimneys, toppled stoves, severed electrical wires, and broken gas pipes. "A fire seemed so small next to our earthquake," according to one woman, "that but little attention was paid to it."[3] Soon, however, little notice would be taken of anything else. Even though the fire alarm system was not working, firemen and concerned citizens eagerly chased down all signs of smoke. They worked without direction—fire chief Dennis Sullivan had been fatally wounded in the earthquake. Still, they battled heroically and were only defeated because there were just too many fires—and, as it turned out, hardly any water. Pipes had shattered during the earthquake and precious water was now draining away through thousands of breaks and holes.[4]

The fiercest blaze moved rapidly westward through the wooden hotels, factories, warehouses, and homes south of Market. There was no

FIG 5. View east down Market Street from near Stockton and Ellis Streets during San Francisco fire of 1906. From Online Archive of California, http://ark.cdlib.org/ark:/13030/hb2s200628.

mad dash for safety as there had been during the Great Chicago Fire of 1871, but flames did overtake a few unfortunate souls before they could be rescued from the rubble. One mining engineer was particularly rattled by "the futile struggle of a policeman and others to rescue a man who was pinned down in burning wreckage. It was a race with the fire and a losing race. The helpless man watched it in silence till the fire began burning his feet. Then he screamed and begged to be killed. The policeman took his name and address and shot him through the head."[5] The account may not be true in every detail—many such stories were embellished for publication—but these and similar incidents provided the most horrifying moments of the disaster. Most of the area south of Market was leveled before noon.

A second fire edged forward through the concrete and brick buildings of the wholesale district north of Market Street, while a third blaze broke out in the west later in the morning when a woman tried to cook breakfast at a broken fireplace. She inadvertently set fire to her flue, and then had to evacuate her home before it burned to the ground. The Ham and Eggs fire spread quickly through the thickly clustered wooden houses of the Hayes Valley and then burned east toward the city center. A temporary hospital at the Mechanics' Pavilion lay across the path of the fire, and it took a furious evacuation effort by medical staff and helpers to save the wounded from a roasting. Corpses had to be left to the inferno. The fire swept on through the ruins of the city hall before merging with the south of Market fire.

On the first day, flames climbed two hundred feet into the sky, scattering ash and cinders over the retreating refugees. Firemen, soldiers, and volunteers worked furiously to stop the fires but only managed to save a handful of buildings, most notably the Southern Pacific terminal at Townsend and Fourth Streets (a vital depot for incoming supplies in the days ahead) and the U.S. Mint at Fifth and Mission. In the latter case, men labored for seven hours, damping the roof with water pumped up from tanks in the basement and creating a clearing around the building. They stuck to their posts, even when it became certain that they were going to be encircled by flames. This was a rare triumph on a day of "forlorn-hope stands." For, as one commentator recalled, the campaign against the conflagration took on "more the character of a massacre than a battle."[6]

A plentiful supply of water might not have prevented the conflagration from annihilating the city once it got out of hand. The fire was so hot that one hundred thousand gallons of water pumped into the flames from a cistern at First and Folsom evaporated on impact.[7] What the shortage of water did ensure, however, was that officials would have to rely on riskier strategies. And so they did, turning to dynamite and gunpowder to create backfires in front of the advancing flames. For many survivors the earsplitting explosions would become one of their most vivid memories of the disaster. At first, the dynamiting was ineffective. As one officer complained, firefighters "worked too close to the fire and used no tamping so that little was accomplished except to splinter the buildings and make them burn quicker and to break all windows within a radius of 5 blocks."[8] Until city officials allowed them to demolish buildings more than a block ahead of the flames, the powder did more to start fires, and spread existing ones, than to put them out.[9]

By midnight on Wednesday, the business district, Chinatown, Hayes Valley, and all of the area south of the Market had sunk beneath the flames. One hundred thousand people had seen their homes burn and had scattered through the city in search of sanctuary. A river of refugees had flowed toward the Ferry Building hoping to find a way across the bay to friends and families in Berkeley and Oakland; many more streamed into city parks at Golden Gate, the Mission, and Lafayette, or onto open ground at the Presidio and Jefferson Square. The exodus continued throughout the day with men, women, and children winding their way slowly up and down the steep hills of the city carrying or pulling trunks, boxes, bundles, babies, birds, animals, beds, sewing machines, even pianos—anything they were able to salvage from their homes.

Few slept on the first night. Many could not get comfortable on the hard ground, while others were repeatedly awakened by the endless shattering explosions. Matilda Murphey remembered "living in mortal dread every moment." Josephine Baxter clung to the earth, bracing herself for aftershocks, for the approach of the fire, for the assault of thieves, for a whole host of imagined calamities.[10] Those who remained awake often found themselves captivated by the terrible beauty of an inferno that lit up the night sky. "Imagine," one woman wrote, "half the sky clear and starry—the other half masses of great flame-colored clouds. It was magnificently horrible. The horrible predominated."[11] Another observer, gazing ruefully on the fire from a vantage point at the top of Russian Hill, found the spectacle devilish but also "Soul-stirring" and "sublime." "It would," he thought, "have been worth all that it cost could we only have afforded it."[12]

By Thursday morning, fires were advancing on two fronts. One blaze made its way slowly southward through the Mission District, getting as far up the hill as Twentieth Street before firefighters turned water on it from an uncovered spring. The fire north of Market was even more dangerous. Firemen and soldiers put up determined resistance at several points, but each time the flames swept over their defenses. Late on Thursday, officials resolved to make a last stand at Van Ness Avenue, hoping at least to save the Western Addition, a densely populated middle-class residential district that was home to 150,000 San Franciscans. Men demolished the fashionable residences along the east side of the wide boulevard, but flames leapt across the clearing on at least two occasions. Still, firemen, soldiers, and civilians battled gamely, snuffing out sparks wherever they came across them, helped by water from a newly operational hydrant. (Sanitation crews had been working around the clock since Wednesday to fix the water mains.) By dawn on Friday morning the Western Addition was safe. Firefighters, some of whom had been on their feet for fifty-five hours, dropped to the ground and slept, surrendering at last to their fatigue.

Just as it seemed that the fire had finally run its path, however, a few stray embers sailed over Washington Street to the north, starting a fire that would rage through Russian Hill and North Beach for two days. Homeowners put up pockets of resistance:

They chopped and broke down fences and small outbuildings that might afford a pathway to the fire; they achieved the successful destruction by dynamite of a small barn; they wet blankets, rugs, and carpets with small quantities of water that had previously been collected in pails and bath-tubs, and one by one, as sparks fell or shingles caught, they beat out the flames. A dipper of water here, a stroke with a wet cloth there—that was all—enough.[13]

In this way several homes were saved, but once again the successes were few and far between. On Friday, there was a heart-stopping moment when several thousand people in the Italian North Beach area were trapped at the edge of the bay, surrounded by walls of flame with no possibility of escape except by sea. It took a concerted effort to assemble the boats that would ferry them to safety. On Saturday morning, the fire finally burned out as it was beginning to sweep southward once again, picking through the buildings that had escaped the first fire. Most of the docks and piers were still standing. This, like the survival of the Southern Pacific terminal, was a matter of no small comfort: it was over sea and rail that desperately needed relief supplies would come to the city in the weeks ahead.

This was not the first conflagration in San Francisco's short history. The city had burned down so many times in its early years that citizens had emblazoned a phoenix on their official seal in 1850. But this was far and away the most destructive fire, leaving behind a gutted city that resembled nothing so much as the "ruined cities of the east."[14] The city registrar, Cameron King Jr., left a vivid record of the destruction. On the second day of the disaster, he and his family picked their way through the scorched city center in an effort to get to his brother's house in Alameda across the bay:

> Our path led through the district that had burned the day before. Where block on block of populous frame houses had stood was now only a smoul-dering ash-strewn plain. Only like headstones and monuments in a cem-etery, but blackened and ugly on each lot stood a chimney, the melancholy reminder of once cheerful firesides, now desolate and perhaps destroyed forever. Block after block of this and then the gaunt, grim hideous piles, the gigantic skeletons, the massive walls of the business district.[15]

Other observers followed a similar rhetorical descent into morbid sen-timentalism, like the writer who imagined the devastated "Argonaut" city as "a Crescent moon set about a black disk of shadow." He wrote that "a Saharan desolation of blackened, ash covered, twisted debris was all that remained of three-fifths of the city that four days ago stood like a sentinel in glittering, jeweled armor, guarding the Golden Gate to the Pacific." He painted a grim picture of a ravaged city lying prostrate before the shell of its largest structure: "The Call building stood proudly erect, lifting its whited head above the ruin like some leprous thing and with all its windows, dead, staring eyes that looked upon nothing but a wilderness."[16]

This was by far the worst natural disaster in the United States (up until that point) in terms of property damage. The city engineer calculated that the fire had burned over 4.7 square miles, one and a half times the area covered by the Chicago fire. The fire had devoured 508 blocks and 28,188 buildings at a cost of at least $500 million.[17] The Sub-committee on Statistics counted 674 dead (315 bodies found in the ruins, 6 men executed for criminal acts, 1 shot "by mistake," and 352 others reported missing), but the death toll was probably closer to 3,000.[18] And San Francisco had not suffered alone. Oakland, Berkeley, and Alameda had sustained little damage, but other towns and dwellings along a two-hundred-mile stretch of the San Andreas Fault had been badly shaken. Santa Rosa, sixty miles north of San Francisco, was almost completely destroyed by earthquake and fire, and many of the fine new buildings at Stanford University were now rubble. In one of the most appalling single episodes of the calamity, one hundred patients and staff were killed when the state mental asylum at San Jose collapsed on top of them.

San Francisco was the ninth largest city in the United States, the biggest in the West. And now half of its four hundred thousand residents were homeless, with fifty thousand more unable to return to temporarily uninhabitable homes. There was no (or very little) available gas, electricity, or water. The transportation system was in shambles and it was very difficult to deliver the few foodstuffs remaining in the city to an increasingly hungry population. Authorities responded forcefully to the crisis. The mayor empowered policemen and soldiers to break into stores and give away everything that could be eaten, tiding San Franciscans through a difficult Thursday. Some resourceful civilians took matters into their own hands, like the men who captured and cooked the ornamental ducks that had hitherto bobbed happily on Lake Merced. Over the long run, famine was averted by the swift response of the American public. The first of an eventual two thousand carloads of food, clothing, and supplies started arriving in the city on the very night of the earthquake. In all, Americans would send $9 million in donations to the city, with Congress appropriating a further $2.5 million to cover War Department expenses.[19] The availability of such a large relief fund saved the people of San Francisco from starvation and destitution, but it did not solve the problem of reconstruction. Could the city ever recover? Where would the money come from to rebuild homes and businesses? What cultural and emotional impact would the devastating disaster have? As we shall see, the San Francisco earthquake and fire focused and intensified many of the anxieties of the modern age; more surprisingly, perhaps, it also generated a surprising amount of optimism . . . and even delight.

2

What Comes Down Must Go Up

DISASTERS AND THE MAKING OF AMERICAN CAPITALISM

We predict that for those who five years hence shall behold the brand-new splendor of the resuscitated capital, the earthquake of 1906, with all its unparalleled destructiveness, will serve only to point a moral and adorn a tale.

DAVID HARVEY, "Comment," *Harper's Weekly*, May 6, 1906

George Harvey, the editor of *Harper's Weekly*, was strangely unshaken by the San Francisco earthquake and fire of April 1906. Confronted by news reports of one of the greatest calamities in American history, his response was to sit down and write a "comment" on the inevitable future splendors of San Francisco. The California city was in ruins. Nearly five miles of stores, offices, factories, hotels, and homes had been destroyed, and many hundreds of people were dead, but Harvey's attention was captured by the new and improved city that he foresaw emerging from the rubble. In just five years' time, he predicted, his countrymen would stand in awe before "the brand-new splendor of the resuscitated capital."[1]

A talent for seeing mangled bodies and burned-out buildings as signs of progress was widely shared among Harvey's class. Many professionals and businessmen agreed that this "so-called catastrophe" was more a boon than a misfortune. Time only confirmed this happy assessment. As one spokesman for real estate interests observed three months after the earthquake, it was still a "commonplace" to maintain that the destruction of San Francisco was "a blessing in disguise." "Instinctively," he declared, "we feel that the heavy hand of fate which has so ruthlessly fallen on us has fallen for our good, if not for our comfort."² Why should so many merchants, industrialists, and entrepreneurs have viewed the San Francisco disaster as an opportunity for urban development rather than as an obstacle to growth? How do we explain this startling determination to overlook the appalling wreckage and to focus instead on the promise of reconstruction?

The tendency of middle- and upper-class Americans to regard disasters as "blessings" can be traced back to the endeavors of early American religious leaders to emphasize the corrective uses of "providential" afflictions. This religious genealogy is significant. Even in the twentieth century, American expectations about the benefits of destruction continued to rest as much on faith, or at least habit, as on rational calculation. My main concern here, however, is to explain how and why so many modern Americans came to view disasters as sources of economic growth and as agents of progress. I believe a hint of an answer can be found in the unintentional double meaning of George Harvey's phrase "resuscitated capital," which can be read not only as a reference to the soon-to-be-restored capital city of the West but as an allusion to the revitalizing role of the calamity for American capitalism.

In recent years, economists, urban historians, and geographers have written extensively about the "geography of capital" and the "production of space," seeking to explain how capitalist economies shape built environments. Surely the most compelling concept to emerge from this scholarship is that of "creative destruction," the notion that modern capitalist systems require the continual obliteration of outmoded goods and structures to clear space and make way for new production and development. Creative destruction (according to powerful apologists like former Federal Reserve chairman Alan Greenspan and persistent critics like *Nation* correspondent William Greider) is the dialectic that keeps the wheels of industry turning.³ Traditionally, economists have deployed this concept to explain entrepreneurial innovation, industrial restructuring, and planned obsolescence, but more recently scholars have begun to appreciate the role of creative destruction in shaping and reshaping modern urban environments.⁴ If capitalism does depend for its survival on the endless ruin and renewal of physical structures, this is surely a matter of interest for those who seek to understand modern ways of imagining and managing disasters.

Within this framework we can begin to appreciate natural disasters as events that transform space in ways that promote economic expansion and present (some) investors and businesses with opportunities for the accumulation of capital. Indeed, we can begin to understand why so many social thinkers have turned to calamities in search of metaphors to convey the destructive and reconstructive logics of modern capitalism. In his dazzling critical account of modernity, *All That Is Solid Melts into Air*, political theorist Marshall Berman was much taken by the saturation of Karl Marx's writings with calamitous images: the endless parade across his pages of "abysses, earthquakes, volcanic eruptions, crushing gravitational force." Berman speculated that Marx deployed these analogies to compel his readers to "feel" the dizzying, crashing power of a transformative modernity, but these images were also surely the most compelling ones available for conveying the dynamic and propulsive qualities of modern capitalism and, in particular, the embroilment of its creative and destructive forces.[5]

So deeply ingrained has the link between disaster and development become that even those who have fought most vigorously to contain the ravages of capital have tended to view further destruction as the necessary precondition for healing modernity's harms. Thus it was that Lewis Mumford could fear that the bombing blitzes of World War II would prove *insufficient* to flatten the grimy cities of Europe to the extent necessary to transform modern urban sites from "dreary infernos" into "life-centered environments." "There is a sense," he wrote in 1942, "in which the demolition that is taking place through the war has not yet gone far enough. . . . We must . . . continue to do, in a more deliberate and rational fashion, what the bombs have done by brutal hit-or-miss, if we are to have space enough to live in and produce the proper means of living."[6] By the middle of the twentieth century, even Mumford, the ardent and humane critic of capitalism, was convinced that (controlled) destruction was a good thing, that responsible planners had to become destroyers before they could build a better world.

To explore the complex and sometimes surprising connections between disaster, capitalism, and urban development in the industrial age, I look especially closely at two episodes, the New York fire of 1835 and the San Francisco earthquake and fire of 1906. I conclude by drawing some implications from these case studies for our understanding of the evolving relationship between capitalism and calamity in our own time.

The Economics of Disaster

How did Americans learn to view calamities as economic opportunities? The seeds of an answer can be found in the colonial period. In 1727, an earthquake ripped through New England. Most inhabitants were understandably upset by this fearsome "affliction," but a surprising number were rhapsodic. The prominent Boston clergyman Cotton Mather, for example, gushed, "O Wonderful! O Wonderful! Our GOD instead of sending *earthquakes* to destroy us as He justly might, He sends them to fetch us home unto Himself, and to do us the greatest Good in the World!"[7] What exactly was this good that God intended? As we have seen, the early settlers interpreted fires and storms and earthquakes as divine punishments for their sins and transgressions, but there was a twist in this theology that enabled ministers to recast calamities as blessings: the supposition that God sent disasters to recall his chosen people to the path of righteousness.

Significantly, Puritans claimed to be especially gladdened by the fact that disasters destroyed property—reminding communities of the transience of worldly goods, freeing them from the distractions of material possessions, and refocusing their thoughts on the one thing that really mattered: salvation. Disasters were blessings because they assisted colonists along the path to God's kingdom, inspiring moral and spiritual reformation, and promising them a final *transcendence* of space and time. Or so official sermons proclaimed. In truth, Puritans often found it easier to assert than to feel this particular blessing of destruction. When fire razed the North End of Boston in 1676, the prominent minister Increase Mather might have claimed vindication for his repeated warnings that the "inordinate Affection to the World" of his congregation foredoomed them to an awful calamity, but in his private correspondence he admitted his deep distress at the loss of his home and the incineration of his goods: furniture, clothes, and winter provisions.[8] He was hopeful that the wealth of the community would be restored as soon as he and his neighbors had repented of their sins and abandoned their lustful pursuit of worldly goods and pleasures.

What Mather, like other pious settlers, was unable to fathom was that calamities could promote economic prosperity. From the beginning of the European settlement of America the impulse to transcend the physical world had coexisted uneasily with countervailing religious and political injunctions to tame the wilderness, and, in New England at least, to construct the sort of orderly towns that manifested and made possible a proper devotion to God. It was thus both a civic and a religious duty to rebuild homes and cities as well and as solidly as possible in the wake of calamities. This injunction was not always easy to realize. In the days before fire insurance, dependable relief, and easy credit, it often took years for householders and communities to recover from the devastations of arson, wars, or natural disasters. On occasion, however, unexpected destruction spurred rudimentary adventures in urban renewal. In the wake of the 1676 fire, after all, Boston authorities seized the opportunity to make improvements that would contribute to the city's emergence as a prosperous commercial center.[9]

If disasters played an important role in the (re)shaping of urban space throughout the colonial period, they also sometimes facilitated the accumulation of profits, and not only for profiteers but also for respectable entrepreneurs. Because ministers were so skillful at exploiting the fears stirred up by calamities to bully congregations into cultivating virtuous habits of self-discipline and hard work, disasters could (in classic Weberian fashion) boost productivity and economic development. Indeed, endless disaster sermons or "jeremiads" eventually persuaded colonists that crises and misfortunes were necessary and welcome catalysts for a distinctively American brand of "progress" that was measured in terms of personal betterment and social improvement.[10] Reassuring experiences of recovery gave credence to these improbable assertions, and over time Americans learned to treat disasters as both religious *and* economic blessings. By 1871, it seemed the most natural thing in the world for Henry Ward Beecher, the nation's most prominent clergyman, to declare that the United States could not afford to do without the Great Chicago Fire. He was hardly alone in his conviction that disasters were part of an essentially comforting divine plan, apparent afflictions that were actually sent to promote spiritual, moral, and material progress.[11]

Although faith in the blessings of disaster was already widespread by the end of the colonial period, speedy recovery from calamities could not be taken for granted until the spread of communications systems, credit networks, insurance companies, and all the other apparatuses of industrialization in the nineteenth century. As Progressive reformers wryly pointed out at the end of the century, this resilience was just as well because one city after another was being devastated by conflagrations brought about by unregulated economic and urban growth in the era of competitive capitalism. Still, while cities might fall, they never just died. By 1906, *Harper's* editor George Harvey had seen Chicago, Boston, Charleston, Galveston, and Baltimore all bounce back after being "laid waste by conflagrations, earthquakes, or tidal waves" over the previous thirty-five years.[12] When the San Francisco earthquake struck, he had practically been conditioned to treat calamities as economic opportunities. He was confident that Americans would invest whatever labor and capital was necessary to build a better city over the ruins of San Francisco. No less a force than the logic of capitalism demanded the creation of a magnificent new city in the Bay Area. But what was this logic? And how exactly did it shape responses to calamity in the age of industry?

As early as 1848, John Stuart Mill spelled out the uses of disasters for industrial economies in his influential work *Principles of Political Economy*. Mill argued that in a free market system in which capital was constantly being consumed and reproduced, there was "nothing at all wonderful," or surprising, about "the great rapidity with which countries recover from a state of devastation; the disappearance, in a short time, of all traces of the mischief done by earthquakes, floods, hurricanes, and the ravages of war." As long as the population remained productive and the infra-structure was not completely destroyed, then "rapid repair" was always likely.[13] In fact, Mill expected disasters to produce long-term benefits by obliterating old stock and encouraging manufacturers to introduce new efficiencies into their production processes, adopting better technologies and building more efficient plants. Mill did not discuss the New York fire of 1835, but few events corroborated his theory more amply.

The New York Fire of 1835

On December 16, 1835, during the coldest night in half a century, a warehouse in downtown Manhattan burst into flames. The fire spread quickly through the narrow and congested streets of the business dis-trict, destroying seventeen city blocks and burning so brightly that the glare was visible as far away as Philadelphia and New Haven.[14] Although religious leaders made familiar noises about the benevolent disciplining effects of providence, businessmen were not yet conditioned to see *eco-nomic* opportunity in the ruins. The *New York Herald* reported the grim conviction of prominent merchants that the development of their city would be set back by at least twenty years. For its part, the newspaper forecast hard times ahead, warning readers that "the destruction of sev-enteen millions of property cannot pass away as a summer cloud."[15] But pass away it did—or at least it seemed to.

By the first anniversary of the fire, five hundred new and more splendid buildings had risen from the ruins, streets had been widened, a solution to chronic downtown pollution and water shortages was in sight, and busi-ness was better than ever.[16] Although a town such as New Madrid was unable to recover from earthquake and flood in 1812, the situation was quite different in a vibrant commercial metropolis such as New York. Many merchants emerged wealthier from the calamity than they had been on its eve. A building boom quickly and dramatically raised rents in the burned-out district.[17] One proprietor, returning from Europe under the impression that he had been ruined by the destruction of his proper-ties, discovered instead that he had become a very rich man.[18] Just two

THE GREAT FIRE of THE CITY of NEW-YORK. 16 DECEMBER 1835.

FIG 6. "The Great Fire of the City of New York, December 16, 1835." Image downloaded from Wikipedia. Original at Library of Congress Prints and Photographs online catalog, at http://hdl.loc.gov/loc.pnp/cph.3a06226.

months after the fire, twenty empty lots were sold for $765,000; before the conflagration, the property had been worth just $93,000. Philip Hone, businessman, socialite, former mayor, and prominent member of the re- lief committee, marveled to see how these lots commanded "the most enormous prices, greater than they would have brought before the fire, when covered with valuable buildings."[19] To be sure, not everybody ben- efited from this inflation. Despite the construction boom, most working people suffered a net decline in real wages, as rising rents and food prices outpaced modest gains in earnings. But one thing seemed undeniable: the disaster had spurred business activity and economic growth. How had this happened?

In 1835, New York City was still enjoying the wave of economic expansion that had been stimulated by the opening of the Erie Canal ten years before, and businesses were generally prosperous enough to absorb the costs of the conflagration.[20] More important, living in the nation's financial center, well-connected New Yorkers enjoyed singular access to international capital, as well as to the abundant credit made available by the expansion of state and "wild-cat" banks in the aftermath of President Andrew Jackson's successful campaign to terminate the monopoly of the Bank of the United States over the money supply. The tide of speculation that washed over these years indicates a broad faith in the expansive potential of the American economy.[21] With abundant credit available, there was every indication that the business district was going to be swiftly restored (and even modernized with improved streets and services), and few merchants hesitated to rebuild their downtown enterprises.

As a result of the commercial revolution of the early nineteenth century, a whole new infrastructure was in place—railroads, telegraphs, insurance companies, financial networks, and charity organizations—that made it easier than ever for Americans to rectify the physical damage caused by natural disasters. Insurance (the industry that depends most directly on catastrophe for its very existence) played an especially central role in changing the rules of economic and urban development, even as it changed the rules of disaster management. Fire insurance came late to the United States, and no coverage was available for floods or earthquakes until the twentieth century.[22] It was not until the establishment in 1792 of the nation's first stock insurance firm, the Insurance Company of North America, that fire insurance became available to the general public.[23] By 1804, there were forty insurance companies in the United States, with hundreds more established in the following decades.[24]

Although most New York businesses carried insurance in 1835, it quickly became apparent that few claims would be honored. In a protectionist move, the state government had followed a precedent set by Massachusetts, requiring out-of-state insurance companies to pay a 10 percent tax on all policies in New York. As a result many of the nation's most reliable firms had been unable to compete for business in New York, and the city was covered largely by undercapitalized local companies. When the business district burned in 1835, all but three of these twenty-six insurance companies were forced into bankruptcy after paying only a fraction of what they owed to policyholders.[25] The experience of silk merchant and abolitionist Arthur Tappan was typical. His textile house lost $40,000 worth of coverage as a result of these failures, and he was one of the more fortunate or shrewd entrepreneurs because he was carrying insurance with more reliable out-of-state companies. Insurance company stockholders were in even worse shape; Philip Hone, for example, lost $11,000 worth of investments.[26] By contrast, those fire insurance firms that survived the calamity were soon able to harvest windfall profits. The directors of the Aetna insurance company, for example, dug deep into their own pockets to ensure that all claims were paid, and having thus earned the trust of their clients were well positioned to take advantage of the huge demand for policies activated by the fire itself.[27] Learning from the calamity, states began to reverse earlier rulings in the hopes of putting the insurance industry on a sounder footing. Massachusetts again took the lead in reforms, resolving in 1837 to withhold licenses to businesses that lacked sufficient reserves to cover extensive losses. This restored the competitive edge of larger firms—though wild rate-cutting practices ensured the continued vulnerability of individual companies to urban conflagrations throughout the nineteenth century—and the industry as a whole flourished.[28]

Fire insurance dramatically transformed the way Americans felt about disasters and development. Overall, the diffusion of insurance engendered a sense of security in the face of nature's recurrent harms, by spreading the costs of calamities from individual victims to communities. As a result, it most likely encouraged the sort of risk-taking behaviors on which capitalism depends. If, as Alexis de Tocqueville surmised, "restlessness" was the spirit of the age, then insurance was its institutional scaffolding, enabling and encouraging risk and providing a measure of protection against the severest consequences of failure. At the same time, insurance companies, much like Puritan ministers of yore, depended for their own success on their ability to impress customers with the precariousness of life and property in this world.[29] Disasters provided them with their best advertisements; insurance companies would certainly play their part in persuading Americans that they lived in a land of (always imminent) calamity.

In any case, an industry now existed with the organization and power (and economic incentive) to take serious steps toward dealing with the persistent menace of fires. To preserve profit margins, insurance companies lobbied aggressively for the enforcement of building codes and safety standards, even as they established and outfitted private fire brigades with the latest firefighting equipment.[30] Firms also found that they could influence building practices by withholding coverage from structures they deemed to be hazardous. So not only did they help to ensure that disasters produced reforms, they provided a context within which aggressive urban and commercial redevelopment was financially and emotionally appealing.

In such an economy, even if entrepreneurs and financiers were not yet fully aware of the fact, calamities presented opportunities for capital accumulation. New York was already renewing itself every few years, with city blocks being demolished and rebuilt with astounding frequency. In many respects, the great fire simply accelerated the process by which obsolete buildings were replaced with more up-to-date structures. In 1845, Philip Hone reflected ruefully on this phenomenon. "Overturn, overturn, overturn!" he pronounced, "is the maxim of New York. The very bones of our ancestors are not permitted to lie quiet a quarter of a century, and one generation of men seem studious to remove all relics of those which preceded them."[31] Hone, who had managed to sell his downtown home in the aftermath of the conflagration for a staggering profit, was a beneficiary of this turbulent state of affairs, but he never fully came to terms with the emotional costs of living in a city devoted to the constant erasure of the past. As we shall see, this discomfort was itself one of the most profound effects of the transformative forces of modernity and an intimation of struggles to come that would pit sentimental local attachments against the interests of capital throughout the nineteenth and twentieth centuries.[32]

For now, to make sense of the rhythms of ruin and renewal, Hone turned, like many compatriots of his class, to the comforting axioms of Harriet Martineau, the celebrated British writer he met while she was visiting the United States in the spring of 1836. She had been greatly interested in the fire, noting with some admiration that "it seems now as if the commercial credit of New York could stand any shock" short of a cataclysm like the earthquake that had obliterated Lisbon in 1755. This was evidence enough of the capability of an expansive economy to overcome any obstacles to growth, though Martineau did admit to some uneasiness about the long-term effects of the game of "wild speculation" that seemed to preoccupy so many Americans in this period.[33] Her misgivings proved well founded. The correction, when it came in 1837, precipitated a devastating financial panic that tipped the country into a severe recession.[34]

There was a stunning lesson here: in an advanced capitalist economy, paper transactions could present more of a threat to prosperity than a fire or an earthquake.[35] What sort of a world was it where natural disasters could produce prosperity while a contraction of credit could bring the economic activity of a nation to a virtual halt? In short, it was a world that was coming to be dominated by industrial and finance capitalism.

Destructive Creation

The material benefits of destruction would not be widely appreciated until Western economies entered their abundance stage at the end of the nineteenth century, producing many more products than consumers needed or thought they wanted. At this point, disasters became blessings because they approximated and amplified those dynamic forces that inspired Austrian economist Joseph Schumpeter to compare modern capitalism to a "gale of creative destruction."[36] A century after Mill, Schumpeter made the case that destruction was a necessary and desirable agent of invention and renewal in an expansive economy. He celebrated the bold and unceasing innovations of entrepreneurs that ensured the constant outdating of old commodities and their replacement by new ones. Schumpeter was concerned with changes over time rather than changes across space and would surely have balked at the idea that it was a good thing to tear down and rebuild *cities* with any great frequency. According to a growing number of recent geographers, however, this latter phenomenon has been absolutely essential for the survival of capitalism.

Putting a Marxian spin on creative destruction, scholars such as David Harvey, Neil Smith, and Edward Soja have insisted that modern capitalism thrives on the constant reshaping of urban space, to the point, we must presume, where calamities can be good for business. They base this conclusion on analyses of the process that Marx described as the "epic of overproduction"—the tendency of capitalists to glut successful markets, drive down prices, and thereby provoke business failures and recessions.[37] Apologists and critics disagree about whether capitalist systems move through boom-and-bust cycles toward increasing economic strength or toward ultimate collapse, but they do share an appreciation for the role of crises in restructuring and restoring health and efficiency (however temporarily) to the economy.

According to Marx, one of the most valuable functions of a crisis is to ensure the "enforced destruction of a mass of productive forces."[38] If we substitute "calamity" for "crisis," we end up with a sentiment that sounds remarkably like Cotton Mather's old claim that disasters were good because they destroyed property—but for modern economists, of course, the destruction of goods is valuable not as an inspiration for spiritual reformation but as a foundation for economic production and expansion. We have moved decisively here from transcendence to the conquest of geographic space. But how exactly does capitalism change the land, and what is the value of destruction? According to Harvey, capitalism requires the constant, if uneven, development of physical environments to survive. In the nineteenth century, the key to economic growth was urbanization. New metropoles such as Chicago boosted output and productivity by enabling economies of scale, by massing workforces near factories, and by clustering consumers into conveniently large markets, speeding up the production, distribution, and exchange of goods and services. In the twentieth century, however, cities also put up increasing obstacles to the accumulation of capital by concentrating and intensifying social conflicts, becoming congested and dangerous, and freezing capital in obsolete structures.[39] This obsolescence, it should be pointed out, has little to do with the suitability of buildings as living or working environments and everything to do with capital flows and profit margins.

In a financial capitalist system of the sort increasingly predominant in the twentieth and twenty-first centuries, profits are increased by the circulation of capital; the more capital circulates, the more possibilities there are for profits. (We are witnessing this mobility of capital on a global scale today as multinational corporations and investment firms move money, people, and resources across the planet in search of marginal advantage.) In such a system urban development offers investment opportunities, but infrastructure also tends to tie capital down. One of the primary benefits of a calamity is that it destroys urban environments and thereby liberates and recycles capital that has "ossified" in fixed structures, thus clearing space for new development and opening up new investment opportunities.[40] Of course, particular owners rarely welcome this destruction. After all, they have little incentive to demolish and rebuild their own buildings, and in fact, unless they have unusually good insurance coverage, can rarely afford to do so until their initial property investments have paid off.[41] The beauty of disasters is that they render irrelevant any objections of individual property owners to renewal. And so it is that disasters are good for capitalism, if not for all capitalists. In such a system, as Marshall Berman contends provocatively, "our lives are controlled by a ruling class with vested interests not merely in change but in crisis and chaos," and catastrophes become "lucrative opportunities for redevelopment and renewal."[42]

San Francisco's Fortune: The Earthquake and Fire of 1906

Theories of creative destruction can help us to understand not only why capitalism promotes the constant and dramatic reshaping of modern urban space but why good bourgeois men like George Harvey might welcome the San Francisco earthquake as an investment opportunity. After all, he was not only an influential editor, he had also played a small but important role in implanting modern financial institutions in the United States during his tenure as state commissioner of banking and insurance in New Jersey in the 1880s. Although a vigorous critic of monopolies, he was a friend of J. P. Morgan and crony enough to big business to campaign, only half-jokingly, for a "holiday for capital" to complement the existing Labor Day.[43] He was certainly familiar enough with the workings of a credit economy to appreciate that the 1906 calamity presented a "promising investment" for capitalists and financiers who were on the lookout, in a time of low interest rates and high market confidence, for new ventures and risks.[44]

As one might expect, the notion that disasters were good for the economy was hardly uncontested in 1906. The editor of the *New York Times*, in fact, was exasperated by the "absurdity" of the idea that a great fire "was an actual advantage." Although the recent Baltimore fire of 1904 had stimulated construction and provided that city with a "clean slate" for improvements, it had done so at "somebody's cost." Failing to grasp the principle of productive expenditures, the editor adamantly resisted the idea that debt-financed development increased the wealth of the nation. "Destruction of capital," he concluded unequivocally, "is never beneficial, not even in a successful war."[45] The insurance companies that found themselves suddenly liable for over $200 million worth of claims in San Francisco had narrow reasons for agreeing, as did those corporations with extensive local interests such as the United Railroads or the Southern Pacific, both of which saw their stocks fall significantly when news of the conflagration reached New York City.[46] Indeed, investors as a group were distinctly unnerved by the calamity. Even as financiers, stockbrokers, and industrialists gathered in their clubs to pledge tens of thousands of dollars in donations for San Francisco, misgivings about the larger implications of the disaster precipitated "heavy selling" of stocks on Wall Street.[47]

The collapse, however, was never likely to be more than momentary in the bullish market of 1906, and within three days stocks were moving upward again.[48] One writer, struck by this turnaround, decided to research previous "catastrophe markets" and discovered, to his surprise, that rapid recovery of stock prices after a major disaster was the rule rather then the exception.[49] San Francisco soon began to look like a promising field of investment. Eastern financiers and firms lent significant sums to the City, and the federal government had to import $45 million in gold from Europe to cover the drain on bank holdings as firms withdrew deposits to pay insurance claims and construction costs. This expansion of the money supply made possible a tremendous upsurge in business activity in San Francisco, doubling employment in the building trades and dramatically increasing banks' clearings in the Bay Area, though it may also have fueled the national speculation frenzy that led to the "rich man's panic" in the spring of 1907.[50]

Although some prospective investors were concerned about future earthquakes, there was general agreement that San Francisco would recover because it was a "natural metropolis," destined for a glorious future by virtue of its location on a harbor and its possession of a large hinterland. It was these "natural advantages" rather than "artificial enhancement by investment," according to the editor of the *Times*, that guaranteed the recuperation of San Francisco. More sophisticated observers recognized that it was a combination of geography and artificial enhancements such as railroad connections, credit flows, and trade networks that ensured the continued prosperity of the city.[51] As a writer for *Collier's* pointed out, San Francisco's resources were by no means "confined to the little blackened tip of land by the Golden Gate." On the contrary, this plot of land was "the focal point at which her streams of wealth converge." "San Francisco capital," in fact, was "breeding revenue all the way up and down the Pacific, from Panama to Alaska, and across from the Rocky Mountains to China."[52] San Francisco, then, was bound to be restored, but what was the new metropolis going to look like? And whose interests were going to be served and sacrificed by the reconstruction of the city?

If some outside investors can be said to have had a stake in the constant ruin and renewal of cities such as San Francisco, merchants and manufacturers believed that they required *more* substantial cities (with fixed assets such as railroad lines and stations, factories, offices, parks, and stores) to facilitate the production and distribution of their goods and services, to boost the purchasing power of consumers, and to promote the social peace that they believed was necessary for the orderly conduct of business. These individuals seized on the disaster as an opportunity to build a more, not less, permanent city. They wished to harness and control rather than unleash the forces of creative destruction, and they were driven as much by sentimental as by economic motives.

One of the defining characteristics of modern (and postmodern) history is the resistance to creative destruction of those classes that have benefited most from it. Many powerful and wealthy residents of turn-of-the-century San Francisco were eager to contain the disintegrative forces of capitalism, to bring an end to the constant mutation of their living and working spaces. A combination of disgust at the chaotic physical and social evolution of their city and a sense of alarm provoked by the deep recession of the 1890s had induced a group of influential citizens to form the Association for the Improvement and Adornment of San Francisco in 1904. These progressive-minded industrialists, merchants, and professionals were determined to bring an end to unregulated development, to build a beautiful city that blended artistic form and efficient function. Accordingly, they commissioned Daniel Burnham, chief architect of the neoclassical White City at the 1893 Chicago World's Fair, to draw up plans for a more permanent city, a pleasing and orderly city of boulevards and parks and monuments. In the words of Hubert Howe Bancroft, the new city was going to be "modern and up to date, with some widened streets and winding boulevards, gardens hanging to the hillside, parks with lakes and cascades, reservoirs of sea water on every hilltop; public work and public service, street cars and lighting being of the best."[53]

In effect, Progressives wished to achieve in San Francisco the sort of improvements that Baron Haussmann had famously accomplished in his rebuilding of Paris fifty years before, during the reign of Napoleon III, an enterprise that had inspired contemporaries to apply the phrase "creative destruction" to modern development for the first time.[54] Burnham, like most of the Improvement Association leaders, was an enthusiastic admirer of Haussmann's work, so it is worth briefly reminding ourselves of his contribution to urban planning. Essentially, Haussmann transformed Paris in the 1850s and 1860s from a medieval city of nooks and crannies into a modern metropolis of grand avenues and stately buildings. His genius was to harness the forces of creative destruction for the purposes of the imperial state. He relished his role as wrecker, using cannons to demolish entire neighborhoods so that he could cut his trademark boulevards across the old city. He was, in his own words, an "artist of demolition," destroying so that he might create.[55] But he also saw himself as an agent of order, attempting to bring an end to chaos by constructing a rational, efficient, and more durable urban environment. Few would deny that Haussmann's endeavors reflected a sincere determination to save the city from an urban crisis brought about by population growth, overcrowding, and inadequate public services. His magnificent water supply and sewage system, in particular, led to significant health improvements, helping to ensure, for example, that the horrifying cholera epidemics that had gripped Paris in 1832 and 1849 would become a thing of the past.

But Haussmann also sought stability and control over the city and particularly over what he viewed as its unruly working class. Part of his plan was to provide employment in order to appease the "rabble," and many thousands did indeed find work on his projects. At the same time, however, he also tore down slums and wiped out many vibrant working-class districts, replacing them with bourgeois neighborhoods. This early exercise in gentrification saw most of the working poor retreating to the cheaper edges of the city as downtown rents escalated. Haussmann was fully aware that urban design was a political weapon, and although he was personally more interested in aesthetic, health, and commercial matters, he knew that his beautiful boulevards would make it easier for the Napoleonic regime to impose its authority on the city, facilitating not only the flow of goods and services but the flow of troops to quell disturbances, making it harder for mobs to riot or to put up barricades.[56] In other words, although Haussmann, the artist of demolition, was fully prepared to use creative destruction to build a better city, he was also trying to tame some of the annihilating forces of capitalism, seeking to discipline the working class as well as to place limits on profit-driven development.

Progressives in San Francisco hoped to achieve the same effect with the Burnham plan: a more rational and efficient city that would facilitate the conduct of business, elevate the moral character of the inhabitants, and bring an end to chronic instability and conflict.[57] Obstacles to their scheme, however, were forbidding. The legal machinery for condemning and improving property was cumbersome, and the cost of demolition and construction promised to be so high that even Burnham thought his plan would take fifty years to implement. "And then," as California author Gertrude Atherton put it, "Nature stepped in."[58] In the words of one leading citizen, blending religion and real estate in a now conventional way, the calamity was "almost like a visitation of Providence to give complete scope and liberty to the Burnham plan for rebuilding the city."[59] Disasters had been appreciated before. French emperor Napoleon III had envied the English for the great fire that had incinerated grubby medieval London in 1666, and he had essentially ordered Haussmann to reproduce, in a controlled fashion, the conditions of a conflagration in Paris.[60] He deliberately exploited the prestige of the throne to shelter the baron from any constitutional or democratic checks that threatened to hinder his mandate to destroy by decree.

Lacking the imperial authority to tear San Francisco down, local Progressives seized on the disaster as their best chance for urban improvement. Freshly printed copies of the Plan for San Francisco had been delivered to City Hall just hours before the earthquake struck, and reformers moved quickly to seize this opportunity. For a brief moment it looked as if Burnham's design would reshape the new city. After all, who could find fault with clean streets, convenient throughways, parks, improved municipal services, and attractive and sturdy buildings? Despite the endorsement of some of the most powerful men in the country, however, the plan never made it off the drawing board. What went wrong? Why was this American city unable to replicate Haussmann's model of urban design and development? A good part of the responsibility rests with the contradictory priorities and goals of the reformers themselves.

Burnham and his supporters were deeply committed not only to beautification but to economic expansion. The architect Louis Sullivan was not always Burnham's most sympathetic critic, but he was on the money when he wrote about his rival's "intense commercialism."[61] At every turn, proponents of adornment insisted on the increased tourist revenues and commercial profits that were sure to be generated by planned cities. Just look, they said, at what Haussmann's monuments and boulevards had done for earnings in Paris.[62] Former city engineer Marsden Manson produced the numbers. In a report recommending the immediate widening and extension of key streets in San Francisco, he calculated that improvements costing as little as $7,821,580 would add $75 million to the value of city property within a decade.[63] Improvement, it seemed, paid. But there was a contradiction here between the pursuit of profits and the quest for a city design that would endure, in Burnham's words, "for all time to come."[64]

The economic arrangements that reformers made to promote commercial activity in San Francisco inevitably undermined their efforts to control urban development. In an expansive economy, especially one marked by overaccumulation, planned obsolescence, and constant technological innovation, there would always be pressure to build new and changing urban structures: factories, railroads, stores, restaurants. Highway construction alone would lead to demand for new bridges, parking lots, service stations, and bus depots. Moreover, rising downtown ground rents would introduce irresistible incentives for the construction of skyscrapers as well as transit systems and suburban developments for overflow populations. Finally, there was always bound to be pressure on downtown commercial and professional interests to gain an edge on competitors by building more distinctive and prestigious show stores, office blocks, and business districts. Burnham should have known this. After all, in the 1890s his own company designed and built the first of San Francisco's skyscrapers, which would come to overshadow the city's downtown monuments, parks, and thoroughfares by the 1920s.[65]

Progressives tended to view the city as a stage upon which life and economics were performed, but space cannot be permanently fixed in a dynamic capitalist system. Walter Benjamin once wrote that "in the convulsions of the commodity economy we begin to recognize the monuments of the bourgeoisie as ruins even before they have crumbled."[66] What he meant to suggest by this cryptic remark was that fixed structures could never be ends in themselves in a capitalist economy. The imperial city envisioned by Daniel Burnham as a physical manifestation of modern progress always threatened to stand in the way of the flow of capital, presenting an obstacle to continuing downtown commercial development.[67] Hence the opposition to monumentalism by so many of San Francisco's businesses.

The conservative *San Francisco Chronicle* mobilized resistance to the Burnham plan, insisting that the best guide to reconstruction was the "plain, common-sense of our best business men."[68] And most of these businessmen were "rapid reconstructionists," keen to throw up new warehouses, factories, and offices as quickly as possible in order to get back to trading and making money. It soon became clear that these men would be able to raise the money necessary to rebuild by drawing on savings, insurance claims, bank loans, and Eastern capital.[69] In retrospect, these impatient men were more in tune with the logic of creative destruction than the luminaries of the Adornment Association. Indeed, it is hard to avoid the conclusion that the impulse to beautification and order was an anxious and nostalgic reaction of a corporate class to the disintegrative forces of capitalism, even though reformers surely deserve credit for their sincere ambition "to make San Francisco a more agreeable city in which to live."[70] It would be tempting to view the labors of Progressive planners as a worthy instance of the mobilization of local interests against the ravages of "placeless" capital but for two things.[71] First, they did more than any other group to increase the presence and power of outside capital. Second, these reformers tended to be insensitive to the desires and needs of less advantaged citizens, proposing initiatives that stood to damage and displace many ordinary San Franciscans.

Those entrepreneurs and downtown shopkeepers who opposed urban planning found unlikely allies among those of the city's working people who were likely to be harmed by the Burnham plan. Their hostility would not have been so surprising to reformers if they had paid more attention to the outraged response of ordinary citizens to Haussmann's rebuilding of Paris. One of the prefect's most important acts was to remove obstacles to the circulation of capital through the French economy. To fund his gargantuan projects, he had discarded old bourgeois pieties about living within one's means and built on credit, gambling on unending economic expansion (and increasing tax revenues) to pay off the debts he acquired. In so doing, he promoted cycles of deficit financing, speculation, forced economic growth, and capital instability that have since become trademarks of the global economy.[72] Many Parisian property owners and investors grew rich, but laboring people did not fare as well. Although the great rebuilding added significantly to the city's housing stock, it paradoxically contributed to a worsening housing crisis by dramatically increasing downtown property values. Just as hundreds of thousands of rural migrants were pouring into Paris in search of work, landlords took advantage of improvements and a growing pool of bourgeois tenants (civil servants, professionals, and white-collar workers who enjoyed rising incomes during the Second Empire) to raise rents. Most of the poorer residents, as we have seen, were driven from their former homes into outlying districts that were remote from their places of work. Those who stayed were sealed into slums quite as bad as the ones that had existed before the renovations.[73] Haussmann's policies only intensified the problem. Although he had been willing to regulate the size and appearance of the building fronts that looked out onto his new boulevards, he was unwilling to interfere in what he viewed as the private housing market, resisting appeals for rent controls or quality housing statutes. Huge profits for landlords went hand in hand with deteriorating housing conditions for the working population.

Haussmann was wont to contend that his improvements offered something for all classes of society: "Foreigners and provincials would be attracted to the fine new city, would flock there to spend their money and would pay the expense of the new buildings. The shops would reap a harvest, the bourgeoisie would invest their money in the ground rents of the new streets, and the working classes would have full time employment; everyone would prosper."[74] But many did not prosper. Even Robert Moses, the American developer who was later reviled by many critics for destroying urban neighborhoods as he thrust great roadways through the heart of New York City in the mid-twentieth century, was troubled by the prefect of Paris's tendency "to neglect the lower middle class and the poor."[75] The economic forces Haussmann unleashed and the resentments they inspired exploded in 1871 when the laboring people of Paris took over the city and established the Commune. More destruction would follow. The communards themselves set fire to the city as they fled before murderous Versaillais soldiers during the May massacres, though in this case Karl Marx, for one, was sympathetic, contrasting the "vandalism of defense in despair" to the more destructive "vandalism of Haussmann, razing Paris to make place for the Paris of the sightseer."[76]

The important point here is that "improvement" or "beautification" was bitterly contested in France, that there were winners and losers, and that rebuilding programs helped to determine who prospered and who languished. Similar conflicts plagued the reconstruction of San Francisco, but whereas Haussmann could ignore opposition, building by edict, such an option was not available to officials in the California city. The Progressives who lobbied for adornment could be quite as contemptuous of democracy as the prefect of Paris. A correspondent for *Collier's* gave voice to the frustrations of many wealthy Americans, fantasizing about establishing "an enlightened despotism" to ensure that reconstruction was dictated by the public interest rather than the individual search for

the "quick profit." San Francisco, however, had unusually strong democratic traditions and a municipal council that depended on working-class
votes for its survival.[77]

From the beginning, this constituency mobilized against those parts
of the Burnham plan that threatened to drive ordinary families from
their homes. The demands of reformers to ban wooden structures from
downtown promised to produce a more fireproof and attractive city
center, but few working people could afford to build brick houses.[78] In
this case, market logic (and a political voice) protected the interests of
working-class householders much more effectively than the deeds of
civic-minded reformers.[79] Labor mobilized against the new building
regulations, and the municipal authorities abandoned proposals to ex-
tend the city's fire limits—a zone from which wooden buildings were
excluded. Progressives lost interest in the political reforms that might
have made the Burnham plan possible when it dawned on them that an
amendment to the state constitution allowing San Francisco to widen
streets over the objections of property holders would place expansive
new powers in the hands of politicians beholden to working-class con-
stituents. Fearing that urban planning might become the thin end of a
socialist wedge, reformers surrendered their imperial ambitions.[80]

In the end, George Harvey of *Harper's* was correct in his prediction:
investors and insurance companies poured enough money into San
Francisco to ensure that the city was rebuilt in less than five years.[81] But
while there were several improvements in design and structure, these
owed more to the ambitions and whims of individual entrepreneurs and
to a pool of talented architects who had flocked to the city to exploit the

FIG 7. Aerial view of San Francisco's business district after the earthquake and fire, 1906.
Photograph courtesy of Harry Myers.

FIG 8. Aerial view of San Francisco's rebuilt business district, 1909. View is shifted slightly to the east. Photograph courtesy of Harry Myers.

sudden demand for their services than to any Haussmannic planning.[82] The old street layout was little changed, and there was not even sufficient will to pass a bond issue for a new city hall until 1912, when prominent citizens were suddenly faced with the task of turning their city into a site impressive enough to host the impending 1915 Panama-Pacific International Exposition. Seeing immense potential for growth in the opening of the Panama Canal and eager to promote San Francisco as a city of global importance, residents finally voted to fund the construction of a monumental Beaux Arts civic center, one of the final achievements of the beautification movement. Still, Progressives could hardly claim to have imposed a rational design on San Francisco.

One of the sources of their undoing, reformers believed, was the callous behavior of Eastern corporations that seemed determined to put short-term profits ahead of responsible development. At the time of the earthquake, for example, United Railroads, a New York–financed company, was lobbying vigorously to defeat proposals that would have required it to house electrical lines for its trolley cars in expensive underground conduits, rather than in cheaper and unsightly overhead wires. For members of the Improvement and Adornment Association this was proof of the folly of leaving development to "foreign interests," to brokers and bankers on Wall Street and in Europe who cared nothing for living conditions in San Francisco.[83] Only if development was left to the community-minded citizens of San Francisco, reformers reasoned, would it be possible to build a city that expedited the pursuit of commerce without sacrificing quality of life.

Hence the eagerness with which influential local reformers sought to control all money raised to finance the rebuilding. As a first step, they dispatched Senator Francis Newlands to Washington to try to arrange a loan from the federal government. When this failed, Newlands and other San Francisco businessmen approached New York investors directly, hoping to secure an advance of $100 million with which to implement the Burnham plan.[84] This initiative also foundered, and it soon became clear that reconstruction was to be funded by private capital, acquired by businesses on a case-by-case basis. At first, individual companies would have to rely on the forbearance of suppliers. The merchant proprietor of Livingston Brothers, for one, later recorded that his business could not have survived without the willingness of Marshall Field and Company of Chicago to waive "the usual 60 day credit term."[85] Over the long haul, money was indispensable, and fortunately it arrived in abundance. Ultimately, about half of the costs of construction (about $200 million) were covered by fire insurance, $115 million of which reached businesses and householders within six months of the earthquake. Relief donations and federal contributions covered a further 2 percent of costs with the rest of the money coming from private savings and borrowings.[86]

When it became clear that they would not have a vast reconstruction fund at their disposal, reformers turned their attention to raising Eastern capital for their private enterprises. James Duval Phelan, banker, property owner, former mayor, and president of the Adornment Association, lobbied to change provisions in the California Constitution that had hitherto given preferential mortgage terms to residents of the state and thus deterred outside investment. Similarly, he and his allies secured the repeal of special taxes on the stocks and bonds of non-California corporations.[87] As so often in the twentieth century, the imperatives of development encouraged local leaders to try to entice outside investment by dismantling obstacles to the movement of capital. Their unintended legacy was to increase the influence of financiers over development patterns in a city once proud of its independence from Eastern investors.[88] A city, according to William Issel and Robert Cherny, that had "enjoyed economic autonomy" to an extent surpassed only by New York City at the end of the nineteenth century would find itself increasingly subject to national and international capital flows that accelerated the very cycles of ruin and renewal that Progressives abhorred.[89]

The merchants, professionals, and industrialists of the Adornment Society were willing to use the power of the state to promote private enterprise and to build the infrastructure they believed was necessary for the effective prosecution of commerce, but they remained profoundly uncomfortable with any intervention that threatened to distort what they viewed as a "free" market in wages or rents. Like Haussmann, in fact, their greatest failure lay in their inadequate response to housing problems. In the conditions that prevailed after the disaster, with a drastically reduced housing stock, market forces offered a strong economic incentive to landlords to supply overpriced and undermaintained accommodations for the refugees. The unburned Western Addition began its transformation from a comfortable middle-class district into a "blighted area," as property owners turned homes into lodging houses, cramming tenants into every available room and basement, and rented space to workshops, stores, and even dangerous industries. "Every condition that would make a modern city planner shudder," one historian later lamented, "was soon to be found in exaggerated form: indiscriminate mixture of land uses, excessive density of population, substandard housing, traffic congestion."[90]

And these middle-class tenants were the lucky ones. The destruction of some 55 percent of the city's housing stock hit blue-collar workers and their families especially hard. One of the unexpected effects of the calamity was to speed up the deindustrialization of the city as manufacturing firms moved out to the suburbs or across the bay to Oakland in search of cheaper ground rents, surrendering the city center to banks, insurance companies, and other financial institutions. Not only did many working people thus lose their jobs but they lost their homes too, as the financial district expanded by about 44 percent in the aftermath of the fire, taking over sites that had formerly been occupied by low-income housing.[91] Poorer families were left in a precarious position.

The prominent charity worker Edward T. Devine, head of the American Red Cross operation to aid San Francisco, lobbied vigorously to release relief funds for the construction of simple but good quality housing that could be made available cheaply to working-class families. As he pointed out, and as was plain to see, the private sector was simply unable to supply the needs of working-class refugees for affordable shelter in the aftermath of the conflagration. Eight thousand houses were built in the year and a half following the calamity, but these were almost all taken by middle-class residents. Sadly, several months after the calamity, Devine had to report that a "golden opportunity" had been missed to spend aid surpluses on decent homes for "the working men of the community." The reason: the local business leaders responsible for the distribution of relief funds could not bring themselves to interfere with the private property market. Instead, they paid for the erection of "temporary" and often unsanitary shacks that became, as Devine predicted, lasting scars on the San Francisco landscape.[92]

Meanwhile, in part as a result of their efforts, San Francisco began its evolution from a manufacturing center to an increasingly important financial center; by 1975, it would be home to the second largest concentration of international banks and financial institutions in the country, after New York City. It was these institutions that would push through plans to renew, or "Manhattanize," downtown San Francisco in the years after World War II, throwing up huge structures of steel, concrete, and glass, and producing finally the sort of imposing skyline that businessmen believed was worthy of this capital of capital. All this redevelopment accelerated the obliteration of low-income accommodation (ensuring that the city would suffer the highest housing prices in the country), while ensuring the disappearance of open spaces and the intensification of downtown congestion.[93]

Market forces, however, would not rule unopposed in San Francisco. If Adornment Association leaders failed to follow through on their ambition to impose limits on capital, activist communities over the twentieth century would enjoy considerable success resisting highway developments or building projects that threatened to destroy the neighborhood character of their city.[94] Such resistance to mobile capital, however, has not been without costs and may partly explain the increasing shift of money, people, and industries from the Bay Area to more "flexible," development-driven Los Angeles in the years since 1906.[95] The legacy of the disaster was thus an ambiguous one, revealing the crucial influence of capitalist logics in restoring a devastated metropolis and promoting business interests at the expense of the poor, but also bringing to the surface profound and enduring discontents with the destructive aspects of capitalist development that would spur ongoing resistance to the relentless remaking of San Francisco to suit the needs of business.

The story of San Francisco's reconstruction substantiates the growing critical consensus that there has always been a vital spatial dimension to capitalist development and that some of the most urgent social conflicts of the twentieth century and beyond have been organized around concerns of space and place. The logic of creative destruction, in particular, helps to explain why so many well-positioned Americans at the turn of the last century expected conflagrations to produce material benefits, even if those benefits were not shared by all.

In many respects, things have changed little since 1906. As the *Wall Street Journal* reported in 1999, calamities continue to generate economic gains that outweigh losses: "Afterward, retail sales soar as ruined goods are repaired or replaced, and construction is fueled by an influx of insurance money and federal disaster relief. Moreover, insured homeowners and businesses, already facing insurance-financed repairs, often seize the occasion to improve their properties." From 1989's Hurricane Hugo to the earthquake that shook Northridge, California, in 1994, the effects were the same. According to Steve Cochrane of Dismal Sciences, Inc., natural disasters invariably generate "a rapid rise in employment and income." And yet, calamities still ruin many individuals, and even those people who profit "would rather not face the risk."[96] A financial windfall rarely compensates for the loss of treasured possessions or for the stresses of renovation.

In the world made by late capitalism, disasters continue to mimic (and perhaps even burlesque) the destructive forces of capitalism, breeding a nostalgic preoccupation with order, permanence, and continuity, even as they promote economic growth and the expectation that ruin leads to renewal and improvement. But if calamities enable progress, "progress" itself often seems only to increase human vulnerability to increasingly severe calamities.[97] Nowhere has creative destruction contributed more to the shape of economic and urban development than in San Francisco's southern rival, Los Angeles, and nowhere, significantly, have disasters become such a persistent presence.

Until recently, as Mike Davis points out in his book *Ecology of Fear*, few have appreciated the costs of radically transforming the landscape according to the whims of capital. Viewing disasters as opportunities for development and exhibiting a reckless disregard for environmental limits, Americans have too often failed to heed the warnings that calamities bring. As a result, there have never been enough checks on unregulated, ecologically irresponsible construction: "Historic wildfire corridors have been turned into view-lot suburbs, wetland liquefaction zones into marinas, and floodplains into industrial districts and housing tracts." Meanwhile, Californians have continued to build homes, highways, and even nuclear power plants over fault lines. "As a result," as Davis concludes, "Southern California has reaped flood, fire, and earthquake tragedies that were as avoidable as the beating of Rodney King and the ensuing explosion in the streets."[98]

At the beginning of the twenty-first century, calamities (social and natural) are becoming such regular features of Southern California, and American, life that old optimisms about the benefits of disaster are finally wearing thin.[99] Faith in progress seems to be waning, and as a result more and more Americans view disasters as threats rather than as blessings, or at best as spectacles without moral or meaning. There is little sign, however, that we will see an end to the constant transformation of urban space any time soon. Many businessmen and financiers continue to heed Alan Greenspan's enthusiastic appraisal of creative destruction as the engine of an ever-innovating and expanding American economy, though there are also critics aplenty who insist that unending growth is an environmentally unsustainable option that may well produce a calamity that finally buries rather than invigorates capitalism.[100]

Destruction has enabled capitalist development. Over the last century and more, it has facilitated extraordinary economic expansion and invention, affirming many Americans in their long-standing conviction that calamities are blessings. The benefits, however, have not been spread equally, and we all have to find a way to live with and under a capitalist system that must constantly destroy to create, and which at times seems to create solely in order to destroy.

3

"That Enchanted Morning"

OR, HOW AMERICANS LEARNED TO LOVE DISASTERS

I can suggest no better "cure" for those that live where nature has practically forgotten them and civilization has become as great a vice as too much virtue, in whom a narrow and prosperous life has bred pessimism and other forms of degeneracy, stunting the intelligence as well as atrophying the emotions, than to spend part of every year in earthquake country.

GERTRUDE ATHERTON, 1906

For several years after I wished that there would be another earthquake so that I could hear things smash again.

RUTH WORNER, San Francisco earthquake survivor, 1919

How I wish that to every life there might come, if once only, such days of change and freedom, so deep and intoxicating a draught of realities, after all the artificialities of civilization and society. . . . Everyone talking together, disheveled, excited, running to see what was happening elsewhere, running back, endlessly diverted, satiated for once with excitement.

KATHLEEN NORRIS, San Francisco earthquake survivor, 1932

At twelve minutes past five on the morning of Wednesday, April 18, 1906, the ground suddenly shifted along a two-hundred-mile stretch of the San Andreas Fault, triggering an immense earthquake in northwestern California. Fortuitously for historians, and for him too it seems, William James was visiting Stanford University at the time. Like countless others, the eminent psychologist awoke to find his bed shuddering and furniture crashing all around him. Despite being lifted up and thrown face down on his bed, however, he could barely contain his excitement: "The emotion consisted wholly of glee and admiration; . . . I felt no trace whatever of fear; it was pure delight and welcome."[1] His wife, Alice, was not quite so buoyant, later describing the earthquake as a "most terrifying experience," but she verified her husband's joyous response, noting that as soon as the shaking had stopped he had run into her room, asking, "Are you frightened?" and then assuring her proudly, "I am not, and I am not nauseated either."[2] William remembered urging the earthquake on: " 'Go it,' I almost cried aloud, 'and go it stronger.' "[3] And stronger it had gone, peaking at an impressive 8.25 on the Richter scale, reducing much of the university to ruins and leaving two students dead under the rubble.[4]

San Francisco, thirty-five miles to the northwest, was in even worse shape. Later in the day, James took a train in to "the City" to survey the damage. He discovered that the earthquake had torn gaping holes in the streets and felled rows of chimneys and buildings. More ominously, tremors had also crippled the water supply system and ignited fires that would blaze through the city for three days. By the time the flames were finally extinguished, most of San Francisco was rubble and ash: twenty-eight thousand buildings had been gutted, over two hundred thousand people (half of the city's population) were destitute, and three thousand were dead—a catalog of material destruction unprecedented for a single event in the United States during peacetime.[5] One might imagine that the sheer scale of this tragedy would have had a sobering effect on James, but the distinguished professor clung to his first impression of the disaster as a "memorable bit of experience."[6] Sifting through his feelings in an essay written a few weeks later for *Youth's Companion*, he chose to play down the horrors of the calamity, emphasizing instead the pleasures of the initial shock.[7] This, he assured his youthful readers, was an encounter he "wouldn't have missed . . . for anything."[8]

What should we make of these curious confessions? It is tempting to dismiss James's glee as the perverse reaction of a man uniquely susceptible to the charms of chaos and confusion.[9] But letters, diaries, and memoirs reveal that he was by no means exceptional in savoring aspects of the disaster. James was struck by the ebullience of his fellow survivors at Stanford: "Everybody was excited, but the excitement at first, at any rate, seemed to be almost joyous. Here at last was a *real* earthquake after so many years of harmless waggle!" So welcome was this ferment, in fact, that most sought to prolong it, sleeping out of doors for the next few nights not, according to James, for any anticipated safety benefits, but "to work off their emotion, and get the full unusualness out of the experience."[10] Meanwhile, Americans across the country were thrilling to newspaper reports, film footage, and even theatrical reproductions of the calamity.

Where did these enthusiasms come from? Before James, most philosophers and psychologists would have looked for an answer in human nature.[11] James, however, recognized that emotional responses varied from person to person and that they were to a large degree culturally constructed. How people sensed, felt about, imagined, or responded to any given spectacle depended on such variables as their moods, experiences, and expectations.[12] Disaster sentiment, in short, had a history.[13] This is an invaluable insight that provides the starting point for my own cultural analysis of calamities. Indeed, stated most boldly and abstractly, my thesis in this chapter is that modernity created a "love" of disasters. Moreover, and perhaps more surprisingly, I hold that this enthusiasm for disasters was in turn a crucial ingredient of the modernizing process—enabling, specifically, the corporate reconstruction of American society and the emergence of a mass consumer culture. We see here the assembly of a culture of calamity that offers an imaginative counterpart to a modern economic and social order governed by processes of creative destruction.

It is important to emphasize at the outset that the "pleasures" of the San Francisco earthquake and fire were by no means universally felt, and they were almost always tinged with, or haunted by, revulsion and sorrow. As William James recognized, the satisfactions of disaster depended on assurances of one's own safety and the safety of loved ones. The disaster, it hardly needs to be said, was devastating for many who lost family members, friends, careers, savings, and homes, or who beheld grim scenes of death and destruction. After investigating cases of hysteria two weeks after the calamity, the *San Francisco Chronicle* predicted that some poor souls would never recover from the trauma: "The memory of the catastrophe will never leave their disordered minds."[14] And many of those who escaped with their sanity intact struggled to come to terms with their experiences. One young mother, who had feared for her baby's safety, was still reeling when she wrote to her parents five days later: "I can never describe or forget that horrible minute. It seemed an eternity; I thought we were doomed; every shake we were gone. Oh! I hope I shall never feel another like it."[15] Another woman who had witnessed the destruction of her house and her husband's business admitted to finding the affair "awful," and hard to bear.[16]

For such people, the disaster instilled a strong craving for a return of order, and most citizens were sufficiently disturbed by the turmoil to welcome the swift appearance of well-drilled and determined-looking troops on their streets. "The will of the people was toward authority," one writer observed, "and everywhere the tread of soldiery brought a relieved sense of things orderly and secure."[17] Indeed, a normally fractious and independent citizenry willingly renounced its constitutional freedoms and political rights, applauding when armed soldiers and policemen were authorized to evacuate buildings, close saloons, confiscate food for the hungry, and even shoot looters on sight.[18] And hardly a voice of opposition was heard when a committee of industrialists, professionals, and relief experts seized control of the city (with the mayor's later consent), implementing centralized relief and reconstruction programs to facilitate the most "efficient" distribution of aid supplies and the most "methodical" restoration of the city.[19] Reformers, in fact, were soon writing parables of organization that presented the disaster as a symbol of the perils of chaos and the blessings of modern planning. "If our civilization means anything," prominent "muckraking" journalist Ray Stannard Baker, for example, concluded, "it means an increasing ability of men to mitigate the blind operation of natural law; it means the coming of a time when men, clear-eyed, will see that service, self-control, cooperation, will accomplish the same end at which selfish competition now aims—and fails to reach."[20]

These responses provide some confirmation for Robert Wiebe's venerable "search for order" thesis, illustrating how turn-of-the-century experiences and fears of natural and social disorder won Americans over to bureaucratic values of "continuity and regularity, functionality and rationality, administration and management."[21] President Theodore Roosevelt persistently identified the paramount task of the age as one of removing chaos from the world and achieving "security" for the American people, and when he received news about the San Francisco calamity he immediately called for relief efforts to be organized along systematic lines.[22] The great problem facing the modern United States, according to Roosevelt, was "the problem of national efficiency, the patriotic duty of insuring the safety and continuance of the nation."[23] The earthquake advertised the virtues of control, seeming to substantiate Walter Lippmann's later claim that a "new science of administration" was required to protect Americans from depressions, social conflicts, and "natural catastrophes."[24] Even the most devoted champions of social and economic consolidation, however, harbored some misgivings about the desirability of a world entirely given over to "order."

Some of those present, in fact, insisted that the San Francisco earthquake was one of the most exciting, thrilling, and delightful experiences of their lives. This response is not entirely surprising. This was, after all, an age in which cultural leaders were openly reacting against the stifling influence of Victorian personal prohibitions and industrial routines, celebrating instead martial values, frontier ways, wilderness excursions, and any manner of intense experiences. Other historians have alerted us to the anxieties about "overcivilization" that pervaded middle- and upper-class society in this period.[25] I am concerned here with a specific aspect of this sentiment—a cult of chaos or search for *disorder*—that induced many Americans to greet natural eruptions as welcome cultural interruptions at the dawn of the twentieth century.[26] In the 1890s, William James had suggested (somewhat scurrilously) that only an event as startling as an Armenian massacre could rescue Americans from the stupor of living in an "uninspiring" civilization burdened by excessive "security, intelligence, humanity, and order."[27] He was famously appalled, of course, by the actual massacres and sufferings of the 1898 Spanish-American War, but he did find some satisfaction in the toppling of California's largest city eight years later, an event that supplied drama, excitement, and thrills aplenty.

Unfolding in three distinct stages—earthquake, fire, and aftermath—the San Francisco calamity appealed variously as an occasion for adventure, escapism, and entertainment. This was a matter of no small interest for social commentators. Was this simply a passion for nihilism (and annihilism) at play? James, for one, thought not. Indeed, he insisted that the cult of chaos and the search for order were dialectically linked, physiologically and socially. As a good Darwinian, he had long suspected that the faculties of the mind had evolved so as to be "adapted in advance to the features of the world in which we dwell, adapted . . . so as to secure our safety and prosperity in its midst."[28] Thus did humans find themselves especially jolted by and attentive to threatening objects and incidents. Disasters were rousing precisely because they were dangerous; the excitement produced by a fire or an earthquake originated in a powerful fear response. For modern men and women, however, spared most of the hazards that daily confronted their prehistoric ancestors, this shiver might well be experienced merely as an agreeable rush, as a welcome flood of feeling rather than an impulse to flee. This was especially likely to be the case for those, like the Boston boy, who encountered the calamity not directly but at a safe remove, through the images and stories purveyed in newspapers, theatrical performances, movies, and "the gossip of loquacious folks."[29] An instinct for self-preservation, it seemed, structured the thrill response that could turn calamities into entertainments.

And this was a good thing, according to James, who hoped that the emotions unleashed by disasters would provide a propulsive force—motive and desire—for the march of American progress.

Whereas many of his Victorian contemporaries continued to insist that the repression of strong emotions was necessary for the cultivation of virtue and the preservation of civilization, James had come to believe that repression, even if it was possible, would lead only to social stagnation. He thought it best to indulge, or at least provide an outlet for, unruly passions, harnessing them for the civilizing process. Thus it was that this apostle of chaos exulted in San Francisco in "the rapidity of the improvisation of order out of chaos."[30] As much as he feared the stagnations of "order," he celebrated the heroic task of "ordering." Indeed, he sensed that modern life could be salvaged from insipidity only if it was kept moving. And a dynamic society was, by definition, a destructive one. To bring about a new and better civilization, it was necessary to obliterate elements of the old, and James seems to have intuited that a society founded on creative destruction had to develop a cultural appreciation for annihilation.[31]

James hoped that thrill seekers would be the most alive and the most productive of citizens; what he did not fully anticipate was the role of disorderly desires in fuelling a mass culture oriented toward entertainment and commodity consumption rather than improvement, social justice, and democracy. But this is exactly what happened. One San Francisco woman remembered being "immensely" pleased when her tin boxes crashed to the floor during the great quake. "For several years after," she admitted, "I wished that there would be another earthquake so that I could hear things smash again."[32] Hers was no doubt an extreme reaction, but this yearning to hear and see things smash has become a recognizable staple of twentieth-century emotional life, exploited and inflamed by all sorts of commercial entertainments, from disaster movies and staged train wrecks to demolition derbies and news broadcasts.[33] By the 1900s, movie directors, newspaper editors, and amusement park operators were already aware of the immense profits that could be earned by catering to a public taste for chaos. To be sure these cultural entrepreneurs insisted that they were contributing in their own way to the preservation of those middle-class values of decency and hard work upon which modern civilization supposedly rested, contending that spectacles of disaster and thrill rides were necessary distractions from such competing and debilitating attractions as sex, alcohol, and idleness.[34] This was an argument supported by the work of Simon N. Patten, a prominent economist who was also an architect of Progressive disaster relief.[35]

Patten was perhaps the only important scholar of his day to hazard a formal connection between the cult of chaos and the rise of the industrial state, between modern emotional life and modern economics. Patten identified the shift from a scarcity economy to one of abundance as the defining transformation of the age, a pleasing outcome to one who hoped that industrial surpluses would enable the abolition of poverty and misery in the United States; but he worried, like Roosevelt and James, and like the early Puritan settlers, that "material success" might lead to personal and social degeneration. In his popular book, *The New Basis of Civilization*, which he and his wife were editing for publication at the time of the San Francisco earthquake, Patten celebrated an industrial revolution that had increased human productivity and promised the final mastery of nature. But if "efficiency," "discipline," "science," and "technology" had made progress possible, progress had also bred discontents that threatened to send working people running to the barricades or to dissipating vices such as alcohol. How were workers to be kept both happy and productive? William James had recognized that overcivilization had imbued the middle classes with longings for excitement; Patten similarly believed that "the barren industrial grind" had filled laboring people with a desire for an "emotional corrective," a yearning "to feel intensely." This, he recommended, should be satisfied by mass entertainments that recruited thrilling spectacles of chaos for the purposes of "social control." He anticipated that the immensely popular disaster shows and thrill rides at Coney Island, for example, would "stir and spur" the emotions, creating consumer desires ("new wants") that would revitalize the industrial economy, energize the workforce, and save the "young industrial civilization" from disintegration.[36] The culture of calamity, in this view, was an accomplice of an energized corporate capitalism.

Most historians and sociologists of "thrill" culture have emphasized its contribution to the narrowing of American life, bemoaning the substitution of a mass culture of vicarious pleasures for the more authentic satisfactions of life in a participatory republic.[37] Patten, no doubt, was insufficiently critical of both corporate society and mass culture, but what he did glimpse was the role of a modern enthusiasm for spectacles of chaos in promoting social and political activism. Many consumers of reports of the San Francisco earthquake, as we shall see, were sufficiently inspired by sensational stories and pictures of suffering to throw themselves into relief efforts. Compulsively drawn to representations of this spectacular disaster, people far from the scene found their attention fixed on the plight of the victims, and felt compelled to help.

A cultural history of natural disasters that is attentive to the cata-strophic logic of modernity raises a series of questions: Would the nation have become so preoccupied with security and safety in the twentieth century if American culture had not been saturated with images of calam-ity? Was a cult of chaos a necessary component of the search for corpo-rate order? Did it also structure or animate the consumer sensibility on which this corporate order depended for its survival?

Romancing Disaster

Reading about William James bouncing joyously up and down on his bed while the earth moved, it is tempting to wonder if this encounter with disaster was not, for him, the moral equivalent of sex. After all, James was wont to speak of the passionate relations between man and nature, or "bridegroom" and "bride," as he put it. And his wife's account of the earthquake is endlessly suggestive to the post-Freudian reader: "Our little frame house simply tossed and shook, shook and waved, and so vindictive was the process that I felt as if we must reach some climax—be shaken elsewhither or even be swallowed by the heaving earth."[38] It is possibly inappropriate to couple natural convulsions and sexual passions so glibly, but the link between destruction and desire is one that deserves close critical attention. For Freud, human desires for stimulation and sensory gratification were by definition chaotic and destructive, and had to be repressed, or channeled, for the sake of civilization.[39] And yet, the human condition was such that these instincts could never be entirely contained or forgotten, and could at any time erupt to disrupt the social order. Norman O. Brown, one of Freud's most influential American in-terpreters, cautioned that if our patently chaotic drives were repressed, they would return to galvanize a collective neurotic obsession with vio-lence and annihilation.[40] This sort of (psycho)analysis, of course, defies rigorous empirical validation and is impaired by the presumption that passions are a primordial force, when recent scholarship makes it clear that a change in social conditions and cultural systems can produce new structures of desire.[41] It does, however, provide a useful starting point for a historical investigation into the erotics of disaster, suggesting that there is a close psychological relationship between desire, chaos, and pleasure, and that we must look to the conditions of industrial civilization if we are to understand the rise of a distinctively modern appetite for destruction.

Americans have always been fascinated by disasters, but the nature of that fascination has changed considerably since the days of the Eu-ropean conquest and settlement of this continent. The Puritans, for all their reputed solemnity, eagerly devoured tales of calamity, supporting a lively trade in sensational stories from the earliest years of settlement in New England. The clergy fully recognized that the best way to grab the attention of parishioners was to pepper sermons with spine-tingling accounts of destruction and suffering.[42] Into the eighteenth century, the publishers of immensely popular almanacs eagerly filled their pages with accounts and promises of calamity to further feed and exploit interest in extreme events.[43] Although the colonists were no doubt titillated by the sheer drama of these tales, the intense fascination of the age with storms, fires, and earthquakes stemmed primarily from the conviction that God spoke most loudly and urgently through such events. And this, as we have seen, was often reassuring for believers. After all, as Increase Mather had explained to the readers of *Remarkable Providences*, "They that are in Christ, and who make it their design to live unto God, need not be dismayed at the most terrifying thunder-claps, no more than a child should be afraid when he hears the voice of his loving father."[44]

Faith in the providential purpose of disasters encouraged believers to look upon natural eruptions with awe, wonder, and enthusiasm. Before his conversion, Jonathan Edwards, for example, remembered being "struck with terror" whenever he "saw a thunderstorm rising." Afterward, God's excellency, purity, wisdom, and love "seemed to appear in everything; in the sun, moon, and stars; in the clouds, and blue sky; in the grass, flowers, trees; in the water and all nature."[45] And what of nature's harms? Significantly, he found particular sweetness in those occurrences that had formerly terrified him the most: thunder and lightning. "I felt God at the first appearance of a thunderstorm. And used to take the opportunity at such times, to fix myself to view the clouds, and see the lightning play, and hear the majestic and awful voice of God's thunder: which oftentimes was exceeding entertaining, leading me to sweet contemplations of my great and glorious God."[46] A true Christian filled with divine grace, he asserted, was bound to find these displays not simply instructive but beautiful. Edwards was surely not the first American to become excited in the presence of nature's fury, but he was the first influential thinker to theorize about the splendid affect of these events. Indeed, he was developing an aesthetic appreciation for nature's violence that would only become more widely shared as the eighteenth century unfolded, anticipating those romantics who would cherish the intense emotional state provoked by disasters as evidence of an authentic relationship with nature and with God.

There is certainly much truth in Simon Schama's observation that "born from the oxymoron of agreeable horror, Romanticism was nursed on calamity."[47] Reacting against the scientific rationalism of the industrial revolution in the late-eighteenth and early-nineteenth centuries, these philosophers and bards celebrated calamities as "sublime" events that could stimulate the senses and inspire appreciation for the mysteries of life.[48] Resisting the secularizing tendencies of their age, they projected yearnings for spiritual transcendence onto the wildest and most unruly forces of nature. As early as 1757, in a work that greatly influenced romanticism, Edmund Burke had pronounced that "there is no spectacle we so eagerly pursue as that of some uncommon and grievous calamity."[49] Burke's theory of the sublime is too complex to discuss at length here, but two points are worth emphasizing: his careful distinction between pleasure and delight (only the latter was experienced in the presence of calamity), and his insistence that delight was only felt by those spectators who were essentially safe from danger. Whereas a sense of spiritual immunity (the "very sumptuousity of security," as William James called it) had enabled Jonathan Edwards to feel joy in a storm, Burke's sublime feeling depended on an expectation of physical safety.[50] Burke understood that disasters were exciting to the extent that they were rare and different from "those things which a daily and vulgar use have brought into a stale and unaffecting familiarity," alternatives, in short, to the banalities of contemporary life. But it was not until the arrival of romantic poets like Wordsworth that sublime emotions came to be viewed as a possible *remedy* for the alienations of modern life.[51]

In other words, the march of "progress," and the supposed subjugation of the natural world, fed a consuming interest in calamities. As social and environmental historians have amply demonstrated, one of the most important consequences of the conquest and settlement of America was the transformation of trees, animals, and land into resources or commodities valued according to the price they could command in an emerging Atlantic market economy.[52] It appears that the more colonists commodified the American environment—cataloguing, expropriating, and "improving" the "wilderness"—the more they came to appreciate earthquakes, hurricanes, and other uncontrolled natural forces as sacred, sublime, and exciting happenings.[53]

This appreciation for the thrills of calamity filtered only slowly and unevenly into everyday American life. As Lewis O. Saum has shown, before the Civil War most ordinary men and women held to an outlook that was "fundamentally pre-Romantic." They clung tenaciously to a providential understanding of calamities and were too preoccupied with the task of taming nature to appreciate it in its more violent and unruly guises. Still, as Saum also documents, the words *romantic* and *sublime* did enjoy an

increasing vogue over the middle years of the nineteenth century as people began to write more often about the stirring emotional impact of fires,
floods, and earthquakes.[54] By the nineteenth century, a hunger for sensational disasters was becoming a prominent feature of everyday American
life.[55] The New York fire of 1835 impressed the young George Templeton Strong, for example, as a "splendid spectacle."[56] It also inspired the
young firefighter Nathaniel Currier to produce a print, "The Burning
of the Merchant's Exchange," that inaugurated Currier and Ives's long
career selling pictures of calamities in the emerging mass print market.
Most portentously of all, the conflagration spurred the New York *Herald*, launched by James Gordon Bennett the previous spring, to print its
first ever illustration, a sketch of a ruin, as a memento.[57] Bennett also
moved accounts of the fire to the front page rather than page two, where
American newspapers had always placed lead stories in the past.[58] This
was the first of many sensational events exploited by the *Herald* on its way
to establishing itself as the largest circulation newspaper in the world by
the end of the decade, guided by its manifesto to "exhilarate the breakfast
table."[59] And just as disasters sold newspapers, so did newspapers feed
appetites for disaster. By the 1840s, fires had become reliable fixtures
in the entertainment world of the American city. As a Swedish visitor to
New York noted, people would plan their evenings around a good local
blaze: "It was like deciding to go to the theater to see a play that had been
announced and that could be counted on with certainty to come off. And
sure enough, we did not have long to wait for the spectacle."[60] As the century drew on, stereographs and photographs of violent and catastrophic
scenes were increasingly welcomed into Victorian parlors. When the
movies arrived in the 1890s, audiences were most eager to watch films
that featured such "exciting" subjects as fires and firefighters.[61]

By the dawn of the twentieth century, repeated exposure to sensational representations of calamity in newspapers, nickelodeons, and even
amusement parks had primed Americans to become thrilled, and even
entertained, by disasters. These commodified images, I believe, had prepared people to experience the adrenaline rush provoked by a calamity
as an agreeable tingle of excitement. This was new. As recently as 1871,
most Americans had viewed the Great Chicago Fire as a providential
drama, literally as an act of God.[62] Although a festival atmosphere had
prevailed in the early hours of the conflagration, political and religious
leaders had entreated all citizens to exhibit stoic fortitude and self-control
during and after the disaster.[63] Many boys and youths reveled in the confusion, but few adults would admit to taking any pleasure in the disaster.[64]
Things were quite different in 1906.[65] Americans in this corporate age

certainly viewed disasters as hazards to be overcome through hard work and collective endeavor, but even respectable commentators appreciated the San Francisco earthquake and fire as an occasion for adventure and welcomed its commodification in books, newspapers, souvenirs, and films, maintaining that the heightened emotions it aroused might bring personal and cultural revitalization.

Many men and women in San Francisco savored their experiences of the calamity. They had various motives. Some viewed the disaster as a bearer of life. One man, having lost everything, later wrote happily to his sister about the benign influence of the crisis. "The fresh air and out door roughing it" had made him feel fitter than ever; in the three weeks since the fire, he had been "free from asthma, my direst enemy."[66] Most of those who reflected on the restorative powers of the calamity, however, were more impressed by its invigorating emotional impact. The disaster brought a touch of drama, excitement, and intensity into colorless lives. The earthquake and fire carried people out of the ordinary and into the extraordinary, opening them to intense, barely recognizable, emotions. One Berkeley student, making his way alone into San Francisco while it burned, was overwhelmed by the strangeness of the sensation: "I was not frightened, but rather exhilarated. At the same time I had an eerie feeling that this was not real, that I was in another dimension, or in another existence."[67] Others thought that the disaster had introduced a world somehow *more* real. An architect, for example, recalled that the conflagration "fascinated, thrilled, took one out of oneself and made him part of another life; another life in which might is mightier, time quicker and things altogether on a more stupendous and potent scale than here on this little, slow, imperfect earth."[68] Although this man was clearly stirred by the sublimity of the disaster, achieving a fleeting transcendence, more onlookers were glad simply of the excitement.

San Francisco had its fair share of modern romantics, men like Charles Ross who had grown up on a diet of dime novels and adventure stories and who were grateful to be present during such a tremendous calamity. Ross, a printer and a union organizer, found the chaos and confusion exhilarating, and he went out of his way to court danger, enlisting as a special policeman and patrolling the city with a pistol on his hip. He explained to a friend that he had come out West to "see the world, to get literary color, to broaden my mental horizon, to seek adventure!" And he had found it in scoops. Joyously, he thanked the heavens: "The gray old gods are giving their child his wish. I could not ask for more. And I like it all—the excitement, the uncertainty, the danger, the adventure." In fact, the disaster had given him a taste for further adventures: "I expect greater lessons; we are here today—where tomorrow? Kismet! Well, so be it. For myself I must say that I am ready for anything, and my courage is good." Like many young men of Jack London's generation, and London coincidentally was also in San Francisco at this time, Ross was determined to live life to the fullest, and even though he experienced moments of uneasiness, he clearly could not believe his luck when the disaster struck.[69]

The calamity provided Ross with an opportunity for adventure and self-assertion, as well as the satisfaction of defending civilization in its hour of need. This was very much a gendered pursuit for him. Disasters enabled men to be men. His letters, indeed, betray an anxious preoccupation with manly bearing and masculine courage, his description of an incident at a refugee camp being typical: "Out of the tents came frightened, screaming women, and a man or what ought to have been a man yelling that we were all lost and that a tidal wave would soon come and drown us!" For Ross, to be a "man" was to be courageous; a man without courage was like a woman.[70] There were plenty of women, however, who would have argued this point with him. Indeed, one of the most surprising features of the 1906 earthquake is the response it drew from "ladies," many of whom turned out to be just as eager as men for adventure and for release from the banalities of domestic life.

Few expressed the rapture of the disaster, "that enchanted morning," as powerfully as Kathleen Norris, a respectable young woman who married Charles Norris, brother of the novelist Frank Norris, in 1909 and later won renown for herself as a writer of popular romances. Writing twenty-five years after the earthquake, she began a memoir with familiar descriptions of falling chimneys and crashing china—signs of a "world gone mad." Before long, however, she switched gears and sank into a warm reverie about the joys of the disaster: "How I wish that to every life there might come, if once only, such days of change and freedom, so deep and intoxicating a draught of realities, after all the artificialities of civilization and society. . . . Everyone talking together, disheveled, excited, running to see what was happening elsewhere, running back, endlessly diverted, satiated for once with excitement."[71] One thing that appealed to Norris, as to William James and Charles Ross, was the fact that the disaster forced the abandonment of suffocating conventionalities. For Norris this was experienced as a release from domestic chores.[72] In the weeks after the earthquake, San Franciscans were prohibited from cooking indoors (the combination of damaged chimneys and broken water mains made a renewed conflagration a genuine threat), and she couldn't have been more pleased: "Youth led forbidden forays into the forbidden kitchens, came forth to cook at curbstones, realized at last its rebel dream of the tiresome old office burning down!" Stifling duties were left behind, at least for the time being, and as Norris pronounced, "to certain hearts wearied with routine and responsibility these conditions spell complete satisfaction with life."[73]

Norris discloses an ardent antimodern sensibility in her memoir, trotting out clichés about the artificiality of civilization and waxing lyrical about the "reality" of this intoxicating disaster.[74] There surely was something elemental about the earthquake and fire. As flames swept through the city, men, women, and children fled for their lives. For once, many comfortable citizens were forced to reflect on matters of sheer survival. On the second day of the fire, as hunger set in and the prospect of famine began to loom, as refugees began to scour the city for food, city dwellers also surely became freshly aware of their dependency on the natural world for sustenance. The disaster stripped away some civilized illusions, reminding people of the limits to their control over nature, over suffering, over their world. But what did it mean for Norris to argue that this extraordinary disaster had introduced a "draught of realities"? What did it mean to imply that everyday life was unreal? For most Americans, stating that modern life was inauthentic was simply a way of saying that it had been drained of emotional vitality. What appealed about the disaster was its ability to provoke sweeping passions. When Americans expressed appreciation for the "reality" of this overwhelming experience, they were responding to its emotional impact, not venturing ontological opinions. What they wanted was to *feel* something real, to get in touch with an authentic sense of self.

In California, it was perhaps inevitable that such longings should be expressed in pioneering terms. At the turn of the century, a nostalgia industry was emerging in the United States that presented the West as a landscape of extremes, as the last environment that could inflame intense emotions.[75] For many survivors of the earthquake, not the least exciting feature of their disaster was that it seemed to restore the Old West, at least for a while. William James uttered a commonplace when he ventured that California was uniquely equipped to deal with calamity: "If such a disaster had to happen, somehow it couldn't have chosen a better place than San Francisco (where everyone knew about camping, and was familiar with the creation of civilizations out of the bare ground)."[76] Many citizens, in fact, were oddly pleased to return to what they believed were frontier conditions, hoping for a revival of the spirit of '49. "Our fathers and mothers," one woman explained, "migrated from that cold and over-civilized East to reach this free Western land of the sunset." But "overcivilization," a state more deplorable even than "savagery" where people at least had "air to breathe and space to turn around in," had over-taken them even here.[77] Perhaps, she hoped, the restoration of pioneer-ing ways—living in tents, struggling for survival—would help settlers to get back in touch with the elemental forces of life, recovering in the process the unvarnished ways that had built the West.[78]

The earthquake and fire, of course, did not really bring about a resto-ration of the "wild" West. The refugee tent cities were as much Frontier-land as frontier: carefully planned and closely supervised. But the disaster did at least offer an occasion for outdoor adventuring. The Sierra Club was emerging in California at this time, drawing its membership from well-to-do Americans who had grown "restive under the restraints of cities and conventionalities."[79] A number of refugees appreciated the San Francisco calamity for bringing the wilderness to the city. Sierra Club activist Ruth E. Praeger traced a lifetime's passion for camping to her experiences in a tent in the aftermath of the disaster: "That was a great experience for me, and I enjoyed it a lot. . . . I could run around and enjoy the out-of-doors."[80]

For all of the rhetorical tributes to pioneering self-reliance, what ap-pealed most about the disaster to many citizens was the opportunity to forge a genuine community. Although the antimodern rebellion against orderliness in San Francisco was usually couched in universal terms, it may well be more appropriate to view it as an expression of dissatisfaction with the emerging corporate industrial order. Countless San Franciscans recalled the joys of assembling around the stoves of neighbors, making friends, helping one another.[81] Food was free and divided according to need; all ranks had to stand in line to receive rations. San Franciscans of all classes were mesmerized by the *apparent* sweeping away of class and ethnic divisions, of "every artificial barrier," during the disaster.[82] One man, later the director of the German hospital in Alameda in the East Bay, wandered through Union Square on the day of the earthquake and found it jammed with people of all types: "White people and negroes and Chinese and Japanese all mixed without prejudice—one bench in the park might harbor all the chief races and no-one seemed to be aware of it."[83] For some this glimpse of a world without (fundamental) difference was profoundly liberating. One woman was sure that the disaster had brought San Franciscans a little closer to Jesus: "All artificial restraints of our civilization fell away with the earthquake's shocks. Every man was his brother's keeper."[84] People reached out across cultural distinctions and experienced a powerful union of concern, a quiver of compassion, a harmony of interest. One man helped an Italian bootblack he did not know and was later himself assisted by a stranger—this, he thought, was evidence of the sweet "kinship of suffering."[85] "For a few days at least," wrote Charles Keeler, "the millennium had come to San Francisco. The brotherhood of man was not a misty ideal but a beautiful reality. Caste and creed were thrown to the winds. There were no rich and poor, no capitalists and laborers, no oppressed and oppressors. All extraneous things were gone, and the greatness of human hearts, meeting a common loss, facing a common peril, and buoyed up by a common hope, was sublime."[86] "Would that it could always be so!" another commentator wrote.[87]

But did San Franciscans really want to dwell indefinitely in this state of happy anarchy? Not really. It was fun to imagine a nation without distinctions and conflicts, but few among the upper classes were willing to give up the privileges these distinctions gave them.[88] The charms of this "Utopia" were fleeting.[89] The pleasures of privation, in particular, quickly paled. Sleeping under canvas might at first present itself as a great adventure, but most San Franciscans quickly began to pine for running water and fresh changes of underwear.[90] As one poet wrote of the refugee camps, "Ten thousand khaki tents or more / The parks' green hillsides scattered o'er / To the idealist might seem / Idyllic as a shepherd's dream," but tent life had its drawbacks: "The simple life in them pursued / Proves both disquieting and crude; / That which in art is picturesque, / For living proves a coarse burlesque."[91] Before long, the inconveniences of life in the camps had most refugees longing for the comforts of civilization. Kathleen Norris's rebel dream of the office burning down was, for the most part, a fantasy of the privileged. And if privileged men and women found the disaster exciting, they also found it unsettling. It did not take long for fears about social anarchy, violence, and disorder to convince most disaster enthusiasts that too much turmoil and disruption was a bad thing. Comfortable men and women wanted to tour through confusion, not surrender to it.

From the beginning, the pleasure that San Franciscans took in the disaster had depended on assurances of safety, of protection from physical harm. Norris's enthusiasms were underpinned by an expectation that the army would protect her and her family from crime and hunger. "Delight of delights," she remembered, "nobody could make beds or dust on that enchanted morning!" And why? Because the army had turned them out of their houses. "Authority," she remarked joyously, "was in the saddle by six."[92] For William James, too, a feeling of security was crucial for his enjoyment of the earthquake. As he rocked in his bed, it was his faith in the sturdiness of his "frail little wooden house" that enabled him to yield to the pleasures of the shaking.[93] The same went for a wealthy mining magnate who had also enjoyed the earthquake, satisfied that he was in no danger high up in the St. Francis Hotel. In the following year, this man experienced another earthquake in Italy in which his life really was endangered. On that occasion, he admitted, he was truly "frightened."[94]

Although the longing for release from the disciplinary routines of daily life spread through all sectors of society, the most joyous discourses on the pleasures of the San Francisco calamity were written by men and women such as William James and Kathleen Norris who could count on a degree of security from life's hazards.[95] America's working poor lived rather too intimately with want and hardship on a day-to-day basis to find much cheer in the compound dangers of a natural disaster. For immigrant families like those who populated Upton Sinclair's famous portrait of Chicago's Packingtown in *The Jungle*, a novel that was electrifying readers in the spring of 1906, life itself unfolded as a series of catastrophes. People who were unable to afford dependable shelter against the ravages of winter storms were hardly likely to place a high value on the primitive delights of a natural disaster. The desperation of one female worker who was unable to find work in the weeks following the earthquake is illustrative here. Lavinia Robbins, a young woman with few friends and no family to call on for support, gave no indication of any pleasure in the calamity—on the contrary, she "had the blues for days and days"—and she was greatly relieved when her former employers reopened for business and invited her back to work.[96]

Similar anxieties afflicted the embattled Chinese community. According to Erika Pan, author of the most detailed study of Asian responses to the earthquake, most Chinese men and women believed a malevolent Earth Dragon had caused the earthquake, crying, "Day Loong Jun Ah! or The Earth Dragon trembles!"[97] Whatever terrors the supernatural realm might have inspired, there was plenty of cause for apprehension in the here and now. As the only community to be segregated by race in San Francisco, and as the only ethnic group to endure overtly discriminatory treatment in the aftermath of the earthquake and fire, the Chinese had a particularly complex set of responses to the 1906 disaster.[98] On the one hand, the vast majority of them were migrants or the children of migrants, risk takers who were quite accustomed to dealing with adversity and unexpected challenges. Moy Jin Mun, for example, had worked as a gold miner and lived through anti-Chinese riots, and when his business burned down in 1906 he responded with the stoicism expected of a "pioneer," cutting his losses and vowing to rebuild his fortune.[99] But few of his neighbors were quite so sanguine. After two decades of legal and extralegal campaigning to "exclude" Asians from the West, and as the victims of constant (and often violent) harassment, most of the remaining fifteen thousand residents of Chinatown viewed it as a sanctuary, and when the district burned down on the first night of the disaster, they felt, and indeed were, vulnerable to further exhibitions of white racism.[100]

Memories of the bubonic plague episode of 1900 did little to reassure them that they could expect fair or just treatment from the authorities. On that occasion, although no proof was ever offered of any link to the disease, Chinatown had been quarantined for three weeks, causing great economic hardship and even several cases of starvation.[101] Confronting a hostile political and social environment, there was little hope that this new disaster in 1906 would turn into a great adventure. Officials, in fact, treated the Chinese as a social problem rather than as a community in need of support, herding them from location to location to mollify whites who objected to their supposed smell or who were fearful that these interlopers would settle permanently in their neighborhoods.[102] Chinese men were pressed into work gangs as a matter of course and were frequently harassed by the armed soldiers who patrolled the city. As a final indignity, because they were denied passes to return to their homes, they could only look on while national guardsmen and "respectable" white citizens looted the embers of Chinatown for souvenirs.[103]

In such a context, it is hardly surprising that the Chinese found few delights in the calamity. The memoir of Hugh Kwong Liang, who later achieved fame as a vaudeville performer, reads as a chronicle of fear and hopelessness. Fifteen years old in 1906 and alone because his mother had moved back to China and his father had recently died, he found the calamity traumatic, collapsing into tears and wondering "what was to become of me, now that I was left penniless and all alone in this mess?" The sight of the conflagration presented no charms. "As I looked down the hill and saw the whole of Chinatown burning, including the building on Washington Street where I was born and spent my childhood, a feeling of true sadness and awe came over me." There was nothing to do, he concluded, but join "the slow march with the other refugees." Even at the Presidio, under the protection of the army, the survivors spent an anxious night praying that the flames would not catch them, and Liang resolved to drown himself at the waterfront. As luck would have it, however, he came across a boat and stole aboard as a stowaway. The only joy he felt that day was when he realized he had escaped from the burning peninsula: "No words can adequately describe my feelings that morning, when I realized I was at last out of the nightmare in San Francisco."[104]

When San Francisco subsided beneath the flames, the future looked bleak for Hugh Kwong Liang and for Lavinia Robbins.[105] They were too preoccupied with chasing the elusive domestic comforts that so oppressed Kathleen Norris and her kind to find much enchantment in the calamity. The men and women who wrote most lavishly about the thrills of the disaster, understandably, were those who felt stifled by bourgeois social conventions and who were yet relatively removed from privation and uncertainty and had some control over their destiny. Indeed, it was middle-class opinion shapers who made the case for the emotional benefits of American disasters—and they tended to make this case on behalf of the middle classes rather than the masses, who they suspected were quite excitable and disruptive enough as it was.

The popular writer and columnist Gertrude Atherton (who was married to one of the wealthiest men in the Bay Area) argued forcefully in an article for *Harper's Weekly* that those who had lived through the San Francisco disaster had truly "lived," not "merely existed." "Everybody," she claimed, "looks back upon the era 'before the earthquake,' as a period of insipidity, and wonders how he managed to exist." Atherton went so far as to recommend a dose of disaster for people who had never seen nature at its most furious: "I can suggest no better 'cure' for those that live where nature has practically forgotten them and civilization has become as great a vice as too much virtue, in whom a narrow and prosperous life has bred pessimism and other forms of degeneracy, stunting the intelligence as well as atrophying the emotions, than to spend part of every year in earthquake country." Emotional excitement was a good thing, but Atherton was not ready to endorse thrills for their own sakes. On the contrary, she wrote glowingly about the earthquake experience precisely because she expected it to reinvigorate Americans for the urgent labor of building a more orderly modern world. She was, after all, writing in *Harper's Weekly*, a magazine that billed itself as "A Journal of Civilization." The passions stirred by the calamity were acceptable to her only to the extent that men arose "refreshed, wider awake and more determined to conquer than ever before."[106]

Respectable American men welcomed an excuse for enjoying the calamity, and Atherton provided one when she revealed how these passions could revitalize the civilizing process. She was echoing William James here. He too was drawn to chaos because he believed it could ignite the strong passions that would invigorate a civilization devoted (ideally) to the "immemorial warfare against nature." At Stanford University, just two weeks before his earthquake adventure, James had premiered his seminal paper on "The Moral Equivalent of War," warning about the "cultural degeneration" that lay ahead unless American men could escape from the scented trappings of comfortable civilization and revitalize themselves by living life on the edge, or *"in extremis."*[107] His concern, however, was to help men live in the modern world, not to escape from it. The San Francisco earthquake appealed to him not only as a source of excitement but also as an occasion for arduous (manly) endeavor—for turning chaos against chaos.

If romantics loved disasters for their sublimity, it was sublimation that enabled modern Americans such as James to love disasters. At the outset of the twentieth century, it seems, many middle-class men and women were beginning to intuit that irrational desires were unavoidable, but, happily, that they were salvageable for "constructive" ends.[108] James's theory of moral equivalents, as Walter Lippmann explained in 1913, was in fact a theory of "sublimation" that revealed how unruly instincts could be put to productive uses.[109] Disasters, by this reasoning, were not just moments of chaos to be overcome; they were events that liberated and channeled the chaotic passions that propelled the civilizing process. One of the elements that most reassured James about human nature in the aftermath of the San Francisco earthquake was the speed with which order was restored, but it is not clear that he ever really wanted to win the war against nature.[110] It was the war itself, the ongoing presence of adversity, the shadow of calamity, in short, that made life worth living. On occasion, it seemed as if James might be satisfied enough with the mere impression of adversity.

James distrusted all sentimentality that did not produce deeds, believing that stimulated emotions were only acceptable if they helped to build character and to produce virtuous behaviors.[111] But in spite of himself he was swept up in the sheer excitement of the California disaster. Indeed, this peaceful apostle of strenuousness found the spectacle of calamity at San Francisco as stirring as the physical challenge. He may, in fact, have been more comfortable as a consumer of disaster than as a warrior against nature. In his celebrated, oft-cited essay "What Makes a Life Significant" (1899), he had penned a withering critique of the tranquil, safe, and unspeakably dull bourgeois community he had visited at Chautauqua, New York, in 1896. What was missing from this "middle-class paradise," he sighed, was "the element of precipitousness, so to call it, of strength and strenuousness, intensity and danger." But as his critique unfolded, it became clear that his principal concern was the restoration of "moral style, expressiveness, and picturesqueness." He wanted a world that could excite what he called, in a revealing phrase, "the looker-on at life." For James, the line separating doing and seeing, or acting and spectating, was not always firmly drawn: "What our human emotions seem to require," he concluded, "is the *sight* of the struggle going on."[112] He wanted to see spectacles of chaos. In fact, like others of his era, he found it hard to see a calamity as anything other than a spectacle.

Significantly, many San Franciscans responded to their disaster as spectators, experiencing many of the same chills and thrills as the millions of men, women, and children across the country who purchased and read sensational newspaper reports or who entertained themselves in theaters watching reproductions of the event. For Mary Hawgood, the fire presented a "gorgeous sight" through her bedroom window.[113] Cameron King Jr. also found the "terrible and magnificent" scene compulsively alluring. "I tried to lie down and sleep," he wrote, "for I was foot-sore and my legs ached with exhaustion, but the spectacle drew me with irresistible power to a coign of vantage."[114] Even those who were struggling to save their possessions or to protect their homes sometimes fell into the role of spectators. "Right here," according to the writer Mary Austin, "if you had time for it, you gripped the large, essential spirit of the West, the ability to dramatize its own activity, and, while continuing in it, to stand off and be vastly entertained by it." Such detachment enabled residents to take some satisfaction in their extraordinary predicament: "In spite of individual heartsinkings, the San Franciscans during the week never lost the spirited sense of being audience to their own performance."[115]

Few artifacts capture this spirit better than a photograph taken of the fire from Sacramento Street on the first day of the disaster. In the picture, a crowd of men and women are seated in rows of chairs on the hilly street (creating something of an amphitheater effect). Their expressions are hard to read, but the lasting impression is of an audience watching what one insurance salesman described as "the greatest spectacular drama ever staged."[116] The picture was taken by the celebrated photographer Arnold Genthe, later to win fame for his pictures of old Chinatown, whose fancy had been caught by the composure of these onlookers, and by the way they would calmly move back a block up the street every time the fire drew closer. Especially pleased with this picture, he later recounted how in subsequent years he had been asked whether it was a "still from a Cecil De Mille picture." "No," he had replied, "the director of this scene was the Lord himself."[117] It was a fine jab, but perhaps his inquisitors had not been so far off the truth. De Mille, of course, was yet to arrive on the American cultural scene in 1906, but the celebrated filmmaker's taste for spectacular productions was cultivated in much the same environment that had instilled in Genthe an appreciation for the aesthetics of disasters.

FIG 9. "Looking down Sacramento Street—April 18th, 1906." Photograph of the San Francisco fire by Arnold Genthe. Courtesy of the Steinbrugge Collection of the Earthquake Engineering Center, University of California, Berkeley.

Genthe became so absorbed shooting the conflagration that he forgot to save his belongings from his studio before it burned. This degree of distraction, or preoccupation, was unusual. According to one correspondent, there were few cameras on the streets when the fires were most out of control. But once the immediate danger was past, amateur photographers were everywhere, flashing away with their portable Kodak Specials, "apparently afraid the fire would be subdued before they secured all the pictures they wanted." "The probabilities," this reporter deduced, "are that never since cameras were first invented has there been such a large number in use at any one place as there has been in San Francisco since the 18th of last April."[118] What was so appealing about this event? Why was it so photographed? Clues can be found in the fervent exhortations of a fellow camera enthusiast:

> The time for making the best pictures of the desolated city is passing; the tottering walls are being pulled down and the battered ironware is being gathered into neat little piles that are fatal to beauty. . . . Instead of beholding one of the mighty tragedies of history, we shall soon be spectators at a common-place, every-day drama. . . . So, my good brother photographer, before the halcyon days in which we are living pass away, never to return in our time, get out with your "picture-box" and record some of the wonderful sights of the modern Herculaneum.[119]

In an orderly and predictable world, scenes of chaos assumed a rare loveliness.

This ability to perceive the fire as an artistic composition or as a dramatic spectacle seems to have steadied men and women as they beheld the disaster.[120] After all, spectacle is not only a way of seeing the world but a strategy for ordering its unruly aspects.[121] Through the framing device of spectacle, spectators in San Francisco could gaze at the conflagration and enjoy, as one observer phrased it, "something almost pleasant in looking at a monster."[122] The word *monster* has etymological links with the word *monitor*: we tame monsters (the chaotic forces beyond reason and the customary) by monitoring them.[123] Spectacle, in other words, has a therapeutic dimension. But there were limits to its power to calm. Appreciation for a "splendid view of the burning city" from a vantage point at the top of McAllister Hill did not spare an exhausted Mormon youth from nightmares on the first night of the fires: "I dreamed I was in a burning building with no chance to escape."[124] And a spectatorial perspective rarely survived direct encounters with carnage, as the experience of Lutheran pastor George A. Bernthal reveals. He volunteered for nursing duties at a makeshift hospital and witnessed a series of horrors. "Whole wagon loads of injured and dying," he recalled, "were constantly coming in, such as could be pulled out of the ruins. I stood for hours at the operating tables and was downright splattered with blood. It smelled like only in a slaughterhouse as, again and again, legs, arms, and other limbs were amputated and whole piles of amputated limbs were lying around. How I could stand it, I do now know; but finally my senses became completely numb." Writing to his brother, he attempted to put a brave face on the experience, but clearly the events had taken some toll. "We are all still well and cheerful," he maintained, but admitted that "people tell us that this trauma has aged us by years."[125]

Still, the frame of spectacle helped many eyewitnesses to distance themselves from the horrors of the disaster and, crucially, thereby to extract some pleasure in the unfolding sights.[126] An Oakland man, wandering through San Francisco during the fire, was so impressed by the good nature and merriment of the survivors that he wondered whether he "had not made a mistake and fallen in with an excursion to Coney Island."[127]

Commercializing Disaster

The reference was not as far-fetched as he probably thought. New York's great amusement park was awash in disaster shows in 1906, with huge crowds turning out to watch reproductions of the Johnstown flood of

1889, the Galveston hurricane of 1900, and the eruption of Mount Pelée, which killed thirty thousand people on the island of Martinique in 1902.[128] We cannot understand how Americans felt about the real San Francisco earthquake and fire without considering the role of amusement parks in presenting or re-presenting disaster as commercial entertainments. As many social commentators and scholars of the age were beginning to realize, these parks, which were springing up all across the country in this period, revealed something profound about a modern psyche that seemed to be structured in some way by a desire to watch spectacles of calamity and to enjoy the shivering pleasures of thrill rides—that approximated nothing so much as the experience of earthquakes.[129]

Once shunned as a den of iniquity by respectable folks, Coney Island had begun to reinvent itself as the quintessential modern playground with the opening of Steeplechase Park in 1897, but it was the arrival of Luna Park and Dreamland in 1903 and 1904 that launched the "great age of spectacle."[130] Dreamland, always trying to outdo Luna, advertised itself as the home of the "superspectacle," putting on such gargantuan shows as "The Fall of Pompeii," which simulated the ancient volcanic eruption and its forty thousand deaths using real explosions, real flames, and real smoke. Luna Park's extraordinarily popular "Fire and Flames" set the standard for these shows. Spectators would fill a large grandstand to watch one thousand actors enact a tenement street scene, awaiting the inevitable outbreak of a fire, a tumultuous affair of dense smoke, explosions, and screaming women that would cue the dramatic arrival of seventy firefighters, with steam engines and the latest firefighting equipment, to subdue the flames.[131]

Most of the disaster shows were accompanied by informative lectures put on by proprietors eager to defuse criticism that they were promoting voyeurism or offering thrills simply to titillate audiences.[132] But the crowds that came to these performances were clearly in search of something more visceral than edification. "There is emotion in such scenes as the Galveston Flood and the Johnstown Flood," Theodore Waters observed in *Harper's Weekly*, an emotion that audiences were willing to pay for. Waters, in fact, was "amazed" to discover that New York's own great calamity—the burning and sinking of the *General Slocum*, which killed over one thousand excursionists on the East River in 1904—had not yet been reproduced when he visited Coney Island one year later. "What an opportunity," he wrote, "to give the *blasé* New Yorker the sensation of his life by putting him on a stage steamboat, letting it burn to the water's edge, and rescuing him at the last moment with a stage police-tug, while dummy passengers burn to death in real fire or drown in real water." The desire to encounter calamity, in controlled settings, ran so deep, according to Waters, that even the survivors of the original tragedy would be unsure whether to denounce or patronize "such a horror."[133]

The recruitment of disaster for the purposes of entertainment was a matter of considerable interest to observers of the American scene. Few commentators offered more penetrating insights into this phenomenon than Rollin Lynde Hartt, an early authority on the history of leisure, who visited Coney Island for the *Atlantic Monthly* in 1907. Hartt identified three principal types of "joy" at the resort: "wonder," "vicarious terror," and "the first-hand hair's breadth 'scape," recognizing that customers sought stimulation not only for the eye but for all of the senses.[134] The park promised sensations much like those experienced during the 1906 earthquake. Coney Island's "specialty," according to a *Munsey's* writer, was "to toss, tumble, flop, jerk, jounce, jolt, and jostle you by means of a variety of mechanical contrivances."[135] Indeed, the whole point of Coney Island, according to Waters, was to disorientate and excite the senses: "'Shake 'em up! Shake 'em up!' yells the barker, . . . and that is what they are doing all over the Island—'shaking them up.'"[136] No wonder the Foolish House (where "the floor wallows and shakes. Horrifying bumps confront your feet") was such a favorite with the patrons.[137]

What exactly was the appeal of the shaking houses and the stomach-churning roller coasters? Edwin Slosson, trying to explain these strange pleasures to the respectable readers the *Independent*, turned to physiology for answers, concluding that "modern entertainers" catered to an "obscure sense, only recently recognized by psychologists, the sense of equilibrium, the sense of which is affected when the motion of the body is changed in direction or speed, a sense located in part in the semi-circular canals of the ears." Where overstimulation of this sense was "a source of acute misery," it seemed that a gentle agitation could produce "a sensation of pleasure," even a "delight of danger."[138] This explanation was convincing enough as far as it went, but most other observers insisted also on the important influence of historical, or at least evolutionary, factors. Hartt invoked both Darwin and the psychologist G. Stanley Hall as authorities for his belief that crazy houses and thrill rides were popular because they gratified "primitive" urges for stimulation. In a singular turn of phrase, Hartt called these rides "thanatopses" (which he translated as "death traps," but which might also be translated as death drives), portraying Coney Island as a site of regression where destructive passions could be gratified.[139]

Crucially, however, Hartt recognized that the desire to flirt with danger was not driven by an actual death wish or a genuine desire for annihilation. On the contrary, audiences wanted only "a brush with death," the sort of brush that made "life unutterably precious."[140] For jaded moderns, such encounters could be exhilarating:

> Flaming sympathies, wild upsurgings of desire, and mad jubilance, — when the dread crisis has passed, — give the spectator a panoramic view of his own soul. Incapable, commonly, of introspection, he has experienced an interval of dazzling, astounding self-revelation. Out of his littleness, he rises to momentary greatness — feels himself terribly, almost epically, alive.[141]

Surviving danger and conquering one's fears, as William James had argued at Stanford, made life worth living.[142] Indeed, the thrill-seeking desires that drew people to chaos and danger surely had as much to do with a drive for mastery as with any regressive capitulation to "primitive instincts" for disorderly fun.[143] It is tempting to argue that disaster shows, like disasters themselves, appealed in part because of the opportunities they presented to work through the anxieties produced by living in a dynamic and dizzying modern world, and perhaps even that the process of learning to court and master the unexpected played a role in producing the risk-taking personalities required by an expansive industrial capitalist economy.[144]

What does seem clear is that disaster attractions could not be experienced as thrills unless their dangers were believed to be more apparent than real, or when the "dread crisis," as Hartt put it, had passed.[145] This in turn meant that they had to be carefully staged. If a ride was "not thrilling or intimate enough," it failed, but it also failed if it was too frightening.[146] Accordingly, shows and rides had to be planned down to the smallest details, and although Coney Island became known as the home of "ten cent chaos," it was, more properly, the home of controlled chaos.[147] The three "syndicated" amusement parks were actually showcases for modern technology and the industrial method, modeled after the great manufacturing concerns of the day.[148] To enjoy the thrills of chaos, people had to trust big business and embrace technological progress. The cult of chaos led back once again to the search for order and the creation of American capitalism.[149] Of course, not everyone was happy with this. When Maxim Gorky went to Coney Island in 1907 he was mesmerized by the effect produced at night by a million electric lightbulbs, describing Coney as a "city of fire." But it was an artificial fire, in his view, that could produce no "transport" or "joy," and he found himself longing for a more genuine contact with nature: "The soul is seized with a desire for a living, beautiful fire, a sublime fire, which should free the people from the slavery of a varied boredom."[150] It was no longer clear, however, whether a real fire could produce "authentic" emotions that were recognizably different from those generated by Coney's entertainments. The proof came in 1907 when Steeplechase Park burned to the ground. Spectators, perhaps inevitably, treated the blaze as an attraction, and the entrepreneurial owner, George C. Tilyou, capitalized on this interest the next day, charging customers ten cents to tour the ruins.[151]

In the 1890s and 1900s, amusement parks, like sensational newspapers and the movies, had helped to inculcate and to legitimate a popular appetite for spectacles of chaos. And commentators were already beginning to worry about the effects of this new cultural phenomenon. Edwin Slosson, for one, foresaw a bleak future: "Our feeling for the dangers and sufferings of others is easily jaded, so the feats must each year be more and more dangerous to excite the interest of the spectators." He was not quite sure where "the cultivation of this appetite" would end, but he anticipated a decline of "squeamishness" and compassion.[152] This has become a familiar lament, but perhaps he was missing something important here. Hartt was almost alone in resisting the temptation to condemn those "white savages" who slaked their thirst for disasters at Coney Island. He suspected that these individuals were *more* likely to help the victims of real disasters than were those "more delicate individuals who pass by, with averted faces, too tender-hearted to witness pain." He considered the case of a street accident: "When somebody gets under the fender of a trolley car, the same blind instinct brings the same seekers after shudders; yet, once there, they lift the car bodily, rescue the sufferer, and exhibit civilized mercy almost simultaneously with prehistoric savagery!" The lesson was perhaps unsavory, but unavoidable: "However vile the horror-thirst, its ulterior purpose (if you sanction that degree of teleology) is beneficent."[153] This is an insight that we should keep in mind as we return to the San Francisco disaster and its influence on Americans outside of the stricken city.

There are striking similarities, it seems, between responses to the real earthquake and fire and those to the replica disasters at Coney Island. In both cases, spectators were drawn to the spectacle of destruction, and in both cases, it seems, their enjoyment depended on a sense of insulation from personal danger. Most disaster enthusiasts were searching for what Russel B. Nye has called "riskless risk"; they wanted the thrills of danger without the harms.[154] But in an actual calamity, of course, there was always the possibility that people might be killed, injured, or impoverished. So calamities had to be made safe. One might imagine that the men and women who were so excited by news of the destruction of San

Francisco would have been disinclined to support measures to manage and contain nature's chaos, but they tended to be among the staunchest supporters of relief programs. The search for riskless risks went hand in hand with a growing social commitment to risk management.

But how exactly did the modern cult of chaos stimulate endeavors to tame disasters and to restitute victims? To answer this question we must examine the thoughts, feelings, and actions of ordinary Americans who experienced the calamity through cultural mediations and representations.[155] News of the San Francisco earthquake and fire spread quickly across the United States—as it did, indeed, throughout the "civilized world"—through telephone wires and telegraphs, and within a day Americans from New York to New Orleans were devouring sensational newspaper accounts and even film footage of the destruction.[156] Entrepreneurs wasted no time in turning the calamity into money, tapping into a huge market for stories, pictures, and performances of the earthquake. Thirteen years after the event, one Berkeley student could still vividly recall her excitement as a young girl in Salt Lake City, watching paper boys run through the streets "calling out Extra! Extra!" For days, her mother had been thoroughly absorbed in reading about the "terrible disaster"—"Nobody talked about anything else for weeks."[157] Much of the "information" about the disaster took a sensationalistic form, exaggerating the horrors of an already dreadful event, and readers with friends and relatives inside the burning city were often frantic with worry until reassured of the latter's safety. William James learned only belatedly about the "extremity of anxiety" felt by his novelist brother Henry, how the latter was "unable to settle down to any other occupation, the thought of our mangled forms, hollow eyes, starving bodies, minds insane with fear, haunting you so." William found evidence here for his belief that the greatest emotional agonies produced by calamities were felt by those at a distance rather than those in the midst of things.[158] What he underestimated were the strange delights of the earthquake and fire for distant spectators.

Salesmen everywhere tried to capitalize on public interest in the great earthquake, like the man who called one day at the home of a Kansas girl to sell her family a book with "a wonderful description of the San Francisco disaster."[159] And even respectable lecturers tried to entice audiences to come to their talks by showing moving pictures of the cataclysm.[160] Throughout the summer, numberless Americans flocked to movie houses or theaters to watch shows featuring the calamity. Lucile Garrett, for example, accompanied her parents to a theater in Minneapolis to see a reproduction of "the Quake" a few months after the event. Her description is worth recounting at length because it captures so vividly the pleasures of such a show:

> On the stage was a miniature reproduction of San Francisco, on the night of the fire. Myriads of little lights shone from as many little windows, and my mind was deeply impressed by the "doll houses," then suddenly we were favored with a great rumbling! The hills on which the city was built shook and crackled! The highest buildings shook and tottered! This lasted for several agonizing seconds. Finally the hills cracked open, the tottering buildings fell, and the whole city burst into flames. It continued to burn for some minutes and at last they lowered the curtain on the glorious blaze.

"I'm sure," she later recounted, that "I held my breath through the whole act, and I know that the delicious horror stayed with me for months, even years."[161] Some, like Donald Abbe Pearce, a California boy who found news of the conflagration "terrible but very thrilling," were so excited by the first reports of the disaster that they yearned to visit the burning city.[162] Others, as the *San Francisco Examiner* reported, acted on the impulse: thousands of "sightseers" poured into the burned-out city for the "holiday of their lives."[163] Although some resourceful San Franciscans took advantage of this intense curiosity, selling relics to eager souvenir hunters, the invasion was disturbing to others, who found something sordid in tourists taking pictures of their suffering. What they did not realize was that those who found the spectacle of chaos most entertaining were often the very same people who most energetically devoted themselves to the task of helping the disaster victims.

A legion of historians and social scientists have denounced the sensationalization of disasters, claiming that it cheapens the experience of adversity, turns suffering into entertainment, and encourages passivity in the face of horror. Daniel Bell's observations about television coverage of disasters in our own time conveys some of the flavor of these criticisms: "The visual media . . . invites not purgation or understanding but sentimentality and pity, emotions that are quickly exhausted, and a pseudo-ritual of a pseudo-participation in the events. And as the mode is inevitably one of over-dramatization, the responses soon become either stilted or bored."[164] There is surely a good deal of truth in this assessment, but what is striking about representations of the San Francisco earthquake and fire are the resolute acts of charity they inspired.

Spectacular interest in the San Francisco disaster energized philanthropic acts. American men, women, and children may have stood transfixed before representations of the earthquake and fire, but they were also filled with desires to understand the disaster, to grasp its natural causes, and to alleviate its harms. Nearly every community in the United States sent food or money or clothes to the people of San Francisco to help them through their misfortune. The experience of Helen Sanders, a Montana woman, was typical. She responded to news of the disaster first with sentiment and then with deeds: "All over-wrought with excitement and grief, I fled to my little sanctum, and there in sweet silence, I sat down and began to write some lines. Then it struck my sense of the ridiculous — this making of rhymes when a city was threatened with destruction and a multitude of people — aye, and not strangers, but 'mine own people' — were homeless in the ruined streets." So she resolved to "help them materially," throwing herself fervently into fund-raising activities.[165] Sensational accounts, pictures, and performances brought the sufferings of earthquake victims to the attention of people throughout the country and established vicarious, but powerful, bonds between spectators and sufferers; these images made "strangers," as Sanders put it, "mine own people."

As Benedict Anderson has argued in his work on nationalism, the media has been pivotal in the formation of imagined communities, prompting citizens to develop strong emotional commitments to the fellow citizens (even strangers) that they read about in their newspapers.[166] Disaster reporting clearly had an important nation-building role to play in this respect. But I do not believe that men, women, and children in 1906 donated time and money (entirely) as a reasoned or virtuous response to publicity about the misery of their fellow Americans. On the contrary, involvement in charitable activities seems to have been closely linked to the pleasure people took in the spectacle of suffering. It is certainly striking how closely involved theaters were in efforts to raise money for the people of San Francisco. Typical was the experience of Lars Bennett, a Massachusetts boy, who discovered that part of his admission fee for a show about the earthquake went directly to the relief fund. Kids who went to the playhouse, he wrote, "'killed two birds in one shot.' They helped the San Francisco victims and received amusement all for the same dime." This particular boy was candid enough to admit that he had a "merry time" not because he "was helping someone, but for the simple reason that it was the first time I had ever been inside of a theater."[167] Charitable contributions depended here on the commodification of the disaster.

A public eager to see words, pictures, and performances of the San Francisco earthquake, it seems, could not easily ignore or turn its back on the sufferers. Charity professionals, recognizing this, were not above exploiting the dramatic appeal of disasters to maximize donations. Simon Patten, in a series of lectures at the New York School of Philanthropy in 1905, had chastised social workers for failing to make use of "vivid methods" to raise funds for charitable endeavors.[168] His student Edward T. Devine, famed welfare scholar and head of Red Cross operations in San Francisco, had reservations, however, fearing that the spectacularization of suffering would draw attention away from the routine calamities of everyday life. "When there comes an urgent call for aid from a distance," he warned, "the continuing, and possibly equally imperative, needs at hand resulting from more ordinary causes should not be forgotten."[169] But forgotten they often were. The 1900s was an inauspicious decade for public assistance. Federal and state courts were striking down laws that mandated better conditions for workers; labor unions, losing faith in the goodwill of the government, were resisting campaigns to involve the state in the provision of unemployment benefits; and reformers were reluctant to establish pension programs that might present opportunities for graft by supposedly corrupt political machines.[170] But very few Americans objected to the lavish distribution of aid to the survivors of the San Francisco disaster.

Why should disaster victims command a singular sympathy, and why do they continue to do so?[171] It certainly helped that calamities were the sort of afflictions that struck the worthy and unworthy alike. Most donors clearly found it easier to identify with disaster victims than with, say, the "dangerous poor." Moreover, disaster relief promised to be a one-time deal: sufferers could be given a temporary hand up, and then left to sink or swim. There seemed to be little danger that recipients of aid would become permanent dependents on charity. On the contrary, disaster relief seemed to be consistent with the principles of social insurance that were coming to govern welfare thought at the beginning of the twentieth century: the spreading of risk in order to make the American capitalist system more productive and efficient.[172] But it was publicity, above all, that ensured that special attention would be paid to the suffering of disaster victims.[173] Who could avoid thinking about such sufferers when stories of their pain and anguish dominated magazine and newspaper coverage for weeks after a calamity? The half-horrified enthusiasm of middle-class Americans for spectacles of destruction, it seems, underpinned the growing public commitment to more effective and efficient disaster relief.

To trace the origins and influence of this enthusiasm, it should be said, is hardly to explain the shape of Progressive relief, let alone to account for the rise of the welfare security state. Those occurrences had as much to do with religion, class politics, and the demands of capitalism as with sentiment, as much to do with social control as with the exercise of compassion. Most donors in 1906 were happy to turn the administration of relief contributions over to the newly nationalized American Red Cross, an indication that Americans were beginning to believe that disaster operations ought to be administered by qualified experts, perhaps even by the federal government.[174] And while welfare experts, businessmen, and professionals may have appreciated the role of aroused emotions in inducing Americans to donate money, they were determined to ensure that the distribution of this largesse was a strictly "rational" endeavor, one that promoted discipline and corporate order by *containing* unruly passions. Not only were the majority of refugees denied any say about how donations should be spent or how supplies should be allotted, they were compelled to meet strict standards of "decency, order, and cleanliness" if they were to stay in the "concentration" camps.[175] A cult of chaos might be tolerated and even indulged in the case of the respectable and wealthy, but regimentation and surveillance was the fate of the poor.

The San Francisco earthquake and fire helped to promote the expansion and professionalization of emergency management that culminated with the establishment of the national security state after World War II. But it also had a wider cultural impact and significance. This disaster dramatically underscored the hazards of a natural and social world out of control. Witnessing the calamity, many Americans, especially Progressive reformers, were renewed in their conviction that constant vigilance was necessary to surmount the hazards of the modern world. Civilization, it seemed, was in crisis, and only the rational management of nature, economy, society, and individual behavior could recall citizens to the path of progress. By reminding Americans of the need for civilized restraints, disasters served an industrial society that offered security in exchange for self-discipline, conformity, and application at the workplace. But the disaster also underscored the tedium of a world in control, providing a release from routine, making the world exciting, offering an enchanting diversion from the demands of an overly ordered world.

It is a commonplace to assume that disaster has been the mortal enemy of civilization (viz. William James's "immemorial warfare against nature"), but in fact spectacles of chaos like the San Francisco earthquake may well have enabled the survival of corporate society by providing an outlet for modern discontents. Once again, the link to Coney Island is suggestive. The historian John Kasson has emphasized the "safety valve" function of the great amusement park, arguing that it served as "a mechanism of social release and control that ultimately protected existing society."[176] To some extent, the real San Francisco earthquake supplied a similar safety valve for simmering modern discontents, relieving social and psychic as well as seismic tensions. But perhaps we should interrogate the "safety valve" metaphor more closely and challenge the presumed rivalry of civilization and its discontents.

Desires may well be chaotic and subversive by definition, but they have often benefited modern corporations and businesses that have learned over time to exploit images of destruction to sell practically every product under the sun.[177] While the American infatuation with disaster in the 1900s threatened to destabilize an emerging corporate order founded on economic discipline and social control, these impulses were rather easily, if incompletely, commodified and transformed into a quest for cheap thrills.[178] Cultural historian Alan Trachtenberg writes that the origins of American consumerism can be dated by tracking the changing meanings of the word *consumption* at the end of the nineteenth century. "From its earlier sense of destruction (as by fire or disease), of squandering, wasting, using up," he notes, "by the 1890's consumption had won acceptance as a term designating such goods as food and clothing, 'all those things which directly satisfy human needs and desires.'"[179] Disasters by this point, appropriately, were no longer simply events that consumed, but also events to *be* consumed—in newspapers, movies, and Coney Island shows.

In Henry James's novel *The Ambassadors*, the starched Victorian Mr. Waymarsh intermittently surrenders to his civilized discontents, to his "sacred rage," and responds by making "extraordinary" purchases that enable him to feel free. Many turn-of-the-century Americans assuaged a profane rage for destruction by consuming disasters so as to achieve a sense of liberation, a sense of having felt something real, of having lived.[180]

The imagination of disaster, it seems to me, has operated as a modern unconscious, as a repository of the chaotic desires that have invigorated an industrial system that depends on a dynamic balance of productive discipline (figured as order) and consumer abandon (figured as excess or chaos or catastrophe). While they were learning to love disasters, Americans were learning how to be modern—turning themselves into the hard-working, thrill-seeking citizens who would sustain, even as they chafed against, an emerging corporate consumer society and national security state.

4

The Modern Way of Disaster

THE NUCLEAR AGE AND THE ORIGINS OF FEDERAL
EMERGENCY MANAGEMENT

Ours is indeed an age of extremity. For we live under continual threat of two equally fearful, but seemingly opposed, destinies: unremitting banality and inconceivable terror.

SUSAN SONTAG, "The Imagination of Disaster," 1965

I feel that urgent action must be taken by Congress to assure that in the future Americans will not need to live in fear that all their possessions, savings and hopes may vanish in a single catastrophic blast.

SENATOR HERBERT LEHMAN, August 27, 1955

The truth is that once the Government goes into business to meet some emergency, real or fancied, it almost never gets out.

Saturday Evening Post, August 20, 1955

The Northeast was still reeling from a record-breaking heat wave when a series of hurricanes swept through the region late in the summer of 1955. Hurricane Connie saturated the drought-parched soils of the Northeast on August 13, and a few days later the remnants of Hurricane Diane brought record-breaking rainfall and severe flooding.[1] Highways, bridges, dams, factories, and houses were damaged and washed away in Pennsylvania, New Jersey, New York, Connecticut, Rhode Island, and Massachusetts. All told, twenty thousand homes were wrecked or damaged and nearly two hundred people died in what the press excitedly dubbed the nation's first "billion dollar disaster."[2]

The floods seemed made for television. Newscasts were soon awash in images of ferocious winds, churning waters, collapsing buildings, exploding factories, and daring evacuations. By the time President Dwight D. Eisenhower addressed the nation by radio on August 23 to report on his visit to the disaster area, he could take it for granted that Americans already knew all about the calamity. "Like the rest of you," he announced, "I read in the papers, saw on television, and heard on the radio about this great disaster."[3] Although he insisted that it was impossible to appreciate fully the scale of the destruction without seeing it for oneself, or at least talking to survivors, his comments acknowledged that the United States was now a mass communications society and that disaster was now a media staple. Spectacle was in the ascendant. Americans were coming to demand and expect photographs or live footage with their "news," whether in newspapers, in enormously popular magazines such as *Life*, or on television, a new medium that was well on its way to becoming the nation's primary source of entertainment as well as of information about current events.[4] And disasters were securely established at the center of the news-gathering enterprise.

As we have seen, a sensational interest in calamities was already commonplace in 1906 when San Francisco shook and burned to the ground. Since then, decades of attending movies had reinforced the tendency of Americans to establish a consumer relationship to images of chaos. Significantly, actual footage of the Bay Area calamity had failed to find a wide audience because it was unable to compete with a more dramatic fake depiction produced in New York by the Biograph Company.[5] The lesson was not lost on the producers of the "newsreel," an influential compendium of current affairs, lifestyle pieces, and sports coverage that became an integral part of the movie theater experience after 1911. Newsreels fed on and heightened a public appetite for spectacular destruction, featuring calamities prominently from the very beginning. This was not simply a matter of editors' catering to established or imagined consumer tastes and demands. What could be seen on newsreels, and later on television news programs, was restricted by the edicts of censors, the meddling of sponsors, and the paramount need to turn a profit.[6] Government prohibitions against the distribution of war footage, official censorship of sexual and violent images, and the decision of producers to avoid "controversial" topics that might alienate audiences ensured that disasters would assume a privileged position among news topics as exciting events that could be

FIG 10. The set of the fake documentary movie of the San Francisco earthquake produced by Biograph in 1906. Reproduced by permission from Raymond Fielding, *The American Newsreel* (Norman: University of Oklahoma Press, 1972), 24.

displayed on the screen.[7] Politics, economics, and culture, in other words, were thoroughly interwoven in the mass representation of disasters.

Because newsreels were designed to attract the attention of movie-goers and to entertain them, editors unsurprisingly took their aesthetic cues from Hollywood. As a result, news coverage of the 1955 floods often had the look and feel of a movie. A Warner Brothers "News Magazine Special Report," distributed to theaters soon after the calamity, is typical in this regard.[8] It is unabashedly sensationalistic, making ample use of dramatic images, breathy voice-overs, and stirring music to get the pulse racing. The narrator falls silent for long stretches as viewers are invited to sit back and watch scene after scene of churning waters and devastated urban landscapes.

The heyday of the newsreel was already over in 1955, but as a cultural force it had already established and refined the look that would prevail in television news and current events magazines.[9] All of these formats processed and transmitted information by linking dramatic headlines, captions, and sound bites to arresting pictures. In so doing they subordinated event and analysis to the visual (and, in the case of television, aural) and thereby introduced an unmistakably cinematic dimension into the imagination of disaster. This had an enormous impact on how viewers perceived and experienced floods and storms and fires.[10]

Although news coverage of disasters was supposed to be exciting, even entertaining, it was also presumed to be socially valuable. Susan Sontag has written incisively about the "heroism of vision," a distinctively twentieth-century veneration of photojournalists whose task it was to make the world a better place by documenting its miseries so as to prompt compassion, moral commitment, and social activism.[11] The media, in this view, had an indispensable role to play in the march of civilization. This, perhaps, is why the editors of the Warner Brothers newsreel were "proud" to present "the most complete motion picture record yet shown of the terrible flash floods which swept through the American Northeast."[12] This heroic model of disaster reporting was sustained by a widespread conviction in the 1950s that modernity was generating the sort of technological and institutional advances that promised nothing less than a mastery of nature. Even as hurricanes were slamming into the southern and eastern coastlines of the United States, prominent scientists and commentators were announcing that control of the weather was imminent. Some even anticipated an end to natural disasters. And if hurricanes, floods, tornados, fires, and droughts could not be avoided entirely, it did seem that an organized society—one founded on a collaboration of science, industry, government, and the military—would soon be able to manage extreme events so as to avert their most damaging effects.

But this was also, as the poet W. H. Auden and the theologian Paul Tillich famously dubbed it, the age of anxiety. Optimism coexisted with profound uncertainty about the fate of the modern world. The atom bomb, first tested and used in 1945, haunted the imagination of disaster. Introducing the iconic image of the mushroom cloud, *Life* magazine announced that August 6, the day the bomb was dropped on Hiroshima, was "the day men formally began a new epoch in their history."[13] It certainly introduced a new epoch in the politics of disaster. The editors, like many other commentators, invoked the myth of Prometheus to explain the parameters of this new world: "No limits are set to our Promethean ingenuity, provided we remember that we are not Jove. We are not ants either; we can abolish warfare, and mitigate man's inhumanity to man. But all of this will take some doing. And we are in a strange new land."[14]

FIG 11. Mushroom cloud produced by the atomic bombing of Hiroshima on August 6, 1945. Photograph courtesy of AP Images.

When the Soviet Union successfully tested a bomb in 1949 matters took an even more ominous turn, precipitating an arms race that threatened mass human extinction. Even Eisenhower confided to his diary the "conviction" that the world was "racing toward catastrophe."[15] Nuclear fission might present the most potent symbol of human progress in this era, but the mushroom cloud presented an equally vivid symbol of the disaster to end all disasters.

Catastrophe, then, was unsurprisingly a central preoccupation of the nuclear age. The Warner Brothers newsreel conveys both the hopes and fears of the era. It opens with footage of a wing and a propeller and shifts quickly to a close-up of the aircraft's passenger, the president of the United States, who is pictured poring over a map, consulting with a companion. A somber voice explains what is going on: "Winging low over the flood-ravaged Northeast, President Eisenhower leads a shocked nation in helping the six states stricken in one of the worst disasters in American history." After a brief aerial shot of the floodwaters, audiences see "Ike" peering through a window at the havoc below. His expression is concealed, but the narrator assures viewers that "the president is grim-faced as he flies over the complete and utter devastation." This is a classic modern tableau: the strong and compassionate leader, armed with maps and technology, determined to use all resources at his disposal to prevail against calamity. The newsreel symbolically pits industrial American society against the untamed forces of nature. And it turns out that the man accompanying Eisenhower is Lewis L. Strauss, chairman of the Atomic Energy Council. He was there to brief the president on the Atoms for Peace conference concurrently taking place in Geneva, Switzerland.[16] Like most Americans, these two leaders believed, or wished to believe, that the nuclear age was going to be one of unprecedented comfort and security.[17] One month before, Strauss had thrown the "switch releasing the first surge of atomic generated electric current over commercial power lines."[18] But this scene offered more than a glimpse into the workings of the modern state.

Significantly, this newsreel moment was choreographed for the cameras. This cues us in to a radical transformation in the politics of disaster, as indeed of all politics, in the age of mass media. Although the documentary has every appearance of being an objective record of events, this segment was a public relations exercise. Newspapers later reported that Eisenhower was unable to see much at all of the "devastation" because of heavy cloud cover. But this did not ultimately matter much because the point was to be seen rather than to see. Ike was the first president to cultivate a favorable image to enhance his approval ratings in the television age.[19] He employed a team of media consultants, skilled in matters of wardrobe, "cosmetics, studio direction, and proper lighting," to ensure that he projected strength and trustworthiness on screen; he hired celebrity actor Robert Montgomery to teach him how to carry himself with authority. He engaged an advertising agency to market test as well as publicize his policies.[20] The image of the strong and vigilant president presented in this newsreel was manufactured. A camera crew had been invited onto the *Columbine III*, the president's official aircraft, to film the leader's response to the calamity. Although Eisenhower's pictured concern and resolve was undoubtedly genuine, he was purposely posing for the public. This disaster, in other words, was a staging ground to perform the role of a modern man of action and of compassion. At the same time, this media glare imposed a condition:

that he make good on public demands for vigorous measures to help New England recover from the floods.

Boosting national morale was an important presidential duty, but Eisenhower was also taking advantage of the calamity to justify and promote the exercise of executive power. Disaster coverage was an occasion for presenting an activist federal government in a favorable light. Certainly it helped to render any alternatives unthinkable. Awareness, for example, that disaster policy was the product of political choices or the interplay of material interests was concealed under a rhetoric that cast rescue and relief as the heroic struggle of "man" against "nature." At the same time, an efficient response to disasters probably did more to convince Americans of the value of civil defense than contrived and absurd nuclear drills.[21] Television, it should be said, was a willing accomplice in all this. Despite formal independence, the commercial networks eagerly promoted controversial modern civil defense agendas in these years.[22] Disaster coverage contributed more generally to the formation of an imagined national community for the cold war era. It presented the United States as a strong, united, and caring nation at a time when it was under fire from new postcolonial governments at the United Nations for its domestic racial policies and imperialist ventures abroad. It offered a more positive image than the media spectacles of racial violence that would accompany the movement of civil rights to the center of national concern in the aftermath of the Supreme Court's order to desegregate schools in 1954. Spectacles of calamity, in sum, were thoroughly political.

One of my tasks in this chapter is to examine the modern politics of disaster within the context of a radical expansion of government bureaucracy and authority in the aftermath of the New Deal and World War II and amid the security concerns of the cold war. Just as the imagination of disaster in this period was haunted by the unprecedented prospect of global nuclear annihilation, so too was the management of disaster utterly transformed by the emergence of the national security state. The presence of civil defense institutions and agendas changed the rules of disaster. When commentators and politicians had talked about "security" in the Progressive era or during the New Deal in the 1930s, they were usually thinking about social security, about welfare; in the 1950s, the term acquired a more sinister resonance, conjuring up breaches of national "security" and the demands of Senator Joe McCarthy and his acolytes to curtail civil liberties so as to suppress "un-American" dissent. Both of these conceptions of security—welfare and national defense—

collided in complex ways to encourage Washington to assume greater control over the politics of catastrophe.

Hurricane Diane was the first major disaster administered under the provisions of the Disaster Relief Act of 1950. Although little was made of it at the time, this law played a significant role in launching the age of federal emergency management.[23] I will first trace the developments that led to the passing of this act, paying particular attention to the Mississippi flood of 1927 and the long history of federal flood control in creating a political and cultural framework for the advent of federal emergency management. I then consider the vital role of a massive new civil defense infrastructure in providing the impetus and institutional machinery for an activist politics of disaster. An examination of the Northeastern floods of 1955 reveals the effect of these new laws and agencies on the management of a disaster. This incident establishes just how important disasters remained as occasions for rethinking and revising the proper role of government and the organization of the economy. And, as we shall see, the dominant framing of calamity sustained a vision of modernization that emphasized the expansion of government authority as well as relentless capitalist development with limited consideration for social or environmental costs.

This is not to say that there were no counternarratives. On the contrary, this disaster also focused criticism of the status quo. For social dissenters and environmentalists, devastating floods suggested that modernity itself was a catastrophe to the extent that technology and industrial organization were destroying the cohesion of society and the ecological balances of the natural world. To be sure, in the 1950s these voices remained marginal, but they hearkened back to older jeremiad traditions and thus enjoyed considerable cultural resonance. Disasters would continue to be sites where the meaning of America was debated and contested, where modern American values and social arrangements were articulated and assembled. Because a good deal of this debate occurred in the mass media, in this chapter I offer an aesthetic and ideological analysis of an emerging postmodern culture of calamity.[24]

The implications of this cultural rewiring for the politics of disaster would not achieve their full force until later in the century, but it is important to emphasize here that it is no accident that disaster movies became a mass phenomenon at the very same time that a national security state became the preferred means of achieving protection against natural and man-made catastrophes. Both were responses to the opportunities and challenges of the nuclear age and, more broadly, to the conditions of modernity. The implications were profound. Over time, an overinvestment in spectacular calamities helped to ensure that disaster victims rather than, say, the homeless, the poor, and other victims of economic misfortune, would be deemed uniquely worthy of attention and support from government, the public, and philanthropic organizations. The modern regime of disaster management was established by media preoccupations as well as by an intricate combination of constitutional considerations, economic interests, and security commitments.

The Mississippi Flood of 1927 and the Politics of Flood Control

Eisenhower did not think twice before proclaiming the Northeast a disaster zone and declaring that Washington would take a prominent role in the relief and recovery of the region after the 1955 hurricanes.[25] But it is worth pausing over this announcement because it signals a decisive shift in the politics of disasters. After the Great Chicago Fire of 1871, leading citizens and local politicians had accepted help from the U.S. Army, but they flatly refused more substantial federal assistance, fearing precedents, in the words of the *Chicago Tribune*, that were "dangerous to the future well-being of the state."[26] Similarly, when earthquake and fire decimated San Francisco in 1906, a coalition of businesses leaders and city officials thwarted Progressive efforts to secure extensive congressional funding to cover the costs of reconstruction and opposed the intrusion of federal bureaucrats and planners into local affairs. Fifty years later, the president was explicitly empowered by law to authorize substantial aid. And almost all sectors of society—government officials, businessmen, media commentators, social scientists, and ordinary citizens—agreed that it was entirely appropriate for Washington to take a leadership role in local disasters.

Congressional politics helped to determine what form this contribution could and should take. A key innovation was the Disaster Relief Act of 1950. As a legislative response to a specific local flood, it provides evidence of the continuing contribution of catastrophes to the expansion of government authority. It also speaks to a new consensus that the nation-state should protect its people from unexpected misfortunes. At the same time, the terms of this law reveal that any attempt to establish a role for Washington in the management of disasters had to be consistent with constitutional restrictions and capitalist principles that set limits to the exercise of federal power.

Lawmakers and the courts had long agreed that flood protection, unlike other federal disaster programs, was permitted by the Constitution on the grounds that it facilitated interstate commerce. In 1950, Washington already had over seventy years of experience with flood management. Here, more than anywhere else, the precedents were set that led the government to take an active role in disasters. In 1879, Congress created the Mississippi River Commission to avert flooding along the vital channel of trade that connected the industrial centers and agricultural hinterlands of the Midwest to the Gulf Coast. The Army Corps of Engineers, established in 1802 to build national defenses and fortifications, worked with civilian technicians to subject the river to human mastery, building hundreds of miles of earthen walls, or levees, to contain this vast and periodically flooding river.²⁷ These men brought modern scientific principles to bear on the problem of disasters, exhibiting extraordinary faith in technology and planning. The renowned engineer James Buchanan Eads, for example, testified before Congress in 1874 that "disasters and serious accidents" were "always evidence of bad engineering." Man, in his view, was fully "capable of curbing, controlling and directing the Mississippi, according to his pleasure."²⁸ All that was needed was the right plan and adequate resources. Of course, there were plenty of skeptics. Mark Twain was particularly scornful of Eads's endeavors to "fetter and hand cuff" the river. "Ten thousand river commissions," he wrote in his 1883 book *Life on the Mississippi*, "with the mines of the world at their back, cannot tame that lawless stream, cannot curb it or confine it, cannot say to it, Go here, or Go there, and make it obey; cannot save a shore which it has sentenced; cannot bar its path with an obstruction which it will not tear down, dance over, and laugh at."²⁹ For all his derision, even Twain admitted that Eads had accomplished great feats with his jetties at the mouth of the Mississippi. Lawmakers in Washington, D.C., were even more impressed, authorizing $71 million in the forty-eight years after 1879 to build a system of fortifications along the river, a sum that added to $170 million raised by taxpayers in the South.³⁰

Over time, these measures accustomed Americans to expect a larger role for the federal government in other areas of disaster management. This was in spite of the fact that the celebrated levee policy actually helped to create one of the worst disasters ever seen along the river. The Mississippi, as Twain wrote, is "always changing its habitat *bodily*—is always moving bodily *sideways*." So dramatic is this westward drift that there was "*good solid dry land*" where the river had flowed just two hundred years before.³¹ It was hubris that convinced the engineers that they could fix this vast waterway in place simply by building walls around it. But build they did. And once the levees were in place they required constant and expensive maintenance. Confined within an artificially narrow channel, the waters of the Mississippi began to rise to unprecedented heights and to move with increased velocity. Blocked from access to its natural floodplains, the river constantly threatened to overspill its banks during heavy rainfall. The only way to protect towns and settlements along the river within such a system was to raise and reinforce the levees; when these failed the flooding was more severe than it would have been in the absence of man-made constraints.

This was the case when torrential rains struck in the early months of 1927; floods on the Ohio, Missouri, and upper Mississippi rivers created an immense wave of water that rolled southward on a devastating thousand-mile journey to the sea. Scores of levees were breached and riverfront communities were pounded in seven states, with especially extensive damage in Mississippi, Louisiana, and Arkansas. The Mississippi valley, in the words of popular Southern writer Lyle Saxon, was turned "into a series of lakes, several of which could have cupped a European nation apiece without showing a rim of foreign ground." Sixteen million acres of land were submerged, 221,994 homes and other buildings were damaged or destroyed, and at least one thousand people died.[32] The calamity, according to a testy letter in the *Outlook*, was not an "act of God but the work of man." "Had our sole object been to flood out our neighbors on

FIG 12. "A typical highway scene, Mississippi River Flood of 1927." Album, Mss 4373069d. Photograph courtesy of Louisiana State Library.

FIG 13. "Refugee Camp on the Levee." Louis Link Papers, Mss 343103. Photograph courtesy of Louisiana State University.

the lower Mississippi," this Midwesterner charged, "we could have done nothing that we have not done for years to bring about this catastrophe."[33] Modern disaster policy, in this case, was the mother of disaster. But this was not the lesson that most Americans took from the deluge.

The 1927 Mississippi flood was a turning point, clearing the emotional and political space for a modern system of disaster management. Intense media attention encouraged the public to invest emotionally in the flood and to demand that politicians do whatever they could to help the victims. The American Red Cross launched an aggressive publicity campaign, including the first national radio appeal transmitted on stations owned by the National Broadcasting Company and the Columbia Broadcasting System, and federal officials worked hard to keep the story of the relief effort on the front pages of the newspapers. The Red Cross took advantage of this attention and raised an impressive sum of $17,500,000 to pay for the care of over 325,000 refugees in camps across the region and to supply food to 300,000 more in private homes.[34]

The scale of the destruction encouraged federal officials to take a more active role than was customary. President Coolidge appointed Secretary of Commerce Herbert Hoover to coordinate rescue and relief operations, overseeing the efforts of private organizations and state governments as well as such federal agencies as the Army Corps of Engineers, the Coast Guard, the Weather Bureau, and the Red Cross—a private agency that was subject to federal oversight. Hoover assumes a pivotal role here as a distinctively American Faust. After achieving exceptional success as an engineer, he acquired a reputation as "the Great Humanitarian" for his extraordinary achievements in getting food and supplies to European civilians during World War I as head of the Commission for the Relief of Belgium and later as head of the American Relief Administration.[35] A Progressive with an extraordinary faith in science and organization, he seized on the 1927 Mississippi flood as a "blessing in disguise," as a valuable opportunity to bring progress to what he viewed as a backward region of the South. In the wake of the flood, the American Red Cross was already mounting a public health campaign (vaccinating against smallpox, immunizing against typhoid fever, providing hygiene education) and supplying seeds to farmers to diversify the region's agriculture in the hope of achieving "significant advances in the public health service and the promotion of social and economic welfare."[36] Invoking "cooperative group effort," "planning," and "human engineering," Hoover went even further, dreaming of a "reconstruction" program that would permanently modernize the Mississippi Delta.[37]

Taking advantage of his extraordinary position as the director of a "highly centralized and coordinated" organization with emergency powers, he set about arranging for vast sums of credit from federal institutions and regional and national banks to pay for agricultural reforms and crop diversification.[38] He was successful at pressuring lending agencies into making money available for these purposes, but very few recipients (most of whom had endured substantial financial and property losses) were able to raise the necessary collateral to secure loans.[39] And in the end, Hoover, averse to any measures that suggested socialism, was unwilling to countenance a more assertive role for the government such as underwriting loans or grants. As he was to discover, a free market system could not solve the problem of capital accumulation in the aftermath of a great catastrophe. For now, there was no question of the federal government directly spending taxpayers' dollars on relief or reconstruction operations. As Hoover recalled, defensively, in his *Memoirs*, "Those were the days when citizens expected to take care of one another in time of disaster and it had not occurred to them that the Federal Government should do it."[40] But this was only a small part of the problem.

Although the nation's newspapers properly marveled at the achievements of the relief effort, attempts to distribute aid equally and fairly ran up against entrenched class interests and racial prejudices. Despite a formal commitment to equality, Hoover and the Red Cross were often unable to see, let alone avert, state and local policies and practices that favored whites at the expense of a black population that accounted for over half of the flood's victims.⁴¹ Inequities and abuses were legion. Black men were forced by white men with guns to work on levees even as they were about to break, causing many deaths. In Greenville, Mississippi, planters prevented African Americans from boarding empty steamboats and evacuating along with whites to safer locations. Planters, it turns out, were willing to risk the lives of these men, women, and children in order to keep close at hand the manpower on which they depended to rebuild the town and to harvest what was left of the cotton crop. Relief camps were segregated and unequal. Whites routinely took the best of the donated food and supplies brought in by the Red Cross; blacks could pick through what, if anything, was left. The Red Cross camp established at Greenville, Mississippi, became, in the terse assessment of historian John M. Barry, "a slave camp." African Americans were routinely beaten and the hungry were sometimes denied food. Canned peaches, sent by donors from outside the region, were explicitly withheld from blacks on the grounds that it would "spoil" them. Local planters, businessmen, and politicians were primarily responsible for these measures, but it was Red Cross officials who gave them control over the distribution of provisions and who did little to stop these community leaders, for example, from commandeering donated supplies and selling them to blacks.⁴²

The scandal of race did not figure significantly in newspaper reports of the calamity (except in black journals), but it did reveal the limits of government to conduct an impartial disaster relief operation in a society beset by legal and social racism and inclined to place commercial interests above the claims of justice. A failure of disaster policy, and of politics more generally, accounted for the most dramatic contribution of the flood to social and economic change. It was destitution rather than opportunity that led tens of thousands of African Americans to join the Great Migration to the urban centers of, among others, Chicago, Detroit, and Los Angeles.

What did capture the national imagination was the idea that the government should do more to protect Americans against natural hazards. Although conservative newspapers and business journals tended to oppose any expansion of government responsibility for disaster victims (invoking the familiar argument that this would cause "moral injury" and "a rapid sapping . . . of initiative"), most newspapers came out in favor of a special session of Congress to appropriate funds to help with recovery and reconstruction. President Coolidge held firm and refused to convene the Congress, but a significant number of Americans were beginning to demand federal support in these extreme circumstances, whatever the Constitution, or free market economists, might have to say on the topic.

The weight of these demands and expectations came to bear on the one area where the federal government clearly did have a mandate to act: flood control. Noting that the war to end all wars had not stopped nations from arming for the next war, Lyle Saxon, in his popular book *Father Mississippi*, claimed to speak for his entire region when he argued that all concerned had to make sure that this disaster would really turn out to be the "flood to end floods." The problem was not engineering per se but a flawed program. The levee-only policy had failed. The only solution was a new system that included controlled spillways. This, admittedly, was going to be enormously expensive to build and would depend on federal funding. Saxon argued that it was a moral and economic necessity to save this rich agricultural region (one enriched, ironically, by centuries of flooding); he went so far as to insist that the South "had a right" to ask this much from the U.S. government.[43] This was an entitlement. And key congressional figures agreed. For Frank R. Reid of Illinois, the chairman of the House Committee on Flood Control, disaster relief was a categorical imperative. Who, he asked, "can stand idly by and see that land devastated and depopulated, business interests destroyed, commercial intercourse cut off, and people starved and degraded."[44] Few could.

When Congress passed the Lower Mississippi Flood Control Act the federal government assumed full legal responsibility for building dams, levees, and reservoirs on the river as part of a new and even more comprehensive program of flood protection. The act, signed into law by President Coolidge on May 15, 1928, appropriated $325 million for the plan and set a precedent for the later expansion of federal programs during the New Deal era—the establishment of the Tennessee Valley Authority; efforts to restore farmlands decimated by the Dust Bowl; and a raft of welfare legislation including the provision of Social Security—as well as additional flood control laws in 1936 and 1938 that extended the government's reach into flood management across the whole country.[45] Billions of federal dollars would now be available for flood control. And the measures taken were often very successful at providing a margin of security for those who lived in flood zones. But this was hardly a comprehensive solution to disasters. For one thing, it was very expensive to build floodwalls and, as we have already seen, this approach committed Americans to costly long-term maintenance and renovations. It also tended to encourage development in floodplains, the paving over of wetlands and the stripping of forest cover that had hitherto offered natural protection against floods. This augured ill for the future. Floods would keep on coming, as would earthquakes, tornadoes, fires, and other natural hazards that the federal government had no formal role in averting.

The Disaster Relief Act of 1950 and the Origins of Federal Emergency Management

Before 1950, disaster relief and recovery tasks were handled locally and paid for out of individual savings, business loans, church funds, union contributions, mutual aid society payments, insurance monies, and town or state treasuries. Congress was empowered to pass special relief acts, and did so on 128 occasions between 1803 and 1950, offering a variety of benefits from tax exemptions to relief payments in response to a list of calamities that included floods, fires, earthquakes, explosions, and "Indian deprivations."[46] But this was an ad hoc arrangement that sat uneasily with the planning and preparedness preoccupations of the post–World War II era.

When floods submerged North Dakota and Minnesota in April and May of 1950, Representative Harold C. Hagen of Minnesota did not simply ask Congress for local aid. He proposed a "broad general program for the whole country where emergencies of any kind, whether bombing or flood, hurricane, or cyclone, may hit or strike a community, perhaps where you gentlemen represent."[47] The inclusion of bombings in this list speaks to the decisive role of civil defense imperatives in promoting a more activist politics of calamity in the age of the cold war, a matter to which I will return. But the request for a "broad general program" also reveals the influence of the notion, forged during the Progressive era, the New Deal, and World War II, that Washington should play a more active role in promoting the welfare of the American people.

The modern politics of disaster owe as much to institutional habits and constitutional limits as to any philosophy of activism. Hagen was a shrewd politician who understood how to frame a policy initiative to win approval in Congress. He built support for a disaster bill with an appeal that blended emotional, moral, and financial considerations. He emphasized the misery caused by the floods, claiming that the damage was in the hundreds of millions (in fact it was closer to $33 million) and stating, or overstating, that this was "a national disaster of major proportions, one of the most serious disasters that has confronted the nation in all its history."[48] He explained that local governments, businesses, and individuals lacked the resources to cover the costs of the calamity. His constituents had endured floods in 1943, 1945, 1947, 1948, and 1949, and, according to Hagen, there were no funds left to repair roads and bridges and buildings. Treasuries were empty, and it was not possible to raise funds by taxing residents because they were already struggling to cope with private losses. The federal government alone had the resources to pay for repairs. More important, it had a moral obligation to step in. Other local officials agreed. "To ask these people who are suffering every year financial damage to try to increase their burden by additional taxes locally is unfair and unjust," Lyman Brink, the county attorney from Kittson County, Minnesota, maintained.[49] Rather than request a special relief program that might be rejected in Congress for giving preferential treatment to one area of the country, Hagen's proposal promised benefits to districts all across the country. Members of Congress could anticipate similar assistance if their own constituencies were ever to be hit by a calamity. At the same time, Hagen was careful to emphasize the conservative nature of the bill, assuring the Committee on Public Works, for example, that there was "ample precedent for this sort of legislation."[50]

The Disaster Relief Act that was approved by Congress on September 30, 1950, was a modest proposal, but it was an important step on the path to the institutionalization of federal emergency management, a process that would quickly lead to the formation of bureaus and organizations with a professional interest in ensuring that disaster management remained a primary federal function. The act authorized the president to declare as a major disaster "any flood, drought, fire, hurricane, earthquake, storm, or other catastrophe in any part of the United States" that was, or was likely to be, damaging enough "to warrant disaster assistance by the Federal Government to supplement the efforts and available resources of States and local governments."[51] The point of the act, according to the Committee on Public Works, was to provide "a framework for the Federal Government under which prompt action can be taken in meeting the needs of stricken areas." Rather than improvise a response to calamities after they occurred, the intention was to "establish a general Government policy in respect to emergency relief in all future disasters."[52]

At the same time, the act was deliberately limited in its scope. It confirmed that local and state governments had primary responsibility for responding to disasters; any "assistance" from Washington was "supplementary," and could not be disbursed without a formal request from the governor. Moreover, states and local governments were expected to give "assurance of expenditure of a reasonable amount" of their own funds before they could receive federal aid.[53] And there was no question of using taxpayers' money to cover the losses of private businesses or of individuals. Federal involvement was restricted to "work essential for the preservation of life and property, clearing debris and wreckage, making emergency repairs to and temporary replacements of public facilities of local governments damaged or destroyed."[54] This was the sort of contribution that could be justified as an attempt to maintain the infrastructure that was required for the functioning of business and civic life.

It is important to emphasize that the federal government was supposed to restore property but not make good the losses of individuals. This tended to implicate the government in the maintenance of existing property relations. And while the sums involved were initially expected to be small—the president was only authorized to spend $5 million "to carry out the purposes of this Act"—the stage was set for a massive expansion of federal financial aid.[55] By shifting power from the legislative branch to the executive, by leaving it up to the president to "coordinate in such manner as he may determine the activities of federal agencies in providing disaster assistance," the act helped to ensure that money and resources would be available to repair or restore public facilities without waiting for Congress to pass an appropriations bill.[56] The easier it was to distribute taxpayers' money to disaster victims the more generous federal contributions became.

In all, the Disaster Relief Act was a key step on the path to a new arrangement whereby the burden of paying for local disasters would be shifted from local governments and survivors to U.S. taxpayers as a whole. "In the process," as geographer Rutherford H. Platt explains, "an implicit new social compact was gradually forged between government and the citizenry in which the former assumed a large share of disaster losses arising from the bad luck or bad judgment of the latter."[57] But this transformation was not simply guided by domestic policy objectives. When Hagen proposed legislation for dealing with disasters he deliberately included bombing among the hazards of the modern age. Although the definition of disaster included in the final act did not specifically mention such military assaults, it was, as the General Services Administration observed, broad enough "to include disasters engendered by war, enemy attack, or subversive action."[58]

This linkage of calamity and civil defense was one of the most important elements driving the federalization of emergency management. The development of modern disaster policy is utterly bound up with the foundation of the national security state. The threat of nuclear attack by the Soviet Union raised the stakes and changed the rules of catastrophe; henceforth disaster relief would be absorbed into a civil defense apparatus that made a vast and lavishly funded new infrastructure available for dealing with calamities, even as it created the emotional and cultural conditions that inclined Americans to federal emergency management. This was a new age. As one civil defense policy report explained, "For Americans the development of long-range bombing and the invention of super-explosives and bacteriological weapons have brought about a new concept of total war. For the first time in history, a potential enemy is capable of striking at the American homeland."[59] In response to this threat the United States increased its production of nuclear weapons, built an elaborate strategic defense infrastructure, and assembled a national security state.[60] This required a much greater integration of federal, state, and local governments than Americans were accustomed to, and this in turn dramatically enhanced the ability of federal agencies to respond to local calamities.

The foundation of what sociologist Robert Bellah described as a "national defense state within a state" changed the legal and institutional context for managing disasters.[61] It authorized a massive concentration of funds and the formation of an elaborate network of agencies and offices. It justified greater federal oversight of state and local governments in order to ensure a "uniformity of equipment and practices" for the operation of civil defense programs across the country.[62] States quickly established civil defense acts and organizations. In accordance with the new 1950 civil defense law, Connecticut, the state that was to be the worst hit by hurricanes in 1955, was among many states to set up an advisory commission and mobile support units; within a year, voluntary police, firefighting, and radio units were available to respond to a range of crises from air raids to floods and fires.[63] In 1953, the "lead agencies" for managing disaster relief were formally located in the Federal Civil Defense Administration.[64] Disaster relief and national security would be tied together legally, administratively, and symbolically.

New civil defense laws and institutions enhanced federal authority to respond to disasters, but they also encroached on civil liberties.[65] Although this was intended to improve the efficiency of disaster response, it was now possible to suspend civil rights even during *simulated* disasters. On June 15, 1955, many cities around the country participated in Operation Alert, which required citizens to take shelter in subways from an imagined thermonuclear attack. This was part of a series of efforts designed to persuade Americans that it was possible to survive and win a nuclear war, a central premise of the whole civil defense project. In New York City, twenty-nine people protested in front of city hall. They insisted that nobody could survive such a catastrophe and that civil defense exercises, to the extent that they suggested otherwise, were extremely dangerous. All were arrested and jailed under the terms of the New York

State Defense Emergency Act of 1951, and although their offense was technically a misdemeanor, Judge Louis Kaplan called them "murderers" and set bail at fifteen hundred dollars each, before jailing the protestors to await trial. Although most newspapers overlooked this story, the editors of the liberal Catholic journal *Commonweal* were outraged. "If," they asked, "as in this case, our most basic freedoms may be abrogated by executive proclamation of a simulated emergency, what meaning has the Constitution in America today?" Was the United States moving toward "an authoritarian society"? To what extent, they wondered finally, might "the Bill of Rights be suspended and the police power be invoked against free speech and free assembly during a *mock* emergency?"[66] These were important questions to ask of civil defense and of disaster laws, but they were raised all too rarely in the 1950s.

What is important to emphasize is that these tendencies toward political authoritarianism were tempered by a powerful commitment to an American brand of industrial capitalism. The Disaster Relief Act, in particular, was designed to ensure a response to emergencies that interfered as little as possible with private property and the workings of the free market. Much of this was couched in the rhetoric of states' rights. Thus, while the Department of Agriculture might extol the bill as "a business-like approach" to the challenge of disasters—high praise in this age of business—the Committee on Public Works was eager to prevent the enactment of Section 6 of the proposed bill because it proposed a "grant program for the permanent construction of public utilities."[67] This would have empowered the government to intervene in local affairs without the justification of clear and present danger.[68] Elmer B. Staats, the assistant director of the Bureau of the Budget, explained the implications by dividing disaster response into "three phases." The first involved bringing the crisis under control and rescuing survivors; the second encompassed the immediate aftermath when debris had to be cleared, laws upheld, health preserved, and temporary repairs made. These stages had long been recognized as matters of proper federal involvement, "based," he contended, "upon the feeling that when American lives are threatened by disaster, it is the duty of all authorities to take direct action to alleviate the ensuing hardship." Matters became more complicated during phase three "when, in the absence of a direct threat to lives and property, the community plans and undertakes the permanent restoration of all essential public facilities." Although it was a federal responsibility to restore federal buildings, Staats argued that the reconstruction of local government buildings ought to remain the responsibility of local authorities. The only exception was when the repair of roads or bridges was necessary to avert a "major threat" to "the national interest."[69] The secretary of commerce and the Bureau of the Budget agreed that Section 6 raised "the question of the proper role of the Federal Government as against that of the State and local governments in the permanent reconstruction of local public facilities." But they were also concerned that this might turn out to be the thin end of the wedge toward an expansion of federal financial obligations in areas best left to local or private sources.[70] The specter of socialism haunted these debates. In the end, this provision was deleted from the bill, and the federal government retained only the power to assist state and local governments in making temporary repairs to public facilities. For the time being state and local governments had to pay for the reconstruction of nonfederal public buildings.

Although bureaucrats and politicians were surely correct to sense that disaster legislation would provide an enhanced role for Washington in the domestic affairs of the nation, in retrospect federal disaster policy is probably best understood as an attempt to manage the natural environment and the economy in ways that suited American business. A commitment to regulation, centralization, rationality, and control were hallmarks of the evolving "Fordist" restructuring of the economy under way in this period—one that produced infrastructural and legal conditions congenial to corporate capitalism and acceptable to powerful American unions.[71] The restoration of roads and bridges and public buildings was consistent with the consensus that the federal government should help to build the infrastructure for a thriving industrial economy.

When this began to seem inadequate, lawmakers set out to fill the gap with the Small Business Act in 1953, a classic piece of capitalist engineering that was ostensibly designed to provide loans to assist small businesses in peacetime, but which became one of the most important sources of federal support for disaster victims throughout the twentieth century. Government loans had first been made available to finance the reconstruction of public facilities after disasters during the New Deal in 1934; the Disaster Loan Program authorized the Small Business Administration to make loans to individuals who had suffered losses "because of floods or other catastrophes."[72] And it did so at a discount. Whereas the rate for regular business loans was 6 percent, the rate for disaster victims, including homeowners and tenants, was 3 percent. Direct aid was still off limits, but there was a growing sense among politicians, business leaders, and the public that helping disaster victims might be a practice consistent with the stimulation of the economy. Once this principle was accepted, the stage was set for a broader assumption of powers by the federal government to promote the security and welfare of the American public.

"Who Pays?" The Politics of the Northeastern Floods of 1955

When floods rolled over the Northeast in 1955, an unprecedented array of laws and institutions were in place to facilitate and finance rescue and relief operations. Local and state authorities (including police, firefighters, National Guardsmen, and civil defense forces) were quickly deployed, and they were soon joined by U.S. troops with orders to assist in the evacuation of survivors and the protection of property. Martial law and states of emergency were declared in a number of towns to discourage looting and to broaden the powers of mayors and governors to respond to the crisis.[73] *Time* was especially impressed by the extent of military activity. "Swarms of helicopters and Army amphibious 'ducks,'" the magazine reported, "were pressed into action."[74] Soldiers even dusted off bridges designed for the invasion of Germany during World War II to temporarily replace structures that had succumbed to the flooding. They also supplied generators, water purification systems, and blankets.[75] Indeed, the army acted as if it were engaged in combat maneuvers, turning against this natural disaster the might of a modern war machine that had been assembled to win World War II and to contain the Soviet Union during the ongoing cold war.

FIG 14. "Naugatuck, August 19, 1955," after the floods following Hurricane Diane. Notice the military helicopter, a sign of the militarization of disaster management. 55 Flood 19, Connecticut State Library, Hartford, Connecticut.

Americans had been prepared by over two decades of government activism (and, more recently, by civil defense propaganda) to believe that it was the responsibility of the government to protect them from sudden catastrophe. Of course, states and localities still had primary responsibility for relief and recovery—"the community" was primarily imagined in state rather than national terms—and these moved quickly to raise money for relief. The State of Connecticut announced that there was no "sound" (that is to say legal) way to make direct grants to individuals, though it managed to channel about $2,280,000 to victims through the abatement of property taxes or by offering low-interest mortgages or low-rent housing.[76] Officials did move quickly to release funds for the restoration of infrastructure. The Massachusetts legislature passed a $55 million bond issue, and Connecticut reallocated $35 million in state construction funds to free up money to pay for the recovery.[77] About half of the state money was diverted to municipalities for the repair of roads, bridges, schools, and other public properties, and a similar amount was disbursed to state agencies to repair state highways, bridges, parks, and so forth. But while the political will was in place, states simply did not have the resources to finance the recovery. So they turned to the federal government for help. And when Washington offered $25 million to Connecticut, for example, Governor Abraham Ribicoff publicly complained that this amount fell far short of what was needed.[78] He certainly did not consider this aid a threat to his own authority.

There were limits, however, to the support the federal government was able to provide. "This is a case," Eisenhower declared, "where the Federal Government, the State government, the county government, the city government will do every possible thing they can. But they operate under laws * * * laws made by your representatives. And those laws are necessarily limited in the scope of authority they delegate."[79] Still, he felt pressured to promise that the government would take aggressive steps to assist the region. Although his Republican Party was committed in this period to reversing the expansion of federal power that had taken place during the twin emergencies of the Great Depression and the Second World War, he was willing to grant that disasters presented a special case. The task was to find creative ways to make money and assistance available. Eisenhower even agreed to consider convening a special session of Congress. Significantly, Senate Majority Leader Lyndon B. Johnson of Texas opposed this option on the grounds that it would "merely waste time."[80] A disaster demanded a temporary suspension of politics as usual. In an emergency, as Val Peterson, the head of the Civil Defense Administration, put it, the task was to "cut the red tape and get things done in a hurry."[81] In accordance with the terms of the Disaster Relief Act of 1950, agencies were able to divert $100 million from other accounts to cover the contributions of the Army Corps of Engineers to the "restoration of such public facilities as water systems, schools and sanitary systems, and for clearing flood debris."[82] But even this did not satisfy popular demand. Lt. Gen. S. D. Sturgis Jr., the officer in charge of Army Corps of Engineers operations, had to keep reminding the public that the federal role was "one of assistance to the local governments and not a complete acceptance by the Federal Government of all responsibility for work in affected areas."[83]

Most of the requirements of individuals would be met, as in the past, by private charities and especially by the American Red Cross. This, Eisenhower insisted, was exactly as it ought to be. Voluntary disaster relief was to be judged not solely in terms of its effectiveness but also as an expression of modern American values. With one eye on the cold war and another on the free market principles of his party, he laid out his vision in a speech to the American Bar Association in Philadelphia. "We stand," he declared, "in the shadow of the hall in which was written the Constitution of the United States. Implicit in that document is the conviction, the belief, the faith, that Americans would perform by voluntary cooperation those deeds which in other governments had to be performed by direction, by regimentation, by order of government." Disasters had once been a test of individual morality; now, clearly, they were a test of American civilization. Invoking Woodrow Wilson's premise that "the highest form of efficiency is the spontaneous cooperation of a free people," he declared the recent catastrophe to be "one of those most unusual opportunities to exhibit that spontaneous cooperation." The management of disaster was not simply a matter of need but an ideological imperative. Eisenhower called on Americans to donate generously to the Red Cross "to make certain the disaster is alleviated, that the morale of all those people in those destroyed villages or towns will understand that America's heart has not forsaken them; that we are proud to help."[84] This calamity was a chance to consolidate an imagined American community for the cold war era, one that emphasized the United States as a free market capitalist society (in contrast to the command economy of the Soviet Union) and established Americans as a "free" and good people. This was an occasion to "prove that the American people, regardless of governments, regardless of limitations on them, can meet an emergency and do it well."[85] In the end, donors did do well, sending $16 million to the Red Cross to cover the bulk of the $18 million spent on rescuing, feeding, and sheltering 144,000 people as well as repairing houses, replacing furniture, and other such rehabilitation measures designed to get families "back to normal life."[86] But there was much more to be done.

Faced with enormous losses, the "big question," as *New York Times* reporter Charles Grutzner put it, was "who is going to foot the bill?"[87] This, of course, was an urgent practical consideration for victims and administrators alike, but it was also a matter of broad philosophical and political significance. At stake was nothing less than the proper administration of a complex industrial society at a moment of transition. This disaster, like those before and since, was an occasion for contemplating, debating, and revisiting the premises of social and economic policy.[88] As in the past, most officials and commentators made it clear that those individuals and companies affected by the calamity would (and should) be primarily responsible for their own restitution. "The costs of recovery, for the most part," as *Newsweek* explained, "would have to be paid out of future income. Heavy tax deductions would ease the blow—but these would raise no immediate cash. Only a few big companies could afford to repair damages out of capital; others must rely on banks or some kind of state or Federal loans."[89] Indeed, in a credit-fueled economy the victims of the floods were doubly penalized. Even if they lost their homes or shops or factories they were still legally bound to keep up interest and mortgage payments on these ruined properties. And banks, reportedly, fully intended to foreclose on those who could not pay their debts.[90]

Newsweek sent a reporter to Washington, Connecticut, one of many small towns hit hard by the floods, to evaluate the capacity of people there to finance the restoration of their communities. The reporter emphasized the determination of the residents to rebuild, but he was struck by the obstacles they faced. Readers were introduced, for example, to a local garage owner, Mr. Machno, whose establishment was located on a street of businesses and shops that had been inundated by rising waters:

> Two walls and the roof were all standing, but the river had torn apart the rear of the building and the front. The floor was blanketed with mud, and mud filled the grease pits. Some of the equipment had been washed away and nearly all the supplies. Out of 60 cases of oil, Mike Machno could find only 2 quarts. What equipment remained was soaked with water and caked with mud, and useless.

He vowed to rebuild, but this was not going to be easy because, like many other local business owners, he was already in debt. He had borrowed money to set up his garage three years before. His story, according to the reporter, was typical. This community of twenty-three hundred incurred losses of at least $3,215,000. And it was not clear how the costs would be covered. The predicament of the Washington Furniture Shop's owner pointed to more general problems. He was "wiped out" and could not say for sure whether he would be in a position to rebuild. He could borrow more money, but he was sure that he would "starve to death paying it back." And, like his neighbors, he could not collect flood insurance because there was none.[91]

As we saw in chapter 2, discussions about the restitution of disaster victims had long been absorbed into larger debates about the proper distribution of risk in a modern capitalist society. By the twentieth century it seemed both unfair and uneconomical to require individuals and private businesses to bear the full costs of "unforeseen" natural calamities. The advantage of insurance was that it spread risk without involving the government. It encouraged capital investment and innovation; it was the safety net that made industrial capitalism work. Although the insurance industry offered comprehensive coverage for fires, earthquakes, tornadoes, hurricanes, and even radioactive contamination in 1955, however, there was no cost-effective flood insurance. San Francisco had been rebuilt with help from insurance monies after it burned down in 1906; the victims of the killer hurricanes of 1954 had received hundreds of millions of dollars from the insurance industry. But only 5 to 10 percent of the $1.6 billion in damage to railroads, factories, businesses, and houses by the 1955 floods was covered.[92]

Continuing his investigations at the *New York Times* into the economics of the floods, Charles Grutzner acknowledged that this was a source of continuing public astonishment. "Every disastrous flood," he noted, "is followed by a public gasp of surprise that so little of the damage is covered by insurance." Time and again such disasters were greeted with "mutterings that something must be wrong with the $20,000,000,000 insurance industry." In fact, he assured his readers, there were compelling economic reasons operating here. Quite simply, flood insurance did not pay. All Americans were susceptible to fires, and most were willing to pay premiums for protection; this kept insurance rates down even as it ensured profits for the insurance industry. By contrast, floods wrought "their havoc only in valleys, along river or ocean shores or upon what the geologists call flood plains." They were geographically localized. The risk was not spread widely enough.[93] The insurance industry was unyielding. It was not good business to devise an arrangement whereby the "man who lived on a hill would be subsidizing the river bank dweller."[94] The best that adjusters could offer was the advice to heed the lessons of nature and avoid settling in floodplains. As one Manhattan insurance agent put it, "The Bible tells you to build your house on a rock. I guess you'd better be sure the rock is a high one."[95] Those who did not were expected to pay the consequences.

The insurance industry was driven by the bottom line to advocate for an environmentally responsible approach to development. But this was not a suggestion that most Americans were willing to accept. Life was not supposed to be so precarious in an advanced industrial civilization. As we have seen, there was a legal mechanism in place that enabled the federal government to provide cheap loans for disaster victims, but the calamity exposed the limitations of these measures and created the political context for reform. The Federal Housing Administration (FHA) authorized special loans for public works and private housing repair, the Farmer's Home Loan Association had a $121 million disaster fund, and the Labor Department offered $20 million to help workers who lost jobs in the calamity. But the main institution for channeling capital to businesses and individuals in devastated areas was the Small Business Administration.[96] When it was realized that the Small Business Act of 1953 limited the amount that could be spent on any disaster to $25 million, lawmakers and business leaders insisted that this was not enough. Congress revised the law to make all SBA holdings (at that date $175 million) available for disaster loans. Some members of the Committee on Banking and Currency feared that all these funds might end up being diverted to disaster relief, leaving none for the development of small businesses, which had been the primary goal of the original law. But officials at the agency forced the issue by offering loans to disaster victims at 6 percent, promising that the rate would be reduced to 3 percent once lawmakers approved an amendment. Congress, prodded by members from afflicted states, agreed to rubber-stamp the disaster loans.[97] In the public glare of a disaster, few politicians were willing to stand in the way of such measures to help survivors.

Indeed, most accepted that even more had to be done. Although it was still not possible in this legal and cultural climate to countenance direct federal aid for disaster victims, a strong conviction prevailed that other remedies had to be devised. "The question facing Congress," according to Representative Thomas J. Dodd of Connecticut, was "basically to find a solution to the problem of how the Federal Government can offer some degree of economic protection against loss from floods and other natural disasters to all its people and still do so without spending large Federal subsidies."[98] This involved a complex diplomatic and political dance. Dodd's solution was to introduce a bill calling on Washington to subsidize flood insurance.[99] Supporters insisted that the benefits of such a solution could not simply be measured in economic terms. "To those who say that insurance against the hazards of floods is unrealistic and un-workable," Federal Housing Administration commissioner Norman P. Mason announced, "I say that the least we can do for American families facing such overpowering loss in the future is to explore every possible means of protection."[100] Anxieties about atomic obliteration permeated the debates. Supporting a federal program of insurance that would cover not only floods but also "atomic bomb attacks," Senator Herbert H. Lehman of New York, for example, argued that Congress had to act im-mediately "to assure that in the future Americans will not need to live in fear that all their possessions, savings and hopes may vanish in a single catastrophic blast."[101]

Congress responded to the popular demand by passing the Flood Insurance Act in 1956, but once the moment of intense scrutiny elapsed, it declined either to fund or to implement it. The Federal Flood Insur-ance Administration, in the words of one journalist, "passed out of ex-istence with the record of being the shortest-lived government agency in U.S. history. It never wrote a single policy. It never did a single one of the things it had been created to do."[102] Strict economic accounting prevailed. This was entirely acceptable to most "insurance men," ac-cording to A. L. Kirkpatrick, insurance director for the U.S. Chamber of Commerce, who continued to "hold that the best flood insurance is flood control."[103] A combination of constitutional law, economics, and precedent once again pointed to flood control as the proper sphere for federal activism.[104]

In many respects, faith in organization reinforced the traditionally optimistic American view of disasters. While a booming economy pro-vided the foundations for this confidence, there was wide consensus that a helping hand from experts was required to ensure that a calamity would turn out to be a blessing. Towns across Connecticut assembled commit-tees to build what the *New York Times* called "new better communities."[105] Governor Ribicoff called on townsfolk to plot reconstruction carefully: "You have an opportunity to rebuild, so rebuild soundly. Get the maxi-mum economical and social benefits out of this. Through a planning commission or some other such group, make plans so that out of this will come a better Winsted, a better Torrington, a better Waterbury, and a better Naugautuck. If industry has to be rebuilt, ask yourself if there is a different area in which it should be located."[106] In a world where new was better, and where planning was the answer to chaos, destruction re-mained a principle of creation.

The Modern Imagination of Disaster

Mounting hopes for the planned technological society in the 1950s encouraged some commentators to anticipate nothing less than control of the weather. Congress had actually been mulling over proposals for meteorological manipulation since 1850. One hundred years later the federal government and private companies such as Better Weather Incorporated were conducting full-scale experiments in weather modification. In 1953, the President's Advisory Committee on Weather Control was established to study and evaluate these initiatives. Results, it turned out, had been decidedly mixed. In 1947, the military dropped two hundred pounds of dry ice into the center of a hurricane that was approaching Florida, hoping thereby to "over-seed" the clouds and prevent rain. The storm shifted direction soon afterward and careened into Savannah, Georgia. According to historian Ted Steinberg, that luckless city may thus have been "on the receiving end of modernity ascendant: the first engineered hurricane disaster."[107]

The remarkable faith exhibited here in technology and engineering tended to go hand in hand with a disregard for long-term environmental consequences. The shocking insensitivity to biological processes that Rachel Carson was soon to expose in her pathbreaking study *Silent Spring* was fully operational in suggestions for the management of hurricanes. According to the *New York Times*, one idea under consideration was to saturate ocean waters with oil. "Hurricanes," the writer explained, "die when they travel over land, partly because the landscape hinders the free flow of winds. The oil slick would be a kind of false landscape, intended to slow up some of the air currents that may be influential in deciding the hurricane's forward movement."[108] Meanwhile, Gordon E. Dunn, the nation's "leading hurricane expert," noted that the most popular recommendation for preventing ruinous tempests, as measured by the letters he received, was to break up "baby" storms with A-bombs.[109] While these proposals seem to have been inspired more by science fiction than by science, and while little was then known about the origins of hurricanes, researchers fully expected to close gaps in their knowledge in the near future. Indeed, well-funded hurricane research promised to be one of Diane's "silver linings."[110] Another was the development of a sophisticated social science of calamities. A new field of academic research appeared at this very moment: disaster studies. The Department of the Army and the National Academy of Sciences–National Research Council, for example, began funding investigations by the Committee on Disaster Studies to examine problems that "might result from disasters caused by enemy action," expecting this work to help experts model and manage peacetime disasters more effectively.[111]

The national obsession with planning evidently owed as much to the apprehensions of the age as to its optimism. In August 1947, in the aftermath of the dropping of "the Bomb," the social critic Dwight Macdonald had announced that there was no longer any possibility for believing in "Science" and "Progress." W. E. B. DuBois, writing in the *Chicago Defender*, had offered an even bleaker assessment: "We have seen, to our amazement and distress, a marriage between science and destruction." Science, hitherto the "emancipator" of mankind, was now its "enslaver."[112] Historian Paul Boyer notes that this "Great Fear" had begun to exhaust itself by the end of the 1940s, but it remained a nagging concern throughout the 1950s.[113] Certainly, a growing number of scientists and commentators were beginning to blame "man" rather than nature for disasters.

Conservationists, in particular, took advantage of the interest aroused by the floods of 1955 to instruct Americans about the social and environmental obligations of an industrial society. William Vogt, the former editor of the Audubon Society magazine, for example, echoed Rousseau (and the insurance adjustors of his own day) when he argued that it was foolish to spend money "rebuilding where the destruction has taken place." What was required was greater heed to the rhythms and cycles of nature. "The lesson," he declared, "is that no one should build where a flood has taken place before, or may reasonably be expected to take place in the future, unless he is willing to accept the consequences."[114] Vogt believed that this was unlikely to happen without an abandonment of capitalism. "Free enterprise—divorced from biophysical understanding and social responsibility," as he had contended a few years before in *The Road to Survival*, "must bear a large share of the responsibility for devastated forests, vanishing wildlife, crippled ranges, a gullied continent, and roaring flood crests." This influential book was nothing less than a modern jeremiad, a warning that population was outstripping resources and that the planet was facing "a meeting at the ecological judgment seat."[115]

Such heated rhetoric speaks to the enduring power of apocalyptic rhetoric in the modern age. Indeed, anxiety about impending annihilation also lay behind the dramatic resurgence of evangelicalism in this period. To be sure, the much-heralded religious revival of the decade tended to be more tepid than scorching, the most famous expression of this ecumenical age being Eisenhower's 1954 observation, "Our government makes no sense unless it is founded in a deeply felt religious faith—and I don't care what it is."[116] Certainly, when it came to the 1955 floods, the vast majority of religious organizations and preachers agreed that Christians should put their energy into charitable activities rather than the divination of ultimate meanings.[117] But the prospect of human extinction reactivated a millennial strain of religious thought with deep roots in American culture. In 1949, the Baptist evangelical preacher Billy Graham began to address nuclear fears directly, assuring congregations that the end was near and that repentance was the only solution.[118] Thus the seeds were sown for an extraordinarily influential Christian movement that would leave a deep imprint on the imagination and politics of disaster over the remainder of the century and beyond.

The prominent historian of colonial New England, Perry Miller, placed this revival in a historical context. In an anguished address on "The End of the World" delivered in 1950, he acknowledged continuities between contemporary apocalyptic thought and the millennialism of seventeenth-century Puritans, and even that of early Christians. "Men," he claimed, "have always desired the assurance of an end, and there is good reason to suppose that Christ Himself won the audience by assuring His disciples that the end of the world was at hand." But Miller was struck by the novelty of the nuclear apocalypse. "When the end of the world was a descent from Heaven," he maintained in an extraordinary passage, "it was also a Judgment; if it becomes more and more a contrivance, it has less and less to do with good and evil. Humanity lusts after the conflagration, even after nature seems unlikely to provide it. The human finger actually itches for the trigger. But then, if humanity has to do the deed itself, can it bring about more than the explosion? Can it also produce the Judgment?" Miller was skeptical. "Explosion, in its stark physical simplicity, although satisfying the most venerable requirements for stage effects, turns out to be . . . not what was wanted after all. Not for this was the errand run into a wilderness, and not for this will it end. Catastrophe, by and for itself, is not enough."[119] The Harvard professor of English, owning up to the existential preoccupations that had pulsed though his scholarship, concluded with some dismay that modern people were drifting in a world without "meaning." In this assessment he shared much with the theologian Paul Tillich who, as we saw in chapter 1, was highly critical of the superficiality of postwar American culture and religious thought. But while most ordinary Americans surely did fail to cultivate the sort of sensibility that would have impressed these intellectuals, it is hardly the case that they lived in a meaningless world. Rather they found meaning in family, work, faith, and consumer goods. And many found particular sustenance in the obscure eloquence of what Miller derided as "special effects."

Nuclear anxieties found cultural expression in the popular genre of science fiction movies.[120] These films, as Susan Sontag observed in "The Imagination of Disaster," an important essay from 1965, were really more about calamities than about science.[121] A cultural fascination with representations of destruction, of course, was hardly new, but it assumed a distinctive shape in the twentieth century. Disasters were featured heavily in motion pictures from the earliest days of the industry; films that featured lavish spectacles of destruction were popular enough in Europe and the United States at the beginning of the twentieth century to constitute, in film historian David Annan's phrase, a "cinema of catastrophe."[122] The nuclear age saw a radical increase in the scale of destruction portrayed on the screen. Movies such as *When Worlds Collide*, *This Island Earth*, and *War of the Worlds* lovingly portrayed the annihilation of buildings, cities, and, in one instance, the entire planet. These films further encouraged an appreciation for the aesthetic pleasures of destruction.

As movie and television production values became more sophisticated in the 1950s, simulated disasters began to set the standard for spectacles of destruction. To be sure, most movie representations of calamity still paled before the drama of actual disasters. Science fiction films tended to be cheaply made, with poor special effects. But this was changing. Rudolph Mate's 1951 movie *When Worlds Collide* won a deserved Oscar for special effects for its convincing simulation of the destruction of New York City by tidal waves.[123] One year after Hurricane Diane, audiences were treated to the spectacular obliteration of government buildings and landmarks in Washington, D.C., in *Earth vs. the Flying Saucers*. In an age when movies could offer images of such extravagant destruction, there was a danger that real disasters might seem a pale imitation of these silver-screen versions. A reporter writing in *Life* in 1945 believed that popular culture had taken away some of the drama of the dropping of the atom bombs. "American kids, fans of Flash Gordon, reacted to the news with peanut-butter stares which seemed to say, 'What's all the excitement?' or, '*We've* had it for years.'"[124] As the archive of images of destruction built up over the twentieth century, movies increasingly set the standard for convincing spectacles of destruction.

The 1950s marks a significant shift in ways of seeing natural disasters. The residue of an older modernist outlook was apparent when veterans compared the devastation in Waterbury, Connecticut, to the bombed-out cities of Europe and Japan they had passed through during World War II. But another eyewitness described the same scene as being "like a movie."[125] At this point, we begin to enter the postmodern cultural landscape mapped out in *White Noise*, when even real disasters begin to appear somehow unreal unless they match Hollywood notions of what a disaster should look like. This was an extraordinary reversal. Romantics had taught Americans to view culture as an inferior imitation of nature. Indeed, nature, especially in its most extreme forms, was valued for its authenticity in an artificial and insubstantial world. Thus, as we saw in chapter 3, the San Francisco earthquake and fire offered a welcome burst of "reality" for some. But even in 1906 more and more people were encountering calamities by watching simulated disasters (including one of the San Francisco earthquake) in entertainment venues such as the Coney Island amusement park. Of course, most Americans would have been quite sure that they could distinguish between the real and the fake, trusting that actual disasters would elicit more sincere emotions. Disaster shows were just entertainment. But in the 1950s this distinction between the natural and the cultural was beginning to break down. In a world of weather control experiments and nuclear fission, it was obvious that much that had been taken for granted as being outside of human manipulation was now thoroughly imprinted by social actions. Technology was annihilating the modernist opposition between nature and culture. Disaster movies compounded this ambiguity.

At the same time, they helped to condition Americans' responses to real disasters. The floods of 1955 were responsible for many tragic incidents. In the Poconos, near Stroudsburg, Pennsylvania, a creek swelled thirty feet in fifteen minutes, unleashing a wall of water that swept away more than fifty people.[126] But there were no photographers there to preserve the scene, so national attention fixed instead on events in Putnam, Connecticut, where cameras captured images of rising waters tearing through the industrial district, giving rise to the most arresting television pictures of the disaster: "Hundreds of barrels of burning magnesium floated in the streets, sending geysers of white-hot metal 250 feet in the air."[127] Although no deaths were recorded here, these images ensured that the devastation of Putnam would become the emblem of the calamity and that the town would be the recipient of a disproportionate amount of aid.

A sensational taste for spectacles of catastrophe was shaped by the concerns of the times. "Ours," as Susan Sontag wrote in 1965, "is indeed an age of extremity. For we live under continual threat of two equally fearful, but seemingly opposed, destinies: unremitting banality and inconceivable terror." Spectacles of destruction offered double release from this predicament, helping to "lift us out of the unbearably humdrum and to distract us from terrors—real or anticipated—by an escape into exotic, dangerous situations which have last-minute happy endings."[128] In chapter 3 we traced the process whereby images of chaos came to be embraced as a revitalizing source of stimulation for those dulled by the predictabilities and conventions of modern life. Such a longing for release was more urgent than ever in the conformist society of the 1950s in which, according to social critics such as C. Wright Mills, corporate organization now reached "into every area and detail of daily life."[129] Although life, even in the postwar suburbs, was never as anesthetized or complacent as some critics claimed, filmmakers obviously sensed that ordinary Americans were disaffected enough to wish to see things blow up. Alienation from the gray and administered world of the 1950s was pronounced enough to lend some support to cultural historian Mark Jancovich's contention that the true source of horror in science fiction movies was not the bomb but a world governed by the modern imperatives of science, rationality, standardization, and "order."[130] But the case should not be overstated. The threat of nuclear annihilation undoubtedly added a new dimension to the modern imagination of disaster. A reading of reviews from the period lends support to Sontag's claim that these movies owed a good deal of their fascination to the therapeutic opportunity they presented for working through anxieties about the frightening prospect of global annihilation, particularly because they so consistently supplied happy endings and comforting resolutions.

Disaster movies obviously had complex effects on the politics of disaster. Sontag believed that most science fiction movies taught Americans to accept bureaucratic and totalitarian responses to the challenge of catastrophe. If so, the textual evidence of the films indicates that this acquiescence was driven more by uneasiness than by any assurance about the utopian prospects of an administered technological society.[131] Institutions of authority get blown up too frequently and too gleefully for these films to convey unambiguous enthusiasm for the emerging national security state. Indeed, disaster movies articulated and dramatized resentments about modernity. What we can say is that these movies helped to generate popular interest in spectacular catastrophes. This in turn further encouraged media coverage. And intense media scrutiny of actual calamities pressured government officials to demonstrate competence and caring in their efforts to keep the American people safe from unexpected hazards.

The Contradictions of Federal Emergency Management

In 1955, *Collier's* published an appreciative essay on the efforts of the Eisenhower administration to "retreat from socialism" by reducing economic regulations and reversing the incursion of government into industrial production that had been a hallmark of wartime mobilization. But it also offered a cautionary note, identifying the politics of emergency management as a dangerous obstacle to privatization. " 'National health and safety,' " the correspondent wrote facetiously, "will undoubtedly be invoked to stay the hand of the executive when Government-operated bakeries, hairdressing establishments, brickyards, false-teeth manufacturing plants or steamship lines are threatened with extinction." There seemed to be an unfortunate but unshakable truth here: "Once the Government goes into business to meet some emergency, real or fancied, it almost never gets out."[132] Although emergency management did not provide any justification for the establishment of the sort of Soviet-style command economy feared by *Collier's*, it did facilitate the consolidation of a powerful national security state. This legal and institutional apparatus has done more to promote private business and capitalist development than to inhibit it.

In the years since the Disaster Relief Act was passed in 1950, the federal government has established an impressive array of laws, agencies, and policies to tackle calamities. Washington now provides flood insurance and even direct grants to disaster victims. The list of services and benefits that the government can offer to survivors is lengthy and includes food coupons, unemployment compensation, and mental health counseling.[133] Although states and local governments retain formal responsibility for combating local disasters, Washington has taken an increasingly prominent financial and administrative role in both relief and recovery. The new legal and administrative edifice has transformed the management of disasters. The money and resources are available to respond to calamities as never before.

While the federalization of emergency management is sometimes described as a triumph of reason and justice, as the culmination of a modern quest for control over the natural environment, there are contradictions and complications here that compel us to settle on a more cautious and complex assessment. Public policy has been largely improvised in response to specific calamities and in differing political contexts, and lacks an overarching coherence or clarity of purpose. And while one can only marvel at the resilience of American communities in the face of calamities and (sometimes) at the effectiveness of government responses, modern ways of responding to disasters have also had some ruinous consequences, prompting patterns of development that create conditions for future disasters. The costs can be measured not only in financial terms but also in damage to the environment and to the social fabric.

Constitutional mandates, congressional politics, and ideological expectations have long placed technological solutions at the center of federal disaster management. The edition of *Life* magazine published the day before Hurricane Diane arrived in August 1955 reported that U.S. engineers had finally "tamed" the Big Muddy. Readers learned that, with the completion of the Gavins Point Dam, engineers had "finally clinched their victory over the rampaging Missouri River."[134] A $5 billion flood relief plan had resulted, according to the excited prose of the reporter, in "an intricate and far-flung system of dams, dikes, reservoirs, and levees, a technological achievement which in scale overshadows every feat of engineering in history, from the Pyramids to the Panama Canal." These measures ensured that there would "never be another disaster like the 1952 flood, the biggest ever experienced on the river."[135] Although these and similar projects undoubtedly did help to contain smaller floods, the expenditure of $9 billion on nine thousand miles of levees and two hundred reservoirs during the 1960s was not enough to stop flood-related losses from mounting.[136] As communities along the Mississippi River had learned in 1927, floodwalls must continually be strengthened and raised if they are to keep raging waters at bay. When they breach, as happened again in 1993, the flooding is much more severe than would have been the case if artificial defenses had not been erected. This was one of the unintended consequences of federal disaster mitigation policy. Another was that the greater security promised by flood control encouraged development and settlement in floodplains. Not only was this placing more people in harm's way, it was destroying wetlands that presented a natural impediment to floods. By 1966, it was all too clear that engineering could not, in itself, protect communities from calamities. Thereafter, hoping to control costs as well as to protect vulnerable residents, Washington took steps to regulate and restrict settlement in flood-prone areas.[137] But this would not be easy.

After every calamity, communities demanded restitution. The ongoing love affair of television cameras with catastrophe continued to ensure that local misfortunes captured national attention and sympathy. In response, Washington finally bowed to pressure to underwrite flood insurance. The Flood Insurance Act of 1956 may have withered from neglect, but subsequent disasters like Hurricane Betsy, which flooded one-fifth of New Orleans in 1965, induced Congress to establish and later modify the National Flood Insurance Program in 1968. This was supposed to achieve the double goal of helping flood victims while encouraging responsible settlement. In theory, residents could not receive federal insurance payments if they lived in areas that lacked land-use regulations. But in practice, the regulations proved ineffectual and the insurance payments kept on coming. For the most part, local and state authorities failed to establish or enforce flood-zoning regulations. A lack of political will in the face of aggressive resistance, especially in the 1990s from an assertive property-rights movement that deployed lawsuits, political pressure, and even violence to limit government restrictions on the use or settlement of private land, evacuated federal policies of much of their effectiveness.[138] The long-term effect was that insurance took away much of the financial risk of living or working in places that were prone to flooding.[139]

Much the same was true of federal loan programs. The Small Business Administration subsidized the development of vulnerable shoreline properties in Florida and elsewhere around the country. In 1969, Congress passed the Disaster Relief Act of 1969, authorizing a whole range of direct packages to individuals and, in particular, allowing the SBA to cancel up to $1,800 of the "loans" extended to disaster victims. When added to the millions of dollars spent by the Eisenhower administration on infrastructure in the Florida Keys after Hurricane Donna in 1960, the outcome was a massive expenditure of taxpayers' money for the construction of homes and businesses in parts of the country that were unusually susceptible to hurricanes. This has destroyed natural barriers to tidal flooding, making these locations more vulnerable than ever to "natural" destruction.[140] Disaster mitigation, in other words, has all too often been subordinated to the demands of development. The environmental impact has been severe enough to justify claims that public policy has helped to create conditions that make future catastrophes more likely.

Although federal emergency management was rooted in the social welfare sympathies of the middle years of the twentieth century, in recent years it has provided cover for policies that redistribute resources from the poor to the affluent. Because loans and grants have tended to go to middle-class families, there is reason to agree with a bemused recipient of federal largesse who once described modern disaster relief as a system of "welfare for the wealthy."[141] Washington's share of the costs of local disasters has spiraled over the past thirty years, even though lawmakers have made repeated efforts to control spending in this area. But a media spotlight that rewards those politicians who advocate generous aid to the victims of spectacular catastrophes, alongside a legal arrangement that makes it possible for the president to authorize emergency expenditures without regard to budgetary constraints, has made it very hard to be parsimonious in the aftermath of calamities. Legislators tend to respond quickly when asked to pass bills that enable special disaster relief. Because they have not always authorized extraordinary expenditures, however, these funds have often come out of the general budget. This has had a significant effect on the politics of distributive justice.

In the 1990s, a fiscally conservative Congress began to offset the costs of calamities by slashing social services. To pay for the earthquake that hit Northridge, California, in 1994, for example, Congress made deep cuts in programs that were mostly designed to aid the poor, from low-income housing and job training programs to the Low Income Home Energy Assistance Program, as well as environmental protection programs. As a result, as Mike Davis has argued, federal disaster relief has sometimes functioned as an entitlement program for the rich that doubly penalizes the poor. Not only are the underprivileged less likely than middle-class victims to receive Small Business Administration loans and structural renovations in their neighborhoods, but they also face a reduction in social services as public money is diverted to rebuilding the homes and businesses of the affluent.[142]

Even so, Washington has not always responded effectively to domestic disasters. This is in spite of the establishment of the Federal Emergency Management Agency (FEMA) in 1979 and the passage of the Robert T. Stafford Disaster Relief and Emergency Act in 1988 that radically expanded the resources available for combating natural calamities. One problem is that FEMA, like its institutional precursors in the 1950s, has often had its attention and resources diverted from natural disaster protection to national security agendas. Between 1982 and 1991, for example, $3 billion was allocated to defense matters, mostly for civil defense, including protecting government officials from an anticipated nuclear attack (Oliver North, apparently untainted by his role in the Iran-Contra scandal, was heavily involved in these plans), while only $243 million was spent on disaster relief. Champions of this security emphasis defended this "dual use" approach on the grounds that it would improve natural disaster preparedness.[143] But FEMA was evidently not equipped to respond effectively to Hurricane Hugo when it battered South Carolina in 1989 or to Hurricane Andrew when it decimated South Florida in 1992. This gave rise to some bitter humor: "Every hurricane, earthquake, tornado and flood, the joke went, brought two disasters: one when the event occurred, and the second when FEMA arrived."[144]

The controversial civil defense preoccupations of the agency were addressed in the 1998 blockbuster movie *X-Files: Fight the Future*.[145] This film, while exemplifying the ongoing obsession of the entertainment industry with spectacles of destruction, ruffled a few official feathers with its dark mutterings about the secret world of disaster politics. "Are you familiar with FEMA? What the Federal Emergency Management Agency's real power is?" a scientist asks the leading character, an FBI agent. "FEMA allows the White House to suspend constitutional government upon declaration of a national emergency. It allows creation of a non-elected government. Think about that, Agent Mulder." In the 1980s and '90s, left- and right-wing Internet sites buzzed with reports about potential abuses of FEMA's power, and much was made of the agency's reported involvement in proposals to establish an unelected shadow government should the president ever declare a national state of emergency.[146] Although the idea that the politics of disaster might be subordinated to the demands of an authoritarian national security state was likely to provoke more mirth than serious inquiry by the 1990s, the question would erupt again with renewed urgency in the aftermath of the terrorist attacks of September 11, 2001. At the end of the twentieth century, disaster historian Rutherford Platt looked back on the extraordinary expansion of federal emergency laws and institutions over the previous fifty years and concluded that "nothing except national security commands more public support than helping people and communities struck by disasters."[147] After 9/11 this distinction itself dissolved, with enormous implications for the politics of disaster and the social organization of the United States.

5

The Ends of Disaster

THE CULTURE OF CALAMITY IN THE AGE OF TERROR

I turned on the television.
I lowered the volume until it was silent.
The same pictures over and over.
Planes going into buildings.
Bodies falling.
People waving shirts out of high buildings.
Planes going into buildings.
Bodies falling.
Planes going into buildings.
People covered in gray dust.
Bodies falling.
Buildings falling.
Planes going into buildings.
Planes going into buildings.
Buildings falling.

JONATHAN SAFRAN FOER, *Extremely Loud and Incredibly Close*, 2005

An airliner piles into the North Tower of New York's World Trade Center at 8:46 a.m. on the luminous morning of September 11, 2001. The building bursts into flame. Sixteen and a half minutes later, a second jet sweeps along an irresistible arc and plows into the South Tower. It too burns fiercely. By 10.30 a.m. each skyscraper has crumpled to the city floor, unloosing a storm of glass and steel and concrete and body parts on the surrounding neighborhoods. These scenes, edited into a rapid sequence, and interspersed with footage of the Pentagon in flames after it has been hit by a third plane at 9.37 a.m., are broadcast over and over again to U.S. (and global) television audiences throughout the day.

By their own accounts, viewers are overwhelmed by this extraordinary series of events. They are sickened, saddened, terrified, enraged, disbelieving.[1] Yet many also feel an odd stirring of recognition; it is as

FIG 15. The destruction of New York's World Trade Center, September 11, 2001. Photograph courtesy of AP Images.

if they have seen this somewhere before. And in a sense, of course, they have. After all, as *Rolling Stone* movie critic Peter Travers reminds his readers soon after the attacks, "images of mass destruction have been the film industry's bread and butter for decades."[2] These images can indeed be found everywhere in our culture of calamity: in movies, computer games, television shows, news broadcasts, magazines, art galleries, comic books, music videos, the Internet. What is surprising, perhaps, is that so many people should grasp this actual horrifying event as if it were unfolding on a Hollywood set. Noticing that eyewitnesses and news reporters alike were recycling phrases from blockbusters to describe the destruction of the twin towers, *New Yorker* film critic Anthony Lane was one among many to insist that people "saw—literally saw, and are continuing to see, as it airs in unforgiving repeats—that day as a movie."[3] He allowed:

> Of course you could argue that last Tuesday was an instant dismissal of the fantastic—that people gazed up into the sky and immediately told themselves that this was the real thing. Yet all the evidence suggests the contrary; it was the television commentators as well as those on the ground who resorted to a phrase book culled from cinema: "It was like a movie," "It was like 'Independence Day.'" "It was like 'Die Hard.'" "No, 'Die Hard 2.'" "'Armageddon.'" And the exclamations from below, from the watchers of the skies caught on video, as they see the aircraft slice into the side of the tower: where have you heard those expressions most recently—the wows, the whoohs, the holy shits—if not in movie theaters, and even on your own blaspheming tongue?[4]

Testimonies from Ground Zero confirm this observation; many of them are written with an uneasy fascination bordering on relish that would not look out of place among the excerpts from *White Noise* with which I opened this book. Just read the following eyewitness recollection, published in the same edition of the *New Yorker*: "Policemen kept saying that the situation was dangerous, that nobody should be there, and yet for a short while one had the strange feeling—clichéd, shaming, and inevitable—of watching a movie, an outlandish disaster film in which the grave threat would increase and increase and then all the tension would be released when the action hero shot his way through and clipped the wires and set the world right."[5] Or the recollection of the reporter who "felt I was reviewing a movie—reporting what I was seeing scene by scene. I almost expected Bruce Willis to arrive in a heat-resistant helicopter and land on top of the tower to rescue all the people."[6]

Passages like these seem to confirm the ascendancy of a distinctively "postmodern" imagination of disaster. Postmodern critics have drawn attention to the crisis of reality in our age, especially an inability amid an unending accumulation of media impressions and digital simulations, to distinguish reliably "between the 'true' and the 'false,' the 'real' and the 'imaginary.'"[7] According to standard accounts of this "hyperreal" imagination, we in the West have been programmed by unrelenting exposure to media sights and sounds to become sensation-seeking consumers, we have been conditioned to respond to actual events in the same way we respond to simulated ones, as passive and disorientated spectators, and we have exchanged critical awareness for an unthinking (or perhaps desperate) trust in technology, experts, and heroes—in those authorities whose job it is to keep us safe, to "set the world right." An aspect of this postmodern outlook is a compulsion to process and evaluate real experiences by measuring them against virtual ones—so that the emotional impact of a disaster depends on its resemblance to a movie spectacle.[8]

Does this account adequately explain American responses to disaster in our times? Has disaster become an entertaining spectacle? Is it possible that television viewers, as Ted Rall proposed in a provocative

FIG 16. Ted Rall's syndicated editorial cartoon, November 15, 2001. RALL © 2001 Ted Rall. Reprinted with permission of Universal Press Syndicate.

cartoon, "secretly" thought that footage of the World Trade Center was "cool"?[9] (Anecdotal evidence suggests that it is. Art Spiegelman witnessed two schoolboys excitedly "high fiving": " 'They hit the Pentagon,' says one. . . . 'Cool!' says the other.")[10] Is this evidence for a radical alteration in the historical relationship between the imagination and management of disaster, so that calamities are now more likely to provoke terrors and exhilarations than to enable insight or progressive social development? Critics such as Fredric Jameson certainly believe so. And his prognosis is bleak. In his view we are left spinning in a free-floating (media-generated) culture of fear that cultivates an emotional habitat in which a repressive political order can flourish.[11]

In this chapter I draw on and develop some of these premises even as I suggest some limitations of this characterization of contemporary culture. To be sure, I do acknowledge a profound shift in popular structures of desire over the past generation or so, and I allow that *postmodern* is as good a term as any to describe the sensibility that governs emotional responses to catastrophe today. Moreover, I agree that our culture of calamity has critical implications for the emergence of the disaster-security state and the consolidation of corporate power in the age of globalization. But disasters have not become mere spectacles, evacuated of meaning and context. On the contrary, they continue to be exceptionally meaningful, producing what passes for "insight," and prompting vigorous social and political activity. Spectacle, indeed, has become thoroughly implicated in the traditional galvanizing functions of catastrophe.

In this chapter I offer a sketch of the contemporary imagination of disaster. I address concerns about the "reality" of the events of September 11 in order to reveal how disasters are made meaningful in the moment of spectacle, how certain "catastrophic" events have come to exert such a compelling hold on public attention and popular concern. I pay particular attention to the outlook of evangelical Christians, an influential social group unaccountably overlooked in most studies of postmodernity, in order to emphasize the decisive contribution of two modes of seeing, the apocalyptic and the hyperreal, to the culture of calamity. I investigate the role of the culture of calamity (and what some critics identify as its primary effect, a culture of fear) in nourishing and, rather less frequently, challenging the authoritarian and centralizing tendencies of capitalist political and economic organization in the age of globalization. I examine these broader developments through an analysis of the commercialization of the "news," a development that has altered the representation and meaning of disasters and restricted the circulation of information about economic processes and geopolitical events to the detriment of deliberative democracy. Indeed, although September 11 was framed almost exclusively as a political crisis, the reforms it prompted had vital, and mostly disguised, economic implications, leading to changes in regimes of regulation and taxation that enhanced the profit-making capabilities of multinational corporations at the expense of social welfare services, civil liberties, and environmental protections. In other words, even as the cultural framing of 9/11 turned it into a symbolic event that bound the American people into an imagined community, the political reaction facilitated by cultural representations enabled an enormous concentration of government and corporate power that has eroded the accountability of big businesses and the state to "the people."

Any attempt to understand the contemporary imagination of disaster must begin at the interface of the culture of calamity, the disaster-security state, and a capitalist economic system that continues to depend for its success on processes of creative destruction (and on spectacles of destructive creation). Many commentators insisted on the singularity of 9/11, arguing that the attacks had hurled Americans into a new world, a new era. The mantra was "this changes everything."[12] The implication was that the past had little or nothing to teach us about this latest crisis. To a remarkable degree, however, responses to September 11 were assembled out of habits, expectations, beliefs, laws, and institutional routines established in encounters with disasters (wars, famines, earthquakes, fires, hurricanes, technological accidents, and so forth) over centuries, and certainly over the past fifty years.

Of course, a terrorist attack is very different from an earthquake or a hurricane. It introduces darker and more unsettling anxieties; it demands a distinctive set of military, intelligence, and community responses. At the same time, the boundary between man-made and natural catastrophes is one that seems to matter less and less to most people in postmodern America. Hollywood, for example, encourages us to treat wars and natural disasters alike as thrilling spectacles; many evangelical Christians insist that wars are more like than unlike earthquakes as tests of faith, or as signs of the apocalypse, or as manifestations of the decomposition of the secular modern world; meanwhile, scientists and social scientists are busy dismantling distinctions between the natural and the cultural, insisting that disasters always have social dimensions, to the extent that even hurricanes are believed to be increasing in intensity as a result of global warming, which in turn is accelerated by the carbon dioxide emissions of industrial societies addicted to fossil-burning fuels. In any case, the destruction of the World Trade Center was routinely described and imagined in government documents as a "disaster" and federal responses were authorized and governed by laws designed to meet the challenge of natural disasters.[13]

Although it is important to recognize that the events of September 11, 2001, constituted a different type of social and political crisis than a natural disaster, widespread insistence that the attacks demanded resolute action, that it was an opportunity for moral, cultural, and political revitalization, and that it cleared space for urban renewal, locates it squarely within the historical narrative I have been sketching here. This, finally, is why the frame of modernity (in an enduringly apocalyptic guise) has so much to teach us about American ways of imagining and managing contemporary disasters.[14] But the imagination of disaster has taken on distinctive traits in the age of the corporate mass media. The idea of the hyperreal, in particular, can help us understand emotional and political responses to the terrorist attacks, even of those who claim to be most resistant to commercial entertainment culture. Evangelical Christians, for example, might often define themselves against Hollywood's moral values, but most have been thoroughly converted by Hollywood's production values; they have learned to grasp "disasters" (whether the destruction of the twin towers or the anticipated devastations of the apocalypse) through the visual and emotional language of the blockbuster. A postmodern lexicon, in other words, sits surprisingly well with religious perspectives that are too often characterized simply as antimodern. In fact, apocalyptic and hyperreal ways of seeing both contribute to the powerful and, as we shall see, troubling conviction that disasters are singularly "real" and deserving of unique attention in a world otherwise lost to artifice, superficiality, and illusion. This has contributed to extraordinary political mobilization and involvement. It also has tended to encourage the view that dramatic disasters deserve more of our concern and attention than such chronic or invisible structural problems as poverty, unemployment, or environmental degradation, and that the perils of our times are best grasped in terms of a moral (and sometimes explicitly theological) struggle between good and evil instead of, say, class or race politics, the geopolitical competition for scarce resources, or anything as abstract as "the logics of capitalism." At the same time, however, disasters continue to prompt others to the contrary conclusion—that catastrophic events are symptoms of the catastrophe of modernity.

This reminds us that the contemporary "imagination of disaster" is multiple rather than singular. There is evidence that marginalized communities within the United States (Arab Americans, for example, or African Americans) registered the events of 9/11 in distinctive ways even when seeing the same images.[15] While the editors of an important collection of black responses, *The Paradox of Loyalty*, noted significant generational differences, with older contributors much more likely than younger ones to prioritize race as a prism through which to view and interpret the attacks, they claimed that race inflected the emotional and intellectual impressions of all members of this community.[16] This was certainly the case for the prominent critic Cornel West, who saw the second plane hit the towers. While he acknowledged being "deeply upset about the precious lives in the World Trade Center and the possible even probable attack" on his hotel, he insisted he had not been "afraid." He attributed this not to any banal optimism but to his bitter experiences as a black man in America. The history of race relations in the United States had accustomed him to outrages: "I felt I had been in this situation before—many times." The attacks were hardly likely to present themselves as an unprecedented act of terrorism on American soil for descendents of slaves who had confronted racists, or what West pointedly referred to as "domestic terrorists." "To be an American 'nigger,'" he explained, "is to be unsafe, unprotected, subject to arbitrary violence and hatred." His final assessment was thus startling and powerful, if a little disingenuous: "I concluded that 9/11 had initiated a painful process of the 'niggerization' of America—we are all now unsafe, unprotected, subject to arbitrary violence and hatred." Still, he had no doubt that African Americans would have a distinctive take on the attacks and the subsequent war on terror as a people who had been "terrorized by the very government that now declares a war against terrorism around the world."[17] Had he broadened his purview to include non-Americans, he might have recognized that even after September 11 all Americans remained relatively insulated from acts of violence when compared to those who lived outside of the developed world. Indeed, he might have wondered at instances of jubilation outside of the United States by groups watching or hearing about the destruction of the World Trade Center in the Middle East and also in places as varied as Nicaragua, Greece, and China. While the media were quick to seize on such images as evidence of the malice and depravity, in particular, of anti-American Muslims, Tariq Ali argued that these incidents, rare enough as they were, articulated the resentments and hurts of disenfranchised peoples in a world dominated by global capital and American military power. What is clear is the extraordinary variety of reactions to 9/11. While there is analytical value in deploying terms such as "hyperreal culture" or "the imagination of disaster," we must insistently historicize emotional and political responses, paying attention to social fissures and grasping the culture of calamity as a field of conflict rather than simply an expression of a universal modern or postmodern response.[18]

Disaster and the American Real

Exasperated by the maddening tendency of onlookers to treat 9/11 as a spectacle, Anthony Lane berated the entertainment industry for having "lied" to audiences, for turning out an endless series of disaster movies that treated violence and destruction as sources of amusement rather than as occasions for compassion or insight or understanding. Avoiding the all-too-easy temptation to lay the blame exclusively at the feet of Hollywood, Lane proposed a broader cultural explanation for the American appetite for destruction. "We are talking," he claimed, "of the indulgence that will always be extended to an epoch blessed with prosperity—one that has the leisure, and the cash, to indulge its fantasies, not least the cheap thrill of pretending that the blessing could be wiped out." He found reason for optimism here. For if American enthusiasm for spectacles of destruction was sustainable only in a world where disasters were hidden away, surely the events of September 11 would shatter this unseemly structure of desire. Indeed, he allowed himself to hope that "the disaster movie" would be "shamed by the disaster" and be cast into oblivion. "The aesthetic habit had cracked," he declared, "and there was no going back." Indeed, in a pointedly biblical turn of phrase, he insisted that this was the "bitter redemption" of disaster: "What happened on the morning of September 11th was that imaginations that had been schooled in the comedy of apocalypse were forced to reconsider the same evidence as tragic." He recognized that mass-media conditioning made it difficult to summon up authentic emotional responses to calamity—"It was hard to make the switch; the fireball of impact was so precisely as it should be, and the breaking waves of dust that barreled down the avenues were so absurdly recognizable"—but he also trusted that this disaster would puncture the film of unreality that had settled over contemporary life. His elegant and elegiac essay was not simply a nostalgic lament for a lost age when feelings were reliable and vision was true but a longing for informed, responsible, and proportionate responses to world events. The problem of reality, in other words, was the problem of deliberative democracy. If images had become our primary means of understanding the world, and if images lied, what was to be the fate of deliberative democracy in the United States?[19]

Lane titled his essay "This Is Not a Movie." It is striking just how many Americans felt compelled to make the obvious point that the events of 9/11 were not simulated. Many of those who first saw images of the attacks on television—from television personality Larry King to Iraqi ruler Saddam Hussein—recalled that they were initially uncertain whether they were watching news coverage or a movie trailer.[20] In the age of digital media it has indeed become increasingly difficult to distinguish actual from virtual images; amid a glut of airbrushed and pixilated representations it is hard to know which pictures to trust, which ones are true or false or trivial or worthy of our attention. There was more at stake here, however, than establishing what had happened. When observers and survivors insisted in their reports, letters, and memoirs that the disaster was "real," they were making a statement about what it *meant* and how it made them *feel*. They were contrasting the substantiality of the catastrophe with the insubstantiality of everyday consumer life. Baudrillard, among others, has argued persuasively that the fakeries of postmodern culture have implanted a powerful compensatory desire to seek out "authentic" experiences and artifacts. In a society in which marketers are always seeking to capitalize on the allure of the real—the real thing, the real world, "keeping it real," reality TV, and so on—the unassailable there-ness of a catastrophe was sure to capture the attention of the public in a very particular way.

To be sure, this anxiety about "reality" is not a problem exclusive to our times. Puritan settlers, as we have seen, mistrusted the evidence of their eyes, suspecting that the invisible (spiritual) world was more real than the visible (material) world. Much of their interest in disasters derived from an assurance that here stood revealed God's awesome truth in a world of false appearances. Eighteenth-century romantics welcomed calamities to the extent that they promised unique access to authentic feelings, enabling a deepening of a self that seemed to be imperiled by the bland materialism and alienating workplace experiences of the emerging modern world. The American real has been a long time in the making, and from the beginning it has been contrasted not so much with the unreal as with the superficial. There is a long history behind the widespread expectation that September 11 might release us from the frivolous preoccupations of daily life in an entertainment-engorged consumer society, that it might enable us to salvage a lost sense of meaning, truth, and purpose.

The destruction of the twin towers was bound to present itself as an urgently "real" event, one that revealed something elemental about the ways of the world and the conditions of our existence. Although true up to a point, this notion demands scrutiny. The terrorist attacks did not so much end up disclosing reality as providing an occasion for constructing a sense of "reality" ("the symbolic coordinates," in Žižek's well-chosen phrase, "which determine what we experience as reality") that validated some ideologies and feelings while casting others as insignificant, inauthentic, and lacking in moral urgency.[21]

The Hyperreal Apocalypse

For many Americans, the "reality" revealed by the disaster was an apocalyptic one. The word *apocalypse* literally means a lifting of the veil, a "revelation," and the catastrophe owed a good deal of its cultural power to the promise that it could reveal things as they really were. According to a Time/CNN poll conducted in 2002, a quarter of all Americans believed that the events of 9/11 were predicted in the Bible. The same survey found that 59 percent of Americans expected the world to end as prophesied in the Book of Revelation.[22] It is uncertain just how reliable these statistics are, but it is clear that no study of the "postmodern" culture of calamity can ignore the deep imprint of Christian imagery and teachings on popular ways of seeing.

Interpreting the destruction of the twin towers as an act of God, many religious commentators resorted instinctively to the rhetoric of the jeremiad. On the Sunday after the attacks the Reverend David Wilkerson preached a sermon at Times Square Church in New York City that would have sounded familiar to the congregations of Increase Mather three centuries before. He opened with expressions of compassion: "I wept at the sight of the utter devastation. I pleaded with God for mercy."[23] And he celebrated the energetic labors of his congregation in assisting sufferers by setting up a relief tent at Ground Zero. But such charitable acts were less important than the lessons: "I've experienced a grief that's even deeper than the mourning for innocent people dying. It's a grief that says if we miss God's message, if we turn a deaf ear to what he's loudly proclaiming, then much worse is in store for us." The jeremiad tradition has always encouraged interventions into the realm of public policy, and Wilkerson was happy to editorialize on the blessings of the recent conservative Christian political ascendancy: "I thank God we have a moral President leading our country. I thank the Lord for all the devout Christians who serve in high office." His message was a distinctively modern one—end abortion—but his was an age-old warning: repent and reform or expect worse disasters in the future. "Many readers," he recognized, "won't receive the word I'm about to deliver. They'll think it heartless, cruel, unkind in a time of grieving. But, I tell you, if we don't hear God's truth and face it, our nation is doomed." In fact, such jeremiads did impress most Americans as heartless and cruel. When the Reverend Jerry Falwell seized the opportunity to scapegoat liberals two days after the attacks during an interview with Pat Robertson on the *700 Club* he provoked widespread revulsion even among conservatives.[24]

At the same time, the popular tendency to treat 9/11 as a test of character and as a call to action suggests that the jeremiad continues to inform habitual American reactions to calamity. Lately, however, it has been supplemented by a potent prophetic tradition. Wilkerson claimed that the "pastoral staff" of his church had been "forewarned" by the Holy Spirit that "a calamity was coming." According to his faith, any great disaster was a sign of the approaching millennium. As far back as 1727, as we have seen, Cotton Mather had cast an earthquake in New England as a "Praemonition" of the apocalypse, as a series of "convulsions" that heralded the Second Coming. Mather, notably, had been reluctant to talk too freely about his eccentric brand of millennialism for fear of being "much mocked," but broad sections of the American public now take such beliefs for granted.[25] "Political events, diplomatic missions, wars, earthquakes, floods, and other natural disasters," as cultural critic Amy Frykholm puts it, "are not random, but woven into a complex narrative about the world's approaching end."[26]

At the center of this theology is the idea of "the Rapture." Many born-again Christians live in the expectation that any day now they are going to be spirited away ("raptured") to Heaven. This, it must be emphasized, is a relatively novel notion dating back to the end of the nineteenth century that has only become widely influential over the past few decades.[27] According to most contemporary advocates, the Rapture is to be followed by seven years of "tribulation" (earthquakes, plagues, famines, wars) that will only come to an end when the Antichrist is defeated at the Battle of Armageddon by the armies of heaven and Christ finally embarks on his thousand years of rule on earth.[28] Disasters play a central role here, and because they are supposed to accumulate as the end of days approaches they can assume an oddly cheering aspect. Consider the Rapture Ready website that tabulates wars, disasters, famines, and other prophetic indicators in order to calculate exactly when the apocalypse will happen. "You could say," the founder explains, that "the Rapture Index is a Dow Jones Industrial Average of end time activity, but I think it would be better if you viewed it as a prophetic speedometer. The higher the number, the faster we're moving towards the occurrence of pre-tribulation rapture." The index peaked on 24 September 2001, a moment of anticipation as well as anxiety. Nancy Gibbs, investigating religious responses to the attacks for *Time* magazine, concluded "the horror of Sept. 11 was experienced differently by people primed to see God's hand in all things." She related the story of a Jerusalem-based evangelical, Doron Standberg, who "was 'joyful' that the attacks could be a sign that the End Times were at hand. 'A lot of prophetic commentators have what I consider a phony sadness over certain events,' he says. In their hearts they know it means them getting closer to their ultimate desire."[29]

The evangelical imagination of disaster owes a great deal to the conditions of modernity. It is no accident that apocalyptic literature has flourished amid world wars, atrocities, famines, and fears of looming environmental collapse and nuclear annihilation. Hal Lindsey's *The Late Great Planet Earth*, the number-one nonfiction best seller of the 1970s, was among the first of this genre to speak to these terrors and to insist that destruction could be a source of hope rather than of despair: "This is the reason that in spite of the headlines, in spite of crisis after crisis in America and throughout the world, in spite of the dark days which will strike terror into the hearts of many, every Christian has the right to be optimistic!"[30] Prophetic literature, in other words, was explicitly marketed as a consolation for the catastrophes of modernity. Certainly, vast numbers of Americans looked to religious texts for solace and explanation, and Christian bookstores worldwide reported surging sales for apocalyptic literature.[31] The *Pre-Tribulation Newsletter* insisted that this was entirely inevitable. Christianity spoke with particular force during times of crisis: "When it comes to explaining *why* the events of September 11, 2001, occurred in history, the Bible, especially Bible prophecy, provides a framework for making sense of this tragic mess."[32]

Postmodern critics have paid little attention to American evangelicalism. And it would be easy to present the disparity between religious and postmodern ideas of calamity as another instance of the impassable cultural rift supposedly dividing the United States into two estranged and mutually uncomprehending camps: red states, blue states, and so forth. But apocalyptic thinking is inextricably woven into the fabric of contemporary American culture; it is, in Catherine Keller's persuasive assessment, a "habit" that exerts an influence well beyond fundamentalist Christian circles.[33] D. W. Griffith's notorious 1915 movie *Birth of a Nation*, the first American blockbuster, was deliberately organized around apocalyptic themes of struggle, defeat, retribution, and redemption. Although ostensibly about the American Civil War and the restoration of the virtuous white South, the final scene depicted the Second Coming of Christ. Griffith's 1916 film *Intolerance*, an account of oppression through the ages, was quite as explicit, concluding with a bright Christian cross appearing over a battlefield and images of the angelic host looking down on the scorched earth, clearly promising a future of peace and harmony. Although this degree of literalism has rarely been approached in subsequent years, Hollywood has stuck by this formula ever since. At the same time, apocalyptic thinking has itself become increasingly cinematic. On occasion Hal Lindsey's book seems to delight in destruction, for example offering an excited, sensational description of the great earthquake expected during the tribulation: "Imagine, cities like London, Paris, Tokyo, New York, Los Angeles, Chicago—obliterated!"[34] This, of course, is exactly what Hollywood has been imagining for years.

Indeed, the postmodern culture of calamity may well be defined by a collision or collusion between the apocalyptic and the hyperreal. It is thus important to resist the temptation to view evangelicals as a group that has opted out of modernity, immune to the imprecations of consumer culture, figured in *White Noise*, for example, as the ludicrous and exotic Jehovah's Witnesses. Although born-again Christians often trumpet their hostility to modernity and its trappings—secularism, materialism, "alternative lifestyles"—most are fully inserted into the consumer grid, watching (and enjoying) Hollywood movies, television shows, mystery novels, and so forth.[35]

Disaster movies clearly exert a particular fascination. Indeed, there is some evidence that conservative Christians are more inclined than liberal Christians to watch movies rated R for violence. This suggests some connection between evangelical imaginings and a taste for spectacles of destruction.[36] Some religious commentators are willing to grant that disaster movies help people to cope with the catastrophes of modernity. Take the following analysis in *Christianity Today*, the most prominent journal of evangelical Christianity: "The imagination of disaster can be twisted into morbid delectation or, even worse, into slick entertainment, as it has in so many Hollywood productions. But it can also take us out of ourselves and return us to our everyday lives purged of complacence. It can even prepare us for times such as this, when imagination yields to dreadful reality."[37] Like Susan Sontag forty years before, this is an admission that cinematic representations of calamity can perform valuable, if problematic, therapeutic work for a modern people living in a world of constant turmoil and turbulence, in a world haunted by violence. This, incidentally, offers an advance on Anthony Lane's suggestion that it is unseemly to fabricate or to take pleasure in simulations of destruction.[38] As I have been arguing throughout this book, there is nothing arbitrary about the American fascination with spectacles of destruction. Exposing oneself to images and accounts of disaster remains, as in the 1950s, a way to work through the anxieties generated by the prospect of personal and collective annihilation.

Perhaps the most intriguing fusion of Rapture theology, entertainment, and spectacles of destruction is the hugely popular *Left Behind* series.[39] By the summer of 2004, when the last of the twelve novels in the series appeared, *Newsweek* reported that total sales had reached sixty-two million.[40] These books are very much a part of the contemporary culture of calamity, and they certainly colored perceptions of September 11—as many as one in eight Americans, only half of whom were evangelicals, had read one or more of the books on the eve of the attacks.[41] The plot of the *Left Behind* series is triggered by a succession of disasters (planes falling out of the sky, car crashes, fires) that are soon revealed to be manifestations of the Rapture. And the calamities of the tribulation are lovingly rendered so as to hook and thrill readers. The tone of the books is insistently sensationalistic: "Horror was not a good enough word for it. . . . Fires had broken out all over the place. They illuminated car crashes, flattened buildings, the earth roiling and rolling like an angry sea."[42] Disaster and destruction, here just as in any Hollywood blockbuster, are designed to entertain.[43] Cloud Ten Pictures, the Canadian Christian film studio that adapted the book into a movie, admitted openly that their task was to turn the prophecies of the Book of Revelation into an exciting contemporary adventure story. The resulting movie, released a year before the destruction of the twin towers, was pure Hollywood. There were heroes and villains, thrilling adventures, sentimental romantic interludes, explosions, and a pop soundtrack to cue the proper emotional responses.

The end of the world had to be cinematic to feel convincing. This has been an accepted principle since the 1970s, when Donald W. Thompson had pioneered the genre of apocalyptic cinema, directing a series of successful prophetic movies like *A Thief in the Night* (1973) that drew heavily on themes taken from the books of Daniel and Revelation. His strategy was to persuade viewers of the immediacy and reality of the end of days by exploiting tricks developed in horror and disaster movies. Accordingly, he self-consciously designed his movies to be chilling and thrilling. His partner, Russell Doughton, whose Hollywood credits also included the 1958 science fiction movie *The Blob*, claimed that these movies led to the conversion of as many as four million people to evangelical Christianity.[44] Among them were the producers of *Left Behind*, who became practicing Christians after watching an evangelical film.[45] They fully shared Thompson's assumptions but were even more concerned with matters of

FIG 17. Still from *Left Behind* DVD (1999). Image reprinted courtesy of Cloud Ten Pictures.

entertainment than with theology. As the narrator of the documentary *Making of Left Behind* explained, the filmmakers "knew they would have to go big in order to tell the story authentically." And this meant adhering to the typical Hollywood practice of favoring spectacle over character, acting, plot, dialogue, or even message. As one of the producers, Peter Lalonde, gushed: "It's not a real movie until you blow something up, and so on the set of *Left Behind* it's been extraordinarily exciting, with one explosion and one effect after another." Indeed, a good portion of the documentary about the making of the movie emphasizes the fun to be had blowing up cars, choreographing death-defying stunts, and so forth.

Significantly, the test of the movie, as far as the film crew and many evangelical commentators were concerned, was not simply (or even primarily) the accuracy of its scriptural message but its resemblance to a big-budget Hollywood epic. Passing quickly over scriptural concerns, Christian viewers and reviewers alike seemed most worried about the movie's "cringe-factor." They dearly hoped the story would be "convincing," and this meant satisfying the expectations of secular viewers, and their own Hollywood-soaked imaginations, about what the end of the world should look like.[46] Any other representation was likely to feel fake and false. It was with mingled relief and self-delusion that one Christian reviewer could declare that the film had "an embarrassment factor of zero."[47] Most, however, were unhappy about the failure of the film as a spectacle.[48] They cared that secular critics might dismiss the movie as "a blundering cringefest."[49] Tim LaHaye was disappointed enough to sue Cloud Ten Pictures because they had failed "to produce a high quality theatrical movie" out of his novel.[50]

Left Behind is just one prominent example of the accommodation of born-again Americans to the postmodern culture of calamity.[51] Evangelicals have long capitalized on this culture's obsessive interest in catastrophe, converting this fascination into profits even as they endeavor to convert consumers into believers. And a religious community accustomed to marketing the apocalypse for its entertainment value is one that is primed to treat actual disasters as thrilling spectacles. A cinematic ("optically correct") catastrophe such as the annihilation of the World Trade Center was surely bound to feel like a movie.[52] In the September 11 Digital Archive, there is an entry from Kathy Dick, an ordinary "God fearing person" working in Panama City, Florida, at the time. Her first reaction to reports of the planes crashing into the twin towers was to pray, but when she finally went home to watch news footage, her primary point of reference was mass entertainment: "I felt as if I was watching a television movie." This response, she was sure, heightened rather than dulled the emotional impact of the tragedy: "There is so much out there that is fiction that seeing it for real is almost unbearable." She cried when watching the coverage. But she insisted on watching the coverage for weeks afterward, mesmerized by the images but also driven by a sense of duty: "It is something that you do not want to forget about ever." Her faith provided consolation and a framework for understanding: "I am a God fearing person and I believe that this terror has called this GREAT NATION back to GOD and PRAYER and patriotism to OUR COUNTRY AND FLAG. Where we need to be. For God has truly BLESSED THE USA." These were the comforts of the jeremiad in its optimistic form. But she was also susceptible to the contemporary prophetic worldview: "It made me think of what it is going to be like when JESUS comes to carry us home. If we think this was CHAOS, just wait until the rapture takes place." Her viewing habits and her beliefs intersected with the crisis to generate an intense emotional response with explicit political implications—in this case commanding allegiance to a God-fearing president. Media exposure and faith reinforced her conviction that 9/11 was an event of profound moral, spiritual, and cultural significance, and that any response would have to be commensurate.[53] Her faith seems to have discouraged her from attempting to understand underlying social processes, or even to involve herself in the deliberations demanded of citizens in a democracy. Her exposure to news coverage seems only to have reinforced her tendency to focus on the moment (and image) of destruction and the impact of the horror on the victims and their families, to resort to an exclusively moralistic rather than analytical framework for making sense of the catastrophe.

Commodifying Calamity

Anthony Lane hoped that the events of September 11 would destroy the public appetite for spectacular images of destruction. He dreamed of a new and redemptive mood of seriousness that would overtake even the entertainment industry. And for a short while it seemed he might get his wish. "News," as media critic Jay Rosen put it, "had entertainment apologizing for itself and its banalities, in those strange weeks after the attacks when Hollywood people were saying (it does not matter if they were totally sincere) how empty their art and industry felt after seeing the destruction in New York and Washington."[54] Warner's shelved the release of the violent Arnold Schwarzenegger vehicle *Collateral Damage*, and the USA network cancelled a planned showing of *The Siege*, a movie about Arab terrorists setting off bombs in New York.[55] It was suddenly unseemly to represent death and destruction in an entertainment venue. And if the news had entertainment apologizing for itself, so too did news shows find themselves apologizing for their own previous incursions into entertainment. Broadcasters took the opportunity to restore blurring boundaries between information and amusement, event and simulation. As Americans turned hungrily to news sources to understand how and why the catastrophe had happened, many broadcasters and print journalists were filled with a powerful sense of their role as servants of the public interest rather than of commerce.[56] It even seemed wrong to interrupt or punctuate news coverage with advertisements. "For a story this big," as a senior vice president of CBS News put it, "it was obvious that you would let that program run an hour instead of a half-hour and that you would have no commercials in it."[57] Indeed, the major networks excluded advertisements from their news programs until September 15. Of course, commercial broadcasters are required by law to operate "in the public interest, convenience and necessity" as the price of access to the public-owned airwaves, but in practice, and with the consent of Congress, media corporations have been allowed to use those airwaves to sell advertising space and to pursue their profits with diminishing concern for educational and informational obligations.[58] In the wake of 9/11, however, for a brief moment, the claims of truth and insight surpassed those of commerce and entertainment. For once, the accountants were silent.

Moreover, while coverage of the calamity tended to the spectacular, a moral calculus inhibited the display of the most shocking images. CNN, like the other networks, adamantly refused to broadcast "graphic" pictures—particularly of workers leaping or falling out of the towers.[59] A WPIX executive producer briefly thought about showing the pictures ("It's happening and it's the truth"), but sensed that this was crossing a line of decency.[60] Indeed, the impulsive sensationalism of American news coverage itself became a target of criticism, with Steve Capus, executive producer of *NBC Nightly News with Tom Brokaw*, insisting that this was no time for the usual hype: "There is a real responsibility right now to just cut out all of that stuff. There is no reason to do it. The language doesn't need to be inflated. The facts speak for themselves and are dramatic enough."[61] Even pictures of the burning towers caused discomfort. "We kept showing pictures of the planes hitting the building," CNN anchor Judy Woodruff recalled. "I began to wince every time I watched that. I thought, 'I hope we don't show that too many times.' "[62] Others were similarly troubled, and after a couple of days ABC refused to show the image of planes crashing into the towers unless it was directly relevant to the story in question; other news agencies promptly followed suit.[63] Woodruff was particularly concerned that coverage of the spectacle would obscure the human story: "It looked so simple: aircraft goes into building, destruction, fire, and smoke. But your mind tried to grab hold of what was happening inside, and it was beyond comprehension."[64] As it turned out, broadcasters turned quickly to the human drama, inserting the disaster into sentimental discourses that were quite as familiar to customers of blockbuster movies as were spectacles of destruction. For a moment, awesome display was displaced by maudlin intimacy as television screens were filled with heartbreaking scenes of weeping mourners and touching testimonials from friends and families of the victims. This restored a valuable emotional dimension to the story, but it gave no greater visibility to the political and historical dimensions of the disaster. Within a week, indeed, the spectacular and the sentimental had been woven into an ethical and aesthetic hybrid entirely familiar to audiences of disaster movies. (Steven Spielberg's lavish 2005 version of *War of the Worlds*, for example, treats the spectacular deaths of millions as a condition for the personal growth of the hero, played by celebrity actor Tom

Cruise; we are asked to expend as much emotion identifying with his tears and fears as on considering the destruction of mankind.)

In this way, the events of September 11 were converted into a human-interest story, into a commodity that could generate substantial profits for commercial news organizations. It is worth reminding ourselves that the television, newspaper, and magazine pictures consumed by the public had owners. Intricate communications and property laws governed the distribution of these images and helped guarantee that the disaster would become a business opportunity.[65] Indeed, a variety of cultural, economic, and political pressures ensured that coverage of this disaster and its aftermath would fall well short of the dreams of serious newscasters. Over the past two decades, the news has increasingly become a venue for converting information into entertainment, or infotainment, and this impulse survived the shock of 9/11.[66] Not only is news a business, it has become a very lucrative one. Indeed, most media conglomerates depend on their news divisions to make money. News has become bait to hook consumers up with the commercials that are the industry's source of revenue. News organizations must attract enough viewers to keep advertisers happy, and they must make a profit in what is essentially a competitive entertainment marketplace, one, moreover, that is diversified and fragmented by a proliferation of cable and Internet offerings. This, according to network bosses, means that the news coverage must stand out, it must be dramatic, it must be arresting. And it has to be cheap. Disasters are relatively cheap to cover, cheaper certainly than foreign news. They fit the mantra of local news ("If it bleeds, it leads") but also bring a cachet of seriousness.

The disaster was rapidly absorbed into the customary entertainment flow and commercials were back on the air by September 15. Having lost as much as $320 million in advertising revenue during the previous week, economic pressures soon became irresistible for a business that measured success in terms of profits. What is striking is how effectively media industries buried awareness of their commercial motives by emphasizing their civic-mindedness. Accordingly, as media critic Lynn Spigel points out, television networks that had implicitly admitted that entertainment and commercials were "in bad taste" were able within days to recast those same phenomena as patriotic: "In short—and most paradoxically—entertainment and commercialism were rearticulated as television's 'public service.'"[67] To attract advertisers, companies began to compete aggressively for ratings, taking this to mean that they had to offer a sensational presentation of the news.

News networks quickly began to deploy entertainment industry devices—dramatic soundtracks, vivid headlines, special effects, hi-tech simulations—to represent the catastrophe and its aftermath. By November, Comedy Central's *The Daily Show* was wringing knowing laughs out of its New York audience with an Ad Nauseam sequence ("America Freaks Out") on the shameless resemblance of newscasts to blockbuster movies. The crisis was deliberately being "jazzed up" to attract larger audiences. "You see," comedian Steve Carell explained, "news is just like any product. It is all about packaging. In this case the product just happens to be our horrible, horrible reality." Disasters were the perfect subjects. "Of course," he continued, "marketing is all about images and the past few weeks have produced some of the most disturbing images in our nation's history." This was "an advertising gold mine." It is worth pointing out that broadcasters read the desires of their audiences with some accuracy. By and large the public seems to have been satisfied with television coverage of 9/11 and its aftermath. According to one *TV Guide* poll, conducted two months after the attacks, for example, 58 percent of respondents judged reports to be "mostly responsible." Only 27 percent judged reports to be "mostly sensational."[68] In fact, the spectacular presentation of the disaster was evidently cathartic for some. Ratings surged for Fox News, the network that offered the most sensational reporting. What is evident is that commercial broadcasters ended up emphasizing image over explanation, appealing to emotions rather than offering complex information.[69]

In a culture that blurs news, commerce, and entertainment a sensational presentation of 9/11 was probably unavoidable.[70] Indeed, for most people raised in the culture of calamity, coverage that did not feature commercials and booming music felt strange, eerie, or even "unreal"—a profound index of the structure of postmodern imaginations.[71] A disaster, in other words, has to be cinematic to meet expectations of authenticity. We know that television reporters assumed they had no information, no news, nothing they could sell, without spectacular images. "I arrived at the scene without a cameraman," one ABC employee later lamented. "Pictures make television, and I couldn't gather any pictures."[72] And not just any picture would do but only one that qualified as a "good shot" or a "great shot."[73] In the case of 9/11, this meant planes hitting buildings or towers burning and falling. Television, but also newspapers and magazines, automatically condensed the catastrophe into a series of iconic images, or logos.[74]

What is clear is that in this mass media society, disasters are most often encountered in a venue that pulls all discussion and representation into the sphere of commercial entertainment. The results are often disconcerting. In December 2004, *TV Guide* listed "The 100 Most Memorable

TV Moments!" promising "magic moments." "You may not agree with all our choices," the editors declared, "but we trust you'll enjoy the view." And what was the number-one event that readers were expected to "enjoy"? "South Tower Collapses." The absurdity of this was obviously not lost on the editors, who omitted the actual picture; instead, the page was dominated by a shot of the number-two event, the moon landing, an altogether more enjoyable spectacle.[75] Although it might be conceded that some of the more nuanced treatments of September 11 and the war on terrorism have occurred in popular culture, the entertainment industry is hardly the best vehicle for presenting the complexity of calamities.[76]

This corporate reorganization of network news has left a deep impression on the way disasters are represented and experienced. A strange brew of market logics, property rights, communications laws, and an apparently rising cultural tolerance, or enthusiasm, for advertising and the dramatic presentation of everyday life has prompted the industry to starve news-gathering services of resources, dramatically curtailing the time devoted to news on network television and the quality of analysis.[77] This has had a particularly devastating impact on international news as foreign correspondents have been recalled and overseas bureaus closed. As a result, news companies were not equipped to treat the attacks of 9/11 with any great substance or insight. "Having thus plucked out their eyes," as Michael Massing wrote at the time, "the networks—suddenly faced with a global crisis—are lunging about in the dark, trying desperately to find their footing."[78] The implications, as he points out, are vast. A functioning democracy requires an informed citizenry. And journalists are supposed to provide the information that enables political engagement. The adulteration of commercial news is a process governed by the economic logics of our times. But disasters, while impressing audiences with the need for reliable reporting about world events, also tend to provoke coverage that is sensational and sentimental and lacking in historical or geopolitical understanding. This contributes to a politics of disaster that favors centralized and authoritarian models. After September 11, the news played a vital role in mobilizing consent for a series of radical policy responses that were sustained more by sentiment than by an understanding of the deeper issues involved and that have had an extraordinary impact on the shaping of the modern, or postmodern, political world.

Emergency Time and the Destruction of Progress

Critics of the society of spectacle from both the Left and Right have tended to insist on the singular passivity of those people who are exposed to a surfeit of dramatic images. "Because of mass culture," as Henri Lefe-bvre famously put it, "by means of a mass culture, everything becomes a *spectacle*, that is, essentially *non-participatory*."[79] Part of my concern here is to substantiate this observation insofar as it speaks to the erosion of deliberative democracy in the age of commercial mass media. But we have to be careful. For if the history of disasters teaches anything it is that spectacles of destruction, even (or perhaps especially) those spectacles displayed in mass culture venues, generate unusually intense emotional attachments and rather vigorous civic involvement. At issue is that this is unlikely to be the sort of revolutionary activity that alone counts, for a leftist intellectual like Lefebvre, as participation. A number of schol-ars have charted the influence on U.S. public policy of round-the-clock cable news coverage of disasters and wars. Piers Robinson, for one, de-scribes how a "CNN effect" can create enough public sympathy to press politicians into taking action to avert humanitarian crises at home and abroad.[80] Certainly, relentless media footage of the burning towers and the suffering of the victims' families ensured that this event remained uppermost in the public consciousness.

One consequence was the greatest outpouring of private charitable aid, up to that point, in the nation's history. The thirty-five largest chari-ties raised over \$2.7 billion for survivors and relatives of the dead, with more than \$1 billion going to the American Red Cross alone; according to surveys, two-thirds of American households contributed time, money, or supplies.[81] Moreover, public sentiment was sufficiently aroused to en-courage Congress to authorize massive federal relief and compensation payments. The 9/11 Fund, for example, disbursed \$7 billion, an aver-age of \$2.1 million in tax-free payments to each family of those killed in the attacks. It also paid out an average of \$400,000 per person to cover 2,680 injury claims, mostly to relief and rescue workers who acquired lung problems after breathing in dust from the debris.[82] These astonish-ing figures can be explained in several ways. One is that legal and institu-tional structures were now in place to make it easy to raise and distribute funds for the victims. The existence of the American Red Cross, for ex-ample, provided an efficient mechanism for raising and spending money. The massive contributions of the federal government, meanwhile, were enabled by a series of laws, most notably the Robert T. Stafford Disaster Relief and Emergency Act of 1988, assembled over the past fifty years to combat natural calamities. Officials in New York City lobbied for new federal laws to meet the unique demands of 9/11, to cover "long-term en-vironmental liabilities and the need for heightened security efforts in the immediate aftermath of a terrorist attack."[83] But the Federal Emergency

Management Agency determined that existing disaster laws contained enough "flexibility" to ensure prompt and appropriate aid from Washington. The president quickly waived the legal requirement compelling states and local governments to contribute a share of FEMA's costs, and Congress appropriated over $20 billion to help New York City recover from the catastrophe.[84]

Conservative commentator Jeff Jacoby was among those who later questioned the arbitrariness of the awards. Why should the federal government have restituted the relatives of these victims, many of whom were affluent, he asked, when aid was not offered to families affected by hurricanes or earthquakes or even the first World Trade Center bombing in 1993.[85] The demand for a strong and generous response in 2001, however, was irresistible. People were filled with a powerful desire to do something, anything, to help. As one commentator explained, "Disaster response and charity giving—from blood donations to soup kitchens and million-dollar payouts to victims' families—were a key part of the American catharsis."[86] But why should Americans have required catharsis? As Fred Jameson points out, there was nothing "natural" about the outpouring of emotion that followed the attacks of September 11. It was not, in his words, "self-explanatory for masses of people to be devastated by catastrophe in which they have lost no one they know, in a place with which they have no particular connections."[87] In fact, as we have seen, this sympathy for suffering fellow Americans had a long history, and media stories about disasters had long contributed to the making of an affective community of compassion and concern. What we can say is that this emotional "devastation" was intensified and given shape by coverage of 9/11.

Just as coverage of the attacks stimulated compassion and concern, so too did it feed unfocused feelings of dread and hostility. According to media critics, the constant parade of disasters and acts of violence across our television screens has produced a "culture of fear" that governs the politics of our times.[88] The exact relationship between public anxiety and public policy is disputed, but antiestablishment filmmaker Michael Moore explains it this way: "We create this culture of fear and it feeds all the wrong things. Ignorance leads to fear and fear leads to hate and hate leads to violence. And that's the equation."[89] Although this analysis has the virtue of clarity, matters are rather more complex. For one thing, as Moore knows, there are useful forms of fear that alert us to genuine dangers, save us from complacency, and produce informed and energetic political involvement. What is really at issue for critics such as Moore, in other words, is not the production of fear per se but rather the manipulation of fear without a proper context.[90]

Although conventional debates about violence on television tend to revolve around the question of whether they desensitize viewers and thereby encourage them to become belligerent—a doubtful claim, at best—what does seem clear is that these images generate what sociologist George Gerbner calls a "mean-world syndrome," whereby exposure to spectacles of chaos produces a sense of disquiet and an abiding suspicion of strangers. Fearful viewers, according to surveys, are more likely to favor strong security measures and favor expenditures on law and order rather than on social programs.[91]

Sensationalist television coverage of September 11 did worry viewers.[92] Moreover, media outlets tended to follow the lead of government leaders and script the disaster and the subsequent war on terrorism according to familiar entertainment industry conventions—converting a fiendishly complex geopolitical situation into a mortal struggle between good and evil. Slapping slogans like "America under Siege" and "America Fights Back" over their broadcasts, CNN and Fox News, in particular, put an explicitly nationalistic construction on the calamity.[93] Meanwhile, CBS anchor Dan Rather openly endorsed the partisan agendas of the Bush administration, announcing on the *David Letterman Show* that "George Bush is the president, he makes the decisions and, you know, as just one American, he wants me to line up, just tell me where." And he recycled Bush's unhelpful explanation for why the terrorists had attacked the United States: "Because they're evil, and because they're jealous of us."[94] Fox News went even further, unapologetically blurring the lines between journalism and politics, adding an American flag to its screen on September 11 and openly supporting "our" war as the only acceptable response to the destruction of the twin towers and the Pentagon.[95]

CNN was not quite so cynical in its treatment of data, but it too massaged the news. According to one frame-by-frame analysis of the first twelve hours of coverage, the network "relied almost exclusively on current and former government officials to provide interpretation of the day's events" and presented the attack in such a way as to create "the impression that war was inevitable and necessary to combat the horror and devastation that Americans had just witnessed."[96] More striking yet, as media historian Robert McChesney noted, the network broadcast two versions of the Afghanistan campaign, "a critical one for the global audience, and a sugarcoated one for Americans." And CNN president Walter Isaacson explicitly ordered his subordinates to defend the war on terrorism on the air.[97] Lacking detailed and complex information about the causes and consequences of 9/11, it is little wonder that few Americans seemed willing or able to subject government responses to judicious and critical evaluation. Attempts to take a nuanced position were likely to be shouted down as treasonous. Thus did the right-wing television personality Bill O'Reilly berate Phil Donahue on an ABC broadcast on October 3, 2001, accusing him of dishonoring the victims of the attacks by proposing that the United States collaborate with the United Nations to construct a multifaceted response to terrorism rather than resort solely to military strikes against targets in Afghanistan.

The entertainment media and apocalyptic theology both tend to present politics and morality in black-and-white terms, treating the world as a place where "innocence" is always imperiled and where retribution is demanded against violators of virtue. Both discourses privilege the sentimental and favor personal morality over political knowledge to such an extent that complexity can begin to feel like the last refuge of fools and the corrupt.[98] And both encourage an inflation of rhetoric such as the vow of the president to capture Osama bin Laden "dead or alive," launching a war with an apocalyptic Hollywood-sounding title (Operation Infinite Justice), while, by some reports, conducting hostilities as if directing a movie.[99] One symptom was the abandonment of the doctrine of proportionate response and the substitution of a retributive politics, wherein ends justified or obscured the means of American foreign policy initiatives.

Disasters, as we have seen, have often put pressure on civil liberties. Tim LaHaye was among those lamenting that the tragedy would "be used by many as an excuse to give 'Big Brother' type enthusiasts an excuse to strip the coveted personal freedoms enjoyed by Americans to allow in the name of 'national security' the right to impose more government restrictions on us." He had no doubt that, in the shadow of calamity, people would "trade personal freedom for national safety."[100] Of course, civil liberties have tended to be restored once a disaster has been brought under control and recovery has been achieved. What makes 9/11 different from other disasters, if not from other hot and cold wars, is the attempt by political leaders to institutionalize the disaster, claiming that it has launched an age of permanent emergency. Jérôme Bindé, director of the Analysis and Forecasting Office of UNESCO, has argued that political decision making is becoming increasingly impaired by "the tyranny of emergency time." Writing before 9/11, he maintained that emergency time had become "the quintessential paradigm of our times and an exclusive value of our societies."[101] As a result leaders were constantly reacting on the fly to crises rather than deliberating how best to mitigate or prevent them. Bindé attributed the origins of emergency time to those technological developments of the modern world that were speeding up the pace of life, but his analysis obviously has implications for the contemporary politics of disaster. Sociologist Henry Giroux explicitly made the link after 9/11, arguing that the main effect of "emergency time in the context of Bush's 'war against terrorism'" had been to displace "radical secularism for a religious rhetoric and discourse." In other words, it had prepared the cultural space for a religious worldview that "dispenses with the task of critically engaging and translating the elaborate web of historical, social, and political factors that underscore and give meaning to the broader explanations for terrorism. Instead, the complexity of politics dissolves into the language of 'crusades,' 'infidels,' 'goodness,' and 'evil.'"[102] And, crucially, such language leaves little room or legitimacy for domestic dissent.

The events of September 11 did lead to a new balance between civil liberties and the security demands of the state. The 9/11 Commission report made it amply clear that U.S. institutions were not equipped to respond effectively to terrorist attacks.[103] Reading the report, it is easy to conclude that reforms were necessary, that greater policing powers and more integration of government agencies might have provided more security against a real and enduring threat. What is striking, however, is that the calamity was seized on as an opportunity to implement a broad program of political initiatives that seemed to have little to do with security and everything to do with political and economic opportunism. Anthropologist John D. Kelly argues that the Bush administration and its acolytes "already, on September 10, 2001, wanted a day one, a new era, a reinvention; it was shopping for a dream."[104] One year before, the Project for the New American Century (PNAC), an influential policy organization that claimed Dick Cheney, Donald Rumsfeld, Jeb Bush, and Paul Wolfowitz among the signatories of its statement of principles, had written a blueprint for the implementation of a neoconservative political agenda that involved the preservation of "American preeminence" abroad, beginning with a war against Iraq, as well as the consolidation of political power at home. The architects of this program understood that the process of realizing their objectives was "likely to be a long one, absent some catastrophic and catalyzing event—like a new Pearl Harbor."[105] Christopher Maletz, assistant director of the PNAC, was asked what this meant. "Without some disaster or catastrophic event," he explained, military leaders and politicians would have rejected the plan.[106] And sure enough, immediately after September 11, Secretary of Defense Rumsfeld was describing the calamity as an "opportunity" to launch a war against Iraq.[107] Richard A. Clarke, the national coordinator for security and counterterrorism, recalled walking into a meeting at the White

House on September 12 and realizing "with almost sharp physical pain that Rumsfeld and Wolfowitz were going to try to take advantage of this national tragedy to promote their agenda about Iraq."[108] To be sure he too viewed 9/11 as an opportunity to improve U.S. defenses in the age of terrorism, but he was aghast at this particular turn of events. "America," as he recognized, "usually waits for a disaster before it responds to a threat. We have had that disaster." But rather than seize the moment to implement the reforms that might secure the United States against future attacks, misadventures in Iraq and the erosion of civil liberties at home had, in his view, made the nation more, not less, vulnerable to "terrorist disasters."[109]

Certainly, at home, the Bush administration took advantage of public outrage and fear to coerce a mostly willing Congress into passing a series of measures that radically expanded the policing powers of military and civil authorities—including the USA Patriot Act, signed into law on October 26, 2001—to facilitate "search and seizure," military tribunals, secret arrests and trials, wiretapping, and the formation of a vast new government agency, the Department of Homeland Security, in the summer of 2002. Whether or not these reforms have made Americans more secure, what is clear is that they have had significant economic implications.

Catastrophes, as we have seen, have been understood as material blessings since the nineteenth century. Faith in economic progress has encouraged business leaders, in particular, to grasp destruction as an opportunity for innovation and revitalization. September 11 generated plenty of talk about the prospects it delivered for political and cultural renewal, but few expected it to promote economic growth. To be sure, some officials and commentators hoped that this latest catastrophe would be an occasion to renovate transit systems and launch a new wave of state-of-the-art construction in Manhattan.[110] But if the American imagination of disaster was shaped throughout much of the twentieth century by an expectation that ruination was a valuable instrument of renewal, observers in 2001 were more likely to suspect that the destruction of the twin towers would trigger a severe and prolonged economic crisis.[111] Much of this gloom, of course, can be explained by the fact that this was an attack rather than a natural disaster. Cities had always been vulnerable to fires and floods and earthquakes, but it could always be expected that new technologies would make them safer. It was much harder to defend against an enemy that was determined to target and destroy buildings by any means necessary, especially structures designed as monuments to American ambition and wealth and power.

Pessimism about the likely economic effects of September 11 also speaks to broader cultural anxieties about the financial and environmental sustainability of the current economic order. In the context of a deepening recession, the destruction of fifteen million square feet of prime office space, the unavailability of 36 percent of downtown office space, and the fact that 14,632 businesses were "destroyed, damaged, or significantly disrupted" by the attacks was a source of despondency for economists, commentators, and ordinary folk alike.[112] Any interruption to commerce presented itself as a mortal threat to the system. No wonder that President Bush should declare on the day of the attacks that he wanted "the economy back, open for business right away, banks, the stock market, everything tomorrow."[113] But the costs of a commitment to economic activity at the expense of other considerations were starkly exposed in this instance. Health matters, in particular, were overlooked as government officials, even those at the Environmental Protection Agency, assured New Yorkers that there would be no "long-term health risks" from breathing asbestos and other pollutants in the vicinity of Ground Zero.[114] Although this was not a story that captured the attention of the media or of politicians, the Natural Resources Defense Council determined that the attacks "constituted an unprecedented environmental assault for Lower Manhattan." Air pollution levels there, according to tests conducted in October 2001, were worse than in Kuwait when the sky was blackened by burning oil fires during the Gulf War.[115] The air was so noxious that more than ten thousand New Yorkers, many of whom were returning to jobs and homes and schools in the days after the attacks, suffered "short-term health ailments."[116] Business as usual, in other words, itself had a calamitous dimension. And some commentators generalized this impression. In August 2002, the Carnegie Endowment for International Peace, for example, concluded that the attacks had little effect on either deepening the existing recession or in facilitating the subsequent recovery. But this was more than the authors could say of huge corporate scandals at energy giant Enron or at WorldCom. "So far," the report noted tersely, "Kenneth Lay, Bernie Ebbers & Co. have been responsible for more damage than has Osama bin Laden."[117]

Significantly, business and government leaders took advantage of the disaster to further "deregulate" the economy, or rather to introduce new legal and institutional mechanisms that released multinational corporations and markets from public oversight and restraint. September 11, in other words, facilitated the concentration of both political and corporate power. As we saw in chapter 2, the destruction of property has tended in the modern industrial age to have some advantageous effects for an economy of overproduction in which obsolescence is a precondition for stimulating consumer demand and for economic innovation. In the 1950s, governments and businesses tended to agree that this dynamic commercial system depended on the stabilizing influence of the state, as manifested in the provision of social welfare and investment in physical infrastructure. By the 1970s, as the crisis of overproduction entered a new phase, businesses faced growing pressures to seek new markets and to develop new and more flexible organizational structures. The exact nature of these conditions is hard to pinpoint with any precision because they are so complex, but according to the persuasive account offered by David Harvey, the economy began to shift in the 1970s from a Fordist system of mass production and standardization (characterized by corporate accommodation to labor unions and a welfare state) to a post-Fordist system of capital accumulation that emphasized "flexibility"—that is, a shift to specialized production, niche marketing, a more opportunistic approach to reducing labor costs (for example, moving U.S. plants overseas), and hostility to the restrictions and restraints of the regulatory state. One consistent demand of post-Fordist corporations was for a rollback of market regulations and assistance in gaining greater access to global labor and resource markets.[118] Deregulation and privatization were the watchwords of the new capitalist dispensation.

One might imagine, then, that businesses would look dimly on any concentration of federal power in the wake of 9/11, but the consolidation of the disaster-security state has if anything been embraced by corporate America. According to sociologist George Steinmetz, this is only to be expected. Sharing Harvey's understanding of capitalism as a system with a built-in tendency to crisis as a result of the constant trend toward overproduction, he argues that a post-Fordist economic system is actually likely to be best served, in the short run at least, by a political order that facilitates the liberalization of global markets while neutralizing opposition to globalization on the terms of U.S. business through a new imperialism of preemptive strikes abroad and a more authoritarian police state at home. Although he tends to be more interested in modeling relationships between modes of capital accumulation and modes of state formation, he maintains that 9/11 provided an opportunity for the "U.S. state to implement the politico-ideological form that is probably the most suitable complement in structural terms to its globally dominant post-Fordist economy."[119] But, as should be clear by now, it is not enough to say that 9/11 was a "contingency" that presented an opening for social experimentation. It was imagined as an opportunity for political and economic elites only because of the long history of representing and imagining disaster as a catalyst for improvement.

Steinmetz is flexible enough to recognize that this new mode of regulation might turn out to be transitory and, moreover, that it would be particularly vulnerable to a sustained economic crisis. Adding a social dimension to this argument, I suggest that an excess of domestic authoritarianism and social chaos might produce sufficient revulsion to compel the government, however incompletely, to restore some of its lost functions as a provider of social welfare. There are some signs of this happening after Hurricane Katrina in 2005, with a resurgence of media and popular interest in problems of race, class, and poverty. In the meantime, creative destruction continues apace, facilitated by a political response to September 11 that seems to have set a stage for future environmental, social, and military catastrophes.

Waiting for the Disaster

After all, disaster is my muse!
ART SPIEGELMAN, *In the Shadow of No Towers*, 2004

Art Spiegelman was compelled by the "disaster" of September 11, 2001, to "make comix" in order to figure out what had happened on that day and what it all meant. Such a response was no doubt obligatory for a politically engaged professional comic book artist, but when we consider the extraordinary determination of Americans to enfold the catastrophe in words and images (letters, memoirs, blogs, novels, poems, songs, prayers, speeches, and so forth), do we not see evidence here for a more general conclusion: that calamity is still an American muse, a source of enormous cultural creativity and an inspiration for social involvement?

If disasters are muses, however, they have also become . . . amusing. They have been absorbed into a mass media industry that treats them as sources of entertainment. Disasters, like everything else in our postmodern world, are instantly commodified. Even Spiegelman, the angst-ridden artist, the inveterate critic of business as usual, circulated his musings in a medium and a marketplace (the profit-driven publishing industry) that mingles message and merriment. While his comix promised insight, they also (necessarily) offered entertainment, albeit of a mordant variety.[120] His text, then, was itself a product of the historical transformations charted in this book that have led to the packaging of spectacular disasters as thrilling products. That is not to say that we should dismiss Spiegelman's art as an exercise in cynicism or opportunism. Like all of us, he has to move through, and think within the terms of, a consumer society.[121] Like all of us, he is an effect of the culture of calamity. But he always endeavors to place his products at the service of studiously acquired political values and philosophical ideas. Indeed, his readers may not be so different from the consumers of Hollywood blockbusters to the extent that they look to his compositions for therapy *and* instruction *and* emotional excitement. We want to know how to cope and survive in a world of calamity. To this end, what may be most valuable about his analysis is his refusal to endorse the official narrative of catastrophe—wherein disaster demands an expansion of government authority (at the expense of civil liberties) and validates ceaseless economic development heedless of long-term environmental and social consequences. Indeed, his task seems to be to find some relief, some release from the grip of the trauma, without sinking into a media-supplied "narcotized normalcy." In his view, television is the source of a therapeutic amnesia that is all the more dangerous for being so appealing. It is what enabled people to cut the events of 9/11 "down to size, to little more than last season's most compelling media event." He believes that it was direct exposure to the calamity that spared him this resolution: "Everyone around the world with access to a television set saw the cataclysmic destruction of those towers, saw it in constant replay, burning—and burning itself into our collective retina. What slowed down my own amnesiac responses is simply that I first experienced those events unmediated by television."[122] He did not see the first plane hit the tower, but heard the crash while walking in lower Manhattan. All the media could offer, according to Marianne Hirsch's reading of Spiegelman's critique, was "the self-blinding of 'percepticide,' we can live with ourselves as we look without seeing, see without doing, understand without saying or writing."[123] Spiegelman himself was clearly determined to create an unsettling art that allowed us to see the disaster responsibly.

Spiegelman's art, like his world, is always darkened (and illuminated) by catastrophe. If *Maus*, the comic book that made him a household name, was an attempt to come to terms with the Holocaust, *In the Shadow of No Towers* is an imaginative endeavor to make sense of the ruination of Manhattan and, more broadly, of the catastrophe of modernity. What is striking and unsettling about his account is its bleakness. This can be explained partly in terms of his location (living in Lower Soho, just blocks away from the stricken towers), his temperament ("I tend to be easily unhinged"), and his personal history as a descendant of Holocaust survivors. It is tempting to locate his work within a lineage of "neurotic" Jewish comedians who expect things to turn out badly. Certainly he was, in his own words, traumatized by the attack, unable to think about the future, let alone to imagine a better one: "That's when Time stands still at the moment of trauma" (2). Initially he was unable to commit himself to long-term projects, though he was able to turn out the extraordinarily moving and powerful black-on-black cover for the first postdisaster edition of the *New Yorker*. But over time he devised a format that suited his uncertainty and bewilderment, the single-page comic strip. As he recorded, "The idea of working in single page units corresponded to my existential conviction that I might not live long enough to see them published." He found a postmodern art form, in other words, that expressed his postmodern disorientation: "The collagelike nature of a newspaper page encouraged my impulse to juxtapose my fragmentary thoughts in different styles."[124]

If disasters past had propelled other Americans enthusiastically into the future, this new catastrophe filled Spiegelman with uncertainty and fear. He was unable to find solace in apocalyptic faith. Judgment Day figured in his work as a calamity to be avoided (3); he satirized yearnings for redemption as the dangerous folly of a government launched on a "war to begin all wars" (7). The Bible offered no solace—this could be found only in the bleaker margins of popular culture, and then only fleetingly: "My 'leaders' are reading the Book of Revelations . . . I'm reading the paranoid science fiction of Philip K. Dick" (7). And yet even Spiegelman looked to September 11 for some secular salvation. For him this was to be measured in terms of a new and more compassionate globalism. Indeed, he was affronted by government's failure to grasp the opportunity presented by the disaster "to bring the community of nations together" (10). Instead of inspiring and enabling a proper modern response (making the world safer, improving the conditions of life) what had ensued was "the same old deadly business as usual" (8). While the corporate media focused unrelentingly on the spectacle of the calamity, conservative political "leaders" had "immediately instrumentalized the attack for their own agendas," reducing 9/11 "to a war recruitment poster" (preface). The disaster had served a national security state that, according to Spiegelman, was more interested in surveillance and social control ("the government began to move into full dystopian Big Brother mode") than in making "America genuinely safer."

Spiegelman, then, is aware of the genuinely energizing and potentially progressive contributions of disasters to modern life, but he does properly insist that we see events like 9/11 as symptoms of a catastrophic modern order that has other devastating consequences: poverty, unemployment, homelessness, and alienation. What is appealing about his

FIG 18. Art Spiegelman laments the failure to heed the lessons of the September 11, 2001 disaster. From *In the Shadow of No Towers* by Art Spiegelman. © 2004 by Art Spiegelman. Reproduced by permission of Pantheon Books, a division of Random House, Inc.

vision is his fierce and principled resistance to the seductions of calamity, to the simple (final) solutions promised by apocalyptic theology and modernization theory—in short, his refusal to trust in disasters to save us from our disasters. It is our challenge, he suggests, to recognize that we dwell in the shadow of calamity and to learn the proper lessons. It is our challenge to cultivate a tragic sense of life, that is to say, to learn to live graciously and courageously and responsibly in a world of disaster, and to resist the actions and reactions that are propelling us toward what Spiegelman, with deliberate theological resonance, calls "the end of the world."

Epilogue

What many people say in this film is that what happened in New Orleans is unprecedented. Never before in the history of the United States has the federal government turned its back on its own citizens in the manner that they did, with the slow response to people who needed help. . . . People in New Orleans are up in arms about [the lack of] progress. People wanna move back. New Orleans was a predominantly African American city, and its black citizens were dispersed to forty-six other states. People wanna come home, but there's nowhere for them to live. They wanna work. The thing is just all messed up.

SPIKE LEE interview about his 2006 HBO documentary on Hurricane Katrina, *When the Levees Broke: A Requiem in Four Parts*

Just four years after the terrorist attacks of September 11, 2001, the United States endured the most devastating natural disaster in its history. At the end of August 2005, Hurricane Katrina smacked into the Gulf Coast with extraordinary fury. With winds whipping through the region at up to 130 mph and waves surging as high as twenty-seven feet, the storm devastated broad swathes of Louisiana, Mississippi, and Alabama. By the time the tempest had passed, almost $100 billion worth of property was in ruins, 300,000 homes were obliterated or uninhabitable, 750,000 people had been displaced, 1,836 people were dead, and a further 750 were reportedly missing.[1] New Orleans was flooded when three of the levees protecting the city were breached; Lake Pontchartrain poured into downtown neighborhoods, leaving 80 percent of the city under as much as twenty feet of water. For the first time in American history, a major urban center was emptied as residents fled inland; tens of thousands of these "refugees" suffered for days without adequate food, medicine, or shelter.

Although federal officials including Michael Chertoff, secretary of the Department of Homeland Security (DHS), quickly claimed that nobody could have anticipated such a colossal disaster, the confluence of public policies, economic practices, and environmental considerations traced in this book suggest that it was more likely to happen than not.[2] Moreover, the Federal Emergency Management Agency itself had funded an exercise the previous summer modeling the impact of a strong hurricane ("Pam") on the city. In some ways this was a curious case of fact following fiction. In the novel *White Noise*, written two decades before, Don DeLillo describes a simulated evacuation conducted by a shadowy, and faintly ridiculous, private company named Advanced Disaster Management. The disaster experts become so absorbed in their graphs and charts that they experience a real calamity as an annoying deviation from the ideal. In New Orleans, the task of simulating Hurricane Pam was farmed out to a real-life private sector concern: Innovative Emergency Management, Inc. But while an influential congressional report would later lament a tendency of government agencies to think too much in abstract terms, arguing that planners had "to stop waiting for the disaster that fits our response plan and instead design a scalable capacity to meet whatever Mother Nature throws at us,"[3] the committee that wrote the report was most struck by how closely the virtual hurricane from 2004 resembled the real thing in 2005. Ominously, disaster specialists had predicted that a strong storm would likely destroy more than half a million buildings and kill as many as sixty thousand people. The problem was that little had been done at local, state, or federal levels to act on this information.[4]

Meanwhile, in the period right before Katrina struck, the *New Orleans Times-Picayune* had run a high-profile series claiming that a major calamity was inevitable unless the federal government reversed cutbacks in funding for storm protection. "No one," the editors asserted after the storm hit, "can say they didn't see it coming."[5] Although the newspaper blamed the Bush administration for diverting money from local engineering projects to pay for the Iraq War and to fund tax cuts for the wealthy, many commentators also noted the deleterious effects of developing the wetlands and barrier islands on which New Orleans depended for natural protection against storm surges. Thus did celebrated local musician Dr. John reject any suggestion that his city had died "a natural

FIG 19. New Orleans submerged after Hurricane Katrina, September 2005. Photograph courtesy of AP Images.

death." On the contrary, he countered, this was a man-made disaster, a "coldblooded murder."[6] Such statements have often been made in the wake of natural disasters, but rarely have they achieved as much traction in the mainstream media as they did after Katrina.

The sheer extent of the destruction and suffering challenged the comforting assumption that disasters were testing times that brought out the best in the American people and its system of governance. To be sure, financial analysts insisted on the long-term economic benefits of this urban catastrophe. Bob Doll, the president and chief investment officer of Merrill Lynch Investment Managers, for example, declared that financial losses would be recovered within months, predicting that the enormous task of rebuilding would stimulate the economy and ultimately add to the gross national product. "The U.S. economy," he explained, "has taken a bunch of hits over time, and history has shown it to be pretty resilient."[7] The spirit of creative destruction, in other words, was alive and well, at least in those financial circles where profits depended on convincing investors that the future is always bright. Despite Congressional Budget Office estimates that four hundred thousand jobs would be lost and that the economy would slow down for one or two quarters, the Dow Jones industrial average was soon three hundred points higher than it had been on the eve of the hurricane.[8]

But even as politicians and media commentators resorted to established conventions in their stories about the hurricane, populating their accounts with heroes and celebrating the fortitude of the American people, they found it harder than usual to absorb Hurricane Katrina into a triumphalist narrative. The covers of current affairs magazines paired images of despair and angry headlines: "The Shaming of America," "Disaster and Disgrace," "System Failure," "Lessons of a National Shame," "Who Screwed Up."[9] Newspaper and television correspondents treated the disaster as a political fiasco. And congressional reports were no less withering in their criticisms. The Select Bipartisan Committee to Investigate the Preparation for and Response to Hurricane Katrina appointed by the House of Representatives concluded bluntly: "Katrina was a national failure, an abdication of the most solemn obligation to provide for the common welfare. At every level—individual, corporate, philanthropic, and governmental—we failed to meet the challenge that was Katrina. In this cautionary tale, all the little pigs built houses of straw."[10] It was clear to most observers that Washington was unable to provide for the safety of the American people in spite of the formidable range of institutional mechanisms and resources mobilized for such a task since World War II. Although the "war on terror" had enabled a massive expansion of the disaster-security state, this did not seem to have made the management of catastrophe any more effective. Hurricane Katrina called into question the whole efficacy of the National Response Plan adopted in February 2003 to coordinate disaster protection in the post-9/11 world. FEMA, in particular, stood exposed as an agency in disarray, run by a director, Michael Brown, who, like many of his colleagues, had been appointed for his political connections rather than for any experience in the field of disaster relief. FEMA was evidently suffering from a neglect driven both by ideological and strategic considerations. After all, Joe Allbaugh, who directed the agency before Brown, had openly disparaged federal disaster relief as "an oversized entitlement program" in 2001.[11] Allbaugh's criticism is best understood within the context of a broad-based Republican-led campaign against "big government," but as we saw in chapter 4, FEMA had in some respects become an entitlement program, and one that disproportionately benefited the affluent. In the 1980s and 1990s, the agency had become a mechanism for redistributing resources from social welfare programs to risk management initiatives. After 2000, however, FEMA had been starved of resources and qualified personnel. In 2003, it was absorbed into the Department of Homeland Security and lost its independent status.[12] Indeed, as in the 1980s, a

FIG 20. The cover of *Newsweek*, September 19, 2005.

preoccupation with national and civil defense had distracted the agency from its mandate to respond to natural disasters.[13]

While there was plenty of indignation about the failure of government to protect the American people, what may be most striking is the

degree to which the hurricane disaster focused attention on the environmental and social costs of modern development. Katrina occasioned a
series of high-profile jeremiads about the perils of capitalism. Writing in
Newsweek, for example, Anna Quindlen insisted that the American way
of life was responsible for turning an unavoidable storm into a major
catastrophe. "New Orleans," by her account, "lived for 80 years with
the granddaddy of all environmentally misguided plans, the project that
straightened out the mighty Mississippi so its banks would be more hospitable to homes and businesses." This had bought short-term benefits,
including a reduction in floods, but it had stored up problems for the
future: "Little by little the seductive city at the river's mouth became
like one of those denuded developments built after clear-cutting. It was
left with no natural protection, girded with a jerry-built belt of walled-
off water, its marshland and barrier islands gone, a sitting duck for a big
storm."[14] According to a report by the American Society of Civil Engineers in 2004, human development had led to the erosion of fifteen
hundred square miles of natural coastal barriers since the 1950s.[15] And
federal flood control was part of the problem. As historian John M. Barry
explained, the success of levees in preventing floods along the Mississippi
had ensured that "the river no longer replenished the land each year with
silt." As a result the parishes of south Louisiana were sinking, with "the
equivalent of the island of Manhattan" disappearing every ten months.[16]
Moreover, engineering initiatives had committed the United States to
the expensive maintenance of an elaborate system of flood defenses in
New Orleans. The city, which is six feet below sea level, had become
increasingly dependent on technological protections, including twelve
hundred miles of levees and floodwalls that quickly deteriorated when
federal funding was reduced, as it had been before Hurricane Katrina.[17]
This suggests that there is not enough money to ensure the protection of
settlements along the Mississippi and the Gulf Coast through engineering means alone. Searching for long-range solutions, news magazines by
and large agreed that wetlands, which act as a sponge and thus provide
a buffer against storm surges, had to be restored if the Big Easy was to
survive future hurricanes.[18]

Although New Orleans is more vulnerable to disasters than most
American cities, Quindlen seized on its fate as a paradigm of the hazards
of modernity. "Everywhere in the country," she contended, "wetlands
disappeared and parking lots bloomed during the past half century of
mindless growth, in which bigger was always presumed to be better."
Like Increase Mather three centuries earlier, she insisted that Americans
were on a course to greater disasters in the future unless they were to

change their ways. She too identified materialism and greed as fundamental problems, but she was more concerned with saving the planet
than with saving souls. "Consumption," she explained, "used to be the
name for a mortal wasting disease. It still is." Whereas past disasters had
tended to reinforce a commitment to capitalist forms of development,
Quindlen argued that this was no longer an option. New Orleans would
be rebuilt, of course, the question was how: "In the heedless, grasping
fashion in which so much of this country has been built in the past 50
years, which has led to a continuous loop of floods, fires and filth in the
air and water? Or could the new New Orleans be the first city of a new
era, in which the demands of development and commerce are carefully
balanced against the good of the land and, in the long run, the good of its
people?"[19] In effect, she was renouncing the logic of creative destruction,
at least in its most expansive forms.

Quindlen was not alone. The challenge of our time, as geophysicist
Klaus Jacob put it, was "to constructively deconstruct, not destructively
reconstruct."[20] And this meant heeding natural limits. Indeed, it suddenly became respectable to acknowledge the connection long apparent
to those in scientific circles between industrial production, carbon dioxide emissions, global warming, and the increasing ferocity of hurricanes.
Environmentalism reigned, at least for a moment, as mainstream commentators argued that the lesson of the fuel shortages caused by damage
to oil platforms and refineries in the Gulf of Mexico was the need for
higher oil and gas taxes so as to cut back on the consumption of dwindling fossil fuels.[21]

Hurricane Katrina also focused demands for the restoration of a social
contract between government and the people. For the editors of the *New
Republic*, the calamity was an occasion to remind politicians of the virtues
of true public service. "American history over the last hundred years,"
they wrote, "is a stirring tale of government in the proud and largely
effective service of compassion." Hence "the ironic history of the Bush
administration," they argued, which had constantly been compelled by
human needs at home and abroad "to betray its philosophy of small and
limited government." Disaster, they asserted, was the best advertisement
and argument for the activist state. "Sometimes," they concluded, " 'we'
cannot take care of our own; only our government can."[22] And here security explicitly included the protection from destitution of the most vulnerable members of society.

The sudden attention by media and politicians to the issues of class,
race, and poverty raised by Hurricane Katrina was especially striking.
After previous disasters, Chicago in 1871 for example, the demands of

reconstruction had tended to obscure the social costs of capitalist development. When the poor did feature in media reports it was likely to be as a source of danger. While television and newspaper reports in 2005 also featured (exaggerated or baseless) stories of blacks looting and pillaging in New Orleans, a more empathetic counternarrative competed for headlines. According to the *New Republic*, one effect of disasters was to reveal "how we live," and the "chilling" lesson here was not only that the poor had been abandoned but that this was symptomatic of a social order that treated the poor in general, and people of color in particular, with contempt.[23] Lt. Gen. Russel Honoré, the black soldier who led the U.S. military effort, added a cultural critique, speculating that help had been late in coming to New Orleans in part because first responders were "afraid of big crowds of poor people." This, he concluded, was not simply a matter of Americans reacting to this disaster as if it were like a movie so much as "people believing the movie."[24] And this movie was evidently as much in the tradition of *Birth of a Nation* as it was that of the disaster blockbuster; it was as much a spectacle of race as it was a spectacle of destruction. After a few days, Hurricane Katrina became a story about the special and unmerited burdens of the poor. Journalists slammed an evacuation plan that failed to make public transportation available for the 35 percent of black households who did not have cars, and they drew attention to the special vulnerability of low-income neighborhoods that tended to be located on low-lying land and shielded, or rather exposed, by defective levees.[25] Craig E. Colten, a geologist at Louisiana State University, condensed this social truth into a memorable sound bite: "Out West, there is a saying that water flows to money. But in New Orleans, water flows away from money." This disaster, in other words, exposed the privileges of power and wealth in American society: "Those with resources who control where the drainage goes have always chosen to live on high ground. So the people in the low areas were hardest hit."[26]

Just as Hurricane Katrina brought environmental matters to public attention, so too did it bring rare visibility to the poor, and in a context that encouraged compassion rather than condemnation. It took a hurricane, Jonathan Alter wrote in *Newsweek*, "a catastrophe like Katrina to strip away the old evasions, hypocrisies and not-so-benign neglect." Most of the victims had been poor and black, but because they could draw on the deep wells of sympathy traditionally reserved for disaster victims, the travails of "the other America" caught the public imagination in a way unknown since the heyday of the War on Poverty in the 1960s.[27] The media spotlight commanded by catastrophe was crucial here. Broadcasters had overlooked the poor for over a decade because their appearance on television screens, in Alter's words, was bad for ratings, causing "viewers to hit the remote."[28] But coverage of Katrina turned poverty and race into a dramatic spectacle. As Noam Scheiber wrote in the *New Republic*, it took a few days to breach "the mental levee blocking comments on the victims' race and class. But once that levee finally broke, it washed away pretty quickly."[29] Not only that, but televised images of the horrendous conditions faced by survivors exposed the falsity of the claims by leading government officials such as Michael Chertoff that things were not as bad as they seemed. "Not that bad?" By way of an answer, all Senate Democratic leader Harry Reid had to say was "Turn on your TV."[30]

In August 1955, President Eisenhower took to the air to survey the damage caused in New England by Hurricane Diane. As we saw in chapter 4, this was an early attempt by the first president of the television age to turn a disaster into a public relations exercise, but it was also an occasion for advertising the power of the modern industrial state as a bulwark against catastrophic threats to order. Fifty years later, on August 31, 2005, President George W. Bush flew over Louisiana to survey the effects of Hurricane Katrina. In an echo of the earlier event, members of the press corps were invited to take pictures of the commander in chief gazing out the window at the carnage below. This was supposed to be a winning publicity event. Bush's senior adviser, Karl Rove, had taken the rare step of allowing cameras inside the forward cabin of *Air Force One* in order to communicate to the public the depth of the president's concern. But, as *Newsweek* would learn, Republican strategists were soon calling "the resulting image—Bush as tourist, seemingly powerless as he peered down at the chaos—perhaps the most damaging of his presidency."[31] A badly managed disaster implied a poorly run administration. Poll numbers began to dip, and an administration ideologically opposed to public programs and big government immediately promised the vast sum of $200 billion to rebuild the devastated region. A Republican-dominated Congress quickly passed a $62.5 billion relief package while assuring the public that there was more money to come.

While the Bush administration was thus catering to a long-standing popular conviction that the federal government is obligated to look after the victims of natural disasters, a vast portion of the money appropriated for Katrina, as Mike Davis pointed out, was likely to be earmarked for Halliburton, Bechtel, and other corporations that specialized in "profiting from disaster." Davis was persuaded that the rhetoric of compassion would cloak an exercise in crony capitalism that would end up gentrifying "New Orleans at the expense of its poor, black citizens." The federal response to Hurricane Katrina was sure to be a lavish one, and it would draw liberally on the rhetoric of social security, but it was unlikely to bear much resemblance to the disaster relief projects of the New Deal.[32] Neither a faith in progress nor a commitment to improvement was required any longer to ensure that catastrophes remained lucrative events for some influential businesses.

Once again, then, a major disaster presented an opportunity to strengthen the national security state while facilitating the corporate accumulation of capital. At the same time, however, an aroused public was pressing the claims of the most vulnerable members of society, seizing on the disaster as a symptom of a failed political and economic order. Significantly, it was not a leftist journal but a center-right magazine, *U.S. News and World Report*, that paused during its account of Hurricane Katrina to invoke the memory of radical folksinger Woody Guthrie and his advocacy for the destitute victims of the Dust Bowl in the 1930s. The article ended with an apocalyptic warning: "For those in public office who failed their fellow Americans so signally—for them, there'll be a reckoning."[33]

Notes

Introduction

1. Don DeLillo, *White Noise* (New York: Penguin Books, 1986), 64.
2. For a sampling of this literature, see Marshall Berman, *All That Is Solid Melts into Air: The Experience of Modernity* (New York: Penguin, 1988); David Harvey, *The Condition of Postmodernity: An Enquiry into the Origins of Cultural Change* (Cambridge, Mass.: Blackwell, 1990); Neil Smith, *Uneven Development: Nature, Capital, and the Production of Space* (Cambridge, Mass.: Blackwell, 1991); Edward W. Soja, *Postmodern Geographies: The Reassertion of Space in Critical Social Theory* (New York: Verso, 1989); and Fredric Jameson, *Postmodernism: Or, The Cultural Logic of Late Capitalism* (Durham: Duke University Press, 1991).
3. Joseph Schumpeter, *Capitalism, Socialism, and Democracy* (New York: Harper and Bros., 1947), 84, 87, cited in Robert L. Heilbroner, *The Worldly Philosophers: The Lives, Times, and Ideas of the Great Economic Thinkers* (New York: Simon and Schuster, 1986), 302.
4. Neil Postman, *Amusing Ourselves to Death: Public Discourse in the Age of Show Business* (New York: Penguin, 1986); Marshall McLuhan, *Understanding Media: The Extensions of Man* (New York: Signet Books, 1964).
5. For the concept of television as "whole flow," see Raymond Williams, *On Television: Selected Writings*, ed. Alan O'Connor (New York: Routledge, 1989); Cecilia Tichi, *The Electronic Hearth: Creating an American Television Culture* (New York: Oxford University Press, 1992); and Mary Ann Doane, "Information, Crisis, Catastrophe," in *Logics of Television: Essays in Cultural Criticism*, ed. Patricia Mellencamp (Bloomington: Indiana University Press, 1990), 222–38.
6. Don DeLillo, *End Zone* (1972; New York: Penguin, 1986), 21.
7. For a parallel project, see Edward J. Ingebretsen, *At Stake: Monsters and the Rhetoric of Fear in Public Culture* (Chicago: University of Chicago Press, 2001).

219

8. For correctives, see George Gerbner, "The Hidden Side of Television Violence," in *What Conglomerate Control of Media Means for America and the World*, ed. George Gerbner, Hamid Mowlana, and Herbert I. Schiller (Boulder: Westview Press, 1996), 27–34, and Robert W. McChesney and John Nichols, *Our Media, Not Theirs: The Democratic Struggle against Corporate Media* (New York: Seven Stories Press, 2002), 57, 59–60.

9. Michael J. Apter, *The Dangerous Edge: The Psychology of Excitement* (New York: Free Press, 1992), 71. Some take this further and seek out truly hazardous "leisure" pursuits.

10. Slavoj Žižek, *Welcome to the Desert of the Real* (New York: Verso, 2002), 15.

11. Ibid., 16.

12. Ibid., 19. My reading of Žižek is heavily influenced by Sarah Kay, *Žižek: A Critical Introduction* (Malden, Mass.: Polity, 2003). For his analysis of the social or "ideological" components of the "real," see *The Sublime Object of Ideology* (New York: Verso, 1989).

13. Sigmund Freud, *New Introductory Lectures on Psychoanalysis* (London: Hogarth Press, 1933), 98.

14. Mary Ann Doane, who believes that television is responsible for our social imagination of disaster, also gestures suggestively at a link between televised calamities and the crisis logic of late capitalism. "Information, Crisis, Catastrophe," 236–37.

15. John Updike, "The Talk of the Town," *New Yorker*, September 24, 2001, 28.

16. BBC News, Entertainment section, September 14, 2001; http://news.bbc.co .uk/hi/english/entertainment/arts/newsid_1544000/1544262.stm.

17. John Updike, "Varieties of Religious Experience: A Short Story," *Atlantic*, November 2002. Also see Robert K. Johnston, "John Updike's Theological World," *Christian Century*, November 16, 1977, 1061.

18. For an argument about the power of images to involve us in the social world, see Michael Warner, *Publics and Counterpublics* (New York: Zone Books, 2002), 89. See also Kevin Rozario, "Delicious Horrors: Mass Culture, the Red Cross, and the Appeal of Modern Humanitarianism," *American Quarterly* 55, no. 3 (September 2003): 417–55.

19. On the important connection between the pleasure of "monopathy"—acting on uncomplicated emotions such as hate and fear and love—and disaster, see Robert Bechtold Heilman, *Tragedy and Melodrama: Versions of Experience* (Seattle: University of Washington Press, 1968), 85–86.

20. "It is pointless to laboriously interpret [disaster] films by their relationship with an 'objective' social crisis, or even with an 'objective' phantasm of disaster. It is in the other direction that we must say it is *the social itself which*, in contemporary discourse, *is organised according to a script for a disaster film.*" Jean Baudrillard, *Simulations*, trans. Paul Foss, Paul Patton, and Philip Beitchman (New York: Semiotext(e), 1983), 75–76n5. (Emphasis in original.)

21. Ibid., 63.

22. For a similar argument, see Stuart Ewen and Elizabeth Ewen, *Channels of Desire: Mass Images and the Shaping of American Consciousness* (Minneapolis: University of Minnesota Press, 1992).

23. *United States Statutes at Large Containing the Laws and Current Resolutions Enacted During the Second Session of the Eighty-First Congress of the United States*

of America, 1950–1951 (Washington, D.C.: U.S. Government Printing Office [hereafter, GPO], 1952), 1109. The number of recorded disasters has regularly increased in subsequent years.

24. Kai T. Erikson, *Everything in Its Path: Destruction of Community in the Buffalo Creek Flood* (New York: Simon and Schuster, 1976), 253–56. See also his later work, *A New Species of Trouble: Explorations in Disaster, Trauma, and Community* (New York: W. W. Norton, 1994).

25. By and large I agree with such critics as Marshall Berman, Fredric Jameson, David Harvey, and Anthony Giddens who view postmodernism as an expression of modernity and the cultural logics of corporate capitalism. As Giddens contends, "Rather than entering a period of post-modernity, we are moving into one in which the consequences of modernity are becoming more radicalised and universalised than before." *The Consequences of Modernity* (Stanford: Stanford University Press, 1990), 3.

26. As Allan Pred and Michael John Watts contend, although there is value in discussing modernity as an abstraction, it is very important to remember that there has been no singular condition of modernity, nor any singular "experience" of modernity. On the contrary, there are "a multiplicity of experienced modernities." *Reworking Modernity: Capitalism and Symbolic Discontent* (New Brunswick, N.J.: Rutgers University Press, 1992), xiv.

27. I take the notion of a modern "project" from Jürgen Habermas, *The Philosophical Discourse of Modernity*, trans. Frederick Lawrence (Cambridge: MIT Press, 1987), xix.

28. Henri Lefebvre, *Introduction to Modernity*, trans. John Moore (New York: Verso, 1995), 2.

29. *Two Very Circumstantial Accounts of the Late Dreadful Earthquake at Lisbon* (Boston: D. Fowle, 1756), 3. For another American account, see *A Genuine Letter to Mr Joseph Fowke, from his Brother near Lisbon, dated November 1755* (London: M. Coliyer, 1755).

30. Kenneth Maxwell, *Pombal: Paradox of the Enlightenment* (New York: Cambridge University Press, 1995), 20–24.

31. Clarence Glacken, in his sweeping survey of European ideas of nature, maintains that "the theme of natural catastrophes, of purposeful and violent changes in the physical nature of the earth as a punishment for sin ... [reached] its climax in the Lisbon earthquake." *Traces on the Rhodian Shore: Nature and Culture in Western Thought from Ancient Times to the End of the Eighteenth Century* (Berkeley: University of California Press, 1967), 160.

32. Maxwell, *Pombal*, 82. Otto Friedrich, *The End of the World: A History* (New York: Coward, McCann and Geoghegan, 1982), 206.

33. Whitefield knew Lisbon well. He had spent a month in the city in 1754, en route to America, and had been fascinated and repelled by the displays of pageantry and "superstition" that he had witnessed. Upset by this "spiritual tyranny," he had consoled himself with reassurances about the ultimate triumph of Protestantism, writing to a friend, "Let us comfort ourselves with this thought, that there is a season approaching, when the Lord God of Elijah will himself come, and destroy this and every other species of antichrist." *Memoirs of Rev. George Whitefield*, ed. John Gillies (Middletown, Conn.: Hunt and Noyes, 1837), 151. When Lisbon fell a year later, however, he allowed a certain sympathy to dilute

his satisfaction at a prophecy fulfilled. "Poor Lisbon!" he lamented. "How soon are thy riches and superstitious pageantry swallowed up." If only the Portuguese had had a true faith, he sighed, the earthquake would have been only "a *rumbling* chariot, to carry the soul to God." Robert Philip, *The Life and Times of the Reverend George Whitefield* (New York: Appleton, 1838), 424.

The founder of the Methodists, John Wesley, was altogether more hostile. Although better known for emphasizing the sweet joys of faith than the terrors of divine anger, he reveled in this act of vengeance: "Is there indeed a God that judges the World?" he asked rhetorically. "And is he now making Inquisition for Blood? If so it is not surprizing, he should begin there, where so much Blood has been poured on the Ground like Water. Where so many brave Men have been murdered, in the most base and cowardly, as well as barbarous Manner, almost every Day." John Wesley, *Serious Thoughts Occasioned by the Late Earthquake at Lisbon* (Dublin: Booksellers, 1756), 4. John Walsh, "'Methodism' and the Origins of English-Speaking Evangelicalism," in *Evangelicalism: Comparative Studies of Popular Protestantism in North America, the British Isles, and Beyond, 1700–1990*, ed. Mark Noll, David W. Bebbington, and George A. Rawlyk (New York: Oxford University Press, 1994), 30.

34. Alexander Pope, *An Essay On Man*, in *Pope: Poetical Works*, ed. Herbert Davis (New York: Oxford University Press, 1978), 249, 245.

35. Jesuit scholars introduced the new word *optimisme* into Western vocabularies in 1737 to describe the philosophy of Gottfried Wilhelm Leibnitz, whose influential 1710 essay on theodicy was the source of the maxim that this was "the best of all possible worlds." Although this observation was taken literally by many supporters and critics alike, Leibnitz was not describing the world from a human point of view. He was quite clear that the world was "optimum" only from God's vantage point. T. D. Kendrick, *The Lisbon Earthquake* (London: Methuen, 1956), 121n2.

36. Voltaire, *Poem upon the Lisbon Disaster*, trans. Anthony Hecht (Lincoln, Mass.: Penmaen Press, 1977), 13.

37. This heightened awareness of the destructive power of nature might have led to despair, as was Goethe's fate. He also traced his retreat from a faith in a benign natural world (and a caring "fatherly" God) to the impact of the Lisbon disaster—when he was a six-year-old child. *The Autobiography of Johann Wolfgang von Goethe*, trans. John Oxenford (Chicago: University of Chicago Press, 1964), 1:24–26. By the time he wrote his famous psychological portrait of the fictional Werther, such suspicions had evolved into a grim conception of nature:

> It is not the great and rare catastrophes of the world, the floods which sweep away villages, the earthquakes that swallow up our towns, that affect me. My heart is wasted by the thought of that destructive power which lies latent in every part of universal Nature. Nature has formed nothing that does not destroy itself, and everything near it. And so, surrounded by earth and air and all the active forces, I stagger on with anguished heart; the universe to me is an ever-devouring, ever-ruminating monster. (Johann Wolfgang von Goethe, *The Sorrows of Young Werther*, trans. Victor Lange [1787; New York: Holt, Rinehart, and Winston, 1949], 49)

38. Rita Goldberg, "Voltaire, Rousseau, and the Lisbon Earthquake," *Eighteenth-Century Life* 13, no. 2 (1989): 5–10.
39. Voltaire, *Candide; Or Optimism*, trans. John Butt (New York: Penguin, 1947), 144.
40. Voltaire, "Author's Preface to the Lisbon Earthquake," *The Works of Voltaire*, trans. William F. Fleming (Akron, Ohio: St. Hubert's Guild, 1903), 36:7.
41. Voltaire, *Candide*, 36.
42. Maxwell, *Pombal*, 24–35.
43. Kendrick, *Lisbon Earthquake*, 32.
44. Pombal strengthened the army and navy, built up the silk and shipping industries, outlawed slavery (in Portugal, not in Brazil), rationalized the legal system, introduced secular education, and modernized the bureaucracy. But if his rule was in many respects enlightened, it was also repressive, exemplifying both the creative and repressive dimensions of the modern disciplinary state. Although he oversaw the expulsion of the Jesuits from Portuguese dominions in 1759, he did not immediately dismantle the Inquisition. On the contrary, he appropriated its police powers to eliminate opposition. The last judicial murder ordered by the Inquisition was that of Pombal's long-term rival, the Jesuit Malagrida. Maxwell, *Pombal*, 82–83, 90.
45. Jean-Jacques Rousseau, "Letter to Voltaire" (August 18, 1756), in *The Collected Writings of Rousseau*, ed. Roger D. Masters and Christopher Kelly (Hanover, N.H.: University Press of New England, 1992), 110. At the end of the century, Jefferson would pick up on this theme, wondering whether outbreaks of yellow fever were not nature's warnings against "unnatural" and undesirable forms of urbanization. Rather than focus on the horrors of a revolting disease that wiped out one-tenth of the population of Philadelphia during a single epidemic in 1793, producing the breakdown of civic institutions, mass evacuations, and pronounced commercial disarray, he satisfied himself that nature was essentially benign and that it turned dangerous only when humans failed to adapt to it. Thomas Jefferson to Benjamin Rush, September 23, 1800, in Henry F. May, *The Enlightenment in America* (New York: Oxford University Press, 1978), 288. On what one historian called "the most appalling collective disaster that had ever overtaken an American city," see J. H. Powell, *Bring Out Your Dead: The Great Plague of Yellow Fever in Philadelphia in 1793* (New York: Time Incorporated, 1965).
46. Allan Bloom, "Rousseau's Critique of Liberal Constitutionalism," in *The Legacy of Rousseau*, ed. Clifford Orwin and Nathan Tarcov (Chicago: University of Chicago Press, 1997), 145. Another "modern" thinker, the young Kant, wrote three papers on earthquakes after the Lisbon calamity, concluding with Rousseau that they were entirely natural and only constituted disasters to the extent that humans failed to adapt to them. Still in his "optimistic" Leibnizian phase, Kant listed such natural benefits of earthquakes as the formation of mineral ores, rationalizing earthquakes as inevitable byproducts of the subterranean fires that kept the planet warm. Kendrick, *Lisbon Earthquake*, 131–33. According to Walter Benjamin, this work "probably represents the beginnings of scientific geography in Germany. And certainly the beginnings of seismology." "The Lisbon Earthquake," in *Walter Benjamin: Selected Writings, Volume 2, 1927–1934*, ed. Michael W. Jennings, Howard Eiland, and Gary Smith, trans. Rodney Livingstone and

others (Cambridge: Harvard University Press, Belknap Press, 1999), 538. Kant later stopped believing that science could demonstrate the indisputable benefits of calamity. "No theodicy," he concluded in 1791, sounding more like Voltaire, "has managed to justify the moral wisdom at work in the government of the world against the doubts which arise out of our experience of the world." Immanuel Kant, "On the Failure of All Attempted Philosophical Theodicies," in *Kant on History and Religion*, ed. and trans. Michel Despland (Montreal: McGill-Queen's University Press, 1973), 290, 293.

47. Sketches of the earthquake circulated throughout Europe, an early instance of a commerce in images of calamity. It should be pointed out, however, that the historian of these representations was able to track down only one openly sensational pamphlet describing the event in the eighteenth century. See *A Collection of the Most Remarkable Ruins of Lisbon As they appeared immediately after the Great Earthquake and Fire, which destroyed that City, November 1, 1755* (London: Robert Sayer, 1755). The unabashedly spectacular interest in the disaster continued to grow in the United States and Europe over the nineteenth century. For example, see the *Description of The Royal Cyclorama, or Music Hall: Albany Street, Regent's Park, opened in MDCCCXLVIII; with numerous illustrations of the Cyclorama of Lisbon, before and after the earthquake in 1755* (London: J. Chisman, 1849).

48. Lawrence J. Vale and Thomas J. Campanella, eds., introduction to *The Resilient City: How Modern Cities Recover from Disaster* (New York: Oxford University Press, 2005), 3.

49. John Winthrop, *A Lecture on Earthquakes* (Boston: Edes and Gill, 1755), 19 note "h." Charles Edwin Clark, "Science, Reason, and an Angry God: The Literature of an Earthquake," *New England Quarterly* 38 (1965): 342.

50. Samuel G. Drake, *The History and Antiquities of Boston* (Boston: Luther Stevens, 1856), 640–41.

51. Charles Chauncy, *The Earth Delivered from the Curse to Which it is, at Present, Subjected: A Sermon Occasioned by the late EARTHQUAKES in Spain and Portugal, as well as New England* (Boston: Edes and Gill, 1756), 10–12. On Chauncy's "liberal" treatment of adversity, see Conrad Wright, *The Beginnings of Unitarianism in America* (Boston: Starr King, 1955), 175–83.

52. Ruth H. Bloch, *Visionary Republic: Millennial Themes in American Thought, 1756–1800* (New York: Cambridge University Press, 1985), 36.

53. Winthrop, *Lecture on Earthquakes*, 27–31, 19 note "h."

54. See Peter Gay, "The American Enlightenment," in *A Comparative Approach to American History*, ed. C. Vann Woodward (New York: Basic Books, 1968), 43.

55. On the Union Fire Company, see *The Autobiography of Benjamin Franklin*, ed. Leonard W. Labaree et al. (New Haven: Yale University Press, 1964), 174–75.

56. Harvey, *Condition of Postmodernity*, 189.

57. Carl Smith, *Urban Disorder and the Shape of Belief: The Great Chicago Fire, the Haymarket Bomb, and the Model Town of Pullman* (Chicago: University of Chicago Press, 1995); John M. Barry, *Rising Tide: The Great Mississippi Flood of 1927 and How It Changed America* (New York: Touchstone, 1998); Mike Davis, *Ecology of Fear: Los Angeles and the Imagination of Disaster* (New York: Metropolitan Books, 1998).

58. Ted Steinberg, *Acts of God: The Unnatural History of Natural Disaster in America* (New York: Oxford University Press, 2000).

59. Henry Adams, *The Education of Henry Adams* (New York: Vintage Books, 1990), 418. Henry James, *Letters to A. C. Benson and Auguste Monod*, ed. E. F. Benson (London: Elkins, Matthews, and Marrot, 1930), 35, quoted in Peter Brooks, *The Melodramatic Imagination: Balzac, Henry James, Melodrama, and the Mode of Excess* (New Haven: Yale University Press, 1976), 153n2.

60. Walter Benjamin, *The Arcades Project*, trans. Howard Elland and Kevin McLaughlin (Cambridge: Harvard University Press, 2002), 906.

61. Susan Buck-Morss, *The Dialectics of Seeing: Walter Benjamin and the Arcades Project* (Cambridge: MIT Press, 1991), 97.

62. Walter Benjamin, "Die Mississippi-Uberschwemmung 1927," in *Aufklärung für Kinder*, ed. Rolf Tiedemann (Frankfurt am Main: Suhrkamp Verlag, 1985), 188, cited in Buck-Morss, *Dialectics of Seeing*, 37. This marks an interesting correction to his treatment of the Lisbon earthquake of 1755 in a radio broadcast for youth two years earlier. At that time, curiously, the lesson he had drawn was that society could depend on technology to "combat" natural catastrophes. "The Lisbon Earthquake," in *Walter Benjamin: Selected Writings, Volume 2, 1927–1934*, 540.

63. Tony Kushner, *Angels in America: A Gay Fantasia on National Themes* (New York: Theatre Communications Group, 2003), 284.

64. Ibid., 142.

65. Quoted in Jameson, *Postmodernism*, xi. Lefebvre's actual words: "At the heart of . . . modernity are inner contradictions, principles of destruction and self-destruction." *Introduction to Modernity*, 182.

66. Ian McEwan, *Saturday* (New York: Doubleday, 2005), 77.

Chapter One

1. Paul Tillich, *The Courage to Be* (New Haven: Yale University Press, 1952), 103.

2. An investigation of providential thought is crucial for understanding American responses to disaster. As Perry Miller reminds us, providentialism was pervasive throughout the colonies. Moreover, variations from Anglican (and African) Virginia to (partially) Catholic Maryland left important traces on emerging American ideas and practices. "Religion and Society in the Early Literature of Virginia," in *Errand into the Wilderness* (Cambridge: Harvard University Press, Belknap Press, 1984), 105–22. Still, as David Hackett Fischer argues, it was surely the Puritans that did most to articulate and formalize the study of calamities (what settlers often called "remarkable providences") in America. *Albion's Seed: Four British Folkways in America* (New York: Oxford University Press, 1989), 126. Moreover, as Lewis O. Saum's investigations into popular thought reveal, Puritanism would frame ordinary American values and attitudes throughout the country well into the nineteenth century. *The Popular Mood of Pre–Civil War America* (Westport, Conn.: Greenwood Press, 1980), xxii. Also, as Peirce F. Lewis shows, colonial New England was the source of many of the most influential ideas of nature as well as some of the nation's most "persistent geographical habits." "The Northeast and the Making of American Geographical Habits," in *The Making of the American Landscape*, ed. Michael P. Conzen (Boston: Unwin Hyman, 1990), 80–81.

3. Albert Murray, *The Blue Devils of Nada: A Contemporary American Approach to Aesthetic Statement* (New York: Vintage Books, 1996), 94.

4. Ronald H. Stone, *Paul Tillich's Radical Social Thought* (Atlanta: John Knox Press, 1980), 112–30. See also Brian Donnelly, *The Socialist Émigré: Marxism and the Later Tillich* (Macon, Ga.: Mercer University Press, 2003).

5. William Bradford, *History of Plymouth Plantation* (New York: Barnes and Noble, 1946), 348.

6. Edward Johnson, *Johnson's Wonder-Working Providence, 1628–1651*, ed. J. Franklin Jameson (New York: Charles Scribner's Sons, 1910), 185.

7. William Bradford, *Of Plymouth Plantation, 1620–1647*, ed. Samuel Eliot Morison (New York: Alfred A. Knopf, 1952), 62.

8. On death in Virginia, see Edmund Morgan, *American Slavery, American Freedom: The Ordeal of Colonial Virginia* (New York: W. W. Norton, 1975), chap. 8, "Living with Death."

9. Dwight B. Heath, ed., *A Journal of the Pilgrims at Plymouth: Mourt's Relation* (New York: Corinth Books, 1963).

10. In the seventeenth century, the world was passing through what climatologists have called the Little Ice Age. See Karen Kupperman, "Puzzle of the American Climate," *American Historical Review* 87 (1982): 1262–89; H. H. Lamb, *Climate, History, and the Modern World* (New York: Methuen, 1982), 201–30; and Emanuel Le Roy Ladurie, *Times of Feast, Times of Famine: A History of Climate since the Year 1000*, trans. Barbara Bray (Garden City, N.Y.: Doubleday, 1971), 129–226. These historians note that this so-called ice age produced not only cold weather but greater climatic variation, including some unusually hot summers. Even promotional accounts conceded that the continent was subject to uncomfortably hot summers and bitterly cold winters; as far south as Virginia, two-thirds of the settlers succumbed in the winter of 1607–08. See, for example, William Wood, *New England's Prospect*, ed. Alden T. Vaughan (1634; Amherst: University of Massachusetts Press, 1977), 27–31.

11. Bradford, *Of Plymouth Plantation*, ed. Morison, 62.

12. As David Laskin writes, "New words, for example 'hurricane,' adapted from the language of the Taino tribe of the West Indies, and 'blizzard,' had to be coined or imported into English to describe weather phenomena unknown in Western Europe. Early descriptions of hurricanes and violent thunderstorms convey some sense of how truly electrifying these weather events appeared to eyes accustomed to the mildness of Western Europe." *Braving the Elements: The Stormy History of American Weather* (New York: Doubleday, 1996), 52–53. New England endured some especially severe storms. As David Hackett Fischer writes, the weather

> was kept in constant turmoil by the continuing collision of warm dry air from the west, cold dry air from the north, cold wet air from the east, and warm wet air from the south. When these air masses met above New England, the meteorological effects were apt to be spectacular. The countryside was lashed by violent blizzards, drenched by thunderstorms, raked by tornadoes, and attacked by dangerous three-day nor'easters which churned the coastal waters of New England into a seaman's hell. (Fischer, *Albion's Seed*, 53–54)

13. Bradford, *Of Plymouth Plantation*, ed. Morison, 122. Cotton Mather also cited this passage in *Magnalia Christi Americana*, ed. Kenneth B. Murdock (Cambridge: Harvard University Press, Belknap Press, 1977), 136.

14. Bradford was inclined to exaggerate adversities to magnify the achievements of the Pilgrims, or perhaps simply to reaffirm (however unconsciously) his abiding conviction that calamity was the inevitable lot of sinful man. Alan B. Howard, "Art and History in Bradford's *Of Plymouth Plantation*," *William and Mary Quarterly* 28, no. 2 (April 1971): 243–48; Norman Grabo, "William Bradford: *Of Plymouth Plantation*," in *Landmarks of American Writing*, ed. Hennig Cohen (New York: Basic Books, 1969), 10. On the gaps between reality and representation in *Of Plymouth Plantation*, see David Laurence, "William Bradford's American Sublime," *PMLA* 102, no. 1 (January 1987): 55–66. There are suggestive affinities here with the tendency of the first settlers to represent America as a wilderness. As Leo Marx perceptively pointed out, this poetic metaphor fortified the aggressive proclivities of the first settlers:

> To describe America as a hideous wilderness . . . is to envisage it as another field for the exercise of power. This violent image expresses a need to mobilize energy, postpone immediate pleasures, and rehearse the perils and purposes of the community. . . . Life in a howling desert demands action, the unceasing manipulation and mastery of the forces of nature, including, of course, human nature. Colonies established in the desert require aggressive, intellectual, controlled, and well-disciplined people. (Leo Marx, *The Machine in the Garden: Technology and the Pastoral Ideal in America* [New York: Oxford University Press, 1967], 43)

On the anxiety and fear generated in early settlers by the wilderness, see Roderick Nash, *Wilderness and the American Mind* (New Haven: Yale University Press, 1982), 23–43; John R. Stilgoe, *Common Landscapes of America, 1580–1845* (New Haven: Yale University Press, 1982), 7–12; and John Canup, *Out of the Wilderness: The Emergence of American Identity in Colonial New England* (Middletown, Conn.: Wesleyan University Press, 1990).

15. On the epidemics, see Charles Francis Adams, *Three Episodes of Massachusetts History* (Boston: Houghton, Mifflin, 1892), chap. 1, and Johnson, *Johnson's Wonder-Working Providence*, 40–41. On the cleared land, see Howard S. Russell, *Indian New England before the Mayflower* (Hanover, N.H.: University Press of New England, 1980), 11–15.

16. Betty Flanders Thomson, *The Changing Face of New England* (New York: Macmillan, 1958), 19–21. As Francis Jennings forcefully reminds us, America was not a virgin land, it was widowed; and the Europeans were not just settlers, they were also conquerors. *The Invasion of America: Indians, Colonialism, and the Cant of Conquest* (New York: W. W. Norton, 1976), 15.

17. See Lewis, "The Northeast and the Making of American Geographical Habits," 82–83, and D. W. Meinig, *Atlantic America, 1492–1800*, vol. 1 in *The Shaping of America: A Geographical Perspective on Five Hundred Years of History* (New Haven: Yale University Press, 1986), 219.

18. Crosby distinguishes usefully between the hardships of individuals and the achievements of Europeans as a group:

Of course, the white pioneers of the United States and Canada would never have characterized their progress as easy; their lives were filled with danger, deprivation, and unremitting labor. But as a group they always succeeded in taming whatever portion of temperate North America they wanted within a few decades, and usually a good deal sooner. Many individuals among them failed—they were driven mad by blizzards and dust storms, lost their crops to locusts and wolves, or lost their scalps to understandably inhospitable Amerindians—but as a group they always succeeded, and in terms of human generations, very quickly. (Alfred W. Crosby, *Ecological Imperialism: The Biological Expansion of Europe, 900–1900* [New York: Cambridge University Press, 1986], 147)

19. Ralph Waldo Emerson, "Nature," in *Selected Essays*, ed. Larzer Ziff (New York: Penguin, 1982), 39. The novelist V. S. Naipaul writes similarly, in a phrase both lovely and keen, that land "is not land alone, something that simply is itself. Land partakes of what we breathe into it, is touched by our moods and memories." *The Enigma of Arrival: A Novel* (New York: Penguin, 1987), 301.

20. Puritan governor John Winthrop also offered a naturalistic account in his journal: "Between three and four in the afternoon, being clear, warm weather, the wind westerly, there was a great earthquake. It came with a noise like a continued thunder or the rattling of coaches in London, but was presently gone. . . . The noise and the shaking continued about four minutes." *The Journal of John Winthrop*, ed. Richard S. Dunn, James Savage, and Laetitia Yeandle (Cambridge: Harvard University Press, Belknap Press, 1996), 257. Like Bradford, he was impelled to describe unusual events like storms in detail because he assumed these events expressed God's will and that they presented an opportunity for reading divine purposes. See Robert M. Benton, "The John Winthrops and Developing Scientific Thought in New England," *Early American Literature* 7, no. 3 (Winter 1973): 273–75.

21. John Josselyn, "Two Voyages to New England," in *John Josselyn, Colonial Traveler*, ed. Paul J. Lindholt (Hanover, N.H.: University Press of New England, 1988), 42. Also see Raymond Phineas Stearns, *Science in the British Colonies of America* (Urbana: University of Illinois Press, 1970), 168.

22. Urian Oakes, "The Sovereign Efficacy of Divine Providence," in *The Puritans: A Sourcebook of Their Writings*, ed. Perry Miller and Thomas H. Johnson (New York: Harper Torchbooks, 1963), 1:352. Perry Miller described the principle economically:

In its simplest form the Puritan concept of secondary causes combined neatly the ideas of order and of divine will. Cause has its effects in the ordinary course of things, and yet the cause does not of itself generate the effect; the will of God determines that when a fire burns, heat will be radiated, but God sustains both the fire and the heat. There is no guarantee that fire will always give heat other than the willingness of God to maintain the sequence. (*The New England Mind: The Seventeenth Century* [1939; Cambridge: Harvard University Press, Belknap Press, 1982], 233)

23. Of course, there was no singular Indian or African way of seeing, or acting in, the natural environment, but there seems to have been a shared general belief

that spirits infused and influenced the "physical" world and that natural events carried religious meanings. According to most Indian and West African belief systems, specific deities and spirits controlled storms or famines or diseases and had to be propitiated accordingly through ceremonies and rituals. On the varieties of Indian views of nature, see William S. Simmons, *Spirit of the New England Tribes: Indian History and Folklore, 1620–1984* (Hanover, N.H.: University Press of New England, 1986). See also Catharine L. Albanese, *Nature Religion in America: From the Algonkian Indians to the New Age* (Chicago: University of Chicago Press, 1990), 19–33; Neal Salisbury, *Manitou and Providence: Indians, Europeans, and the Making of New England, 1500–1643* (New York: Oxford University Press, 1982); and Åke Hultkrantz, *Belief and Worship in Native North America* (Syracuse, N.Y.: Syracuse University Press, 1981). On African spiritual beliefs, see Mechal Sobel, *The World They Made Together: Black and White Values in Eighteenth-Century Virginia* (Princeton: Princeton University Press, 1987), 5, 71–74, and Lawrence W. Levine, *Black Culture and Black Consciousness: Afro-American Folk Thought from Slavery to Freedom* (New York: Oxford University Press, 1978), 1–80. Most of these writers emphasize that European, Indian, and African beliefs mingled with and transformed each other.

24. Simmons, *Spirit of the New England Tribes*, 59.

25. Johnson, *Johnson's Wonder-Working Providence*, 95.

26. "It is not improbable," Cotton Mather wrote, "that *Natural Storms* on the World are often of the Devil's raising." *Wonders of the Invisible World: Being an Account of the Tryals of Several Witches Lately Executed in New England* (1692; London: John Russell Smith, 1862), 53, 60–61. Mather also suspected that the American wilderness had been Satan's realm before the arrival of the English Protestants, and continued to be a land of rare evils and temptations thereafter. Andrew Delbanco maintains that this "Antic fancy of America's being hell" (Samuel Sewall's words) had more influence in the South than in New England, where the devil was seen more as an internal tempter than as an external adversary. *The Death of Satan: How Americans Lost the Sense of Evil* (New York: Farrar, Straus and Giroux, 1995), 42–43. Another important influence on Puritan and popular outlooks was astrology. On Cotton Mather and astrology, see Michael P. Winship, "Cotton Mather, Astrologer," *New England Quarterly* 63, no. 2 (June 1990): 308–14. On the astrological beliefs in Charles Morton's *Compendium Physicae*, Harvard's standard scientific textbook until the 1720s, see Herbert Leventhal, *In the Shadow of the Enlightenment: Occultism and Renaissance Science in Eighteenth-Century America* (New York: New York University Press, 1976), 14–15. Although magic and astrology went underground after the 1680s, they became prominent again when the American Revolution made "the people" sovereign. See Jon Butler, *Awash in a Sea of Faith: Christianizing the American People* (Cambridge: Harvard University Press, 1990), 28, 83, 97.

27. David Hume contended that "every disastrous accident alarms us, and sets us on enquiries concerning the principle whence it arose. . . . And the mind, sunk into diffidence, terror, and melancholy, has recourse to every method of appeasing those secret intelligent powers, on whom our fortune is supposed entirely to depend." This was the paradox of faith: "Convulsions in nature, disorders, prodigies, miracles, though the most opposite to the plan of a wise superintendent, impress mankind with the strongest sentiments of religion." *The Natural*

History of Religion, ed. H. E. Root (Stanford: Stanford University Press, 1957), 31, 42. Jon Butler restates this claim in his history of early American religion: "Above all, religion explained. It explained unprecedented floods, disappearing animals, catastrophic diseases, and the sudden deaths of children and adults." *Awash in a Sea of Faith*, 9.

28. It was an article of Puritan faith that God had stopped performing miracles after biblical times, but it was still believed that God set natural sequences in motion to produce "wonders" (comets, earthquakes, storms, fires, droughts) when he had something unusually important to say. On the distinction between miracles and wonders, see Butler, *Awash in a Sea of Faith*, 71.

29. As the angel Michael would announce in Milton's *Paradise Lost*, thirty years later, "th' inabstinence of Eve" had ensured that human history would be filled for all time with fires, floods, famines, diseases, and other miseries. *Paradise Lost* (1667; Harmondsworth: Penguin, 1989), bk. 11, 268–69. In 1677, Urian Oakes would agree that God had determined "that every man should meet with Crosses and Disappointments; . . . this is the Fruit of the Curse, under which all natural men ly." "Sovereign Efficacy of Divine Providence," in *The Puritans*, ed. Miller and Johnson, 1:366.

30. Saint Augustine had characterized earthquakes, floods, and plagues as exhibitions of divine power and as punishments for human sins. He did not distinguish between "natural" disasters and "social" calamities such as the sack of Rome in 410 AD, interpreting all such afflictions as retributive judgments. *The City of God*, trans. John Healey (New York: E. P. Dutton and Sons, 1931). This providentialism was revived and reinterpreted by Luther and Calvin in the sixteenth century and significantly shaped Protestant ideas of nature, society, and God in the New World. The classic study of the Augustinian strain of Puritan piety is Perry Miller, *The New England Mind: The Seventeenth Century* (Cambridge: Harvard University Press, Belknap Press, 1982), 4.

31. Howard, "Art and History in Bradford's *Of Plymouth Plantation*," 261. An example of Bradford's reticence is his response to a shipwreck during a 1635 storm, "which some imputed as a correction from God." He was more circumspect: "I dare not be bold with God's judgments in this kind." *Of Plymouth Plantation*, ed. Morison, 290. For more on Bradford, see Jesper Rosenmeier, " 'With My Owne Eyes': William Bradford's *Of Plymouth Plantation*," in *The American Puritan Imagination: Essays in Revaluation*, ed. Sacvan Bercovitch (New York: Cambridge University Press, 1974), and *The Puritans: A Sourcebook of Their Writings*, 1:82–91. Edward Johnson, who had a providential explanation for every event, by contrast interpreted the earthquake as a sign that God was preparing to assist the Puritans in their struggles against the Royalists in England, "a signe from the Lord to his Churches, that he was purposed to shake the Kingdomes of Europes Earth." Johnson, *Johnson's Wonder-Working Providence*, 160–61.

32. See, for example, John Higginson, "Attestation," in Cotton Mather, *Magnalia Christi Americana*, 66.

33. John Winthrop, "A Modell of Christian Charity," *Winthrop Papers* (Boston: Massachusetts Historical Society, 1931), 2:294.

34. Miller, "The Marrow of Puritan Divinity," in *Errand into the Wilderness*, 66, 97.

35. Puritans, interestingly, were much more inclined to declare fast days than were Anglicans. For a comprehensive history, see W. DeLoss Love, *The Fast and*

Thanksgiving Days of New England (Boston: Houghton, Mifflin, 1895). Also see Harry S. Stout, *The New England Soul: Preaching and Religious Culture in Colonial New England* (New York: Oxford University Press, 1986), 28, 74–76.

36. Indeed, this remained a reflexive response late into the nineteenth century. After the Chicago fire of 1871 the Presbyterian mayor called upon the people of his burned metropolis to heed a day of fasting and humiliation in language that demonstrates the reach and influence of colonial religious thought well into the industrial age:

> In view of the recent appalling public calamity, the undersigned, Mayor of Chicago, hereby earnestly recommends that all the inhabitants of this city do observe Sunday, October 29, as a special day of humiliation and prayer; of humiliation for those past offenses against Almighty God, to which these severe afflictions were doubtless intended to lead our minds; of prayer for the relief and comfort of the suffering thousands in our midst; for the restoration of our material prosperity, especially for our lasting improvement as a people in reverence and obedience to God. Nor should we even, amidst our losses and sorrows, forget to render thanks to Him for the arrest of the devouring fires in time to save so many homes, and for the unexampled sympathy and aid which has flowed in upon us from every quarter of our land, and even from beyond the seas. (Elias Colbert and Everett Chamberlin, *Chicago and the Great Conflagration* [1871; New York: Viking Press, 1971], appendix B, "Documentary History of the Fire," 500)

According to one writer, the day was well observed, and although the local press did not feature the event prominently, it was reported as far away as England in the *Illustrated London News*. Edgar Johnson Goodspeed, *The Great Fires in Chicago and the West* (Chicago: J. W. Goodspeed, 1871), 474; *Illustrated London News*, November 11, 1871, 446. On religion and the Chicago fire, see Kevin Rozario, "Nature's Evil Dreams: Disaster and America, 1871–1906" (PhD diss., Yale University, 1997), chap. 2. This passage is worth citing in detail because, in its blend of piety and material aspiration, it perfectly captures the strange marriage of faith and worldly ambition that was a legacy of the providential view of disaster.

37. John Robinson, "New Essays; or, Observations Divine and Moral," in *The Works of John Robinson* (Boston: Doctrinal Book and Tract Society, 1851), 1:143.

38. Keith Thomas, *Religion and the Decline of Magic: Studies in Popular Belief in Sixteenth and Seventeenth Century England* (New York: Oxford University Press, 1997), 82.

39. John Calvin, *Institutes of the Christian Religion*, ed. John T. McNeill, trans. Ford Lewis Battles (Philadelphia, 1960), 1:35, cited in Howard, "Art and History in Bradford's *Of Plymouth Plantation*," 243.

40. After dwelling on Isaiah 45:9–10 ("Woe unto him that striveth with his Maker!"), Sewall admitted to being startled by such boldness, by "the daring height of such wickedness." *Diary of Samuel Sewall, 1674–1729* (New York: Farrar, Straus and Giroux, 1973), 1:35.

41. Of course, Puritans were deeply suspicious of individuality. For them, as Sacvan Bercovitch has observed, "self-examination serves not to liberate but to

constrict; selfhood appears as a state to be overcome, obliterated; and identity is asserted through an act of submission to a transcendental absolute." It was through affliction that the Puritans sought to purge and purify themselves. But this obsessive concern with self-denial or conscience cultivated a preoccupation with selfhood: "They defined conscience as 'a mans judgment of himselfe, according to the judgment of God [*krisis*] of him,' but their very insistence on God called attention to the inescapable I-ness in performance and self-judgment —and as their own words imply, in 'krisis' itself." *The Puritan Origins of the American Self* (New Haven: Yale University Press, 1975), 13, 15, 21.

42. Although Winthrop was fully aware on the eve of the great migration that many calamities had befallen earlier colonial enterprises, he was inclined to believe that these ventures had been punished by God for their lust for profits. He expected his religious venture to be blessed with greater prosperity and security. John Winthrop, "General Observations for the Plantation of New England, 1629," *Winthrop Papers*, 2:114, 119, 120.

43. Ibid., 2:139.

44. Johnson, *Johnson's Wonder-Working Providence*, 151.

45. Increase Mather, "An Earnest Exhortation to the Inhabitants of New England," in *Departing Glory: Eight Jeremiads by Increase Mather*, ed. Lee Scheninger (Delmar, N.Y.: Scholars' Facsimiles and Reprints, 1986), 3. On disaster as the special burden of a chosen people, see Sacvan Bercovitch, *The American Jeremiad* (Madison: University of Wisconsin Press, 1978), 7–8, 23, 57–61, and *Puritan Origins of the American Self*, 53–56.

46. Saint Augustine, *City of God*, 16–17.

47. Increase Mather, "The Day of Trouble Is Near," in *Departing Glory*, ed. Scheninger, 29.

48. "It may be hoped," Mather wrote, that "the *Good Impressions* from our *Earthquakes*, will be such that the *Trembling* of the *Earth* under us, will prove the most *useful Dispensation* of Heaven, that ever we have met withal: . . . many *Elect* of GOD who were not yet His *Children*, are made such, by the Earthquakes driving of them, into those Motions of PIETY, which carry them to their SAVIOUR." Cotton Mather, "Boanerges. A Short Essay to Preserve and Strengthen the Good Impressions Produced by Earthquakes. Boston, 1727," in *Days of Humiliation, Times of Affliction* (Gainesville, Fla.: Scholars' Facsimiles and Reprints, 1970), 365.

49. Ibid., 335. This psychological analysis underpinned Mather's explanation for the growing predominance of women at religious services. There were "far more *godly Women*" than men, he contended, because of exposure to the dangers of childbirth. Cotton Mather, *Ornaments for the Daughters of Zion* (1692), cited in Patricia U. Bonomi, *Under the Cope of Heaven: Religion, Society, and Politics in Colonial America* (New York: Oxford University Press, 1986), 111.

50. New Englanders also devoured written accounts and observations of the earthquake. Boston printers published twenty-six such essays in the aftermath of the tremors. These are listed in William D. Andrews, "The Literature of the 1727 New England Earthquake," *Early American Literature* 7, no. 3 (Winter 1973): 294. On earthquake sermons, see Michael Nathaniel Shute, "Earthquakes and Early American Imagination: Decline and Renewal in Eighteenth-Century Puritan Culture" (PhD diss., University of California at Berkeley, 1977), 71–159, and Maxine Van de Wetering, "Moralizing in Puritan Natural

Science: Mysteriousness in Earthquake Sermons," *Journal of the History of Ideas* 43, no. 3 (July 1982): 427–28.

51. "The great GOD by His *Earthquake* to Night has been *shaking* and *jogging* and *pulling* of you, to make you shake of the *slumber*, that may be upon you." Cotton Mather, "The Terror of the Lord. Some Account of the Earthquake That Shook New-England in the Night Between the 29 and the 30 of October, 1727" (1727), in *Days of Humiliation*, 301, 307.

52. Fellow townsman Jonathan Pearson offered a vivid account of his own awakening:

> God has by ye late amazing Earth-quake Layd open my neglect before me yt I see no way to escape. But by fleeing to X for refuge. God in yt hour Set all my Sins before me. When I was Shaking over yt pit looking every moment when ye earth would open her mouth and Swallow me up and yn must I have been miserable for ever & for ever have been reaping ye fruits of my repeated rebellions against him all my Life long. I yn thôt God would spare my Life. I would walk more closely with him. I made vows and promises to God to lead a new life and renew my baptismall vows and obligations wch my parents layd me under In my tender years and wch is ye initiating Seal of ye Covenant and desire now to give up my Self to ye Lord In an ever lasting Covenant.

"The Relation of Jeremiah Eaton" and "The Relation of Jonathan Pearson," in Kenneth P. Minkema, ed., "The Lynn End 'Earthquake' Relations of 1727," *New England Quarterly* 69, no. 3 (September 1996): 483, 490. See also the conversion narratives of Mehitable Osgood and Elizabeth Ahorn in this collection.

53. Stout, *New England Soul*, 177–79. On links between the earthquake and the Great Awakening, see Andrews, "Literature of the 1727 New England Earthquake," 290–91. Richard F. Lovelace dubs Cotton Mather the "John the Baptist of the coming revivalism": *The American Pietism of Cotton Mather: Origins of American Evangelicalism* (Grand Rapids, Mich.: Christian University Press, 1979), 199. Appropriately enough, when the charismatic evangelist George Whitefield visited Boston in 1740, Mather's close friend and colleague Thomas Prince could compare the response only to the excitement surrounding the earthquake thirteen years before. Richard Hofstadter, *America at 1750: A Social Portrait* (New York: Alfred A. Knopf, 1971), 248. On a cautionary note, Butler reminds us that revivalism did not encompass all of the colonies, that it followed different patterns in different regions, and that revivals were not entirely new. There had been awakenings as early as the 1670s. *Awash in a Sea of Faith*, 177–80.

54. John Walsh, "'Methodism' and the Origins of English-Speaking Evangelicalism," in *Evangelicalism: Comparative Studies of Popular Protestantism in North America, the British Isles, and Beyond, 1700–1990*, ed. Mark Noll, David W. Bebbington, and George A. Rawlyk (New York: Oxford University Press, 1994), 21. Puritans had long insisted that emotional displays of piety were a prerequisite to full church membership in New England, but increasingly, spiritual rebirth displaced the legalistic obligations of the covenant as the first concern of religious institutions. Bonomi, *Under the Cope of Heaven*, 68–69.

55. One of the resolutions that guided Edwards's daily conduct was "never to allow any pleasure or grief, joy or sorrow, nor any affection at all . . . but what helps religion." *A Jonathan Edwards Reader*, ed. John E. Smith, Harry S. Stout, and Kenneth P. Minkema (New Haven: Yale University Press, 1995), 278. On Whitefield, see Frank Lambert, *"Pedlar in Divinity": George Whitefield and the Transatlantic Revivals, 1737–1770* (Princeton: Princeton University Press, 1994), and Harry S. Stout, *The Divine Dramatist: George Whitefield and the Rise of Modern Evangelicalism* (Grand Rapids, Mich.: William B. Eerdmans, 1991).

56. "And as the plowman plowes the ground no more and no longer than is needfull to fit it for the seed, . . . so God will afflict His people no more and hold them under affliction no longer than to fit them for spiritual good." Jonathan Edwards, *Images or Shadows of Divine Things*, ed. Perry Miller (New Haven: Yale University Press, 1948), 55. Edwards further argued that the experience of misfortune in the present was necessary to ensure that the elect would fully enjoy a painless existence when it finally arrived. How, he asked, could one appreciate comfort if one had never experienced discomfort? Jonathan Edwards, "Wisdom Displayed in Salvation," cited in Conrad Cherry, *Nature and the Religious Imagination: From Edwards to Bushnell* (Philadelphia: Fortress Press, 1980), 58.

57. Cotton Mather, *Wonders of the Invisible World*, 64. This expectation has been a defining feature of millenarian faith in America. "Those who regard the millennium as imminent," as Michael Barkun has found, "expect disasters to pave the way." *Disaster and the Millennium* (New Haven: Yale University Press, 1974), 1.

58. Cotton Mather, "Terror of the Lord," 309–11; "Boanerges," 372.

59. For an introduction to Jonathan Edwards's millennialism, see his four essays "A History of the Work of Redemption," "The Distinguishing Marks of A Work of the Spirit," "Thoughts on the Revival of Religion," and "A Treatise concerning Religious Affections," in *The Great Awakening: Documents Illustrating the Crisis and Its Consequences*, ed. Alan Heimart and Perry Miller (Indianapolis: Bobbs-Merrill, 1967). On millennial thought in eighteenth-century America, see Ernest Lee Tuveson, *Redeemer Nation: The Idea of America's Millennial Role* (Chicago: University of Chicago Press, 1968), and James West Davidson, *The Logic of Millennial Thought: Eighteenth-Century New England* (New Haven: Yale University Press, 1977). Other important works include Ruth H. Bloch, *Visionary Republic: Millennial Themes in American Thought, 1756–1800* (New York: Cambridge University Press, 1985), and Bercovitch, *American Jeremiad*.

60. Jonathan Edwards, "Notes on the Apocalypse," in *Jonathan Edwards Reader*, ed. Smith, Stout, and Minkema, 50–55.

61. Jonathan Edwards, *An Humble Attempt to Promote Explicit Agreement and Visible Union of God's People in Extraordinary Prayer* (Boston, 1757), 169, cited in Tuveson, *Redeemer Nation*, 101.

62. Bloch, *Visionary Republic*, 25–26, 42–44. See also Donald Weber, *Rhetoric and History in Revolutionary New England* (New York: Oxford University Press, 1988).

63. J. J. Zubly, *The Stamp Act Repealed* (1766), in John F. Berens, *Providence and Patriotism in Early America, 1640–1815* (Charlottesville: University Press of Virginia, 1978), 58.

64. Samuel G. Drake, *The History and Antiquities of Boston* (Boston: Luther Stevens, 1856), 426n.

65. William Hubbard, "A Narrative of the Troubles with the Indians," in *The History of the Indian Wars from the Settlement to the Termination of the War with King Philip, in 1677*, ed. Samuel G. Drake (New York: Burt Franklin, 1865), 291–92. For another account, see Sewall, *Diary of Samuel Sewall*, 1:28.

66. On the rivalry between Hubbard and Mather, see Dennis R. Perry, " 'Novelties and Stile Which All Out-Do': William Hubbard's Historiography Reconsidered," *Early American Literature* 29, no. 2 (1994): 166–82.

67. Darren Staloff, *The Making of an American Thinking Class: Intellectuals and Intelligentsia in Puritan Massachusetts* (New York: Oxford University Press, 1998), 169–88.

68. Jill Lepore, *The Name of War: King Philip's War and the Origins of American Identity* (New York: Alfred A. Knopf, 1998), 76–83.

69. Hubbard, "Narrative of the Troubles with the Indians," 290. Anne Kusener Nelsen, "King Philip's War and the Hubbard-Mather Rivalry," *William and Mary Quarterly* 27, no. 4 (1970): 615–29.

70. Stout, *New England Soul*, 78.

71. David D. Hall, *Worlds of Wonder, Days of Judgment: Popular Religious Belief in Early New England* (New York: Alfred A. Knopf, 1989), 104. As historian Richard Bushman argues, disaster sermons were one of the most important mechanisms for scaring congregations into obedience: "As interpreted by the minister's sermons, even the natural world—the storms, the wolves in the wilderness, and catastrophes at sea—spoke of the war of good and evil and of God's mighty government. Social institutions, conscience, and the forces of nature meshed in the communal experience to restrain rebellious dispositions." *From Puritan to Yankee: Character and the Social Order in Connecticut, 1690–1765* (Cambridge: Harvard University Press, 1967), 17. The reach and influence of ministers' orations should not be underestimated. As religious historian Harry Stout points out, the sermon "stood alone in New England contexts as the only regular (at least weekly) medium of public communication." He calculates that the "the average weekly churchgoer in New England (and there were far more churchgoers than church members) listened to something like seven thousand sermons in a lifetime, totaling somewhere around fifteen thousand hours of concentrated listening." Stout, *New England Soul*, 3–4. Of course, it should also be pointed out that although church attendance was mandatory, much of the population appeared only rarely at services. Darrett B. Rutman, *Winthrop's Boston: Portrait of a Puritan Town, 1630–1649* (Chapel Hill: University of North Carolina Press, 1965), 152.

72. Increase Mather, "Earnest Exhortation to the Inhabitants of New England," 9.

73. Increase Mather, "Day of Trouble Is Near," 5–33.

74. Although Staloff exaggerates when he maintains that to "a remarkable extent, the history of Puritan Massachusetts in its final years is identical to that of the minister of the second church of Boston," he is correct to insist that "between 1675 and 1686, Increase Mather exercised an unprecedented sway over the orthodox Bay regime." *Making of an American Thinking Class*, 169.

75. Michael G. Hall, *The Last American Puritan: The Life of Increase Mather, 1639–1723* (Middletown, Conn.: Wesleyan University Press, 1988), 107.

76. In a letter written a couple of weeks after the fire, Mather told his brother-in-law John Cotton that he had prophesied this fire. He had been so sure that

"desolation by fire was coming where I lived" that he had tried and failed to persuade his wife to agree to move to a safer neighborhood. After yet another sermon fell on deaf ears, Mather wrote that he had fallen into a tearful conversation with God: "I wept there, walking alone before the Lord, and saying O Lord God, I have told the people in Your Name that you art about to cutt off their dwelling, but they will not believe me." By his own account, at least, he had been hopeful that God would overlook the sins of his congregation and save them from the afflictions they deserved, pleading, "Lord spare them etc. That I might appear to be a false prophet among them when I declare such things as these." Increase Mather to John Cotton, Boston, December 13, 1676, Manuscripts Collection, Mather Papers, American Antiquarian Society.

77. W. DeLoss Love, *The Fast and Thanksgiving Days of New England* (Boston: Houghton, Mifflin 1895), 196.

78. *Diary by Increase Mather, March 1675–December 1676*, ed. Samuel A. Green (Cambridge, Mass.: John Wilson and Son, 1900), 39.

79. Increase Mather to John Cotton, Boston, December 13, 1676, Manuscripts Collection, Mather Papers, American Antiquarian Society.

80. Mather, significantly, asked his brother-in-law to keep his confessions about his private anxieties secret. Increase Mather to John Cotton, Boston, December 13, 1676, Manuscripts Collection, Mather Papers, American Antiquarian Society.

81. Increase Mather, "Day of Trouble Is Near," 17, 20.

82. There were limits to such optimism. Mather himself struggled to feel the blessings of calamity; his son Cotton Mather, who was even more adamant about the blessings of afflictions, found it impossible to sustain a cheery outlook when tragedy struck too close to home. Devastated by the death of the eleventh of his fifteen children in 1721, he could only retreat into a "holy silence," wondering how else one could deal with a deity who seemed to reveal himself to humans primarily through miseries. Cotton Mather, *Silentarius* (1721), in Kenneth Silverman, *The Life and Times of Cotton Mather* (New York: Harper and Row, 1984), 348–49.

83. Increase Mather, "Renewal of Covenant the Great Duty Incumbent on Decaying or Distressed Churches," in *Departing Glory*, preface.

84. This was characteristic of his peers. As Samuel Eliot Morison described, Puritans embraced the new science with speed and enthusiasm. *The Intellectual Life of Colonial New England* (New York: New York University Press, 1956), 247. By the end of the 1680s, Charles Morton's *Compendium Physicae* was an established textbook at Harvard, presenting naturalistic (if often speculative and sometimes improbable) explanations for earthquakes, fires, and storms. Stearns, *Science in the British Colonies*, 157.

85. See Lorraine Daston and Katharine Park, *Wonders and the Order of Nature* (New York: Zone Books, 1998), 303–4, 316.

86. Increase Mather, *Kometographia: Or, A Discourse concerning Comets* (Boston: Samuel Sewall, 1683), 18–19.

87. Increase Mather, *Remarkable Providences: Illustrative of the Earlier Days of American Colonisation* (London: Reeves and Strand, 1890), 92.

88. Increase Mather, *Heaven's Alarm to the World: Or, A Sermon, Wherein is Shewed, That Fearful Sights And Signs in Heaven, are the Presages of Great Calamities at Hand* (Boston: Samuel Sewall, 1682), preface.

89. Increase Mather, *Remarkable Providences*, 239. This was, of course, a self-serving conclusion. Whereas he had viewed the survival of churches during King Philip's War as an indication that God wished to spare the pious from harm, when a meeting house burned down in the fire of 1711, he argued instead that "the HOLY ONE seems to put us in mind of that *shameful negligence* with which too many people in this town *treated the weekly lecture there.*" Quoted in Edward L. Bynner, "Topography and Landmarks of the Provincial Period," in *The Memorial History of Boston*, ed. Justin Winsor (Boston: James R. Osgood, 1880), 2:506.

90. In 1685, Sewall wrote in his diary about a Quaker who was prophesying "great Calamities of Fire and Sword" for New England. *Diary of Samuel Sewall*, 1:67.

91. Increase Mather, *Remarkable Providences*, 241–55. See also Hall, *Worlds of Wonder*, 104–8.

92. Carl Bridenbaugh, *Cities in the Wilderness: The First Century of Urban Life in America, 1625–1742* (New York: Ronald Press, 1938), 136–37.

93. *Boston Records*, cited in Rutman, *Winthrop's Boston*, 215; Josiah Quincy, *A Municipal History of the Town and City of Boston* (Boston: Charles C. Little and James Brown, 1852), 5.

94. Quincy, *Municipal History*, 6. Most of these initiatives—building codes, compulsory water containers, and chimney inspections—drew on well-established English practices developed over the previous three centuries. The English preoccupation with aggressive fire control was heightened by the ignition of at least seventy substantial fires in provincial towns between 1600 and 1665. Stephen Porter, "Newspapers and Fire Relief in Early Modern England," *Journal of Newspapers and Periodical History* 8, no. 1 (1992): 28–33.

95. Quincy, *Municipal History*, 6; Charles C. Smith, "Boston and the Colony," in *Memorial History of Boston*, ed. Winsor, 1:234.

96. Bridenbaugh, *Cities in the Wilderness*, 208.

97. Smith, "Boston and the Colony," 231.

98. At first, in 1653, the town ruled that the owners of these properties would not be entitled to sue for compensation, but six years later a new ruling declared that any house demolished during a fire should "again be repayred and made good by the towne." In 1671, for example, the town paid one man £120 for "his house and goods lost in ye great fire blowne up with gun powder." Bridenbaugh, *Cities in the Wilderness*, 58; Quincy, *Municipal History*, 5–6; Winsor, ed., *Memorial History of Boston*, 1:509. It was a fear of liability that inhibited Mayor Sir Thomas Bludworth, and even the king, from acting aggressively to demolish buildings during the London fire of 1666. Property rights and legal complications presented a greater obstacle to firefighting efforts in this case than any deficiency of firefighting skill or knowledge. Stephen Porter, *The Great Fire of London* (Thrupp, England: Sutton, 1996), 40.

99. Paul Robert Lyons surmises that this was "the first time when explosives were used deliberately to destroy buildings and hinder the spread of the fire front." *Fire in America!* (Boston: National Fire Protection Association, 1976), 7. It was a dangerous strategy, of course, and few were surprised when several men lost their lives trying to blow up buildings during the 1711 fire. Bynner, "Topography and Landmarks of the Provincial Period," 2:504.

100. *Johnson's Wonder-Working Providence*, 247–48, 254–56, 259.

101. Increase Mather to John Cotton, Boston, December 13, 1676, Manuscripts Collection, Mather Papers, American Antiquarian Society.

102. Increase Mather, "Earnest Exhortation to the Inhabitants of New England," 15. He purveyed the same message after the fire of 1711: "Let us endeavour after Hearts more Weaned from the World, and more Set upon Heaven." Increase Mather, "Burnings Bewailed: A Sermon Occasioned by the Lamentable Fire Which was in Boston, Octob. 2, 1711," in *Departing Glory*, 34.

103. Increase Mather, "Earnest Exhortation to the Inhabitants of New England," 15.

104. Cotton Mather, *Magnalia Christi Americana*, 143–44. Observing that religion is expensive, Mark A. Peterson has more recently countered that it was economic prosperity that saved the Puritan movement from rapid extinction in the New World. *The Price of Redemption: The Spiritual Economy of Puritan New England* (Stanford: Stanford University Press, 1997).

105. Hubbard, "Narrative of the Troubles with the Indians," 292.

106. Ann Bradstreet, "Upon the Burning of Our House." For a helpful discussion, see Robert D. Richardson Jr., "The Puritan Poetry of Ann Bradstreet," in *American Puritan Imagination*, ed. Bercovitch, 111–12.

107. Increase Mather, "Burnings Bewailed," 25–26. Since 1653, constables in New England were authorized to prosecute anyone traveling, playing, or working between Saturday evening and Monday morning. But an exception was made for fighting fires throughout the colonial period. Bonomi, *Under the Cope of Heaven*, 5–6.

108. Cotton Mather, *Magnalia Christi Americana*, 183–84.

109. Ibid., 183.

110. Hall, *Last American Puritan*, 128–29.

111. Rutman, *Winthrop's Boston*, chap. 8.

112. Smith, "Boston and the Colony," 230–31, and Bynner, "Topography and Landmarks of the Provincial Period," 2:493.

113. Because whites alone could serve with the watch, nonwhites were required to provide this labor as an alternative public service. Bridenbaugh, *Cities in the Wilderness*, 152–53, 155, 163.

114. Dennis Smith, *Dennis Smith's History of Firefighting in America: Three Hundred Years of Courage* (New York: Dial Press, 1978), 3–8.

115. On the 1679 fire, see Drake, *History and Antiquities of Boston*, 431–32.

116. Benjamin W. Labree, *Colonial Massachusetts: A History* (Millwood, N.Y.: KTO Press, 1979), 185.

117. Bridenbaugh, *Cities in the Wilderness*, 150; Matthew Mulcahy, "'A Tempestuous Spirit Called Hurri Cano': Hurricanes and Colonial Society in the British Greater Caribbean," in *American Disasters*, ed. Steven Biel (New York: New York University Press, 2001), 11–38.

118. See Lester W. Zartman, *Yale Readings in Insurance: Fire* (New Haven: Yale University Press, 1909), 1–11; C. F. Trenerry, *The Origin and Early History of Insurance* (London: P. S. King and Son, 1926), 249–53; and Thomas, *Religion and the Decline of Magic*, 651.

119. Hall, *Last American Puritan*, 128–29.

120. See Marcus Wilson Jernegan, *Laboring and Dependent Classes in Colonial America, 1607–1783* (Westport, Conn.: Greenwood, 1980), 175–77, 190.

121. W. K. Jordan, *Philanthropy in England, 1480–1660: A Study of the Changing Pattern of English Social Aspirations* (New York: George Unwin and Allen, 1959), 140.
122. According to Gary B. Nash, it was not until the 1720s that poverty became a major social problem in Boston. *The Urban Crucible: Social Change, Political Consciousness, and the Origins of the American Revolution* (Cambridge: Harvard University Press, 1979), 21–22, 125.
123. *Records of the Town of Boston*, ii, 94, in Smith, "Boston and the Colony," 230.
124. *Boston Records*, cited in Rutman, *Winthrop's Boston*, 219.
125. After a fire swept through Boston in 1683, for example, poorer residents were released from tax obligations. Jernegan, *Laboring and Dependent Classes in Colonial America*, 198.
126. Matthew Mulcahy records the extraordinary response of imperial and provincial governments to the Charleston fire of 1740. South Carolina's lieutenant governor sent briefs successfully requesting charity from Boston, Philadelphia, Barbados, and even the English Crown. Parliament authorized a grant of £20,000 for the victims of the fire, seemingly "the first and only time the English government provided significant disaster relief to any of its American colonies prior to the Revolution." Most of the money went to elite merchants, supporting Mulcahy's argument that the money was offered not as a humanitarian gesture but as a calculated attempt to shore up an important imperial outpost that was vulnerable to Spanish attacks. "The 'Great Fire' of 1740 and the Politics of Disaster Relief in Colonial Charleston," *South Carolina Historical Magazine* 99, no. 2 (April 1998): 136–37, 148–51, 156–57.
127. G. B. Warden, *Boston, 1689–1776* (Boston: Little, Brown, 1970), 150; Russell H. Conway, *History of the Great Fire in Boston, 1872* (Boston: B. B. Russell, 1873), 33, 43.
128. Karl Polyani, *The Great Transformation* (Boston: Beacon Press, 1957), 38. Because few towns were expected to be able to meet their obligations to feed and shelter their own destitute in the wake of a major fire, neighboring towns were supposed to pick up the slack, donating cash and supplies on receipt of news of any calamity. Unfortunately, word of mouth, letters, or "broadsheets" were not always sufficient to spread the news about suffering, and over the seventeenth century it became customary for the Privy Council to compile and distribute briefs describing calamities and urging donations. Throughout the country, churches would then hold collections, and gatherers would go door to door to raise money for the sufferers. When London burned in 1666, Charles II issued proclamations requiring nearby counties to send bread and other foodstuffs to the city and requiring all cities and towns to accept refugees. In this way £10,611 was raised, along with a further £12,794 collected during church services held throughout the country in response to calls for a day of fasting and humiliation. John E. N. Hearsey, *London and the Great Fire* (London: John Murray, 1965), 168–69, 178; Porter, *Great Fire of London*, 83–84, 65.
129. Warden, *Boston, 1689–1776*, 149–51.
130. Winthrop, "A Modell of Christian Charity," *Winthrop Papers*, 2:284.
131. Boston churches raised £700 for 110 families left homeless by the fire of 1711, but Puritan church members were rarely as forthcoming in their assistance to

outsiders. Drake, *History and Antiquities of Boston*, 542. Mark A. Peterson suggests that much of this charity was directed to churches and their members. *Price of Redemption*, 168–69.

132. Cotton Mather, "Advice from Taberah: A Sermon Preached After the Terrible Fire, Which, . . . Laid a Considerable Part of Boston, in Ashes. Boston, 1711," in *Days of Humiliation*, 171.
133. Bridenbaugh, *Cities in the Wilderness*, 143.
134. Hall, *Last American Puritan*, 127.
135. Hofstadter, *America at 1750*, 104; Paul C. Ditzel, *Fire Engines, Fire Fighters: The Men, Equipment, and Machines, from Colonial Days to the Present* (New York: Crown, 1976), 23.
136. Theodore Roosevelt, *New York* (New York: Longmans, Green, 1891), 101. One hundred and fifty-four blacks were arrested during what Roosevelt called this "Bloody Tragedy," which one Massachusetts observer perceptively likened to the Salem witch trials of 1692. Incendiarism was not unknown in New York. During the revolt of 1712, slaves had burned a building while killing ten whites, and there is evidence of at least one case of arson in the summer of 1741. As Thomas J. Davis notes, deep (and legitimate) racial and class resentments did drive some blacks and poor whites to commit crimes against property. "God damn all the white people," he quotes one slave as declaring. "If I had it in my power, I'd burn them all." There is no evidence, however, of a general slave conspiracy. *A Rumor of Revolt: The 'Great Negro Plot' in Colonial New York* (New York: Free Press, 1985), 252. See also Thomas J. Davis, ed., *The New York Conspiracy by Daniel Horsmanden* (Boston: Beacon Press, 1971); Edwin G. Burrows and Mike Wallace, *Gotham: A History of New York City to 1898* (New York: Oxford University Press, 1999), 159–66; and Jill Lepore, *New York Burning: Liberty, Slavery, and Conspiracy in Eighteenth-Century Manhattan* (New York: Alfred A. Knopf, 2005). Significantly, Charleston authorities, still smarting from the Stono rebellion of 1739, opposed the extensive deployment of slaves to rebuild their city after the great fire of 1740. Not only did they (wrongly) suspect that slaves had started the fire, they were unwilling to risk bringing slaves together, even though this meant slowing the pace of reconstruction. Mulcahy, "'Great Fire' of 1740," 153–54.
137. Bridenbaugh, *Cities in the Wilderness*, 368. Silverman, *Life and Times of Cotton Mather*, 281.
138. For one vivid account of the trials of slaves and immigrants in the eighteenth century, see Hofstadter, *America at 1750*, 3–130. Pointing out that immigration was more characteristic of the colonial experience outside of than inside of New England, he writes of newcomers:

> Bearing in mind the poverty and the ravaged lives which they left in Europe, the cruel filter of the Atlantic crossing, the high mortality of the crossing and the seasoning, and the many years of arduous toil that lay between the beginning of servitude and the final realization of tolerable comfort—one is deeply impressed by the measure to which the sadness that is natural to life was overwhelmed by the stark miseries that seem all too natural to the history of the poor. (64–65)

139. Jon Butler, "The Dark Ages of American Occultism, 1760–1848," in *The Occult in America: New Historical Perspectives*, ed. Howard Kerr and Charles L. Crow

(Urbana: University of Illinois Press, 1983), 58–78. Immigration and slave importations ensured the perpetual renewal of European and African "folk" beliefs and practices in the so-called Age of Reason. Significantly, even after many slaves converted to Christianity at the end of the eighteenth century, most of them remained essentially fatalistic. Although there is impressive (and perhaps surprising) evidence that many converted slaves came to imagine themselves as a chosen people bound, if only after death, for the promised land, many spirituals emphasized earthly hardships: "This world is not my home. / This world is not my home. / This world's a howling wilderness, / This world is not my home." Levine, *Black Culture and Black Consciousness*, 32–40. See also Albert J. Raboteau, *Slave Religion: The 'Invisible Institution' in the Antebellum South* (New York: Oxford University Press, 1978).

140. Saum, *Popular Mood of Pre–Civil War America*, 3, 4–26. See also Agnes Marie Silbey, *Alexander Pope's Prestige in America, 1725–1835* (New York: King's Crown Press, 1949), 27–35.

141. David Stewart and Ray Knox, *The Earthquake That America Forgot* (Marble Hill, Mo.: Gutenberg-Richter, 1995), 15.

142. The following account is taken largely from James Lal Penick, *The New Madrid Earthquakes* (Columbia: University of Missouri Press, 1981), and Stewart and Knox, *Earthquake That America Forgot*, with supplementary information from Francis A. Sampson, "The New Madrid and Other Earthquakes," *Missouri Historical Review* 92 (1997–98): 238–53. Stewart and Knox calculate the probable casualty statistics (209).

143. Quoted in Penick, *New Madrid Earthquakes*, 128. According to Walter Brownlow Posey, in Tennessee, Kentucky, portions of Mississippi, Arkansas, Illinois, Indiana, Ohio, and western Virginia, the Methodist Church attracted more than fifteen thousand new members between 1811 and 1812, an increase of 50 percent. "The Earthquake of 1811 and Its Influence on Evangelistic Methods in the Churches of the Old South," *Tennessee Historical Magazine* 1, no. 2 (1931): 107–14. Michael Barkun argues that a series of natural calamities in the 1810s and 1820s contributed to a similar rise of millennialism in the Northeast in this period. *Crucible of the Millennium: The Burned-Over District of New York in the 1840s* (Syracuse: University of Syracuse Press, 1986), 103–12.

144. Simmons, *Spirit of the New England Tribes*, 63, 78.

145. William G. McLoughlin, *The Cherokee Ghost Dance: Essays on the Southeastern Indians, 1789–1861* (Macon, Ga.: Mercer University Press, 1984), 111–35. See also Michelene E. Pesantubbee, "When the Earth Shakes: The Cherokee Prophecies of 1811–12," *American Indian Quarterly* 17, no. 3 (Summer 1993): 198–217. For an engaging popular account of the prophecies, see Stewart and Knox, *Earthquake That America Forgot*, 58–74, 86–88, 98–106, 263–65.

146. John Dunn Hunter, *Memoirs of a Captivity among the Indians of North America* (New York: Schocken Books, 1973), quoted in Penick, *New Madrid Earthquakes*, 122, 127.

147. Colonel Return J. Meigs, "Some Reflections on Cherokee concerns, manners, state, etc.," March 19 (1812), repr. in McLoughlin, *Cherokee Ghost Dance*, appendix F, 148.

148. "Official Mission Diary of the Moravians at Springplace, Georgia, 1811–12," repr. in McLoughlin, *Cherokee Ghost Dance*, appendix E, 142–47.

149. See Penick, *New Madrid Earthquakes*, 14–50, and Stewart and Knox, *Earthquake That America Forgot*, 251–55.
150. Penick, *New Madrid Earthquakes*, 16–29.
151. Charles Lyell, *Principles of Geology* (Chicago: University of Chicago Press, 1991), 1:479. He wrote about his visit to the Mississippi valley in *A Second Visit to the United States of North America* (New York: Harper and Brothers, 1855), 2:172–82. Also see Leonard G. Wilson, *Lyell in America: Transatlantic Geology, 1841–1853* (Baltimore: Johns Hopkins University Press, 1998), 221–62.
152. Charles Lyell wrote about the New Madrid earthquakes in the first edition of *Principles of Geology*, 1:407–8.
153. William Whewell introduced the term *uniformitarian* in an 1832 review to distinguish Charles Lyell from those "catastrophists" who, according to Lyell, misguidedly attributed major changes in the structure of the earth to "paroxysmal violence" rather than "the reiterated recurrence of minor convulsions." Claude C. Albritton, *Catastrophic Episodes in Earth History* (New York: Chapman and Hall, 1989), 49; Lyell's *Principles of Geology*, 3:339. For a critical analysis of Lyell's opposition to progressive geologists, see Stephen Jay Gould, *Time's Arrow, Times's Cycle: Myth and Metaphor in the Discovery of Geological Time* (Cambridge: Harvard University Press, 1987), 99–179.
154. Deploying a metaphor that recalls the optimistic image favored by Jonathan Edwards, Agassiz characterized glaciers as "God's great plough," as, in the words of his biographer, "destructive and chaotic natural forces which signified a beneficent supernatural plan for the universe." Edward Lurie, *Louis Agassiz: A Life in Science* (Chicago: University of Chicago Press, 1960), 98. Agassiz may have believed in the providential design of nature, but he strenuously resisted Darwin's later theory of natural selection, which he viewed as an impious and insupportable attempt to secularize the logic of the pilgrim's progress. C. George Fry and Jon Paul Fry, *Congregationalists and Evolution: Asa Gray and Louis Agassiz* (Lanham, Md.: University Press of America, 1989), 18. On links between geological and biblical catastrophism (or "dispensationalism"), see George M. Marsden, *Fundamentalism and American Culture: The Shaping of Twentieth-Century Evangelicalism, 1870–1925* (New York: Oxford University Press, 1980), 62–66.
155. Clarence King, "Catastrophism and the Evolution of Environment," June 26, 1877, quoted in Thurman Wilkins, *Clarence King: A Biography* (Albuquerque: University of New Mexico Press, 1988), 221–23.
156. Lyell, *Second Visit to the United States*, 2:179.
157. Louis C. Hunter, *Steamboats on the Western River: An Economic and Technological History* (Cambridge: Harvard University Press, 1949), 16, 272–304. See also S. A. Howland, *Steamboat Disasters and Railroad Accidents in the United States* (Worcester, Mass.: Dorr, Howland, 1840).
158. *The Diary of Philip Hone, 1828–1851*, ed. Allan Nevins (New York: Dodd, Mead, 1927), 2:722, 825.
159. Daniel J. Boorstin, *The Americans: The National Experience* (New York: Vintage Books, 1965), 100–107; Jack Larkin, *The Reshaping of Everyday Life, 1790–1840* (New York: Harper and Row, 1988), 228–31.
160. Bercovitch, *American Jeremiad*, 23. Though also see Perry Miller, who argues that jeremiads were more cathartic than motivational. "Errand into the Wilderness," in *Errand into the Wilderness*, 8.

161. Thus calamities become a link between what Max Weber called the "Protestant ethic" and the "spirit of capitalism," though we should not overstate this connection. Margo Todd, for example, has argued persuasively that the so-called bourgeois social values of the Puritans (work ethic, discipline, social reform, etc.) owe more to the influence of Erasmus and Christian humanism than to Calvinist or scriptural doctrine. *Christian Humanism and the Puritan Social Order* (Cambridge: Cambridge University Press, 1987), 17–18, 94–95.

162. Ralph Waldo Emerson, *The Journals and Miscellaneous Notebooks of Ralph Waldo Emerson*, ed. William H. Gilman et al. (Cambridge: Harvard University Press, Belknap Press, 1963), 3:122.

163. Ralph Waldo Emerson, *Nature*, ed. Jaroslav Pelikan (1836; Boston: Beacon Press, 1985), 40.

164. Ralph Waldo Emerson, "Fate" (1860), in *Selected Essays*, ed. Ziff, 362–65, 379–80, 382.

Interlude

1. P. Barrett's account is reprinted in Charles Morris, *The San Francisco Calamity by Earthquake and Fire* (1906; Secaucus, N.J.: Citadel Press, 1986), 66–68. Of the many narrative histories of the earthquake and fire, perhaps the most vivid and entertaining is John Castillo Kennedy, *The Great Earthquake and Fire: San Francisco, 1906* (New York: William Morrow, 1963). The standard illustrated account is still William Bronson, *The Earth Shook, The Sky Burned* (New York: Doubleday, 1959). Also see Monica Sutherland, *The Damndest Finest Ruins* (New York: Ballantine Books, 1959); Gordon Thomas and Max Gordon Witts, *The San Francisco Earthquake* (New York: Stein and Day, 1971); Gerstle Mack, *1906: Surviving San Francisco's Earthquake and Fire* (San Francisco: Chronicle Books, 1981); and Eric Saul and Don Denevi, *The Great San Francisco Earthquake and Fire, 1906* (Millbrae, Calif.: Celestial Arts, 1981). The centenary of the disaster was marked by a flurry of new narrative histories, including vivid retellings by Simon Winchester, *A Crack in the Edge of the World: America and the Great California Earthquake of 1906* (New York: Harper Collins, 2004), and Dennis Smith, *San Francisco Is Burning: The Untold Story of the 1906 Earthquake and Fire* (New York: Viking, 2005). Among the many "on the spot" histories are Frank W. Aitken and Edward Hilton, *A History of the Earthquake and Fire in San Francisco* (San Francisco: Edward Hilton, 1906); Charles Eugene Banks and Opie Read, *The History of the San Francisco Disaster and Mount Vesuvius Horror* (San Francisco: S. E. Thomas, 1906); Marshall Everett, *The Complete Story of the San Francisco Earthquake* (Chicago: Henry Neil, 1906); Richard Linthicum, *Complete Story of the San Francisco Horror* (San Francisco: Hubert D. Russell, 1906); Charles Morris, *The San Francisco Calamity by Earthquake and Fire* (Secaucus, N.J.: Citadel Press, 1986); Frank Thomas Searight, *The Doomed City: A Thrilling Tale* (Chicago: Laird and Lee, 1906); and Sidney Tyler, *San Francisco's Great Disaster* (Harrisburg, Pa.: Minter, 1906).

2. William Ford Nichols, *A Father's Story of the Earthquake and Fire in San Francisco, April 18, 19, 20, 1906* (San Francisco: Foster, 1909), 9.

3. Amy Kahn to Mr. Coop, Oakland, California, April 23, 1906 (unpublished MS), Bancroft Library, 3.

4. There were more than twenty-two hundred "major breaks" in the water distribution system. Charles R. Boden, "San Francisco's Cisterns," *California Historical Society Quarterly* 15, no. 4 (1936): 315.

5. E. Call Brown, quoted in Everett, *Complete Story of the San Francisco Earthquake*, 150.

6. Albert S. Reed, "The San Francisco Conflagration of April, 1906," *Special Report to the National Board of Fire Underwriters Committee of Twenty* (New York, 1906), 1.

7. Kennedy, *Great Earthquake and Fire*, 45.

8. Captain Kelly, "Earthquake and Fire at San Francisco," April 18, 1906 (unpublished MS), Bancroft Library, 2.

9. Chief engineer, San Francisco Fire Department, September 13, 1906, in Frederick J. Bowlen, *Material Relating to San Francisco Fire Department*, Bancroft Library. See also "Experience of J. J. Conlon, Battalion Chief, Ninth District" and "Experiences of Captain T. J. Murphy, Engine # 9" in *Reports of the San Francisco Fire Department on the 1906 Fire*, vol. 7, p. 2, in Bowlen, *Material Relating to San Francisco Fire Department*.

10. Josephine Baxter to parents, San Francisco, April 23, 1906 (unpublished MS), Bancroft Library, 1, 5. Matilda B. Murphey, letter to Frank Fahey, San Francisco, April 19, 1906 (unpublished MS), Bancroft Library, 1–3.

11. Amy Kahn to Mr. Coop, Oakland, April 23, 1906 (unpublished MS), Bancroft Library, 5.

12. Chas B. Sedgwick, "The Fall of San Francisco: Some Personal Observations," *American Builders' Review* 4, no. 1 (July 1906): 201.

13. Henry Anderson Lafler, *How The Army Worked to Save San Francisco* (San Francisco: Calkins Newspaper Syndicate, 1906), 4, 5.

14. William Douglas Alexander to Mary C. Alexander, San Francisco, May 16, 1906 (unpublished MS), Bancroft Library, 6–7.

15. Mary McD. Gordon, "Notes and Documents: Earthquake and Fire in San Francisco," *Huntington Library Quarterly* 48, no. 1 (Winter 1985): 72.

16. Linthicum, *Complete Story of the San Francisco Horror*, 73, 48.

17. Russell Sage Foundation, *San Francisco Relief Survey* (New York: Survey Associates, 1913), 5.

18. *Report of the Sub-committee on Statistics* (San Francisco: April 24, 1907), 3, 16. "The Great San Francisco Earthquake," in *American Experience* #101 (WGBH Educational Foundation, 1988). See Gladys Hansen and Emmet Condon, *Denial of Disaster* (San Francisco: Cameron, 1989).

19. Russell Sage Foundation, *San Francisco Relief Survey*, 33–34. The Red Cross later calculated that $15 million worth of money and goods went for the relief of San Francisco. *Sixth Annual Report of the American National Red Cross* (Washington, D.C.: GPO, 1911), 13.

Chapter Two

1. George Harvey, "Comment," *Harper's Weekly*, May 5, 1906, 616.

2. J. S. Cahill, "The So-Called Catastrophe," *American Builders Review* 4, no. 1 (July 1906): 177.

3. See, for example, William Greider, *One World, Ready or Not: The Manic Logic of Global Capitalism* (New York: Simon and Schuster, 1997).

4. See, for example, Max Page, *The Creative Destruction of Manhattan, 1900–1940* (Chicago: University of Chicago Press, 1999).

5. Marshall Berman, *All That Is Solid Melts into Air: The Experience of Modernity* (New York: Penguin, 1988), 19.

6. Lewis Mumford, *City Development: Studies in Renewal and Development* (New York: Harcourt, Brace, 1946), 191, 160, 157.

7. Cotton Mather, "Boanerges. A Short Essay to Preserve and Strengthen the Good Impressions Produced by Earthquakes. Boston, 1727," in *Days of Humiliation, Times of Affliction* (Gainesville, Fla.: Scholars' Facsimiles and Reprints, 1970), 366.

8. Increase Mather, "An Earnest Exhortation to the Inhabitants of New England," in *Departing Glory: Eight Jeremiads by Increase Mather*, ed. Lee Scheninger (Delmar, N.Y.: Scholars' Facsimiles and Reprints, 1986), 15. Increase Mather, letter to John Cotton, Boston, December 13, 1676, Manuscripts Collection, Mather Papers, American Antiquarian Society, and *Diary by Increase Mather, March 1675–December 1676*, ed. Samuel A. Green (Cambridge, Mass.: John Wilson and Son, 1900), 39.

9. See Charles C. Smith, "Boston and the Colony," and Edward L. Bynner, "Topography and Landmarks of the Provincial Period," in *The Memorial History of Boston*, ed. Justin Winsor (Boston: James R. Osgood, 1880), 1:230–31, 493.

10. Sacvan Bercovitch, *The American Jeremiad* (Madison: University of Wisconsin Press, 1978), 23.

11. Elias Colbert and Everett Chamberlin, *Chicago and the Great Conflagration* (1871; New York: Viking Press, 1971), 445.

12. Harvey, "Comment," 616.

13. John Stuart Mill, *Principles of Political Economy with Some of Their Applications to Social Philosophy*, in *Collected Works of John Stuart Mill* (Toronto: Routledge and Kegan Paul, 1965), 74–75.

14. Edwin G. Burrows and Mike Wallace, *Gotham: A History of New York City to 1898* (New York: Oxford University Press, 1999), 596–601.

15. "The Conflagration," *New York Herald*, December 19, 1835.

16. The opening of the magnificent Croton aqueduct system (capable of supplying ample, clean water to the city, and incidentally reducing downtown fire insurance rates) may well have been the most enduring legacy of the conflagration. This project had first been proposed as a defense against the devastating cholera epidemics that swept through the city earlier in the 1830s. Because the absence of an adequate water system had seriously hampered the efforts of firemen to put out the fire, this one event dismantled opposition to this expensive public project. George J. Lankevich, *American Metropolis: A History of New York City* (New York: New York University Press, 1998), 81–82.

17. According to Edwin G. Burrows and Mike Wallace, the value of registered real estate in Manhattan shot up from $143 million in 1835 to $233 million in 1836. *Gotham*, 576, 598–601.

18. Harriet Martineau, *Society in America* (New York: Saunders and Otley, 1837), 2:74.

19. *The Diary of Philip Hone, 1828–1851*, ed. Allan Nevins (New York: Dodd, Mead, 1927), 199–201.

20. John Austin Stevens, "The Beginning of New York's Commercial Greatness, 1825–1837," in *The Memorial History of the City of New York, From Its Settlement to the Year 1892*, ed. James Grant Wilson (New York: New-York History, 1893), 3:334–63.

21. Reginald Charles McGrane, *The Panic of 1837: Some Financial Problems of the Jacksonian Era* (New York: Russell and Russell, 1965), 43–69, 91.

22. Until the middle of the eighteenth century, even the most successful American merchants had to buy policies in Europe to cover their properties against loss by fire. Nicholas Barbon established the first successful fire-insurance company in London in the aftermath of the great conflagration of 1666; business was so successful that five more enterprises were in operation in England by 1720. Johan Goudsblom, *Fire and Civilization* (New York: Penguin Press, 1992), 151. It was only in 1752, with the founding of Benjamin Franklin's Philadelphia Contributionship for the Insuring of Houses from Loss by Fire (known by its emblem as the "Hand-in-Hand"), that any community was able to avail itself of dependable homegrown coverage. Even this enterprise was little more than a mutual aid society for a small group of professionals and businessmen who contributed fees to a central fund to compensate any associate whose home or business burned down. The firm prospered only because the city of Philadelphia was spared a major conflagration during the company's eighty-five formative years. Nicholas B. Wainwright, *A Philadelphia Story: The Philadelphia Contributionship for the Insurance of Houses from Loss by Fire* (Philadelphia: William F. Fell, 1952). Franklin was not the first to bring insurance to America. The Friendly Society for the Mutual Insurance of Houses Against Fire survived in Charleston, South Carolina, for five years after its founding in 1735 before being wiped out by fire losses. Lester W. Zartman, *Yale Readings in Insurance: Fire* (New Haven: Yale University Press, 1909), 12–40; Dennis Smith, *Dennis Smith's History of Firefighting in America: 300 Years of Courage* (New York: Dial Press, 1978), 13.

23. Marquis James, *Biography of a Business, 1792–1942: Insurance Company of North America* (Indianapolis: Bobbs-Merrill, 1942).

24. Zartman, *Yale Readings in Insurance: Fire*, 21. As William H. A. Carr points out, the vast majority of these businesses failed. *Perils: Named and Unnamed; The Story of the Insurance Company of North America* (New York: McGraw-Hill, 1967), 51. Fire insurance was always the leading edge of this new industry. Whereas life insurance companies were unable to overcome religious objections to a practice that seemed to interfere with God's providences, there was little such opposition to fire insurance. Viviana A. Rotman Zelizer, *Morals and Markets: The Development of Life Insurance in the United States* (New York: Columbia University Press, 1979), 32n, 73–76.

25. Burrows and Wallace, *Gotham*, 598.

26. Robert Sobel, *Panic on Wall Street: A History of America's Financial Disasters* (New York: Macmillan, 1968), 32–33.

27. Zartman, *Yale Readings in Insurance: Fire*, 20–21.

28. Philip Hone endeavored to restore his own fortune after the panic of 1837 by accepting a position as the president of a new mutual insurance company in

1843. The company proved to be a smashing success—until it was wiped out by the New York fire of 1845. *Diary of Philip Hone*, 2:680, 741.

29. For more on this theme, see Zelizer, *Morals and Markets*, 67–89.

30. Zartman, *Yale Readings in Insurance: Fire*, 7–9. Stephen J. Pyne, *Fire in America: A Cultural History of Wildland and Rural Fire* (Princeton: Princeton University Press, 1988), 459.

31. *Diary of Philip Hone*, 2:730.

32. This discomfort was also inflected with social anxieties. In the Age of Jackson, an era of riots, labor activism, and the growing political influence of the "low Irish," Hone reflexively characterized social disturbances in class terms, as "part of the warfare of the poor against the rich." Calamities brought social tensions to the surface. Hone, for example, was disconcerted by the crowds of "miserable wretches" that suddenly appeared on city streets during the fire, attributing this not to the fire itself (or to the disintegrating social forces of capitalism) but to the malign intentions of the poor. The business district was destroyed, and Hone believed this was sure to be a matter of satisfaction to working men who, by his dubious account, reveled in the misfortunes of entrepreneurs: "such expressions were heard as 'Ah! They'll make no more five per cent dividends!' and 'This will make the aristocracy haul in their horns!'" Hone might blame the laboring classes for all that was wrong with his city, but his anxieties speak to abiding discontents about the costs of a social system that had made him such a rich and powerful man. *Diary of Philip Hone*, 1:189–90. This conflagration, like most others in the nineteenth century, had other important class dimensions. According to Sean Wilentz, few social organizations in the 1830s expressed working-class cultural solidarity more completely than the volunteer fire companies on which cities depended for defense against fires. In the eighteenth century, as Franklin pointed out in his autobiography, fire brigades were clubs for "men of property," but in New York, at least, fire brigades were being taken over by laboring men, and fires were becoming occasions for the assertion of working-class pride and influence. Sean Wilentz, *Chants Democratic: New York City and the Rise of the American Working Class, 1788–1850* (New York: Oxford University Press, 1984), 259–63; *The Autobiography of Benjamin Franklin*, ed. Leonard W. Labaree et al. (New Haven: Yale University Press, 1964), 174–75.

33. Martineau, *Society in America*, 2:74–75.

34. Samuel Rezneck, "The Social History of an American Depression, 1837–1843," in *Business Depressions and Financial Panics: Essays in American Business and Economic History* (New York: Greenwood, 1968), 73–100; Sobel, *Panic on Wall Street*, 67.

35. Some commentators blamed the economic distress on the great fire. See McGrane, *Panic of 1837*, 93. It is true that some business ventures were weakened by losses incurred during the conflagration. For example, Arthur Tappan's powerful silk-import house had borrowed heavily to rebuild and expand after the calamity, and the company was forced to declare bankruptcy in May 1837 because it could not recover enough of its loans to cover debts. Lewis Tappan, *The Life of Arthur Tappan* (New York: Hurd and Houghton, 1870), 272–82. It is clear, however, that the fire had little to do with the panic. Interestingly, commentators on the depression borrowed from discourses of natural disaster to understand the logic of this economic misfortune. Ann Fabian argues that weather metaphors

may have helped to naturalize capitalism at such moments of crisis, encouraging people to accept panics, like disasters, as blessings, as agents of ultimate order and well-being. "Speculation on Distress: The Popular Discourse of the Panics of 1837 and 1857," *Yale Journal of Criticism* 3, no. 1 (1989): 132–38.

36. Joseph A. Schumpeter, *Capitalism, Socialism, and Democracy* (New York: Harper, 1950), 83, 82.
37. Karl Marx and Friedrich Engels, *The Communist Manifesto* (New York: Bantam Books, 1992), 24.
38. Ibid., 25.
39. David Harvey, *The Urban Experience* (Baltimore: Johns Hopkins University Press, 1989), 33.
40. See Neil Smith, *Uneven Development: Nature, Capital, and the Production of Space* (Cambridge, Mass.: Basil Blackwell, 1990), 124–30.
41. Neil Smith, *The New Urban Frontier: Gentrification and the Revanchist City* (New York: Routledge, 1996), 83–84. It has never been easy for property owners, singly or collectively, to tear down and replace existing structures or neighborhoods. As Christine Meisner Rosen shows in her comprehensive account of the politics and economics of reconstruction after the Great Chicago Fire of 1871, the Boston fire of 1872, and the Baltimore fire of 1904, even the most concerted efforts to improve districts and buildings were hindered by "frictions" that included the durability of urban buildings, the high costs of demolition and rebuilding, technological limitations, political weaknesses, and market and tax disincentives to improvements. Frustration with these obstacles to renewal helps to explain why so many businesspeople were so enthusiastic about fires that promised to burn away some of these obstacles to change; the persistence of these frictions helps to explain why ambitious plans for reconstruction were so hard to accomplish. *The Limits of Power: Great Fires and the Process of City Growth in America* (New York: Cambridge University Press, 1986).
42. Berman, *All That Is Solid Melts into Air*, 95. Berman challenges Marx's analysis of crisis: "Marx appears to believe that these crises will increasingly cripple capitalism and eventually destroy it. And yet, his own vision and analysis of bourgeois society show how well this society can thrive on crisis and catastrophe" (103).
43. Willis Fletcher Johnson, *George Harvey: A Passionate Patriot* (Boston: Houghton Mifflin, 1929), 32–33. As editor of both *Harper's Weekly* and the *North American Review*, Harvey was one of the most influential opinion makers of his day. "A Holiday for Capital" is reprinted in his book *Women, Etc.: Some Leaves from an Editor's Diary* (New York: Harper and Brothers, 1908), 139–43.
44. George Harvey, "San Francisco," *Harper's Weekly*, May 5, 1906, 619. It is also possible, however, that extraordinarily high returns in the stock markets in 1906 may have discouraged some financiers from investing in California real estate and infrastructures. John Moody, *The Masters of Capital: A Chronicle of Wall Street* (New Haven: Yale University Press, 1919), 134–35.
45. "San Francisco Will Be Restored," *New York Times*, April 20, 1906.
46. As it turned out, the earthquake was a blessing in disguise for the United Railroads corporation, which took advantage of the confusion to bribe "Boss" Abraham Ruef and thereby win a controversial, and long-resisted, trolley franchise in the city. See Walton Bean, *Boss Ruef's San Francisco: The Story of the Union*

Labor Party, Big Business, and the Graft Prosecution (Berkeley: University of California Press, 1952), 130–37.

47. "Heavy Sales of Stock," *New York Times*, April 20, 1906, 7.
48. Henry Clews, *Fifty Years in Wall Street* (New York: Irving, 1915), 783.
49. "Catastrophe Markets," *New York Times*, April 23, 1906, 14.
50. Clews, *Fifty Years in Wall Street*, 783–85.
51. For an exemplary analysis of the geography of capital and the development of another western metropolis, see William Cronon, *Nature's Metropolis: Chicago and the Great West* (New York: W. W. Norton, 1991), 263–309.
52. "Looking Ahead at San Francisco," *Collier's*, May 12, 1906, 24. For a similar argument, see William H. Mills, "Influences That Insure the Recovery of San Francisco," *California State Board of Trade Bulletin* 15 (1906).
53. Hubert Howe Bancroft, *Some Cities and San Francisco and Resurgam* (New York: Bancroft, 1907), 61–62.
54. David Harvey offers a brilliant technical analysis of "creative destruction" in imperial Paris in *Consciousness and the Urban Experience: Studies in the History and Theory of Capitalist Urbanization* (Baltimore: Johns Hopkins University Press, 1985), 63–220.
55. Haussmann, fully aware that many of his peers viewed him as a vandal for destroying so much of old Paris, offered the self-description with some degree of irony at his admission to the Académie des Beaux Arts in 1867: "My qualifications? I was chosen as demolition artist." Quoted in J. M. and Brian Chapman, *The Life and Times of Baron Haussmann: Paris in the Second Empire* (London: Weidenfeld and Nicolson, 1957), 209.
56. Richard Sennett, *The Uses of Disorder: Personal Identity and City Life* (New York: Alfred A. Knopf, 1970), 88–90.
57. On links between urban planning and the quest for moral order and social control, see Paul Boyer, *Urban Masses and Moral Order in America, 1820–1920* (Cambridge: Harvard University Press, 1978), and M. Christine Boyer, *Dreaming the Rational City: The Myth of American City Planning* (Cambridge: MIT Press, 1983).
58. Gertrude Atherton, "San Francisco's Tragic Dawn," *Harper's Weekly*, May 12, 1906, 660.
59. "What the Disaster Means to Oregon," *Oregon Mining Journal* 22, no. 1 (April 28, 1906): 17.
60. Chapman, *Life and Times of Baron Haussmann*, 90. For their part, most influential Englishmen tended to view the London fire, which destroyed 13,200 structures and left eighty thousand people homeless, as a missed opportunity for urban renewal, lamenting the failure of the Crown or Parliament to implement Christopher Wren's ambitious proposals for an "ideal city." See John E. N. Hearsey, *London and the Great Fire* (London: John Murray, 1965), 183–65, and Stephen Porter, *The Great Fire of London* (Thrupp, England: Sutton Publishing, 1996), 104–5, 123–30.
61. Louis Sullivan, *Autobiography of an Idea* (New York: American Institute of Architects, 1926), 314.
62. See, for example, Daniel Burnham, "Presentation to the Merchant's Association, April 13, 1897," in Charles Moore, *Daniel Hudson Burnham, Architect, Planner of Cities* (Boston: Houghton Mifflin, 1921), 2:102.

63. Marsden Manson, *Report of Marsden Manson to the Mayor and Committee on Reconstruction on those Portions of the Burnham Plans Which Meet Our Commercial Necessities and An Estimate of the Cost of the Same* (October 1906).
64. Daniel Hudson Burnham and Edward H. Bennett, *Report on a Plan for San Francisco* (San Francisco: City of San Francisco, 1905), 35.
65. Mel Scott, *The San Francisco Bay Area: A Metropolis in Perspective* (Berkeley: University of California Press, 1959), 79–80. Although some tall buildings appeared in the aftermath of the disaster, few individual owners could yet afford to erect these costly structures, and it was only during the building boom of the 1920s that skyscrapers came to dominate the San Francisco skyline.
66. Walter Benjamin, "Paris, Capital of the Nineteenth Century," in *Reflections: Essays, Aphorisms, Autobiographical Writings*, trans. Edmund Jephcott (New York: Schocken Books, 1978), 162. Marshall Berman makes the same point with similar polemical dazzle: "Even the most beautiful and impressive bourgeois buildings and public works are disposable, capitalized for fast depreciation and planned to be obsolete, closer in their social functions to tents and encampments than to 'Egyptian pyramids, Roman aqueducts, Gothic cathedrals.'" *All That Is Solid Melts into Air*, 99.
67. Hence, as Richard E. Fogelsong shows, Burnham's hometown of Chicago abandoned his City Beautiful proposals for a more commercial City Practical design after 1909. *Planning the Capitalist City: The Colonial Era to the 1920s* (Princeton: Princeton University Press, 1986), 215–16. Interestingly, as David Harvey notes, although Haussmann's own reforms promoted capital accumulation and economic productivity in imperial Paris, his monumental city may have been partially responsible for "the relative stagnation of capitalism in France" in the late nineteenth and twentieth centuries. *The Urban Experience*, 29.
68. "Proposed Street Changes," *San Francisco Chronicle*, April 27, 1906, 4.
69. A. P. Giannini was one banker who saw tremendous opportunity in the disaster, even though his own banking house was burned to the ground. Seizing the chance to increase business at a time when ordinary citizens were desperate for loans and for a safe place to keep their money, he doubled the deposits and transactions of his bank in the summer after the calamity and was easily able to afford the move to an impressive new nine-story headquarters in the new downtown financial district. This was a crucial moment in the transformation of his small neighborhood institution into the world's largest bank by the 1940s. Gerald D. Nash, *A. P. Giannini and the Bank of America* (Norman: University of Oklahoma Press, 1992), ix, 30–36; Felice A. Bondadio, *A. P. Giannini: Banker of America* (Berkeley: University of California Press, 1994), 32–37. As Marquis James and Bessie Rowland James point out, all San Francisco banks increased their business in 1906 during the reconstruction months. *Biography of a Bank: The Story of the Bank of America* (New York: Harper and Brothers, 1954), 31.
70. Burnham and Bennett, *Report on a Plan for San Francisco*, 7.
71. On the "placeless power" of capital, see Allan Pred and Michael John Watts, *Reworking Modernity: Capitalism and Its Symbolic Discontents* (New Brunswick, N.J.: Rutgers University Press, 1992), 11–12.
72. For two fine accounts of the complex financial politics of the rebuilding of Paris that pay attention to the revolution in the national credit system, see David P. Jordan, *Transforming Paris: The Life and Labors of Baron Haussmann* (New York:

Free Press, 1995), 227–45, and Harvey, *Consciousness and the Urban Experience*, 76–82, 97–98.

73. Lewis Mumford's observations on the contradictions of imperial planning are as trenchant today as they were when he composed them eighty-five years ago:

    Historically, the imperial monument and the slum-tenement go hand in hand. The same process that creates an unearned increment for the landlords who possess favored sites, contributes a generous quota— which might be called the unearned excrement—of depression, over-crowding, and bad living, in the dormitory districts of the city. This had happened in imperial Rome; it had happened again in Paris under Napoleon III, where Haussmann's sweeping reconstructions created new slums in the districts behind the grand avenues, quite as bad, if far less obvious, as those that had been cleared away; and it happened once again in our American cities. (Lewis Mumford, *Sticks and Stones: A Study of American Architecture and Civilization* [New York: Boni and Liveright, 1924], 143)

74. Quoted in Robert Moses, "What Happened to Haussmann," *Architectural Forum* 77 (July 1942): 61.

75. Ibid., 6. In his absorbing biography, Robert A. Caro recalls the violent imagery deployed by Moses to justify the immense destruction that accompanied his developments: "You can't make an omelet without breaking eggs," or "When you operate in an overbuilt metropolis, you have to hack your way with a meat ax." *The Power Broker: Robert Moses and the Fall of New York* (New York: Alfred A. Knopf, 1974), 849.

76. Karl Marx, *The Civil War in France* (New York: International Publishers, 1933), 59–60.

77. *Collier's*, May 12, 1906, 6. Michael Kazin's history of the Building Trades Council emphasizes the extraordinary social, economic, and political influence of construction tradesmen in the 1900s and 1910s but complicates the characterization of San Francisco as a "labor city" in *Barons of Labor: The San Francisco Building Trades and Union Power in the Progressive Era* (Urbana: University of Illinois Press, 1987). Incidentally, one obvious reason for the comparative success of plans to rebuild Washington, D.C., in this era was that Congress had virtually imperial powers to impose a design on the nation's capital.

78. Oscar Lewis, *San Francisco: Mission to Metropolis* (San Diego: Howell-North, 1980), 203.

79. When working people stood to benefit financially from beautification projects such as the new civic center of the 1910s, they were much more supportive. Kazin, *Barons of Labor*, 87.

80. Judd Kahn, *Imperial San Francisco: Politics and Planning in an American City, 1897–1906* (Lincoln: University of Nebraska Press, 1979), 184–99, 212. Soon after the disaster, prominent members of the Adornment Society launched the investigation into municipal graft that led to the conviction of Boss Ruef, the man who was leading the campaign to amend the state constitution to increase the power of the mayoralty.

81. The insurance industry eventually paid out about $200 million of the $235 million claimed by property owners, though the money was usually a long time coming and not all residents were covered. Archibald Mac Phail, *Of Men and*

Fire: A Story of Fire Insurance in the Far West (San Francisco: Fire Underwriters Association of the Pacific, 1948), 101–2, 111. At one point, it seemed as if insurance companies would take advantage of earthquake exemption clauses to pay no more than 75 percent of the amount owed to policyholders, but thirty-five of the larger businesses, concerned about their good name, pledged to pay claims "dollar for dollar," and fourteen other companies joined them. Prodded by the newly formed Policy Holders Protective League, the industry paid $115 million in claims in six months. Five companies went bankrupt and seven retired from business. A handful of foreign companies insisted that the disaster was an "act of God" and not their responsibility, and closed down all business in the United States. "The Fire Insurance History of the World's Greatest Conflagration," *Emanu-El* 22, no. 19 (September 21, 1906), 12–17. Also see Christopher Morris Douty, "The Economics of Localized Disasters: An Empirical Analysis of the 1906 Earthquake and Fire in San Francisco" (PhD diss., Stanford University, 1970), 281–98. See also James, *Biography of a Business*, 212–29, and Carr, *Perils: Named and Unnamed*, 70–81.

82. A. C. David, "The New San Francisco," *Architectural Record* 31, no. 1 (January, 1912): 3–26; Richard Longstreth, *On the Edges of the World: Four Architects in San Francisco at the Turn of the Century* (Cambridge: MIT Press, 1983), 297–98.

83. Kahn, *Imperial San Francisco*, 111–27.

84. For details of both initiatives, see *United States Senate Congressional Record*, May 2, 1906, 6244–48.

85. Edward Livingston, *A Personal History of the San Francisco Earthquake and Fire* (San Francisco: Privately printed, 1941), 29.

86. Christopher Morris Douty, *The Economics of Localized Disaster: The 1906 San Francisco Catastrophe* (New York: Arno Press, 1977), 198, 307; J. Eugene Haas, Robert W. Kates, and Martyn J. Bowden, eds., *Reconstruction following Disaster* (Cambridge: MIT Press, 1977), 6.

87. Similarly, Phelan was happy about an amendment to the California Constitution of a mortgage law that had previously "interfered with the freedom of business and only served to keep much foreign money out of the State of California." James D. Phelan, "The Regeneration of San Francisco," *Independent*, June 20, 1907, 1449. For revealing glimpses into the efforts of private business enterprises to raise loans through contacts in New York City, see James Duval Phelan, Correspondence and Papers, Box 1, Bancroft Library.

88. William G. Robbins, *Colony and Empire: The Capitalist Transformation of the American West* (Lawrence: University of Kansas Press, 1994), 166.

89. William Issel and Robert W. Cheney, *San Francisco, 1865–1932: Politics, Power, and Urban Development* (Berkeley: University of California Press, 1986), 203.

90. Scott, *San Francisco Bay Area*, 111.

91. Haas, Kates, and Bowden, eds., *Reconstruction following Disaster*, 75, 94.

92. Edward T. Devine, "The Housing Problem in San Francisco," *Political Science Quarterly* 21 (1906): 596–608.

93. See Chester Hartmann, *The Transformation of San Francisco* (Totowa, N.J.: Rowman and Allanheld, 1984).

94. Issel and Cheney, *San Francisco, 1865–1932*, 215–16. See also Stephen J. McGovern, *The Politics of Downtown Development: Dynamic Political Cultures in San Francisco and Washington, D.C.* (Lexington: University Press of Kentucky, 1998).

95. This statement needs qualifying. Although imperatives of profit and market-driven development played a more prominent role in shaping Los Angeles than they did in San Francisco, it is important not to forget the southern city's "long history of formal planning." The expansion of Los Angeles is inconceivable in the absence of massive (often federally supported) regional planning projects such as the building of the harbor, the aqueduct system, and the vast freeway system. An activist, or "progressive," city council began work on the diversion of potable water from the Owens Valley to Los Angeles in the year of the San Francisco earthquake. Michael Dear, "In the City, Time Becomes Visible: Intentionality and Urbanism in Los Angeles, 1781–1991," in *The City: Los Angeles and Urban Theory at the End of the Twentieth Century*, ed. Allan J. Scott and Edward W. Soja (Berkeley: University of California Press, 1996), 76–105.

96. "'Anthill' Economics: How Natural Disasters Can Change the Course of a Region's Growth," *Wall Street Journal*, October 5, 1999, 1.

97. According to Hervé Kempf, the beneficial economic impact of disasters may be discouraging the developed world from leading the "fight against climate change," although global warming is patently increasing the number and intensity of floods and hurricanes around the world. The repercussions, as he points out, are likely to be especially "appalling" for developing countries that lack the infrastructure or economic resiliency to cope with disasters. As a case in point, he cites the twenty thousand dead left behind by the Venezuelan floods of November 1999. "Every Catastrophe Has a Silver Lining," *Guardian Weekly*, January 20–26, 2000, 30.

98. Mike Davis, *Ecology of Fear: Los Angeles and the Imagination of Disaster* (New York: Metropolitan Books, 1998), 7–9.

99. William Cronon, "Introduction: In Search of Nature," in *Uncommon Ground: Toward Reinventing Nature* (New York: W. W. Norton, 1995), 29–32.

100. When I opened the Testimony and Speeches file at the official Federal Reserve website in April 2000, I found twenty-five references to "creative destruction," most made by Greenspan in speeches celebrating what he views as the remarkable efficiency with which investment markets shift capital toward innovative technologies such as the Internet, technologies that are presumed to be catapulting the world into a new and sustained season of economic expansion. (See www.federalreserve.gov.) At the same time, an increasing number of economists are beginning to prophesy economic or environmental doom ahead for a world trapped in a debt economy, a world "enslaved" by a financial capitalist system that requires ceaseless expansion for its survival, regardless of the consequences for an already strained environment. Taking his theme from a literal, if slightly misleading, translation of the word "mort-gage," Michael Rowbotham, for example, writes vividly about a planet caught in "the grip of death." *The Grip of Death: A Study of Modern Money, Debt Slavery and Destructive Economics* (Charlbury, England: Jon Carpenter, 1998).

Chapter Three

1. William James, "On Some Mental Effects of the Earthquake," *Youth's Companion*, June 7, 1906, reprinted in *Writings, 1902–1910* (New York: Viking Press, 1987), 1215, 1216, 1221. Perhaps the most eloquent testimonial to James's

delight is the simple but exuberantly scrawled entry in his diary for that day: "Earthquake!" William James, Diary, 1906, William James Papers, Houghton Library, Harvard Library.

2. Alice H. James, letter to George B. Dorr, Stanford, April 22, 1906, 2, James Family Correspondence, Houghton Library, Harvard University; and Alice Howe James, April 18, 1906, Vaux Collection, Henry Vaux, Bancroft Library.

3. James, "On Some Mental Effects of the Earthquake," 1216.

4. The Richter scale was not developed until 1935, but detailed geological surveys from 1906 enable an accurate retrospective estimate of the earthquake's intensity. See Andrew C. Lawson, *The California Earthquake of April 18, 1906: Report of the State Earthquake Investigation Commission* (Washington, D.C.: Carnegie Institution, 1908), 2 vols., and C. F. Marvin, "The Record of the Great Earthquake Written in Washington by the Seismograph of the U.S. Weather Bureau," *National Geographic Magazine* 17, no. 5 (May 1906): 296–98.

5. Russell Sage Foundation, *San Francisco Relief Survey* (New York: Survey Associates, 1913), 5. *Report of the Sub-Committee on Statistics* (San Francisco: April 24, 1907), 3, 16.

6. William James, letter to John Jay Chapman, Cambridge, Mass., May 18, 1906, in *The Selected Letters of William James*, ed. Elizabeth Hardwick (Boston: Nonpareil Books, 1980), 226.

7. William James, "On Some Mental Effects," 1215–16.

8. Ibid., 1222.

9. On James as apostle of chaos, see Frederic J. Ruf, *The Creation of Chaos: William James and the Stylistic Making of a Disorderly World* (Albany: State University of New York Press, 1991), and David M. La Guardia, *Advance on Chaos: The Sanctifying Imagination of Wallace Stevens* (Hanover, N.H.: University Press of New England, 1983).

10. James, "On Some Mental Effects," 1218.

11. "Until very recently," he contended, "it was supposed by all philosophers that there was a typical human mind which all individual minds were like, and that the propositions of universal validity could be laid down about such faculties as 'The Imagination.' Lately, however, a mass of revelations have poured in, which make us see how false this is. There are imaginations, not 'the Imagination,' and they must be studied in detail." *Principles of Psychology* (New York: Dover, 1890), 2:49–50.

12. William James, *Psychology: Briefer Course*, repr. in *Writings 1878–1899* (New York: Library of America, 1992), 310.

13. Any plausible phenomenology of disaster, in other words, has to be sensitive to changing social and cultural conditions. For a (relatively) lucid introduction to phenomenology, see Maurice Merleau-Ponty, *Sense and Nonsense*, trans. Hubert Dreyfus and Patricia Allen Dreyfus (1948; Evanston, Ill.: Northwestern University Press, 1964), 48–59. Many prominent twentieth-century philosophers and phenomenologists from John Dewey to Jean-Paul Sartre have presented their work as a corrective to James's "mechanistic" theory, which reduced emotions to physiological reflexes. See Jean-Paul Sartre, *The Emotions: Outline of a Theory*, trans. Bernard Frechtman (New York: Philosophical Library, 1948), 22–40, and Maurice Merleau-Ponty, *Phenomenology of Perception*, trans. Colin Smith (New Jersey: Humanities Press, 1962), 79n. James admitted

these materialistic aspects of his work, but he shared with his critics an appreciation for the crucial role of "meanings" or "preperceptions" in fashioning senses
and perceptions of objects and events. For a fine introduction to "visuality" that
insists on the role of power, class, and culture in shaping what we (think we) see,
see Norman Bryson, "The Gaze in the Expanded Field," in *Vision and Visuality*,
ed. Hal Foster (Seattle: Bay Press, 1988), 91–92. For more on the social construction of the senses, see also Diane Ackerman, *A Natural History of the Senses*
(New York: Random House, 1990), xvi–xviii.

14. "Driven Insane by Fear of Fire," *San Francisco Chronicle*, May 1, 1906, 13. See
also "Broods over Horrors until Mind Gives Way," *San Francisco Chronicle*,
May 4, 1906, 13. James himself fully expected "a crop of nervous wrecks before
the weeks and months are over" but was sure that this would be more exceptional than typical. "On Some Mental Effects," 1222.

15. Josephine Baxter to parents, San Francisco, April 23, 1906, San Francisco
Earthquake of 1906 Collection, Bancroft Library, 1.

16. Kate Brown to Tom and Evva Russell, Danville, California, May 3, 1906, San
Francisco Earthquake of 1906 Collection, Bancroft Library, 2–3.

17. Mary Austin, "The Temblor: A Personal Narration," *Out West* 24, no. 6 (June
1906): 499.

18. See Frederick Funston, "How the Army Worked to Save San Francisco,"
Cosmopolitan Magazine 41, no. 3 (July 1906): 239–48, and Edward T. Devine,
"The Relief of the Stricken City," *American Monthly Review of Reviews* (1906):
683–88.

19. For a comprehensive account of the logistical aspects of relief and reconstruction, see Russell Sage Foundation, *San Francisco Relief Survey*. For two thorough
scholarly accounts, see Christopher Morris Douty, *The Economics of Localized
Disasters: An Empirical Analysis of the 1906 Earthquake and Fire in San Francisco*
(New York: Arno Press, 1977), and Judd Kahn, *Imperial San Francisco: Politics
and Planning in an American City, 1897–1906* (Lincoln: University of Nebraska
Press, 1979).

20. Ray Stannard Baker, "A Test of Men: The San Francisco Disaster as a Barom-
eter of Human Nature," *American Magazine* 73, no. 1 (November 1906): 96.
For similar parables of organization, see Rufus P. Jennings, "Organization in
the Crisis," *Out West* 24, no. 6 (June 1906): 519–20, and Harold French, "How
the Red Cross Systematized Relief Work in San Francisco," *Overland Monthly*
48 (October 1906): 195–206.

21. Robert H. Wiebe, *The Search for Order, 1877–1920* (New York: Hill and Wang,
1967), 170, 295. On the Victorian search for mastery, see also Peter Gay, *The
Cultivation of Hatred*, vol. 3 of *The Bourgeois Experience: Victoria to Freud* (New
York: W. W. Norton, 1993), 424–513. For a fine study tracing links between
disaster and bourgeois ideologies of order in the late nineteenth century, see
Carl Smith, *Urban Disorder and the Shape of Belief: The Great Chicago Fire, the
Haymarket Bomb, and the Model Town of Pullman* (Chicago: University of Chi-
cago Press, 1995).

22. Roosevelt's right-hand man, Gifford Pinchot, summed up the creed of his class
as follows, "The first duty of the human race is to control the earth it lives
upon." *The Fight for Conservation* (Garden City, N.Y.: Harcourt, Brace, 1910),
45. On Roosevelt's endeavors to raise and organize the distribution of funds for

San Francisco, see "Speech to the Senate and House of Representatives," repr. in Frank Thomas Searight, *The Doomed City: A Thrilling Tale* (Chicago: Laird and Lee, 1906), 162–63.

23. Theodore Roosevelt, "Conservation of Natural Resources," May 13, 1908, in *The Call of the Wild, 1901–1916*, ed. Roderick B. Nash (New York: George Braziller, 1970), 45. The president later described the legislative session of the summer of 1906 as a "great" one, hailing the Hepburn Act, the Meat Act, and the Pure Food and Drug Act as evidence that the federal government was at last willing to assume its appointed role as guardian of public safety. Theodore Roosevelt to Benjamin Ide Wheeler, Oyster Bay, July 3, 1906, *The Letters of Theodore Roosevelt*, ed. Elting E. Morison (Cambridge: Harvard University Press, 1952), 5:329. On the rise of "security" as a dominant cultural and political concern, see Martin J. Sklar, *The Corporate Reconstruction of American Capitalism, 1890–1916: The Market, The Law, and Politics* (New York: Cambridge University Press, 1988); Stuart D. Brandes, *American Welfare Capitalism, 1880–1940* (Chicago: University of Chicago Press, 1976); and Robert H. Bremner, *From the Depths: The Discovery of Poverty in the United States* (New York: New York University Press, 1972), 123–39.

24. Walter Lippmann, *Drift and Mastery* (1914; Madison: University of Wisconsin Press, 1985), 41, 147.

25. See, for example, Nash, ed., *Call of the Wild*, 79–84; John Higham, "The Reorientation of American Culture in the 1890s," in *The Origins of Modern Consciousness*, ed. John Weiss (Detroit: Wayne State University Press, 1965); and George Fredrickson, *The Inner Civil War: Northern Intellectuals and the Crisis of the Union* (New York: Harper Torchbooks, 1968). Especially useful for me has been the splendid analysis by Jackson Lears of the emergence of a "cult of violence" and a "pornography of pain" at the turn of the last century. *No Place of Grace: Antimodernism and the Transformation of American Culture, 1880–1920* (New York: Pantheon Books, 1981), esp. chap. 4. Although his analysis sheds much light on the conditions that produced a cult of chaos in this period, and on the importance of intense experience in easing the accommodation of middle- and upper-class Americans to a new corporate industrial social order, much remains to be said about the contribution of what Henry James called the imagination of disaster to a dynamic modern culture driven and riven by competing impulses to order and disorder. Modern life has been characterized by a quest for security as well as by a fascination with spectacles of disaster. The two impulses are finally inseparable—each structures the other—and when studied together they reveal the essentially catastrophic logic of modernity.

26. According to George Steiner, a "great ennui" also afflicted Europe at the end of the nineteenth century, generating a similar fascination with destruction: "Whether the psychic mechanisms involved were universal or historically localized, one thing is plain: by ca. 1900 there was a terrible readiness, indeed a thirst for what Yeats was to call the 'blood-dimmed tide.'" *In Bluebeard's Castle: Some Notes towards the Re-Definition of Culture* (New Haven: Yale University Press, 1971), 24, quoted in Michael Barkun, *Disaster and the Millennium* (New Haven: Yale University Press, 1974), 59.

27. William James, "What Makes a Life Significant," in *Writings, 1878–1899*, 863–64.

28. James, *Psychology: Briefer Course*, 13.

29. Lars Bennett, "Recollections of the San Francisco 1906 Earthquake by his students," George Malcolm Stratton, Correspondence and Papers, 1911–1956, carton 6.

30. James, "On Some Mental Effects," 1220.

31. Although a critic of Western capitalism, Herbert Marcuse similarly argued that an appetite for destruction—which he attributed to the instincts ("aggressive impulses")—provided necessary "energy for the continuous alteration, mastery, and exploitation of nature to the advantage of mankind." *Eros and Civilization: A Philosophical Inquiry into Freud* (Boston: Beacon Press, 1974), 52.

32. Ruth Worner, term paper, 1919, in "Recollections of the San Francisco 1906 Earthquake by his students," George Malcolm Stratton Correspondence and Papers, 1911–1956.

33. In one of the most dramatic manifestations of the desire to see things smash, tens of thousands of Americans paid good money to watch locomotives crash into each other at staged train wrecks in the late 1890s. See Austin C. Rogers, "A Pre-Arranged Head End Collision," *Cosmopolitan* 22, no. 2 (December 1896): 125–29; "A Railroad Wreck for Silver," *New York Times*, September 18, 1896; and "When the Twain . . . Met," *American Heritage* 13, no. 5 (August 1962): 77–79. At the end of the twentieth century, surveys revealed that disasters were still Americans' "favorite news stories." See Susan D. Moeller, *Compassion Fatigue: How the Media Sell Disease, Famine, War, and Death* (New York: Routledge, 1999), 18.

34. This conception of mass entertainment remained influential into the following decade and beyond. Cecil B. DeMille, for example, famously announced that one of his goals in bringing "disasters before the public" in his movies before the First World War was to take people's minds off "sex." Quoted in Lary May, *Screening Out the Past: The Birth of Mass Culture and the Motion Picture Industry* (Chicago: University of Chicago Press, 1983), 207.

35. Patten, *The New Basis of Civilization* (1907; Cambridge: Harvard University Press, Belknap Press, 1968), 143. On Patten's extraordinary contributions to social theory, see the assessment of his one-time student Edward T. Devine, who was the most prominent welfare activist of the age, author of *The Principles of Relief* (1904), and the man appointed by President Roosevelt to head Red Cross operations in San Francisco in 1906. See Devine, *When Social Work Was Young* (New York: Macmillan, 1938), 20, and Daniel M. Fox, *The Discovery of Abundance: Simon N. Patten and the Transformation of Social Theory* (Ithaca: Cornell University Press, 1967), 96–98.

36. Patten, *New Basis of Civilization*, 121–43.

37. For two classic but quite contrasting statements of this view, see Daniel J. Boorstin, *The Image, Or What Happened to the American Dream* (New York: Atheneum, 1962), and Guy Debord, *The Society of the Spectacle*, trans. Donald Nicholson-Smith (New York: Zone Books, 1994).

38. In 1899, James wrote to the president of Stanford University, David Starr Jordan, in sexual terms about the attractions of the California landscape: "The relation of man to that wonderful nature there is so direct. She has been waiting for him all these years and there she stands responsive—the bride, and he the bridegroom. I can imagine a perfect passion." William James to David Starr Jordan, March 22, 1899, Stanford University Archives, cited in Linda Simon,

"William James at Stanford," *California History* 69, no. 4 (Winter 1990–91): 336. Alice Howe James to George Bucknam Dorr, Stanford, April 22, 1906, James Family Correspondence, Houghton Library, Harvard University, 2–3. Another "respectable" woman later recalled her (mock) indignation at the tremors, asking her husband, " 'Will, what are you doing? You kept me up late enough last night without'—by this time I realized what was happening." Elizabeth Maud Nankervis, *One Woman's Experience* (1959), 1; from Online Archive of California, http://ark.edlib.org/ark:/13030/hb196nb112.

39. Sigmund Freud described the id as "a chaos, a cauldron of seething excitement" in *New Introductory Lectures on Psychoanalysis* (London: Hogarth Press, 1933), 98. See also *Civilization and Its Discontents* (1930; New York: W. W. Norton, 1989).

40. Norman O. Brown, *Life against Death: The Psychoanalytical Meaning of History* (1959; Middletown, Conn.: Wesleyan University Press, 1970), esp. chap. 12.

41. The most influential work on the social construction of desires is still Michel Foucault, *The History of Sexuality*, vol. 1, *An Introduction* (New York: Vintage Books, 1990).

42. David D. Hall, *Worlds of Wonder, Days of Judgment: Popular Religious Belief in Early New England* (New York: Alfred A. Knopf, 1989), 52–57. See also Michael G. Hall, *The Last American Puritan: The Life of Increase Mather, 1639–1723* (Middletown, Conn.: Wesleyan University Press, 1988), 136–37. John D. Stevens observes that more than half of the sermons catalogued from colonial New England "were clearly and principally linked to events, often violent and sensational events." *Sensationalism and the New York Press* (New York: Columbia University Press, 1991), 8.

43. Marion Barber Stowell, *Early American Almanacs: The Colonial Weekday Bible* (New York: Burt Franklin, 1977). For an example of the prominent place of calamities in almanacs, see Nathaniel Ames, *An Astronomical Diary, or an Almanac For the Year of Our Lord Christ, 1742* (Boston: John Draper, 1742). For an annotated version, see Edmund Williams, Diaries, 1742–1755, Manuscripts Collection, American Antiquarian Society.

44. Increase Mather, *Remarkable Providences: Illustrative of the Earlier Days of American Colonisation* (London: Reeves and Strand, 1890), 93.

45. Introduction to Jonathan Edwards, *Images or Shadows of Divine Things*, ed. Perry Miller (New Haven: Yale University Press, 1948), 27.

46. Jonathan Edwards, "Personal Narrative" (c. 1739), in *A Jonathan Edwards Reader*, ed. John E. Smith, Harry S. Stout, and Kenneth P. Minkema (New Haven: Yale University Press, 1995), 285.

47. Simon Schama, *Landscape and Memory* (New York: Vintage Books, 1995), 450. To argue that romantics delighted in spectacles of chaos is not to suggest that they believed nature was essentially irregular and disturbed. Wordsworth, for example, was drawn to catastrophic images and events but was increasingly concerned to reveal the orderly patterns, sequences, and harmonious laws underlying these "disturbances." See John Wyatt, *Wordsworth and the Geologists* (New York: Cambridge University Press, 1995), 51, 112.

48. Many romantics took their cue from the philosopher Immanuel Kant who identified tempests, storms, and earthquakes as events awesome enough to provoke the sublime sensibility and lift human thoughts to the "infinite," writing that nature most aroused sublime feelings "in its chaos . . . or in its wildest and

most ruleless disarray and devastation." *Critique of Judgment*, trans. Werner S. Pluhar (1790; Indianapolis: Hackett Publishing, 1987), 122, 99–100.

49. Edmund Burke, *A Philosophical Enquiry into the Origin of our Ideas of the Sublime and Beautiful* (1757; New York: Garland, 1971), 74. See also Tom Furniss, *Edmund Burke's Aesthetic Ideology: Language, Gender, and Political Economy in Revolution* (New York: Cambridge University Press, 1993).

50. James's phrase is quoted in Sidney Hook, "A Philosopher's View," in *Man's Quest for Security*, ed. E. J. Faulkner (Lincoln: University of Nebraska Press, 1966), 4.

51. Burke, *Origin of our Ideas of the Sublime and Beautiful* (London: Routledge and Kegan Paul, 1958), 31. Also see Thomas Weiskel, *The Romantic Sublime: Studies in the Structure and Psychology of Transcendence* (Baltimore: Johns Hopkins University Press, 1976), 81–106, 36. This impulse to gaze upon (and be stirred by) the marvels of nature also animated an emerging American romantic movement. Artists such as Thomas Cole were popularizing a genre of landscape paintings that located God and sublime power in wild nature, calling on Americans to behold nature as a source of emotional delight rather than simply as a congeries of resources or even as a book of didactic divine lessons. Barbara Novak, *Nature and Culture: American Landscape and Painting, 1825–1875* (New York: Oxford University Press, 1981), 34–39.

52. For detailed and sophisticated accounts of this process, see William Cronon, *Changes in the Land: Indians, Colonists, and the Ecology of New England* (New York: Hill and Wang, 1983); Carolyn Merchant, *Ecological Revolutions: Nature, Gender, and Science in New England* (Chapel Hill: University of North Carolina Press, 1989); and Neal Salisbury, *Manitou and Providence: Indians, Europeans, and the Making of New England, 1500–1643* (New York: Oxford University Press, 1982).

53. By the time he wrote *Walden*, Henry David Thoreau could write with some assuredness about the need of civilized societies for the "tonic of wildness." "We can never have enough of Nature," he pronounced, thinking of nature at its most untamed. "We must be refreshed by the sight of its inexhaustible vigor, vast and Titanic features, the sea coast with its wrecks, the wilderness with its living and decaying trees, the thunder cloud." Henry David Thoreau, *Walden* (New York: Penguin, 1983), 365–66.

54. "The language of the sublime gave a positive gloss to the terrible, the vast, and the chaotic, and at least in some small degree it worked an incursion upon the humble loyalty to order, neatness, and restraint." Lewis O. Saum, *The Popular Mood of Pre–Civil War America* (Westport, Conn.: Greenwood Press, 1980), 175–99.

55. On sensationalism in the antebellum period, see John D. Stevens, *Sensationalism and the New York Press* (New York: Columbia University Press, 1991), and David S. Reynolds, *Beneath the American Renaissance: The Subversive Imagination in the Age of Emerson and Melville* (New York: Alfred A. Knopf, 1988), 169–210.

56. The fire sparked a lifelong fascination with conflagrations. Allan Nevins and Milton Halsey Thomas, eds., *The Diary of George Templeton Strong: Young Man in New York, 1835–1849* (New York: Macmillan, 1952), 8.

57. "We desire all our readers to preserve this paper among the archives of their family. Fifty thousand copies only are printed." *New York Herald*, December 21,

1835. According to Paul C. Ditzel, this "was the first of many lithographs of noteworthy American fires and other disasters made in that era before news-paper and magazine photojournalism." *Fire Engines, Fire Fighters: The Men, Equipment, and Machines, from Colonial Days to the Present* (New York: Crown, 1976), 87. There was an expanding market for stereographs and photographs of violence and disaster throughout the nineteenth century, and particularly in the years after the Civil War. Alan Trachtenberg, *Reading American Photographs: Images as History, Mathew Brady to Walker Evans* (New York: Hill and Wang, 1989), 77, 89.

58. Stevens, *Sensationalism and the New York Press*, 33–34.

59. Edwin G. Burrows and Mike Wallace, *Gotham: A History of New York City to 1898* (New York: Oxford University Press, 1999), 526. Disasters also helped to promote the popularity of newspapers, a new print medium, in England in the seventeenth century. Here newspaper proprietors claimed to be providing a valuable public service by printing information about calamities and appealing for donations for the sufferers, but they undeniably laid the foundations for a durable link between journalism and sensationalism. Stephen Porter, "News-papers and Fire Relief in Early Modern England," *Journal of Newspapers and Periodical History* 8, no. 1 (1992): 28–33. In North America, by contrast, even after the establishment of the first continuous newspaper, the *Boston News-Letter*, in 1704, disasters featured more rarely. The first edition opened with a proclamation by Governor Joseph Dudley calling on the people of Massachusetts to participate in a fast day to expiate their sins and win God's favor for the war against the French. *Boston News-Letter*, January 29–February 5, 1704, 1. The *News-Letter* did cover the great Boston fire of 1711, but it buried it at the bottom of its second and last page: *Boston News-Letter*, October 1–8, 1711, 2. On the early American press, see A. Goddard, "The Press and Literature of the Provincial Period, 1692–1770," in *Memorial History of Boston*, ed. Justin Winsor (Boston: James R. Osgood, 1880), 2:387–88, and Samuel Adams Drake, *Old Landmarks and Historical Personages of Boston* (Boston: Little, Brown, and Co., 1906), 16.

60. Quoted in Dennis Smith, *Dennis Smith's History of Firefighting in America: 300 Years of Courage* (New York: Dial Press, 1978), 45.

61. Trachtenberg, *Reading American Photographs*, 77, 89. Charles Musser, *The Emergence of Cinema: The American Scene to 1907* (Berkeley: University of California Press, 1994), 290–91, 327–29. On the movies as a culmination and source of interest in sensational events such as disasters, see Ben Singer, "Modernity, Hyperstimulus, and the Rise of Popular Sensationalism," in *Cinema and the Invention of Modern Life*, ed. Leo Charney and Vanessa R. Schwartz (Berkeley: University of California Press, 1995), 72–99.

62. On the Chicago fire as the "last providential disaster," see Kevin Rozario, "Nature's Evil Dreams: Disaster and America, 1871–1906" (PhD diss., Yale University, 1997), 95–145. The best scholarly studies of the conflagration are Smith, *Urban Disorder and the Shape of Belief*; Ross Miller, *American Apocalypse: The Great Fire and the Myth of Chicago* (Chicago: University of Chicago Press, 1990); and Karen Sawislak, *Smoldering Ruins: Chicagoans and the Great Fire, 1871–1874* (Chicago: University of Chicago Press, 1995).

63. For evidence of delight in the spectacle, see M. A. Shorey, "The Chicago Fire," *Old and New* 5, no. 1 (January 1872): 17–18; Adelade Elizabeth Wadsworth,

"How I Saw the Chicago Fire" (Chicago Historical Society, Personal Narratives, n.d.), 1, 17; "The Story of the Fire as Told by the Men Who Fought It," *Chicago Tribune*, October 9, 1893, 20; and Eugene Seeger, *Chicago, the Wonder City* (Chicago: George Printing Company, 1893), 124.

64. Many children, in particular, thought the Chicago fire was a tremendous escapade, considering it "all a wonderful lark." Frank Loesch, *Personal Experiences during the Chicago Fire, 1871* (Chicago: Privately printed, 1925), 15. Mayor Carter H. Harriman, for example, later reminisced about the fire as "the great adventure" of his youth: "We played, doing all the things a bunch of adventure craving boys wanted to do at such a time, in such a place." *Growing Up with Chicago* (Chicago: Ralph Fletcher Seymour, 1944), 46–47. See also Henry Raymond Hamilton, *Foot Prints* (Chicago: Lakeside Press, 1927), 24.

65. Young lads were still most inclined to experience the earthquake as "a very enjoyable event," but this delight was now no longer viewed as the sole prerogative of youth. "Growing Up in San Francisco Project," *Growing Up in the Cities, 1977–79*, San Francisco Earthquake of 1906 Collection, Bancroft Library, 3.

66. William Douglas Alexander to Mary C. Alexander, San Francisco, May 16, 1906, San Francisco Earthquake of 1906 Collection, Bancroft Library, 1.

67. W. W. Lyman, "Recollections of the San Francisco Earthquake and Fire of 1906" (St. Helena, Calif., 1968), Bancroft Library, 3.

68. Chas B. Sedgwick, "The Fall of San Francisco: Some Personal Observations," *American Builders' Review* 4, no. 1 (July 1906): 201.

69. Jack London wrote a lively account of the earthquake and fire in "The Story of an Eye-Witness," *Collier's Weekly*, May 5, 1906.

70. Charles Ross to A. M. Von Metzke, San Francisco, April 26, 1906, San Francisco Earthquake of 1906 Collection, Bancroft Library, 8–9. Of course, William James too viewed vigor as a "manly virtue." "What Makes a Life Significant," in *Writings, 1878–1899*, 876. For an introduction to the large and growing literature on the cult of masculinity, see E. Anthony Rotundo, *American Manhood: Transformations of Masculinity from the Revolution to the Modern Era* (New York: Basic Books, 1993), chap. 9; Donna Haraway, *Primate Visions: Gender, Race, and Nature in the World of Modern Science* (New York: Routledge, 1989), esp. chap. 3; Michael Kimmel, *Manhood in America: A Cultural History* (New York: Free Press, 1996), esp. chap. 4; and George Chauncey, *Gay New York: Gender, Urban Culture, and the Making of the Gay Male World, 1890–1940* (New York: Basic Books, 1994), chap. 4.

71. Kathleen Norris, *My San Francisco*, 14–18.

72. This recalls the spirited determination of those elite Northern women who volunteered for duty as nurses during the Civil War. As Katharine Wormeley wrote during her time on a U.S. Sanitary Commission ship in 1862, "We all know in our hearts that it is thorough enjoyment to be here—it is life." Kristie Ross, "Arranging a Doll's House: Refined Women as Union Nurses," in *Divided Houses: Gender and the Civil War*, ed. Catharine Clinton and Nina Silber (New York: Oxford University Press, 1992), 102.

73. Norris, *My San Francisco*, 15–18. Journalists reported that women viewed "their cooking in the streets as a matter of sport and never complain about the lack of conveniences." "What Society Is Doing," *San Francisco Examiner*, April 30, 1906. The response of women to the calamity was always ambivalent. After all,

even as growing numbers of women in the 1900s were making their way into colleges and the professions or finding healthy release in sports and outdoor activities, they were still subjected to tremendous cultural pressures to resist high passions and to embrace instead the "sacred" responsibilities of mother-hood. Although Theodore Roosevelt, for example, might praise "strong and brave and highminded" mothers for their heroism, female strength was still defined in terms of self-sacrifice and self-restraint. Significantly, even Kathleen Norris surrendered to the pressures of her times. Only five years after the earthquake, she wrote the popular novel *Mother*, beloved by Roosevelt, about a girl called Margaret who desired above all to escape from conventional routines. The story reached its happy resolution, however, when the girl came to understand that motherly devotion and routine domesticity was the natural and most rewarding destiny of America's women. How was it possible for the author of this fable to write with such fervor about the liberating qualities of the San Francisco earthquake? It is tempting to speculate that she could enthuse guiltlessly about her adventures during the calamity because they were forced upon her, not chosen, and besides she was at that point still young and un-married. Theodore Roosevelt, "The Strenuous Life" (1899), in *The Call of the Wild, 1901–1916*, ed. Roderick B. Nash (New York: George Braziller, 1970), 81. Kathleen Norris, *Mother, A Story* (New York: Macmillan, 1911). For commentary, see Richard Allan Davison, *Charles and Kathleen Norris* (San Francisco: Book Club of California, 1993), and Joe L. Dubbart, "Progressivism and the Masculinity Crisis," in *The American Man*, ed. Elizabeth H. Pleck and Joseph H. Pleck (Englewood Cliffs, N.J.: Prentice-Hall, 1980), 315–16. For context, see Carroll Smith-Rosenberg, "The New Woman as Androgyne: Social Disorder and Gender Crisis, 1870–1936," in her *Disorderly Conduct: Visions of Gender in Victorian America* (New York: Oxford University Press, 1986), 245–96.

74. As Anthony Giddens sensibly reminds us, the notion that modern life is over-safe or "uneventful" is an illusion. Urban industrial life presents numerous and often unprecedented dangers—some as banal as the hazard of crossing a busy city street—but modern men and women learn over time to follow routines, almost unthinkingly, that mitigate and obscure these dangers. *Modernity and Self-Identity: Self and Society in the Late Modern Age* (Stanford: Stanford University Press, 1991), 127.

75. On the landscape of extremes in the Western genre, see Jane Tompkins, *The Inner Life of Westerns* (New York: Oxford University Press, 1992), 69–87. On California, in particular, as a site of antimodernist desire, see Kevin Starr, *Americans and the California Dream, 1850–1915* (Santa Barbara: Peregrine Smith, 1973).

76. William James to Henry James and William James Jr., Cambridge, Mass., May 9, 1906, in *Selected Letters of William James*, 223. For similar sentiments, see John A. Gray, "San Francisco and the Spirit of the West," *Harper's Weekly* 50, no. 2577 (May 12, 1906), 665.

77. Ella Sterling Cummins, *San Francisco Redi-vivus!* (Oakland: Harrington-Mc-Innes, 1907), 8, 9.

78. See also Sara Dean's fictional account *Travers: A Story of the San Francisco Earthquake* (New York: Frederick A. Stokes, 1907), 218. Frederick Jackson Turner had described the frontier as "a fountain of youth in which America

continually bathed and was rejuvenated." "Address," *Weekly Democrat*, January 3, 1896, quoted in Henry Nash Smith, *Virgin Land: The American West as Symbol and Myth* (Cambridge: Harvard University Press, 1970), 254. Many San Franciscans thought the 1906 calamity had introduced similarly regenerative conditions.

79. Willoughby Rodman, "The Sierra Club in the Northwest," *Out West* 24, no. 5 (May 1906): 365.

80. Ruth E. Praeger, "Remembering the High Things," *Sierra Club Women* (San Francisco: Sierra Club History Committee, 1976), 1.

81. Mrs. Carroll J. Beal to Mary Frances Burgess, San Francisco, 1906 (unpublished MS), Bancroft Library, 2–3.

82. Richard Barry, "The Fire Levels All Classes," *San Francisco Chronicle*, April 28, 1906, 4.

83. Adolf to Max, San Francisco, May 7, 1906 (unpublished MS), Bancroft Library, 7.

84. Emma Maxwell Burke, "A Woman's Experience of Earthquake and Fire," *Outlook* 83, no. 1 (May 5, 1906): 277.

85. Rufus M. Steele, "Faith Abounds in United City," *San Francisco Chronicle*, April 21, 1906, 2.

86. Charles Keeler, *San Francisco through Earthquake and Fire* (San Francisco: Paul Elder and Co., 1906), 38. The same sentiment, in almost exactly the same words, appeared in the merchant Edward Livingston's memoir, *A Personal History of the San Francisco Earthquake and Fire in 1906* (San Francisco: Privately published, 1941), 14.

87. Sedgwick, "Fall of San Francisco," 210.

88. Many of the commentators who celebrated the collapse of distinctions in the aftermath of the earthquake seem to have been more interested in denying the significance of social and economic disparities than in redressing the conditions that caused them. Conservatives contended that the crisis had revealed the superfluity of social reforms, convinced that citizens would look after one another in cases of genuine need. The *Chronicle* assured its readers that "the most glorious thing [was] the unification of our people. If there have been social, industrial or civic cleavages they no longer exist. The souls of our people have been welded in one in the terrific heat of a fiery furnace." "Magnificent Optimism," *San Francisco Chronicle*, April 26, 1906, 6. From here on out, the implication was, any social problem could be solved with a bit of goodwill. This rhetoric of brotherhood and equality (though often sincere) meshed all too easily with class interest. Affirming social unity was a way for the privileged to enforce silence about deep-seated conflicts that disturbed their peace.

89. Baker, "A Test of Men," 82.

90. Vesta Marie Daniels to Elton, May 11, 1906, and to daughter, May 20, 1906, Eaton Family Papers, 1862–1906, Bancroft Library.

91. Amelia Woodward Truesdell, "The Simple Life—In Tents," *Francisca Reina* (Boston: R. G. Badger, 1908), 13.

92. Norris, *My San Francisco*, 15.

93. James, "On Some Mental Effects," 1215.

94. Ernest Abram Wiltsee, "Personal Reminiscences of the San Francisco Earthquake, 1906," Ernest Wiltsee Papers, Part 1, Bancroft Library, 2, 10–11. As

another wealthy visitor recalled of the quake, "When it had attained a certain strength and velocity which I considered the polite limit, I expected it to
stop—but when it exceeded this limit . . ., I said 'the son of a gun' and did not
like it so well—as from that moment on I decided I did not know what kind of an
earthquake it would turn out to be." Adolf to Max, San Francisco, May 7, 1906,
Bancroft Library, 2.

95. The most important variable here for predicting who might have found the disaster liberating is not class, in any classical sense, but security. Those men and
women who could depend on family, friends, savings, unions, mutual aid societies, or insurance were more likely to experience some pleasure in the calamity,
and these were resources available to many working people in San Francisco,
though those upper- and middle-class people who enjoyed the most money,
credit, and influence usually felt the most secure.

96. Lavinia Pearl Robbins, "Memoirs," Bancroft Library, 1906 San Francisco
Earthquake Collection, 20.

97. Erica Y. Z. Pan, *The Impact of the 1906 Earthquake on San Francisco's Chinatown*
(New York: Peter Lang, 1995), 34.

98. In 1906, the small number of African Americans were dispersed throughout
the city and were rarely singled out for discussion in the city's newspapers. See
Douglas Henry Daniels, *Pioneer Urbanites: A Social and Cultural History of Black
San Francisco* (Philadelphia: Temple University Press, 1980).

99. Thomas W. Chinn, *Bridging the Pacific: San Francisco's Chinatown and Its People*
(San Francisco: Chinese Historical Society of America, 1989), 74.

100. Lucy E. Salyer, "'Laws as Harsh as Tigers': Enforcement of the Chinese Exclusion Laws, 1891–1924," in *Entry Denied: Exclusion and the Chinese Community
in America, 1882–1943*, ed. Sucheng Chan (Philadelphia: Temple University
Press, 1991), 63.

101. Pan, *Impact of the 1906 Earthquake*, 15–16.

102. Laverne Mau Dicker, *The Chinese in San Francisco: A Pictorial History* (New
York: Dover, 1979), 85.

103. For all of the rhetoric about racial harmony and "earthquake love," the *Chronicle*
was soon stirring up racial animosities again, reminding white San Franciscans
about the "unassimilable" Chinese "menace" in their midst. "The Labor Situation," *San Francisco Chronicle*, April 29, 1906, 6.

104. Hugh Kwong Liang, personal narrative, repr. in Chinn, *Bridging the Pacific*,
199–201.

105. The Chinese should not be viewed solely as victims of the disaster. Facing unique
obstacles and challenges, leaders and ordinary individuals labored aggressively
to protect their interests, suing insurance companies that refused to settle claims
and defeating efforts by leading citizens and the municipal authorities to prevent
their return to Chinatown after the calamity. Pan, *Impact of the 1906 Earthquake*,
103–4. Indeed, Chinese residents took advantage of the destruction of immigration records and birth certificates to make out new papers declaring that they
had been born in the United States. These papers allowed them to bring "paper
sons" over to San Francisco. According to Hay Ming Lee, many Chinese "forged
themselves certificates saying they were born in this country, and then when the
time came, they could go back to China and bring back four or five sons, just like

that!" Victor G. and Brett de Bary Nee, *Longtime Californ': A Documentary Study of an American Chinatown* (New York: Pantheon Books, 1973), 63.

106. Gertrude Atherton, "San Francisco's Tragic Dawn," *Harper's Weekly* 50, no. 2577 (May 12, 1906), 660, 675.

107. William James, "The Moral Equivalent of War," in *Writings, 1902–1910* (New York: Viking Press, 1987), 1285, 1291. James was careful to deny that the mettle displayed during the calamity was uniquely Californian or even American, believing that "every country in a similar crisis" would have acted to restore order as quickly as possible. "On Some Mental Effects," 1221. Other commentators, however, tended to present this civilizing impulse as a peculiar gift of the "Anglo-Saxon race." See, for example, Atherton, "San Francisco's Tragic Dawn," 660. For a perceptive study of the race-ing and gendering of the concept of "civilization," see Gail Bederman, *Manliness and Civilization: A Cultural History of Gender and Race in the United States, 1880–1917* (Chicago: University of Chicago Press, 1995).

108. At the turn of the century, social theorists such as G. Stanley Hall and Simon Patten were beginning to draw attention to the powerful discontent that was being generated by modern social organization. In analyses akin to Freud's theory of the return of the repressed, they insisted that industrial disciplines and bourgeois prohibitions were stirring atavistic cravings for ecstatic release that threatened to undermine the civilizing process. What distinguished their work was their confident assurance that these impulses could be harnessed for productive ends. See, for example, Patten, *New Basis of Civilization*, and G. Stanley Hall, *Adolescence: Its Psychology and Its Relations to Physiology, Anthropology, Sociology, Sex, Crime, Religion, and Education* (New York: D. Appleton, 1904). Hall, in particular, waged a high-profile campaign to liberate (and channel) adolescent passions so as to create a "race" of vigorous and responsible citizens. See Dorothy Ross, *G. Stanley Hall: The Psychologist as Prophet* (Chicago: University of Chicago Press, 1972), 328–36. The celebration of youthful vitality provided some legitimation for the pleasures of calamity. David Starr Jordan, president of Stanford University, attributed William James's earthquake enthusiasms to the fact that the philosopher had "a child's joyous attitude toward every new experience." Jordan, *The Days of a Man: Being Memories of a Naturalist, Teacher, and Minor Prophet of Democracy* (New York: World Books, 1922), 2:174.

109. "Only by supplying our passions with civilized interests," Walter Lippmann warned, "can we escape their destructive force." *A Preface to Politics* (New York: Mitchell Kennerley, 1913), 50. Lippmann became a student of William James's at Harvard shortly after the earthquake.

110. James, "On Some Mental Effects," 1220.

111. James, *Psychology: Briefer Course*, in *Writings 1878–1899*, 149.

112. James, "What Makes a Life Significant," 864. Emphasis added.

113. Mary Hawgood to Mary Frances Burgess, San Francisco, May 1906, Bancroft Library, 8.

114. Cameron King Jr., "Earthquake and Fire in San Francisco" (1906), in Mary McD. Gordon, "Notes and Documents: Earthquake and Fire in San Francisco," *Huntington Library Quarterly* 48, no. 1 (Winter 1985): 74–75.

115. Austin, "The Temblor: A Personal Narration," 501.

116. George W. Brooks, *The Spirit of 1906* (San Francisco: California Insurance Company, 1921), 13.

117. Arnold Genthe, *As I Remember* (New York: Reynal and Hitchcock, 1936), 94. Also see David Wyatt, *Five Fires: Race, Catastrophe, and the Shaping of California* (New York: Addison-Wesley, 1997), 119–21.

118. Edgar Cohen, "With a Camera in San Francisco," *Camera Craft* 12, no. 5 (June 1906): 183, 184.

119. Arthur Inkersley, "An Amateur's Experience of Earthquake and Fire," *Camera Craft* 12, no. 5 (June 1906): 199–200.

120. On the distancing effect of "modern" ways of seeing, see Martin Jay, "Scopic Regimes of Modernity," in *Vision and Visuality*, ed. Foster, 8, and *Downcast Eyes: The Denigration of Vision in Twentieth-Century French Thought* (Berkeley: University of California Press, 1994). On the limitations of Jay's model, to the extent that it is "vacated of any political dynamics or models of subjectivity," see Irit Rogoff, "Studying Visual Culture," in *The Visual Culture Reader*, ed. Nicholas Mirzoeff (New York: Routledge, 1998), 21.

121. See Norman Bryson, "The Gaze in the Expanded Field," in *Vision and Visuality*, ed. Foster, 91–92, and Jean-Christophe Agnew, "The Consuming Vision of Henry James," in *The Culture of Consumption: Critical Essays in American History, 1880–1980*, ed. Richard Whiteman Fox and T. J. Jackson Lears (New York: Pantheon Books, 1983), 83.

122. Frank W. Aitken and Edward Hilton, *A History of the Earthquake and Fire in San Francisco* (San Francisco: Edward Hilton, 1906), 110.

123. "Monster," *Oxford English Dictionary*.

124. Harold Jenson, Diary, April 18, 1906, quoted in William G. Hartley, "Saints and the Earthquake," *Brigham Young University Studies* 23, no. 4 (Fall 1983): 444.

125. George A. Bernthal to John Herman Bernthal, "Letters from San Francisco, 1906–1931," trans. from German by Edward H. Bernthal, *Concordia Historical Institute Quarterly* 66, no. 3 (Fall 1993): 103.

126. Judith R. Walkowitz's observations about the upper- and middle-class male spectator, the flaneur, of the urban scene in late nineteenth century London are highly relevant here: "Always scanning the gritty street scene for good copy and anecdote, his was a quintessentially 'consumerist' mode of being-in-the-world, one that transformed exploitation and suffering into vivid psychological experience." Spectacles of disaster similarly transformed horrors into thrills. *City of Dreadful Delight: Narratives of Sexual Danger in Late Victorian London* (Chicago: University of Chicago Press, 1992), 16.

127. French Strother, "The Rebound of San Francisco," *World's Work* (July 1906): 7779.

128. Edwin E. Slosson noted in 1904 that Coney's most popular "panoramic effects" all featured great calamities, "The Amusement Business," *Independent* 57 (July 21, 1904), 139. The best scholarly studies of Coney Island are John F. Kasson, *Amusing the Million: Coney Island at the Turn of the Century* (New York: Hill and Wang, 1978), and Kathy Peiss, *Cheap Amusements: Working Women and Leisure in Turn-of-the-Century New York* (Philadelphia: Temple University Press, 1986), 115–38.

129. On the emergence of amusement parks as a national phenomenon, see Gary Kyriazi, *The Great Amusement Parks* (Secaucus, N.J.: Citadel Press, 1976), 98–165.

130. The spectacular period lasted until about 1920, when movies, newsreels, and faster automobiles began to make Coney's big attractions seem dated. Lucy P. Gilliman, "Coney Island," *New York History* 36, no. 3 (July 1955): 284.

131. For a vivid description, see Rollin Lynde Hartt, "The Amusement Park," *Atlantic Monthly* 99 (May 1907), 673. The formula was so successful that Dreamland set out to top it with an even larger show, "Fighting the Flames," which employed four thousand actors, six- instead of four-story buildings, and an even larger cast of firemen. Oliver Pilat and Jo Ranson, *Sodom by the Sea: An Affectionate History of Coney Island* (Garden City, N.Y.: Doubleday, Doran, and Co., 1941), 162.

132. The owners of Coney's parks insisted from the beginning that they were in the business of family entertainment and that their thrill rides and disaster shows were intended to divert Americans from unsavory passions. Lamarcus A. Thompson, a Sunday school teacher, had introduced the Switchback Railroad to Coney in 1884, in the hope that the world's first roller coaster would lure young people away from the vice of alcohol. Kyriazi, *Great Amusement Parks*, 34. When George Tilyou founded Steeplechase Park in 1897, he viewed his rides, sideshows, bands, noise, and lights as alternatives to the gambling, drinking, and whoring that had been so prominent in the "old Coney Island." Luna Park and Dreamland took this principle even further, offering morality plays such as "Hell Gate" with its tawdry depictions of the punishments awaiting drunkards, thieves, and flirtatious girls in the next world. For a withering critique of Hell Gate, see Maxim Gorky, "Boredom," *Independent* 63 (August 8, 1907), 313–14. All of the impresarios claimed that the encouragement and indulgence of a public taste for simulated disasters and thrill rides was a way to contain and control the less savory passions and vices of the masses.

133. Theodore Waters, "New York's New Playground," *Harper's Weekly* 49 (July 8, 1905), 977.

134. Hartt, "The Amusement Park," 676. Much of this essay was reprinted two years later in his pioneering cultural history, *The People at Play: Excursions in the Humor and Philosophy of Popular Amusements* (Boston: Houghton Mifflin, 1909).

135. Guy Wetmore Carryl, "Marvelous Coney Island," *Munsey's Magazine* 25 (September 1901): 811–12.

136. He was struck by the fact that the most popular amusements were the ones in which the customer was "juggled with, stood upon his head, or whirled through space, or shot up to the moon, or dropped into the bowels of the earth." Waters, "New York's New Playground," 976, 977.

137. Hartt, "The Amusement Park," 676.

138. Slosson, "The Amusement Business," 137–38.

139. "The passion that gets its satisfaction from these varied deathtraps," he assured readers (no doubt scandalizing many of them), "takes you back to the troglodyte, perhaps even to the ape. Your simian ancestors, swinging from tree-top to tree-top, had much your sensation. They of the Neolithic Age sought it in the chase and battle. A small boy gets it when a kind and thoughtful citizen turns him upside down. And you yourself, by a personal application of Darwinism, find it here and pronounce it glorious." Hartt, "The Amusement Park," 671, 674.

140. Ibid., 674.

141. Ibid., 672.

142. For an illustration of this point, see Albert Bigelow Paine's account of his ride on the notorious Loop-the-Loop, the island's most terrifying roller-coaster. "The New Coney Island," *Century Magazine* 68 (August 1904), 533.

143. For a more recent analysis of the pursuit of dangers as an attempt to experience the thrill of mastery, see Deborah Lupton, *Risk* (New York: Routledge, 1999), 151.

144. Marshall Berman has observed that "under the pressure of the market, modern men and women are forced to grow in order to survive." To survive in the modern world, that is to say, men and women have to become adaptive, questing, risk-taking personalities. "Why Modernism Still Matters," in *Modernity and Identity*, ed. Scott Lash and Jonathan Friedman (Cambridge, Mass.: Blackwell, 1992), 36. See also Anthony Giddens on modernity as a "risk culture," in *Modernity and Self-Identity*, 3, 111–14, 123–24.

145. The psychiatrist Michael Balint is surely correct to argue that amusement park rides are only thrilling for customers who enjoy "the more or less confident hope that the fear can be tolerated and mastered, the danger will pass, and that one will be returned unharmed to safety." *Thrills and Regressions* (New York: International Universities Press, 1959), 23. Robert Sklar attributes much of the popularity of early movies to their ability to give "viewers access to events that happened when they were not there, to the dangerous, the fantastic, the grotesque, the impossible, at a close but safe remove." *Movie-Made America: A Cultural History of American Movies* (New York: Vintage Books, 1994), 21. Some of Coney Island's disaster shows, such as "Fighting the Flames—Dreamland," were filmed and distributed to enthusiastic movie audiences across the country at the turn of the century. It was not until the 1920s, however, according to Lary May, that movie producers mastered the art of selling spectacles of chaos to the American public. *Screening Out the Past*, 103–4.

146. Pilat and Ranson, *Sodom by the Sea*, 213. "The crowd," Hartt noted, "wants only enough hazing to shock the nerves agreeably; give it more and it bolts." "The Amusement Park," 676.

147. The "Fire and Flames" show is a perfect example of controlled chaos, requiring an extravagant outlay for fireproof building materials as well as strict time-management practices. Theodore Waters described what went on behind the scenes: "In each room of the houses is a huge powder blower, operated by compressed air from the tank; so that when the flames burst from the windows they are not the result of haphazard chance, but part of a system which operates like clockwork and is the result of inventive ability on the part of the stage manager." Waters, "New York's New Playground," 980.

148. *Scientific American* ran several features on the rides at Coney Island, marveling at the engineering skills that made the rides, or "thrillers," so safe and so exciting. See, for example, "The Mechanical Joys of Coney Island," *Scientific American* 99 (August 15, 1908), 108–10. See also Robert E. Snow and David E. Wright, "Coney Island: A Case Study in Popular Culture and Technical Change," *Journal of Popular Culture* 9 (Spring 1976): 960–75. For an account of the amusement industry that emphasizes the industry, see Slosson, "The Amusement Business," 134.

149. Simon Patten thought that the desire for Coney Island's pleasures would promote industrialization in yet another way. To afford the attractions, working

people would have to work harder and "submit to the discipline of work." Less convincingly, he also believed that the habits acquired at the workplace would "make the regular life necessary in industry easier and more pleasant." *New Basis of Civilization*, 137–38.

150. Gorky, "Boredom," 309, 310–11.

151. Kyriazi, *Great Amusement Parks*, 81–82. On the other hand, when the more uptight Dreamland burned in 1911, the directors decided to let it die, believing that there was "too much risk" in rebuilding. Pilat and Ranson, *Sodom by the Sea*, 172.

152. Slosson, "The Amusement Business," 138.

153. Hartt, "The Amusement Park," 672. The term "white savages" comes from Gorky, "Boredom," 317.

154. The term "riskless risk" comes from Russel B. Nye's essay, "Eight Ways of Looking at an Amusement Park," *Journal of Popular Culture* 15, no. 1 (Summer 1981): 71. There is a strong correlation between the cultural longing for riskless risks and the rise of what the German sociologist Ulrich Beck calls the "risk society," a late modern society concerned more with the "quest for safety" than with the "creation and equitable distribution of wealth" or with the distribution of "bads" rather than the distribution of "goods." Beck, *Risk Society: Towards a New Modernity*, trans. Martin Ritter (Thousand Oaks, Calif.: Sage, 1992). See also see John Adams, *Risk* (London: UCL Press, 1995), 179.

155. It is always difficult to reconstruct past emotional lives, but we are fortunate in this case to have a marvelous, and apparently uncharted, trove of information in the Stratton papers at the Bancroft Library. In 1919, George Malcolm Stratton, a professor of psychology at the University of California in Berkeley, asked his students, many of whom lived in the East or the Midwest at the time, to write essays on their recollections of the San Francisco earthquake. Most of these students were only about eight years old in 1906, which raises obvious questions about their accuracy and reliability. But the assignment did require students to pay special attention to the difficulties of recovering past events, and most of the essays accordingly exhibit an unusual appreciation for the fallibilities of memory. The assignment was titled "Earthquake of 1906: Where were you at the time?" The paper guidelines were as follows:

> Write as detailed and precise an account as you can of your own recollections of the earthquake and fire of 1906. Tell if you remember them, the events of the day and evening before the earthquake, the doings and thoughts of yourself during and after the earthquake, the doings of your family and neighbors—all these for the days and weeks following until the earthquake no longer figures in the events. Tell nothing that you do not personally remember. If you remember little tell that little carefully. ("Recollections of the San Francisco 1906 Earthquake by his students," George Malcolm Stratton, Correspondence and Papers, 1911–1956)

Stratton himself was one of the nation's leading experimental psychologists, with a formidable reputation for his work in memory and the psychology of perception. George M. Stratton, *Experimental Psychology and Its Bearing upon Culture* (New York: Macmillan, 1903), 102–22. On his "famous" experiments, see Howard C. Warren and Leonard Carmichael, *Elements of Human Psychology*

(Boston: Houghton Mifflin, 1930), 162–63. For his contribution to phenomenology, see Merleau-Ponty, *Phenomenology of Perception*, 244–54.

156. Musser, *Emergence of Cinema*, 478. On the popularity of footage of the earth-
quake in small-town America (as shot on site after the event by the Edison and
Biograph studios) and on the waning interest of audiences exposed to too many
such images by the end of the year, see Kathryn H. Fuller, *At the Picture Show:
Small-Town Audiences and the Creation of Movie Fan Culture* (Washington, D.C.:
Smithsonian Institution Press, 1996), 20–21.

157. Anna Berryman, "Recollections of the San Francisco 1906 Earthquake by his
students," George Malcolm Stratton, Correspondence and Papers, 1911–
1956.

158. William James, letter to Henry James and William James Jr., Cambridge, Mass.,
May 9, 1906, in *Selected Letters of William James*, 223. For the deputy registrar
of voters at City Hall, "The knowledge of friends and relatives at the mercy of
the yellow press sent me quickly to the telegraph office." Cameron King Jr.,
"Earthquake and Fire in San Francisco," (1906), in Gordon, "Earthquake and
Fire in San Francisco," 72.

159. Lira Davis, "Recollections of the San Francisco 1906 Earthquake by his students," George Malcolm Stratton, Correspondence and Papers, 1911–1956.

160. Musser, *Emergence of Cinema*, 447.

161. Lucile Garrett, "Recollections of the San Francisco 1906 Earthquake by his students," George Malcolm Stratton, Correspondence and Papers, 1911–1956.

162. Donald Abbe Pearce, ibid.

163. The newspaper observed that these tourists "jostled the haggard citizens
along the sidewalks, most of them carrying Kodaks or tripods." "The Sight-
Seers Should Not Come Empty-Handed to the City," *San Francisco Examiner*,
April 30, 1906.

164. Daniel Bell, *The Cultural Contradictions of Capitalism* (New York: Basic Books,
1976), 108.

165. Helen Fitzgerald Sanders, "Work of Woman's Relief Committee of Butte for
San Francisco," *Overland Monthly* 48, no. 2 (August 1906): 48.

166. Benedict Anderson, *Imagined Communities: Reflections on the Origin and Spread of
Nationalism* (New York: Verso, 1991).

167. Lars Bennett, "Recollections of the San Francisco 1906 Earthquake by his students," George Malcolm Stratton, Correspondence and Papers, 1911–1956.
Bennett also recalled that the *Boston American* put out a Sunday edition with "a
colored sheet consisting of postcard views of the earthquake's damage," noting that "these were supposed to be clipped out and this became my duty and
delight." Also pertinent is Correlle Stone's account of her evening at a theater
in Wisconsin where audiences watching moving pictures of the calamity were
asked to donate clothes and food for San Francisco. "Recollections of the San
Francisco 1906 Earthquake by his students," George Malcolm Stratton, Correspondence and Papers, 1911–1956.

168. Patten, *New Basis of Civilization*, 211.

169. Edward T. Devine, *The Principles of Relief* (New York: Macmillan, 1904), 468.

170. For background, see Theda Skocpol, *Protecting Soldiers and Mothers: The Political Origins of Social Policy in the United States* (Cambridge: Harvard University

Press, Belknap Press, 1992), and Edward D. Berkowitz and Kim McQuaid, *Creating the Welfare State: The Political Economy of 20th-Century Reform* (Lawrence: University of Kansas Press, 1992), 43–51.

171. Over the twentieth century, support for disaster relief has largely transcended party differences, even in periods of (supposed) fiscal retrenchment. On the day after the 1989 San Francisco earthquake, House Speaker Thomas S. Foley, a Democrat, made it clear that the city could expect federal assistance: "If we have to regrettably increase the deficit, we will have to do that, but we will not have to say to one part of this country or another, 'You have to bear this disaster alone.'" Thomas S. Foley, *Congressional Quarterly Weekly Reports*, October 21, 1989, quoted in Richard Sylves, "Earthquakes," in *Handbook of Emergency Management: Programs and Policies Dealing with Major Hazards and Disasters*, ed. William L. Waugh Jr. and Ronald John Hy (Westport, Conn.: Greenwood Press, 1990), 47. After 1993's Hurricane Andrew, even conservative columnist William Safire, outspoken opponent of welfare programs expenditures, demanded generous federal support for the disaster victims: "When any part of the nation is struck, the whole nation is injured, and disaster relief is the locality's due." "After the Storm," *New York Times*, September 7, 1993, A25.

172. For a good brief discussion of the philosophy of social insurance, see Linda Gordon, *Pitied But Not Entitled: Single Mothers and the History of Welfare* (Cambridge: Harvard University Press, 1994), 149–50.

173. This supports Theda Skocpol's observation about the Progressive Era: "Measures dealing with problems that could be widely and simply dramatized in human terms were the socioeconomic reforms most likely to be enacted in the states." *Protecting Soldiers and Mothers*, 266.

174. "The Work of the American National Red Cross," *Leslie's Weekly* 102, no. 2644 (May 10, 1906), 455.

175. Drinking alcohol, licentiousness, and boisterousness were among the offenses punishable by expulsion from the camps. See Adolphus Greely, *Earthquake in California, April 18, 1906: Special Report on the Relief Operations Conducted by the Military Authorities of the United States at San Francisco and Other Points* (Washington, D.C.: GPO, 1906); Ernest P. Bicknell, "In the Thick of the Relief Work at San Francisco," *Charities and the Commons* 16, no. 9 (June 2, 1906): 296–97; and George A. Soper, "The Sanitary Situation at San Francisco," *Charities and Commons* 16, no. 9 (June 2, 1906): 305–6.

176. Kasson, *Amusing the Million*, 109.

177. Gilles Deleuze and Félix Guattari, *Anti-Oedipus: Capitalism and Schizophrenia* (Minneapolis: University of Minnesota Press, 1983), xxiii.

178. For two excellent studies that explore links between unruly passions and consumer culture, see Colin Campbell, *The Romantic Ethic and the Spirit of Modern Consumerism* (New York: Basil Blackwell, 1987), and Jackson Lears, *Fables of Abundance: A Cultural History of Advertising in America* (New York: Basic Books, 1994).

179. Alan Trachtenberg, *The Incorporation of America: Culture and Society in the Gilded Age* (New York: Hill and Wang, 1982), 130.

180. Henry James, *The Ambassadors* (Rutland, Vt.: Everyman, 1999), 49–50, 53, 138, 198.

Chapter Four

1. "The Tempest," *Time* 66, no. 9 (August 29, 1955), 19. Also see "Deluge," *New York Times*, August 21, 1955, sec. 4, p. 1.
2. According to the *Times*, 184 died, 77 in Connecticut alone. Property damage was estimated at $1.67 billion. "Flood Toll," *New York Times*, August 28, 1955, sec. 4, p. 1. This was by no means the most expensive disaster in real terms. Once inflation is taken into account, calamities such as the 1906 San Francisco earthquake were vastly more destructive.
3. "Remarks Following a Meeting with the Governors of Flood-Stricken States at Bradley Field, Hartford, Connecticut, August 23, 1955," in *Public Papers of the Presidents: Dwight D. Eisenhower 1953–61* (Washington, D.C.: GPO, 1960–61).
4. By 1955, just seven years after the commercial introduction of this new medium of entertainment, 65 percent of American homes had television sets. Lynn Spigel, *Make Room for TV: Television and the Family Ideal in Postwar America* (Chicago: University of Chicago Press, 1992), 1, 32. It was not until 1960, however, that a majority of Americans claimed TV as their primary news source. And it was not until 1963 that the first networks shifted from a fifteen- to a thirty-minute format for the evening news. Stephen Ansolabehere, Roy Behr, and Shanto Iyengar, *The Media Game: American Politics in the Age of Television* (New York: Macmillan, 1993), 44.
5. Raymond Fielding, *The American Newsreel, 1911–1967* (Norman: University of Oklahoma Press, 1972), 24, 42. The company built a miniature set out of cardboard boxes and then set fire to it while a camera was filming.
6. The impact of commercial considerations on aesthetics and programming is a central theme in William Boddy, *Fifties Television: The Industry and Its Critics* (Urbana: University of Illinois Press, 1990).
7. Fielding, *American Newsreel*, 276–87.
8. "A News Magazine Special Report" (Warner Brothers Pictures, 1955). A copy of this newsreel is in the possession of the Aspinock Historical Society of Putnam, Connecticut. A second Warner Brothers newsreel on Hurricane Diane is available at the Sherman Grinberg Library in Chatsworth, California. I am indebted to that library's archivist, Bill Brewington, for information about the production and distribution of Warner Brothers newsreels in the 1950s.
9. For a television show that follows the same formula, see "New England Flood of '55," a "public service" documentary aired soon after the floods by WJAR Channel 10 in Providence, Rhode Island. It opens with shots of churning waters, images of rioting nature, and proceeds through dramatic close-ups and thrilling aerial panoramas. A copy is in the possession of the Aspinock Historical Society of Putnam, Connecticut. The newsreel was on the verge of passing from the scene after nearly half a century as an integral component of the movie experience. Unable to compete with television, only half of the nation's theaters were still booking newsreels when the hurricanes struck, and Warner Brothers dismantled its newsreel operations late in 1956. See Fielding, *American Newsreel*, 23, 48–50. In a withering critique of the news in the 1950s, Erik Barnouw notes that newscasts tended to be slick and diverting but featured pseudo-events, such as press conferences and beauty pageants, rather than hard

news. The exception was "catastrophes of some duration—fires, floods, wars" that could be reached by the handful of "stringers," cameramen who were usually paid based on the amount of film footage shown on the air. *Tube of Plenty* (New York: Oxford University Press, 1982), 168–69.

10. Douglas T. Miller and Marion Nowak, *The Fifties: The Way We Really Were* (Garden City, N.Y.: Doubleday, 1977), 358–60.

11. As Raymond Fielding shows, the notion of the heroic photographer was vigorously promoted in the 1920s by newspapers and magazines. This was obviously a boon to the companies involved, a form of advertising. *American Newsreel*, 144. Perhaps the most intriguing (and gently subversive) illustration of this conception is Buster Keaton's 1928 movie *The Cameraman*.

12. "A News Magazine Special Report" (Warner Brothers Pictures, 1955).

13. "The Atomic Bomb," *Life* 19, no. 8 (August 20, 1945), 87B.

14. "The Atomic Age," *Life* 19, no. 8 (August 20, 1945), 32.

15. Dwight D. Eisenhower, Diary, December 10, 1953, *The Eisenhower Diaries*, ed. Robert H. Ferrell (New York: W. W. Norton, 1981), 262.

16. "Eisenhower Urges Public to 'Pitch In' for Flood Aid," *New York Times*, August 23, 1955, 1. See also "Change of Plans," *Time* 66, no. 10, September 5, 1955, 12. Ike popularized the notion of the "peaceful atom" in a speech delivered to the United Nations in December 1953.

17. Respected scientists were at this very moment transmitting giddy assurances from Geneva that the technological conquest of nature was within reach. Homi J. Bhabha, the president of the conference, for example, ventured "to predict that a method will be found for liberating fusion energy in a controlled manner within the next two decades. When that happens, the energy problems of the world will have been solved forever, for the fuel will be as plentiful as heavy hydrogen in the oceans." "Peaceful Atoms," *New York Times*, August 14, 1955, sec. 4, p. 1. In Geneva, 1,260 delegates from seventy-two nations gathered to hear more than four hundred papers and to visit the world's first "atomic fair." For two enthusiastic contemporary accounts of the conference, see "The Philosophers' Stone," *Time* 61, no. 7, August 15, 1955, 46–51, and "Atom Experts' Shopping Spree," *Life* 39, no. 8, August 22, 1955, 39.

18. "The Common Coin of Peace," *Collier's*, September 2, 1955, 82.

19. On Eisenhower as "master-user of the U.S. mass media," see Craig Allen, *Eisenhower and the Mass Media: Peace, Prosperity, and Prime-Time TV* (Chapel Hill: University of North Carolina Press, 1993), 6, 26, 33. See also Thomas Doherty, *Cold War, Cool Medium: Television, McCarthyism, and American Culture* (New York: Columbia University Press, 2003), 97–104.

20. Allen, *Eisenhower and the Mass Media*, 26, 33.

21. Officials repeatedly expressed concern about the difficulties of generating enthusiasm for civil defense in peacetime. See Carey Brewer, *Civil Defense in the United States: Federal, State, and Local* (Washington, D.C.: Library of Congress Legislative Reference Service, 1951), 54. See also Andrew D. Grossman, *Neither Dead nor Red: Civil Defense and American Political Development during the Early Cold War* (New York: Routledge, 2001), 5.

22. As Nancy E. Bernhard explains, "Much of the news about the early Cold War on television was scripted, if not produced, by the defense establishment." Newscasters were taking a more independent line by the mid–'50s, but few challenged

what was now a "common sense" view that civil defense was a worthy and necessary venture. *U.S. Television News and Cold War Propaganda, 1947–1960* (New
York: Cambridge University Press, 1999), 2, 67. Meanwhile, the Federal Civil
Defense Agency and its successors distributed over five hundred million pieces
of civil defense literature in the 1950s. Grossman, *Neither Dead nor Red*, 54.

23. A case can be made that a series of "killer" hurricanes in 1954, which left 350
dead and destroyed up to $1.5 billion of property, were the first major disasters
managed under the act. "Double Trouble: Connie and Diane," *New York Times*,
August 14, 1955, sec. 4, p. 1. After Hurricane Hazel (October 16, 1954), President Eisenhower had "offered immediate and unlimited federal assistance,"
but the scale of relief and reconstruction was dwarfed by that offered after the
floods of 1955. "Hazel's Fling," *Time*, October 25, 1954, 30.

24. Perry Anderson notes the emergence of the term "postmodern" among intellectuals in the 1950s but adds that the concept did not achieve widespread currency until the 1970s. *Origins of Postmodernity* (New York: Verso, 1998), 7–16.
Recalling the assertion by sociologists David Riesman and Nathan Glazer that
1955 occasioned "a decisive shift in the American mind," W. T. Lhamon Jr.
also attributes to this year the origins of a new "cultural style." *Deliberate Speed:
The Origins of a Cultural Style in the American 1950s* (Washington, D.C.: Smithsonian Institution Press, 1990), 10. Riesman and Glazer were writing in "The
Intellectuals and the Discontented Classes," *Partisan Review* 22 (1955): 48.
M. Keith Booker, following Fredric Jameson, specifically names this style "incipient postmodernism." *Monsters, Mushroom Clouds, and the Cold War: American Science Fiction and the Roots of Postmodernism, 1946–1964* (Westport, Conn.:
Greenwood Press, 2001), 4.

25. This was consistent with his commitment to aspects of the New Deal and its so-
cial welfare programs and his search for a "middle way" between "government
by bureaucracy" and the "untrammeled freedom of the individual." William H.
Chafe, *The Unfinished Journey: America since World War II* (New York: Oxford
University Press, 1991), 138–39; Paul S. Boyer et al., eds., *The Enduring Vision:
A History of the American People* (Lexington, Mass.: D. C. Heath, 1995), 2:964.

26. *Chicago Tribune*, October 14, 1871, 2.

27. *The History of the US Army Corps of Engineers* (Alexandria, Va.: Office of History,
Headquarters, U.S. Army Corps of Engineers, 1998).

28. Quoted in John M. Barry, *Rising Tide: The Great Mississippi Flood of 1927 and
How It Changed America* (New York: Touchstone, 1998), 75.

29. Mark Twain, *Life on the Mississippi* (1883; New York: Signet Classics, 1961),
172–73.

30. Pete Daniel, *Deep'n as It Come: The 1927 Mississippi River Flood* (New York:
Oxford University Press, 1977), 149.

31. Twain, *Life on the Mississippi*, 15.

32. *The Mississippi Valley Flood Disaster of 1927: Official Report of Red Cross Operations*
(Washington, D.C.: American National Red Cross, 1928), 5–7, 73.

33. The modern agricultural practice of clearing forests had compounded the
problem, removing "the great sponge of forest floor that once . . . held the
snow water for gentle delivery all through the summer." T. G. Winter, letter to
the *Outlook* (New York), May 18, 1927. Quoted in Lyle Saxon, *Father Mississippi*
(New York: Century Co., 1927), 399–400.

34. The Red Cross played a part not only in relief and recovery but also in the rehabilitation of the victims, providing clothing, seeds, and livestock, and helping to repair 22,496 homes. *Mississippi Valley Flood Disaster of 1927*, 7–8, 11, 14–15, 61–75.

35. According to his own statistics, the organizations under his direction donated 33,841,307 tons of food and supplies worth $5.234 billion to Europeans during World War I. Herbert Hoover, *The Memoirs of Herbert Hoover* (New York: Macmillan, 1951–52), 1:426.

36. *Mississippi Valley Flood Disaster of 1927*, 92, 8–9.

37. Joan Hoff Wilson, *Herbert Hoover: Forgotten Progressive* (Boston: Little, Brown, 1975), 114–18.

38. *Mississippi Valley Flood Disaster of 1927*, 22.

39. The quotation is from the *Chicago Journal of Commerce*. Barry, *Rising Tide*, 365–377.

40. Hoover, *Memoirs*, 2:126.

41. *Mississippi Valley Flood Disaster of 1927*, 58.

42. For the racial politics of relief, see Barry's devastating account in *Rising Tide*, 308–17, 334, 388–95.

43. Saxon, *Father Mississippi*, 279, 309, 388.

44. Report of the Committee on Flood Control, March 29, 1928, *House Reports, 70th Congress, 1st Session* (Washington, D.C.: GPO, 1928), xi.

45. Rutherford H. Platt, *Disasters and Democracy: The Politics of Extreme Natural Events* (Washington, D.C.: Island Press, 1999), 12.

46. Peter J. May, *Recovering from Catastrophes: Federal Disaster Relief Policy and Politics* (Westport, Conn.: Greenwood Press, 1985), 20.

47. "Statement of Hon. Harold C. Hagen, A Representative in Congress from the State of Minnesota, 'Disaster Relief,'" *Hearings before the Committee on Public Works, 81st Congress, July 18 and 19, 2nd Session, January 3, 1950–January 2, 1951* (Washington, D.C.: GPO, 1950), 44.

48. Ibid., 43. For the official figure, see "Statement of Lt. Col. Earl C. Paules, Representing the Chief of Engineers, United States Army, 'Disaster Relief,'" *Hearings before the Committee on Public Works, 81st Congress, July 18 and 19*, 32.

49. "Statement of Lyman Brink, County Attorney, Kittson County, Minnesota, 'Disaster Relief,'" *Hearings before the Committee on Public Works, 81st Congress, July 18 and 19*, 48.

50. Having consulted "the record," he could assure members that federal aid had been offered after many of the several hundred major catastrophes that had beset the United States since 1803. "Statement of Hon. Harold C. Hagen, 'Disaster Relief,'" 44.

51. Public Law 875, *United States Statutes at Large, 1950–1951*, part 1, "Public Laws and Reorganization Plans" (Washington, D.C.: GPO, 1952), 1110–11.

52. Report of the Committee on Public Works, July 25, 1950, *House Reports, 81st Congress*, 2.

53. Public Law 875, 1109–10.

54. Ibid., 1110.

55. Ibid., 1111.

56. Ibid., 1110–11.

57. Platt, *Disasters and Democracy*, 11.

58. Report of the General Services Administration, July 18, 1950, *House Reports, 81st Congress*, 6.
59. Brewer, *Civil Defense in the United States*, 1.
60. On the ambitions and agendas of the national security state, see the "Blue Book": U.S. National Security Resources Board, NSRB Doc. 128, *United States Civil Defense* (Washington, D.C.: GPO, 1950).
61. Robert N. Bellah, Richard Madsden, William M. Sullivan, Ann Swidler, and Steven M. Tipton, *The Good Society* (New York: Knopf, 1991), 77–78. The key innovations were the National Security Act of 1947 (establishing the Department of Defense, the Central Intelligence Agency, and the National Security Council) and the Federal Civil Defense Act of 1950 (transforming the new Federal Civil Defense Administration into a powerful and independent agency within the executive branch).
62. Although civil defense was imagined as a program that emphasized civilian involvement and the "principle of self-help at every level of society," it was also obvious that such an expensive project would require massive federal funding. The cost of the civil defense program was expected to be $3.1 billion over its first three years, and Washington was tagged to cover 54 percent of the costs ($1,665,000,000), with states paying the balance. Brewer, *Civil Defense in the United States*, 3, 35, 37.
63. Ibid., 64.
64. Between 1950 and 1953, disaster operations were lodged at the Federal Housing and Home Finance Agency, the agency in charge of federal urban renewal programs. May, *Recovering from Catastrophes*, 50.
65. The state of New York, for example, now had at its disposal several radical options during a calamity. Officials, including the governor and county sheriffs and city mayors, were authorized to declare a "state of emergency" when confronted with serious "situations." In these circumstances the National Guard could be deployed and officials could make unauthorized expenditures out of public funds. The governor could also designate a "disaster area" and request federal funding as well as make extraordinary state expenditures. Neither of these measures had any affect on the "ordinary civil rights of citizens," but the governor was also empowered to declare martial rule during which civilians were bound to obey the authority of the National Guard. The president could go one step further and declare martial law, at which point the military "for a limited period" could direct events without regard for civil rights protections and laws. See the commentary of the New York State Civil Defense Commission in "Calamity Aid Set in Proclamations," *New York Times*, August 21, 1955, 51.
66. "The Rights of Non-Conformity," *Commonweal*, July 15, 1955, 364–65. On this and other Operation Alerts, see Guy Oakes, *The Imaginary War: Civil Defense and American Cold War Culture* (New York: Oxford University Press, 1994), 84–96.
67. Report of the Department of Agriculture, May 18, 1950, *House Reports, 81st Congress, 2nd Session, January 3, 1950–January 2, 1951* (Washington, D.C.: GPO, 1950), 10.
68. Report of the Committee on Public Works, July 25, 1950, *House Reports, 81st Congress*, 2.

69. Statement of Elmer B. Staats, the assistant director of the Bureau of the Budget, *Hearings before the Committee on Public Works, 81st Congress, July 18 and 19,* 79–80.

70. Report of the Bureau of the Budget, July 17, 1955, *House Reports, 81st Congress,* 5. The administrator of General Services agreed, drawing on his experiences. He explained how his agency had investigated requests for aid after a recent flash flood in Ohio: "When we went in to get a breakdown as to what the aid would be, the local people of course wanted to replace furniture; they wanted to repaint the jail; they wanted us to restore records; they wanted us to resurface a street where there had been no surface before; they wanted us to rewind a motor; they wanted us to replace highway signs, and such items as that." Statement of Jess Larson, Administrator of General Services, *Hearings before the Committee on Public Works, 81st Congress, July 18 and 19,* 89.

71. The classic analysis of "Fordism" is David Harvey, *The Condition of Postmodernity: An Enquiry into the Origins of Cultural Change* (Cambridge, Mass.: Blackwell, 1990), 125–40.

72. U.S. Congress, House, *Amendment to Small Business Act of 1953. Hearing before the Committee on Banking and Currency* (Washington, D.C.: GPO, 1956), 1.

73. "Many Units Study Easing of Floods," *New York Times,* August 24, 1955, 19. Governor Christian A. Herter of Massachusetts, for example, proclaimed a state of emergency under the state Civil Rights Act in order to acquire "broad powers . . . over food, drugs, transportation and other necessities." "Flood Zone to Get Billion in U.S. Aid," *New York Times,* August 26, 1955, 8.

74. "The Tempest," *Time* 66, no. 9, August 29, 1955, 19.

75. "Huge Relief Needs," *New York Times,* August 28, 1955, sec. 4, p. 1.

76. "Disasters: Sharing the Cost," *Time* 66, no. 20, November 14, 1955, 31.

77. "Huge Relief Needs," *New York Times,* August 28, 1955, sec. 4, p. 1. The state was the proper branch of government to help the victims because, in the words of Connecticut's Flood Recovery Committee, "the material loss to the survivors must be shared if the total community is to survive." "Disasters: Sharing the Cost," *Time* 66, no. 20, November 14, 1955, 31.

78. "Many Units Study Easing of Floods," *New York Times,* August 24, 1955, 19.

79. "The President's Appeal," *New York Times,* August 23, 1955, 15.

80. "100 Million in Flood Grants," *New York Times,* August 25, 1955, 1.

81. "Coping with the Deluge," *New York Times,* August 25, 1955, 22.

82. "100 Million in Flood Grants," *New York Times,* August 25, 1955, 14. Among other measures, the Civil Defense Administration agreed to spare federal housing projects marked for destruction in Waterbury, Connecticut, instead renovating them to house three hundred of the city's 659 families left homeless by the floods. "Flood Areas Ban Autos," *New York Times,* August 27, 1955, 32. And federal officials pledged to pump money into the devastated region, sending "new contracts to disaster areas wherever possible, thus making more jobs in undamaged factories." *Time* 66, no. 11, September 12, 1955, 103.

83. "U.S. Flood Help Not a Cure-All," *New York Times,* August 28, 1955, 67.

84. "Text of Talk by President Eisenhower," *New York Times,* August 25, 1955, 10.

85. "Text of Eisenhower Appeal," *New York Times,* August 24, 1955, 18.

86. *The American Red Cross Annual Report* (1956), 1–2; "Red Cross to the Rescue," *New York Times,* August 28, 1955, sec. 4, p. 8.

87. "Everyone to Bear Flood Cost Bills," *New York Times*, August 23, 1955, 1.
88. Ibid.
89. "Businessmen at Work," *Newsweek*, September 5, 1955, 21.
90. "Insurance Little Help to Victims," *New York Times*, August 28, 1955, sec. 4, p. 4.
91. "To Taste Disaster," *Newsweek*, September 5, 1955, 19.
92. "Everyone to Bear Flood Cost Bills," *New York Times*, August 23, 1955, 1; "Flood Insurance: Underwriters Keep Their Feet Dry," *Time* 66, no. 10, September 5, 1955, 70.
93. It was cost effective for private concerns to offer fire insurance even though fires damaged an average $429 million worth of property per year between 1927 and 1951. But flooding, which caused an annual average of only $160 million worth of damage over this same period, was too costly to cover. Charles Grutzner, "Flood Insurance: Pros and Cons," *New York Times*, August 28, 1955, sec. 4, p. 1.
94. "Flood Insurance: Underwriters Keep Their Feet Dry," *Time* 66, no. 10, September 5, 1955, 70.
95. Ibid.
96. "Huge Relief Needs," *New York Times*, August 28, 1955, sec. 4, p. 1.
97. U.S. Congress, House, *Amendment to Small Business Act of 1953, Hearing before the Committee on Banking and Currency* (Washington, D.C.: GPO, 1956), 2–3.
98. Ibid., 28–29.
99. Ibid., 29. Northeastern politicians and businessmen, according to the *New York Times*, were "talking about Government-backed insurance as the only solution." The governors of Connecticut and New Jersey made a joint appeal to the president for a national system of flood insurance. "Many Units Study Easing of Floods," *New York Times*, August 24, 1955, 19.
100. "Flood Insurance by U.S. Planned," *New York Times*, August 31, 1955, 48.
101. "U.S. Flood Help Not a Cure-All," *New York Times*, August 28, 1955, 67.
102. Howard Kunreuther et al., *Disaster Insurance Protection: Public Policy Lessons* (New York: John Wiley and Sons, 1978), 25.
103. "Flood Insurance: Underwriters Keep Their Feet Dry," *Time* 66, no. 10, September 5, 1955, 70.
104. The Federal Flood Control Act of 1936 already authorized the Army Corps of Engineers to build a system of dams, reservoirs, dikes, and levees in the Northeast. The act promised that "the Federal Government would pay for all the costs of planning and constructing flood-control projects if the states and local governments provided the necessary lands and easements and would maintain the works after completion," but Congress had not allocated the necessary funds. "Huge Relief Needs," *New York Times*, August 28, 1955, sec. 4, p. 2. Part of the blame rested with local governments that were deterred by the high expense of buying the land that the engineers wished to work on. Local companies and householders also proved reluctant to surrender sites with river views or access to riverfronts. "Flood Control Plans Spurred by Disaster," *New York Times*, August 28, 1955, sec. 4, p. 10.
105. "Connecticut Puts Flood Aid First," *New York Times*, August 23, 1955, 14.
106. "Connecticut Acts to Rebuild Cities," *New York Times*, August 22, 1955, 14.

107. Ted Steinberg, *Acts of God: The Unnatural History of Natural Disaster in America* (New York: Oxford University Press, 2000), 127–28. On the science, law, ethics, and political history of weather control, see the essays in Robert G. Fleagle, ed., *Weather Modification: Science and Public Policy* (Seattle: University of Washington Press, 1969).

108. "Northern Hurricanes: A New Weather Pattern," *New York Times*, August 14, 1955, sec. 4, p. 5.

109. Dunn was not impressed, pointing out that this "would add radioactivity to a hurricane's already bulging bag of tricks and there is no assurance that the bombs wouldn't abet rather than destroy the storm's developing ferocity." At the same time, he did believe that science was likely to discover a means for steering hurricanes, "perhaps by some propitious cloud-seeding." "Mr. Big Wind Himself," *Newsweek*, August 29, 1955, 51.

110. Already, after the 1954 hurricanes, Congress had authorized $1 million to finance a detailed study of hurricanes by the Army Corps of Engineers and the Weather Bureau. "Storm's Behavior Studied by Army," *New York Times*, August 13, 1955, 5; "What Diane Taught Us," *New York Times*, August 24, 1955, 26; "Worst Weather Ever?" *Newsweek*, August 29, 1955, 50.

111. Working under its auspices, the sociologist Anthony F. C. Wallace compiled a thirteen-thousand-item bibliography on "human behavior in extreme situations." See Wallace, *Human Behavior in Extreme Situations* (Washington, D.C.: National Academy of Sciences, 1956), iii. Systematic research into the social and psychological dimensions of calamity began in the 1950s with the foundation of such organizations as the Disaster Research Group. For an example of this work, see William H. Form and Sigmund Nosow, *Community in Disaster* (New York: Harper and Brothers, 1958).

112. *Chicago Defender*, September 15, 1945, quoted in Paul Boyer, *By the Bomb's Early Light: American Thought and Culture at the Dawn of the Atomic Age* (Chapel Hill: University of North Carolina Press, 1994), 269.

113. Boyer, *By the Bomb's Early Light*, 101–3.

114. William Vogt, "Preventing Flood Damages," letter to the editor, *New York Times*, August 31, 1955, 24. Others agreed. Disastrous floods, Russell Lipkin argued in a letter to the *New York Times*, were "totally unnecessary." As he explained, echoing arguments that had circulated after the 1927 Mississippi flood, "In a normally well vegetated region like the Northeast the earth should be capable of absorbing even the heaviest rainfall, effecting a gradual release to the streams without any decrease in their stability. The impairment of the earth's plant cover is what destroys that retentive capacity, resulting in a mass surface flow known as flood." The lesson was clear. The problem was not "nature" or "the weather" but human practices. "Let the people cease blaming the weather, and set to work instead to heal every bare acre of farm, forest and hillside. Otherwise they will continue to be victims not of the supposed perversity of the elements but of their own destructive handiwork." "To Prevent Floods," letter to the editor, *New York Times*, August 29, 1955, 18.

115. William Vogt, *Road to Survival* (New York: William Sloane Associates, 1948), 133, 78. Also see Robert Gottlieb, *Forcing the Spring: The Transformation of the American Environmental Movement* (Washington, D.C.: Island Press, 1993), 36.

116. On the "religious boom" of the 1950s, see Miller and Nowak, *The Fifties*, 84–105.

117. Even the American Bible Association, which arranged to send twenty-five thousand Bibles to victims in the Northeast, insisting that "the Bible and the faith it engenders is vital at this time," agreed that it was a religious calling to tend to the material needs of survivors. "Bibles Being Distributed in Flood-Stricken Areas," *New York Times*, August 24, 1955, 20. Cardinal Spellman, in a typical statement, urged Catholics to give generously to the Red Cross. "Christian charity and the spirit of true Americanism," his spokesman declared, "compel us to render such aid and comfort to our stricken neighbors as our means and circumstances permit." Protestant churches took a similar line. "Catholics Urged to Give Flood Aid," *New York Times*, August 29, 1955, 22.

118. Boyer, *By the Bomb's Early Light*, 239.

119. Perry Miller, "The End of the World," *Errand into the Wilderness* (Cambridge: Harvard University Press, Belknap Press, 1956), 239.

120. It was these films, according to movie historian Peter Biskind, "more than any other genre, that caught the hysteria behind the picture window." *Seeing Is Believing: How Hollywood Taught Us to Stop Worrying and Love the Fifties* (New York: Pantheon Books, 1983), 98, 103. Admittedly, science fiction films were by no means the most successful blockbusters of the decade. It was religious epics that truly captured the popular imagination, with *Ben Hur*, *The Robe*, and *The Ten Commandments* among the five biggest grossing films of the 1950s. It is notable, however, that even those movies were full of spectacles of destruction. Alan Nadel, *Containment Culture: American Narratives, Postmodernism, and the Atomic Age* (Durham: Duke University Press, 1995), 92.

121. Susan Sontag, "The Imagination of Disaster," in *Against Interpretation and Other Essays* (New York: Farrar, Strauss and Giroux, 1966), 213.

122. See David Annan, *Catastrophe: The End of Cinema* (London: Lorrimer, 1975), esp. chap. 1, "Born to Disaster."

123. John Brosnan, *Future Tense: The Cinema of Science Fiction* (New York: St. Martin's Press, 1978), 73, 78.

124. "The Atomic Age," *Life* 19, no. 8, August 20, 1945, 32.

125. "When Disaster Struck Connecticut," CPTV documentary, dir. Rich Hanley (1997).

126. "40 Tell of Terror in the Poconos," *New York Times*, August 25, 1955, 13.

127. "The Tempest," *Time* 66, no. 9, August 29, 1955, 19.

128. Sontag, "Imagination of Disaster," 224, 225.

129. C. Wright Mills, *The Power Elite* (New York: Oxford University Press, 1956), 120. For another classic analysis of corporate conformity and blandness in the 1950s, see William H. Whyte, *The Organization Man* (New York: Simon and Schuster, 1956). For a more recent account, see Jackson Lears, "A Matter of Taste: Corporate Cultural Hegemony in a Mass-Consumption Society," in *Recasting America: Culture and Politics in the Age of Cold War*, ed. Lary May (Chicago: University of Chicago Press, 1989), 38–57.

130. Mark Jancovich, *Rational Fears: American Horror in the 1950s* (New York: Manchester University Press, 1996), 2–3.

131. This also is M. Keith Booker's assessment. See *Monsters, Mushroom Clouds, and the Cold War*, 106.

132. "Uncle Sam Seeks Exit from Private Business," *Saturday Evening Post* 228, no. 8, August 20, 1955, 10.
133. May, *Recovering from Catastrophes*, 24–25.
134. "The Big Muddy Tamed at Last," *Life* 39, no. 8, August 22, 1955, 2.
135. "The U.S. Masters the Big Muddy," *Life* 39, no. 8, August 22, 1955, 21.
136. Steinberg, *Acts of God*, 74, 119.
137. Ian Burton, Robert W. Kates, and Gilbert F. White, *The Environment as Hazard* (New York: Oxford University Press, 1978), 61–63.
138. Platt, *Disasters and Democracy*, 111–30.
139. Rutherford Platt invokes the insurance term "moral hazard" to describe the consequences of generous federal assistance, arguing that it helps "to diminish the natural caution that individuals, communities, and businesses might otherwise exercise in adjusting to natural hazards in their investment and locational decisions." *Disasters and Democracy*, 9.
140. For a fine analysis of this process, see Steinberg, *Acts of God*, 86.
141. Platt, *Disasters and Democracy*, 41.
142. Mike Davis, *Ecology of Fear: Los Angeles and the Imagination of Disaster* (New York: Metropolitan Books, 1998), 50–52.
143. May, *Recovering from Catastrophes*, 62.
144. Donald F. Kettl, "Relentless Revolution," Govexec.com, January 1, 2000; http://www.govexec.com/story_page.cfm?mode=report&articleid=15818& printerfriendlyVers=1&. During the Clinton administration, under the energetic James Lee Witt, the agency switched its focus back to natural disasters and responded aggressively to the Midwestern floods of 1993 and the Northridge earthquake of 1994, with, as we have seen, mixed benefits for poor communities.
145. For popular resistance to FEMA civil defense planning in the early 1980s, see David Cortright, *Peace Works: The Citizen's Role in Ending the Cold War* (Boulder, Co.: Westview Press, 1993), 33–39.
146. See, for example, Sam Smith, "'X-Files' Gets It Right," *Progressive Review*, June 1998.
147. Presidents were more and more likely to declare events "major disasters," to the point where there was an average of one such declaration every week in the last years of the twentieth century. Platt, *Disasters and Democracy*, xvi, 279–80.

Chapter Five

1. For some sense of the sheer range of responses, see the thousands of testimonies in *The September 11 Digital Archive* at http://911digitalarchive.org/.
2. Peter Travers, "Hollywood under Siege," *Rolling Stone*, October 25, 2001, 128.
3. Anthony Lane, "This Is Not a Movie," *New Yorker*, September 24, 2001, 79.
4. Ibid.
5. "From Our Correspondents: September 11, 2001," *New Yorker*, September 24, 2001, 55.
6. Jan Fleischer, reporting for WINS–AM in New York. Quoted in *Covering Catastrophe: Broadcast Journalists Report September 11*, ed. Allison Gilbert et al. (Chicago: Bonus Books, 2002), 15. I draw heavily on this fascinating collection of journalistic responses to 9/11 because it reveals both the variety of personal

reactions in "the media" as well as shared institutional and cultural pressures that produce certain conformities of worldview and professional behavior.

7. Jean Baudrillard, *Simulacra and Simulation*, trans. Sheila Faria Glaser (Ann Arbor: University of Michigan Press, 1994), 3.

8. The passages are full of anxiety about our collective failure to summon up authentic feelings in the presence of such an enormous disaster. Indeed, the insistence by all of these commentators that it *is* possible to discern the truth behind the appearances seems only to verify the existence of a postmodern crisis of perception. John Storey, among others, describes the concept of hyperreality as "the characteristic mode of postmodernity." *An Introduction to Cultural Theory and Popular Culture* (Athens: University of Georgia Press, 1998), 178.

9. Ted Rall, cartoon, *Valley Advocate* (Easthampton, Massachusetts), November 15, 2001, 4. Caption: "By evening, people are glued to their television sets. Secretly they think the World Trade footage is cool." "Cool" itself is a distinctively modern, or hypermodern, sensibility. Evans Chan asks rhetorically, "Hasn't the post-Freudian, permissive, globalized modern society bred a sensibility named Cool to cope with the onslaught of image and information?" Of course, there are varieties of cool. There is the knowing modernist sensibility of jazz performers who assume a cool outlook as a means of exerting artistic control over the dizzying fragmentations of modernity. And there is the vernacular cool of Hollywood that is grounded in the twentieth-century taste for diversion. The schoolboys here are operating within the latter universe of feeling and present a twenty-first-century analogue to the San Francisco girl we encountered in chapter 3, who longed for several years after the 1906 disaster for "another earthquake so that I could hear things smash again." Ruth Worner, term paper at the University of California, Berkeley, 1919, in "Recollections of the San Francisco 1906 Earthquake by his students," George Malcolm Stratton Correspondence and Papers, 1911–1956, Bancroft Library, carton 6.

10. Art Spiegelman, *In the Shadow of No Towers* (New York: Pantheon, 2004), 4.

11. See, for example, Fredric Jameson, "The Dialectics of Disaster," *South Atlantic Quarterly* 101, no. 2 (Spring 2002): 297–304.

12. "In the immediate, before-it-sinks-in aftermath of the September 11 attack, one of the first catch-phrases to take hold—and be widely deployed by TV commentators, politicians, and citizen e-mailers—was, 'this changes everything.'" "The Dark Smoke," *Nation*, October 1, 2001, 6.

13. The attacks, according to the U.S. General Accounting Office, "created the most costly disaster in U. S. history." The key legislation guiding the federal response was the Robert T. Stafford Disaster Relief and Emergency Assistance Act of 1988. U.S. General Accounting Office, "Disaster Assistance: Information on FEMA's Post 9/11 Public Assistance to the New York City Area," 2, 12.

14. Notice, for example, the modernist, and in some ways residually Puritan, assumptions of the commissioners appointed by Congress and President Bush to investigate the causes of 9/11, when they referred to this disaster as both a trial and an opportunity for reform and improvement: "That September day, we came together as a nation. The test before us is to sustain that unity of purpose and meet the challenges now confronting us. . . . We have been forced to think about the way our government is organized. . . . Congress needs dramatic change as well to strengthen oversight and focus abilities." *The 9/11 Commission*

Report: Final Report of the National Commission on Terrorist Attacks upon the United States (New York: W. W. Norton, 2004), xvi.

15. This is conveyed nicely by the rich variety of stories, poems, and reminiscences collected in *110 Stories: New York Writes after September 11*, ed. Ulrich Baer (New York: New York University Press, 2002).

16. Julianne Malveaux and Reginna A. Green, eds., *The Paradox of Loyalty: An African American Response to the War on Terrorism* (Chicago: Third World Press, 2002), xiii.

17. Cornel West, foreword to *The Paradox of Loyalty*, xi–xii. See also Roopali Mukherjee, "Between Enemies and Traitors: Black Press Coverage of September 11 and the Predicaments of National 'Others,'" in *Media Representations of September 11*, ed. Steven Chermak, Frankie Y. Bailey, and Michelle Brown (Westport, Conn.: Praeger, 2003), 29–46.

18. This is a point missed by Baudrillard in his totalizing account of Western culture and the binaristic opposition he draws with non-Western cultures, as witnessed by his provocative account of the appeal of the destruction of the World Trade Center. "At a pinch, we can say that they *did it*, but we *wished for* it." Jean Baudrillard, *The Spirit of Terrorism and Requiem for the Twin Towers*, trans. Chris Turner (New York: Verso, 2002), 4–5.

19. Lane, "This Is Not a Movie," 79.

20. Larry King, quoted in Gilbert et al., eds., *Covering Catastrophe*, 35.

21. Slavoj Žižek, *Welcome to the Desert of the Real* (New York: Verso, 2002), 16.

22. Nancy Gibbs, "Apocalypse Now," *Time*, July 1, 2002, 42.

23. David Wilkerson, "The Towers Have Fallen—But We Missed the Message" (October 8, 2001), John Mark Ministries, http://jmm.aua.net.au/articles/1058.htm.

24. "I really believe," he said, "that the pagans, and the abortionists, and the feminists, and the gays and the lesbians who are actively trying to make that an alternative lifestyle, the ACLU, People For the American Way, all of them who have tried to secularize America. I point the finger in their face and say, 'You helped this happen.'" Later, speaking to CNN, Falwell adjusted his position. Responding to intense criticism, he agreed that the hijackers and terrorists alone were responsible for the attacks, but he continued to attack the ACLU and other liberal groups, who, having "attempted to secularize America, have removed our nation from its relationship with Christ on which it was founded." The jeremiad logic was intact: "I therefore believe that that created an environment which possibly has caused God to lift the veil of protection which has allowed no one to attack America on our soil since 1812." *CNN.com*, September 14, 2001; http://www.cnn.com/2001/US/09/14/Falwell.apology. Surprised by the outrage of conservative allies, he temporarily retreated even from this position, stating that his comments were "insensitive, uncalled for at the time, and unnecessary." William F. Buckley, "Invoking God's Thunder," *National Review Online*, September 18, 2001; http://www.nationalreview.com/buckley/buckley091801.shtml. On Falwell, see Susan Friend Harding, *The Book of Jerry Falwell: Fundamentalist Language and Politics* (Princeton: Princeton University Press, 2000), 161–62.

25. Cotton Mather, "The Terror of the Lord," 1727, in *Days of Humiliation, Times of Affliction* (Gainesville, Fla.: Scholars' Facsimiles and Reprints, 1970), 308–10.

26. Amy Johnson Frykholm, *Rapture Culture:* Left Behind *in Evangelical Culture* (New York: Oxford University Press, 2004), 106.
27. Ernest Sandeen, *The Roots of Fundamentalism: British and American Millenarianism, 1800–1930* (Chicago: University of Chicago Press, 1970), 62–70. And, significantly, it reverses the formerly dominant (optimistic) postmillennialist assumption that Christ's thousand-year rule on earth would precede rather than follow the tribulation.
28. The Rapture does not enjoy unambiguous scriptural authorization. It is mentioned only once in the Bible, and not in the Book of Revelation but in 1 Thessalonians 4:17. See Catherine Keller, *Apocalypse Now and Then: A Feminist Guide to the End of the World* (Boston: Beacon Press, 1996), 320n62.
29. Gibbs, "Apocalypse Now," 44.
30. Hal Lindsey, *The Late Great Planet Earth* (Grand Rapids, Mich.: Zondervan, 1970), 138.
31. Stacey J. Willis, "Attacks Have Many Asking 'Is This the End?'" *Las Vegas Sun*, September 17, 2001.
32. Thomas Ice, "Terrorism in America: Foreshadow of End-Time Events," *Pre-Tribulation Newsletter.* To be sure, even the most ardent advocates of prophecy belief insisted that American disasters were "stage-setting" events rather than prophetic ones predicted in the Bible. Tim LaHaye, the publisher of the website, struck a characteristically cautious note:

> One of my major concerns is that someone may rush into print with some wild suggestion that this act of terrorism is "a sign of the soon coming of the Lord" or "a sign of the end." The media would love to have us read into this tragic act of violence more than there is really there. This is not an act of God. It is the act of some religiously sick Muslims who have been deceived into thinking they will earn their way to heaven by killing innocent children, men, and women. It is not a specific prophecy of anything except we are living in increasingly "perilous times," just as prophecy warns. ("The Prophetic Significance of Sept. 11, 2001," *Pre-Tribulation Newsletter*, http://www.timlahaye .com/about_ministry/pdf/lahaye_sept11.pdf).

This was a very important distinction for evangelicals. No American disaster could tell us exactly when the world would end. For one thing, the Rapture was "a signless event"; for another, preachers were reluctant to overstate the scriptural significance of an event that took place so far from the Holy Land. Todd Hertz, *Christianity Today* (posted September 19, 2001, http://www .christianitytoday.com/ct/2001/138/34.0.html). But such an opportunity could not be missed entirely. "We also know," LaHaye added, "there will be several bonafide signs signifying the end of the age and the Glorious Appearing of Jesus to set up his kingdom." And the calculations ensued: "Which is why, when examining stage-setting events like this one, we must deduct at least seven years from the fulfillment of several of those end-time signs. I believe this dastardly event will contribute to the fulfillment of several of those end-time signs." In particular, the attacks could be expected to spur the sort of developments that were (supposedly) prophesied in the Bible: the trends toward a single world government, global commerce, a common world religion, conflicts in the Middle East, and so forth.

NOTES

33. Keller, *Apocalypse Now and Then*, 11.
34. Lindsey, *Late Great Planet Earth*, 166. Grace Halsell claims that Jimmy Swaggart was similarly thrilled by the prospect of Armaggeddon. *Prophesy and Politics: Militant Evangelists on the Road to Nuclear War* (Westport, Conn.: Lawrence Hill, 1986), 8, 17.
35. Frykholm, *Rapture Culture*, 23, 184. According to a 2005 survey by Market-Cast of evangelicals and nonevangelicals, "When it comes to popular music and popular shows, tastes don't differ at all." "The Passion of the Marketers: Studios Give Christians Their Movie Moment," *New York Times*, July 18, 2005, C3.
36. Joseph Helfgot, president of MarketCast, quoted in "Passion of the Marketers," C3.
37. John Wilson, "The Imagination of Disaster," posted on *Christianity Today*, September 17, 2001, http://www.christianitytoday.com/ct/2001/138/13.0.html.
38. Lane, "This Is Not a Movie," 79.
39. Gibbs, "Apocalypse Now," 42.
40. "Religion: The Pop Prophets," *Newsweek*, May 24, 2004.
41. Ibid. Frykholm argues that church leaders largely ignore the books, however (47, 68).
42. Tim LaHaye and Jerry B. Jenkins, *Nicolae: The Rise of the Antichrist* (Wheaton, Ill.: Tyndale House, 1997), 405.
43. As one reader, interviewed by Frykholm, put it, the first book had "a trashy novel-type plot" that reminded her of nothing so much as the Hollywood "movies my husband loved where there are good guys and there are bad guys and the fight scenes and all that." Frykholm, *Rapture Culture*, 56–57. Nancy Gibbs, citing academic sources, speculates that the popularity of *Left Behind* may owe less to its doctrine than to its appeal as a horror story for those uncomfortable with Stephen King or the Harry Potter books; after all, LaHaye famously condemned J. K. Rowland for promoting black magic in her stories. Gibbs, "Apocalypse Now," 47.
44. See Randall Balmer, *Mine Eyes Have Seen the Glory: A Journey into the Evangelical Subculture in America* (New York: Oxford University Press, 2000), 48–70.
45. Ken James, "Left Behind," *Christian Spotlight on the Movies*, 1; http://www.christiananswers.net/spotlight/movies/2000/leftbehind.html.
46. Tony Kushner gently ridicules this notion in his antiapocalyptic play *Angels in America*. After an angel appears in one scene amid a burst of sound and destruction, the human witness can only declare, "*Very* Steven Spielberg." *Angels in America: A Gay Fantasia on National Themes* (New York: Theatre Communications Group, 2003), 124.
47. James, "Left Behind," 2. At least one reader, Dan, forty-five, was reassured: "I agree that there is zero cringe-factor, and that it's probably the best Christian move [*sic*] I've seen, overall" (3). http://www.christiananswers.net/spotlight/movies/2000/leftbehind.html.
48. One self-identified Christian (Paul Kirby, age eighteen) wrote in to say, "The movie was awful. Terrible acting, a poor script (that actually managed to be worse than the book), and subpar directing. This is not a good movie to show people that Christians can make quality entertainment. Non-Christians who see this movie will most likely be disgusted, and conclude that Christians have

285

no taste in entertainment" (5); http://www.christiananswers.net/spotlight/movies/2000/leftbehind.html.

49. This was the assessment of Desson Howe, "'Left Behind': Heaven Help Us," *Washington Post.* Posted February 2, 2001; http://www.washingtonpost.com/wp-srv/entertainment/movies/reviews/leftbehindhowe.htm. Although the producers spent $17.4 million making the film, much of the budget reportedly was devoted to publicity. Accordingly, the special effects have a decidedly low-budget appearance, the direction is plodding, and the acting is wooden. Although loyal Christians bought three million videos, the movie flopped at the box office.

50. To be sure, this was tied to concerns to secure greater franchising profits. "'Left Behind' Co-Author Sues Filmmakers," *Maranatha Christian Journal*; http://www.mcjonile/news/01a/20010221a.shtml. On the lawsuit, see "Portion of 'Left Behind' Suit Dismissed by Judge," Christian Examiner on the Web, May 20, 2003. http://www.christiantimes.com/Articles.Articles%20May01/Art_May03_07.html. In 2005 the producers teamed up with Sony to make the third installment of the series, evidently hoping that Hollywood money and connections would enhance the visual appeal of the movie. "The Passion of the Marketers: Studios Give Christians Their Movie Moment," *New York Times*, July 18, 2005, C3.

51. Significantly, one of the two heroes in *Left Behind* is a prominent television journalist.

52. The phrase "optically correct" comes from Paul Virilio, *Ground Zero*, trans. Chris Turner (New York: Verso, 2002), 31.

53. Kathy Dick, Story #4003, *The September 11 Digital Archive*, September 11, 2002; http://911digitalarchive.org/stories/details/4003.

54. Jay Rosen, "September 11 in the Mind of American Journalism," in *Journalism after September 11*, ed. Barbie Zelizer and Stuart Allan (New York: Routledge, 2002), 29.

55. "Disaster Programming," *Variety.com*, September 21, 2001, 1. See also "Hollywood Revisits Terrorism-Related Projects," *Wall Street Journal*, September 13, 2001, B3. Meanwhile, acerbic comic George Carlin had to change the title of his HBO show from "I Kind of Like It When a Lot of People Die" to "Complaints and Grievances" and cut a planned segment on the delights of watching natural disasters on TV, though he did keep in material about the pleasure of watching car crashes. (See the show [dir. Rocco Urbisci, Mpi Home Video, 2004] and *TV Guide*, November 17–23, 2001, 6.)

56. Eighty million Americans tuned in to ABC, CBS, or NBC news coverage of the attacks on the evening of September 11 (up from the usual twenty to twenty-five million news viewers); a further fourteen million watched cable news. Many newspapers were unable to produce enough copies to meet demand on September 12. Leonard Downie Jr. and Robert G. Kaiser, *The News about the News: American Journalism in Peril* (New York: Alfred A. Knopf, 2002), 63, 112, 145.

57. Marcy McGinnis, senior vice president for hard news coverage, CBS News, New York. Quoted in *Covering Catastrophe*, 217.

58. Robert W. McChesney, *The Problem of the Media: U.S. Communication Politics in the 21st Century* (New York: Monthly Review Press, 2004), 42–43.

59. See the statement by Barclay Palmer, executive producer, CNN, New York, in *Covering Catastrophe*, 214.
60. Wilson Surratt, executive producer, WPIX-TV, New York. "I don't think we ever used the video we shot of people jumping," Tom Flynn, a CBS producer, recalled. "It wasn't my decision not to use it, but I wouldn't have." Both quoted in *Covering Catastrophe*, 52, 54. Similarly, Jules Naudet, the filmmaker of the wrenching video *9/11*, which offered the only footage of the calamity from within the towers before they fell, refused to film a burning woman, though his shot of the first airliner hitting the North Tower was shown repeatedly during the CBS special presentation.
61. Stephen Battaglio, "After the Deluge," *TV Guide*, November 17, 2001, 58.
62. Judy Woodruff, anchor, CNN, Washington. Quoted in *Covering Catastrophe*, 183.
63. This squeamishness contrasts with the U.S. press's graphic treatment of foreign calamities. By the same token, coverage of 9/11 elsewhere in the world was more explicit than U.S. coverage.
64. Judy Woodruff, anchor, CNN, Washington. Quoted in *Covering Catastrophe*, 183.
65. CNN executive producer Barclay Palmer recalled that about two dozen amateur tapes came through his office, most donated "by people who simply felt it was important for the tapes to be seen, as though they had an obligation to share them with the world," but others asked for money. In each case, he had to authorize expenditures and "tried to make sure we had legal release for each tape." In the short run this turned out to be unnecessary because "the network presidents agreed to pool all the tape, so here CNN was paying for it, yet everybody got to show it." But in time this system of exclusive rights was restored, at which point the networks were entitled and indeed expected to make profits out of their investments in footage. Barclay Palmer, executive producer, CNN, New York. Quoted in *Covering Catastrophe*, 214–15.
66. For an engaging analysis of the technological, economic, political, and cultural forces producing the decline of news into infotainment, see Downie and Kaiser, *News about the News*.
67. Lynn Spigel, "Entertainment Wars: Television Culture after 9/11," *American Quarterly* 56, no. 2 (June 2004): 236–37.
68. Battaglio, "After the Deluge," 59.
69. The cathartic aspect of spectacles of destruction perhaps also helps to explain why, even as pundits were "calling for an end to terrorism as entertainment," Blockbuster video stores were announcing "brisk rentals of films that feature terrorists getting their butts kicked—like *True Lies*, in which Schwarzenegger straps an Arab dissident to a missile and launches him through the windows of a Miami high-rise." Travers, "Hollywood under Siege," 128. Disaster flicks such as *The Towering Inferno* were also hugely popular. Spigel, "Entertainment Wars," 236.
70. As host Jon Stewart admitted, even the *Daily Show* was only tolerated by Comedy Central's corporate bosses Viacom (which at the time also owned CBS, Paramount, MTV, VH1, Showtime, Blockbuster, Simon and Schuster, BET, and Nickelodeon) and Time Warner (which owned much of the rest of the media

including HBO and AOL) because it delivered a young consumer demographic to advertisers. For all of its criticism of the media—which is often brilliant—the *Daily Show* has to promote movies and books to court the celebrity guests on whom they depend for ratings. Tad Friend, "Is It Funny Yet? Jon Stewart Measures Comedy against Crisis," *New Yorker*, February 11, 2002, 28–35.

71. On the complex ways in which television frames or constructs "reality," see James Friedman, ed., *Reality Squared: Televisual Discourse on the Real* (New Brunswick, N.J.: Rutgers University Press, 2002). An Edelman Public Relations Worldwide poll of one thousand American adults soon after September 11 discovered that eight out of ten people were relieved to see the return of advertisements to television after a few days of unbroken news coverage of the attacks. *NewsHour Extra*, October 24, 2001; www.pbs.org/newshour/extra/features/july-deco1/culture.html.

72. Lauren Glassberg, reporter, WABC-TV, New York. Quoted in *Covering Catastrophe*, 246.

73. See Christian Martin, producer, NBC News, New York, and Buba Adschiew, producer, NBC News, New York. Quoted in *Covering Catastrophe*, 77, 79, 213.

74. And this, of course, was fully anticipated by al Qaeda planners who evidently staged the spectacle in New York City, the communications capital of the nation, filled as it was with camera crews, to exploit American fascination with explosions. On the project of all terrorists—dramatic spectacle, or, put another way, theater—see Jason Burke, "Theatre of Terror," *Observer*, November 21, 2004; http://observer.guardian.co.uk/review/story/0,6903,1355798,00.html.

75. "100 Most Memorable Moments," *TV Guide*, December 5–11, 2004, 31–32.

76. A perfect example is TNT's *The Grid*, which aired in the summer of 2004 and offered a multifaceted portrait of the war on terrorism that was more sensitive to complex economic and geopolitical contexts than most statements by politicians. But this show was predictably bound by the conventions of its idiom and wound up offering lurid sexual subplots while trying to entice viewers by promising to exhibit "the world's sexiest counter-terrorism experts."

77. CBS News, for example, which devoted 23.20 minutes to news in 1981, cut this back to 18.20 minutes by 2001, with the rest of the time reserved for promos and advertisements. The other networks made similar cuts. Downie and Kaiser, *News about the News*, 113.

78. Michael Massing, "Press Watch," *Nation*, October 15, 2001, 6.

79. Henri Lefebvre, *Introduction to Modernity*, trans. John Moore (New York: Verso, 1995), 337.

80. He defines the CNN effect as "the generic term for the ability of real-time communications technology, via the news media, to provoke major responses from domestic audiences and political elites to both global and national events." He differentiates between "humanitarian" motives such as those governing U.S. involvement in the Bosnian war of 1992–95 and the national security motives shaping responses to events such as September 11. Piers Robinson, *The CNN Effect: The Myth of News, Foreign Policy, and Intervention* (New York: Routledge, 2002), 2, 4.

81. U.S. General Accounting Office, "September 11: More Effective Collaboration Could Enhance Charitable Organizations' Contributions in Disasters," Report Number GAO-03-259, December 2002, 1.

82. "9/11 Fund Chief Faults Payments," *CBS News*, November 18, 2004; http://www.cbsnews.com/stories/2003/09/04/national/main571663.shtml.

83. U.S. General Accounting Office, "Disaster Assistance: Information on FEMA's Post 9/11 Public Assistance to the New York City Area," 7, 34.

84. The largest portion of this, about $7.4 billion, was earmarked for FEMA to pay for such tasks as debris removal and the repair of public building and transportation infrastructure. This was "the largest disaster response in the agency's history," eclipsing the $6.9 billion spent on the Northridge earthquake of 1994. U.S. General Accounting Office, "Disaster Assistance: Information on FEMA's Post 9/11 Public Assistance to the New York City Area," 1–2, 5, 6.

85. Jeff Jacoby, "Why the 9/11 Fund Was a Mistake," Townhall.com: Conservative News and Information, September 27, 2004; http://www.townhall.com/columnists/jeffjacoby/jj20040927.shtml.

86. Nick Cater, "Why 9/11 Was a Disaster for Charities," *Guardian Unlimited*, September 6, 2002; http://www.guardian.co.uk/september11/story/0,11209,798146,00.html.

87. Jameson, "Dialectics of Disaster," 298.

88. See, for example, Stuart Ewen and Elizabeth Ewen, *Channels of Desire: Mass Images and the Shaping of American Consciousness* (Minneapolis: University of Minnesota Press, 1992).

89. "Fear Factor"; http://www.wga.org/craft/interviews/moore.html.

90. To be sure, the fears activated by disaster are not simply media inventions. As Barry Glassner explains, the media tends to address worries that resonate with audiences, but it heightens these fears to promote ratings. *The Culture of Fear: Why Are Americans Afraid of the Wrong Things* (New York: Basic Books, 1999), xxvi. Significantly, similar concerns were expressed about the culture of fear in some evangelical circles. "Fear," as the editors of the leading evangelical journal *Christianity Today* assured readers, "was designed by God to give our bodies the sudden bursts of strength and speed we need in emergencies. But when fear becomes a permanent condition, it can paralyze the spirit, keeping us from taking the risks of generosity, love, and vulnerability that characterize citizens of God's kingdom." "Fear and Hate," posted on *Christianity Today*, September 11, 2001; http://www.christianitytoday.com/ct/2001/137/30.0.html.

91. George Gerbner, "Violence and Terror in and by the Media," in *Media, Crisis and Democracy*, ed. Mark Raboy and Bernard Dagenais (Newbury Park, Calif.: Sage, 1992), 94–107.

92. Stephen Battaglio, for example, examined a random poll of 504 adults with a margin of error +/- 4.5 percent that suggested a "fearful reaction to the nonstop stream of live press conferences with uncertain and at times confused government officials, constant on-screen tickers . . . and doomsday scenarios from expert talking heads." There was a significant gender dimension here with 18 percent of women saying the news was frightening and 5 percent saying it was reassuring; by contrast, 7 percent of men reported that it was frightening while 14 percent found it reassuring; 37 percent of all respondents found it "both reassuring and frightening," and 38 percent "neither." In a related story, the American Psychiatric Association suggested that one way to cope with "bioterrorism anxiety" was to stop watching TV. "After the Deluge," *TV Guide*, November 17–23, 2001, 25, 58–59.

93. Silvio Waisbord, "Journalism, Risk, and Patriotism," in *Journalism after September 11*, ed. Zelizer and Allan, 208.

94. This, of course, as Michael Massing pointed out, violated "every canon of good journalism." "Press Watch," *Nation*, October 15, 2001, 6.

95. Fox News chairman Roger Ailes meanwhile sent a private memo to President Bush offering explicitly political advice about how to recruit public approval for his policy responses to 9/11. Scott Collins, *Crazy Like a Fox: The Inside Story of How Fox News Beat CNN* (New York: Portfolio, 2004), 170–71, 188. Also see Bob Woodward, *Bush at War* (New York: Simon and Schuster, 2003), 207. In return, the chairman of the Federal Communications Commission, Michael Powell (the son of Colin Powell, who, as chairman of the Joint Chiefs of Staff, directed the Gulf War) invoked the "thrilling" nature of Gulf War coverage as evidence for his position that media concentration, of the sort that enriched companies such as Fox, produced better coverage. These same corporations, all too aware that they had a financial interest in protecting politicians who favored the deregulation of their industry, showed a marked reluctance to air programs critical of conservatives. McChesney, *Problem of the Media*, 280.

96. Amy Reynolds and Brooke Barnett, "'America under Attack': CNN's Verbal and Visual Framing of September 11," in *Media Representations of September 11*, ed. Chermak, Bailey, and Brown, 91, 92.

97. Robert W. McChesney, "Thank the Lord, It's a War to End All Wars . . . Or, How I Learned to Suspend Critical Judgment and Love the Bomb," in *9/11 in American Culture*, ed. Norman K. Denzin and Yvonne S. Lincoln (Walnut Creek, Calif.: Altamira Press, 2003), 116.

98. Lee Quinby offers a particularly bleak analysis of apocalypticism as a worldview that

> fuels discord, breeds anxiety or apathy, and sometimes causes panic. Decision-making suffers when it takes apocalyptic form—whether at the level of individual, everyday personal choices or of local, national, and international government, military, and peace-keeping deliberations. What makes apocalypse so compelling is its promise of future perfection, eternal happiness, and godlike understanding of life, but it is that very will to absolute power that produces its compulsions of violence, hatred, and oppression. (*Anti-Apocalypse: Exercises in Genealogical Criticism* [Minneapolis: University of Minnesota Press, 1994], 162)

For a similar view, see Robert Jay Lifton, *Superpower Syndrome: America's Apocalyptic Confrontation with the World* (New York: Thunder's Mouth Press/Nation Books, 2003). After interviewing readers of the *Left Behind* series, Amy Johnson Frykholm, however, warned against a reductive analysis of rank-and-file born-again Christians. "Outside evangelical circles," she acknowledged, "*Left Behind* is frequently viewed as evidence of a perilous shift toward apocalyptic, fanatical, fear-based thinking on the part of the American public." But while this might properly reflect the values of the novels, most readers were also motivated by more kindly Christian values: "I could tangibly sense the way that apocalyptic language and belief in the rapture gave them hope, both cultivated and assuaged fear, and compelled them toward compassion for the world." *Rapture Culture*, 175, 8. Nancy Gibbs concurred that "most Christians, although affected by Revelation, feel led by other Scripture to make the current world a better place and to understand 'love thy neighbor' more broadly than as an order to convert him or leave him to the Antichrist." Gibbs, "Apocalypse Now," 47.

99. The White House, according to journalist Teresa Wiltz, consulted with Hollywood executives "in a much-publicized gathering" about how to fight the war on terrorism. "Playing in the Shadows: Popular Culture in the Aftermath of Sept. 11 Is a Chorus without a Hook, a Movie without an Ending," *Washington Post*, November 19, 2001, C01.

100. Of course, this also had a prophetic silver lining. LaHaye expected these developments to set "the stage for a 'one world order' governed by you know who." And this would bring on the apocalypse. "The Prophetic Significance of Sept. 11, 2001," *Pre-Tribulation Newsletter*, September 2001; http://www.timlahaye.com/about_ministry/pdf/lahaye_sept11.pdf. Another piece, "Terrorism in America: Foreshadow of End-Time Events," in the same journal spells out the likely sequence of events: "More than likely Americans will have to give up more of our individual liberties so that the government can provide safety for its citizens. An increase in governmental oversight of the individual is also preparatory for the global economic control that the Antichrist will exert in the tribulation (Rev. 13)."

101. "Emergency is a direct means of response which leaves no time for either analysis, forecasting, or prevention. It is an immediate protective reflex rather than a sober quest for long-term solutions. It neglects the fact that situations have to be put in perspective and that future events need to be anticipated." Jérôme Bindé, "Toward an Ethic of the Future," *Public Culture* 12, no. 1 (2000): 52.

102. Henry A. Giroux, "Democracy and the Politics of Terrorism: Community, Fear, and the Suppression of Dissent," in *9/11 in American Culture*, ed. Denzin and Lincoln, 247. This aligns with the analysis of religious scholar John Millbank who sought thereby to explain the appearance in the aftermath of the attacks of "so much apparently insane language concerning 'infinite' processes: an infinite war, infinite justice, infinite retribution—sustained in George Bush's terrifying address to Congress. There he declared, for the first time since Hitler's announcement of the Third Reich, a kind of state of perpetual emergency." John Millbank, "Sovereignty, Empire, Capital, and Terror," *South Atlantic Quarterly* 101, no. 2 (Spring 2002): 309–10.

103. *9/11 Commission Report*, 1–46.

104. John D. Kelly, "U.S. Power, after 9/11 and before It: If Not an Empire, Then What?" *Public Culture* 15, no. 2 (2003): 365.

105. The Project for a New American Century, *Rebuilding America's Defenses: Strategy, Forces, and Resources for a New Century* (September 2000), 51; http://www.informationclearinghouse.info/pdf/RebuildingAmericasDefenses.pdf.

106. Christopher Bollyn, "America 'Pearl Harbored,'" *AmericanFreePress.Net*, April 12, 2004, 2; www.americanfreepress.net.

107. Bob Woodward, *Plan of Attack* (New York: Simon and Schuster, 2004), 25.

108. Richard A. Clarke, *Against All Enemies: Inside America's War on Terror* (New York: Free Press, 2004), 30.

109. Ibid., 262, 257.

110. Employing "flexible interpretations" of the Stafford Act, federal officials promised funds not only to restore but to "improve the overall transportation system

in Lower Manhattan." U.S. General Accounting Office, "Disaster Assistance: Information on FEMA's Post 9/11 Public Assistance to the New York City Area," 6.

111. According to a study by the Carnegie Endowment for International Peace, "an economic doomsday was widely feared: a lengthy stoppage of trading, a market plunge, plummeting consumer confidence, capital flight from the United States, borders closed to trade, and a worldwide slowdown or even recession." Jessica T. Mathews, "September 11, One Year Later: A World of Change," *Carnegie Endowment for International Peace Policy Brief,* Special Edition 18, August 2002, 1–3.

112. In addition to the twin towers, fifteen other major buildings at or near Ground Zero were either totally or partly destroyed, along with subway stations and tunnels. Juan González, *Fallout: The Environmental Consequences of the World Trade Center Collapse* (New York: New Press, 2002), 35. The city controller in New York City estimated the cost of the disaster at over $105 billion. The Century Foundation, "Economic Impact of Terrorist Attack: New York City Fact Sheet" (www.tcf.org), 3, 1.

113. Clarke, *Against All Enemies,* 24.

114. Natural Resources Defense Council, *The Environmental Impacts of the World Trade Center Attacks: A Preliminary Assessment* (February 2002), 10; www.nrdc .org/air/pollution/wtc/wtc.pd. On September 18, for example, Environmental Protection Agency administrator Christie Whitman was "glad to reassure the people of New York and Washington, D.C. that their air is safe to breathe and their water is safe to drink." "Whitman Details Ongoing Agency Efforts to Monitor Disaster Sites, Contribute to Cleanup Efforts"; http://www.epa .gov/wtc/stories/headline_091801.htm.

115. It is entirely possible, as investigative journalist Juan González maintains, that the most damaging long-term effects of the disaster will be environmental. *Fallout,* 22.

116. "An intense fire, fueled by thousands of gallons of jet fuel, spewed toxic gases into the air. Asbestos, used in the construction of one of the towers, rained down over the streets. Burning computers and other electrical equipment sent dioxins, mercury and other hazardous substances into the drifting plume. Vast quantities of dust, glass and pulverized cement were blown throughout the surrounding neighborhood." Natural Resources Defense Council, *Environmental Impacts of the World Trade Center Attacks,* 3, 6, 14; www.nrdc.org/air/ pollution/wtc/wtc.pd.

117. Mathews, "September 11, One Year Later," 1–3.

118. David Harvey, *The Condition of Postmodernity: An Enquiry into the Origins of Cultural Change* (Cambridge: Blackwell, 1990), 121–97.

119. George Steinmetz, "The State of Emergency and the Revival of American Imperialism: Toward an Authoritarian Post-Fordism," *Public Culture* 15, no. 2 (2003): 327.

120. Or, as Tom Tomorrow writes of the subversive political art form, "We are cartoonists, and we are expected to be zany and amusing at all times. Even when the subjects with which we deal are crushingly depressing, or maddening, or, most often these past few years, some combination of all these things." Introduction to Ted Rall, *Generalissimo el Busho: Essays and Cartoons on the Bush Years* (New York: Nantier Beall Minoustchine, 2004), 8.

121. His "definition of Commerz" is telling:

> Abbr. com., comm. The buying and selling of goods, especially on a large scale. 2. Intellectual exchange or social intercourse. 3. Sexual intercourse . . . (Old French, from LATIN commercium: com (collective) + merz (stem merc-), merchandise. To find a commix (Abbr. com) free of commerce, an ART that can sustain and also sustain the ARTIST (to make a 'living'). Fuck it. Fuck me. I'm fucked: fukemism. (Quoted in Deborah R. Geis, ed., *Considering Maus: Approaches to Art Spiegelman's "Survivor's Tale" of the Holocaust* [Tuscaloosa: University of Alabama Press, 2003], 11n10)

122. Art Spiegelman, "Re: Covers," in *110 Stories*, ed. Baer, 284.
123. Marianne Hirsch, "Editor's Column: Collateral Damage," *PMLA* 119, no. 5 (October 2004): 1214.
124. All quotations from Spiegelman, *In the Shadow of No Towers*.

Epilogue

1. *The Federal Response to Hurricane Katrina: Lessons Learned* (Washington, D.C.: White House, February 2006), 7–8. For updated statistics, see the entry for Hurricane Katrina in Wikipedia: http://en.wikipedia.org/wiki/Hurricane_ Katrina.
2. This was acknowledged by congressional investigations: "It remains difficult to understand how government could respond so ineffectively to a disaster that was anticipated for years, and for which specific dire warnings had been issued for days. This crisis was not only predictable, it was predicted." *A Failure of Initiative: Final Report of the Select Bipartisan Committee to Investigate the Preparation for and Response to Hurricane Katrina* (Washington, D.C.: GPO, 2006), xi.
3. Ibid., x.
4. "Four Places Where the System Broke Down," *Time*, September 19, 2005, 37.
5. Sidney Blumenthal, "Katrina Comes Home to Roost," *Guardian*, September 2, 2005; http://www.guardian.co.uk/katrina/story/0,16441,1561356,00.html. For an account of the many predictions that New Orleans was doomed to destruction by a major hurricane, see Mike Davis, "Catastrophic Economics: The Predators of New Orleans," *Le Monde Diplomatique*, October 2005; http:// mondediplo.com/2005/10/02katrina.
6. Dr. John quoted in *U.S. News and World Report*, September 19, 2005, 24.
7. "Slowly Recovering," *U.S. News and World Report*, September 19, 2005, 44.
8. Ibid.
9. *Economist*, September 10–16, 2005; *New Republic*, September 19, 2005; *Time*, September 19, 2005; *Newsweek*, September 19, 2005; *U.S. News and World Report*, September 19, 2005.
10. *A Failure of Initiative*, x.
11. "Four Places Where the System Broke Down," 40.
12. According to one survey, 80 percent of FEMA employees believed these changes had weakened the agency. Angie C. Mark, "A Crisis Agency in Crisis," *U.S. News and World Report*, September 19, 2005, 37.
13. Before Hurricane Katrina, 75 percent of federal disaster contributions to states were earmarked for antiterrorism measures. "Four Places Where the System Broke Down," 40.

14. Anna Quindlen, "Don't Mess with Mother," *Newsweek*, September 19, 2005, 76.
15. John Vidal, "Why City's Defences Were Down," *Guardian*, September 1, 2005; http://www.guardian.co.uk/katrina/story/0,16441,1560764,00.html.
16. John M. Barry, "The Prologue, and Maybe the Coda," *New York Times*, September 4, 2005, sec. 4, p. 4.
17. Vidal, "Why City's Defences Were Down."
18. For one typical assessment, see the editorial by Mortimer B. Zuckerman, "Fixing What's Broken," *U.S News and World Report*, September 19, 2005, 68.
19. Quindlen, "Don't Mess with Mother," 76.
20. Klaus Jacob, quoted in Jay Tolson, "Soul Survivor," *U.S. News and World Report*, September 19, 2005, 48.
21. Winds that reached 175 mph knocked out 10 percent of the nation's refining industry and over 25 percent of domestic oil production by shutting down offshore platforms and onshore wells. This had an immediate effect on oil prices. There was talk of a major recession if oil prices continued to rise steeply in the absence of reserves. This revealed the vulnerability of an economy overdependent on dwindling reserves of fossil fuels. See, for example, Robert J. Samuelson, "Why Cheap Gas Is a Bad Habit," *Newsweek*, September 19, 2005, 41, and Jad Mouawad, "Katrina's Shock to the System: It's That '70s Feeling, but the World Has Changed," *New York Times*, September 4, 2005, sec. 3, p. 1.
22. "Katrina," *New Republic*, September 19, 2005, 9.
23. Ibid.
24. "The Military Boss," *Time*, September 19, 2005, 57.
25. Fifteen percent of white households also lacked cars. Jason DeParle, "What Happens to a Race Deferred," *New York Times*, September 4, 2005, sec. 4, p. 4.
26. Ibid.
27. Jonathan Alter, "The Other America," *Newsweek*, September 19, 2005, 42.
28. Ibid., 44.
29. Noam Scheiber, "Poverty Line," *New Republic*, September 19, 2005, 6.
30. "Four Places Where the System Broke Down," 40.
31. Howard Fineman, "A Storm-Tossed Boss," *Newsweek*, September 19, 2005, 38.
32. On the contrary, Bush, as Mike Davis explained, "wooed his political base with a dream list of long-sought-after conservative social reforms: school and housing vouchers, a central role for churches, an urban homestead lottery, extensive tax breaks to businesses, the creation of a Gulf Opportunity Zone, and the suspension of annoying government regulations (in the fine print these include prevailing wages in construction and environmental regulations on offshore drilling" (Davis, "Catastrophic Economics"). See also Naomi Klein, "The Rise of Disaster Capitalism," *Nation*, May 2, 2005, http://www.thenation.com/doc/20050502/klein, and Michael Eric Dyson, *Come Hell or High Water: Hurricane Katrina and the Color of Disasters* (New York: Basic Civitas, 2006), chap. 8, "Capitalizing on Disaster."
33. Anna Mulrine, "Lots of Blame: But It's No Game," *U.S. News and World Report*, September 19, 2005, 35.

Index

9/11, 173, 175–79, 208; business and government leaders used the disaster to further "deregulate" the economy, 23, 180, 202–4; business and government used disaster to concentrate power, 180; commodification of calamity, 192–96; coverage of it fed feelings of dread and hostility, 198; coverage of stimulated compassion and concern, 198; Digital Archive, 191; disaster institutionalized by political leaders, 200; expectation that disaster might release us from the frivolous preoccupations of daily life, 184; extraordinary variety of reactions to, 6–7, 180, 181; federal relief and compensation payments, 197–98; greatest outpouring of private charitable aid in U.S. history, 197; Ground Zero health risks, 203; interpretation of as an act of God, 185–86; major networks excluded advertisements from news programs until September 15, 192–93; marginalized communities within the United States, 182; mass-media conditioning made it difficult to summon authentic emotional responses to, 182–83; media avoided display of most shocking images, 193; media conversion of complex geopolitical situation into struggle between good and evil, 199; media conversion of into human-interest story, 194–96; one-fourth of all Americans believed the events were predicted in the Bible, 185; popular tendency to view as a test of character, 186; sentimental discourses on, 193; served the national security state, 23, 180, 201, 207; tendency of onlookers to treat · as a spectacle, 183; testimonies from Ground Zero, 177. See also World Trade Center, destruction of

9/11 (video), 287n60

9/11 Commission Report, The, 201, 282n14

9/11 Fund, 197

ABC, 193

Acts of God (Steinberg), 24

Adams, Henry, 26

Aetna insurance company, 83

Dick, Kathy, 191–92
Dick, Philip K., 207
Die Hard, 6
disaster: phenomenology of, 254n13; photographs of, 259n57
disaster enthusiasm, ingredient of the modernizing process, 103
disaster films, 106, 166, 167, 183, 287n69; articulate resentments about modernity, 168; and conservative Christians, 188; images of mass destruction, 177; response to conditions of modernity, 142; in the 1950s, 25
Disaster Loan Program, 155
disaster mitigation, subordinated to the demands of development, 171
disaster relief: consistent with principles of social insurance, 131; largely improvised in the face of actual calamities, 23; support for largely transcends party differences, 271n171
Disaster Relief Act of 1950, 11–12, 23, 25, 31, 60, 142, 143, 150–52, 154–55, 158, 169
Disaster Relief Act of 1969, 171
Disaster Research Group, 279n111
disasters: and the American real, 183–85; awarded more concern than chronic or invisible structural problems, 181; belief in the supernatural sources of, 11; commercializing of, 123–32; contribution to modern thought and activity, 14; defined, 11–12; and desire, 108; destruction liberates and recycles capital, 24, 76, 83, 86; diminished boundary between man-made and natural in postmodern America, 180; distinctions between natural and man-made, 12, 164; economics of, 77–80, 81, 87, 202; enjoyment of depends on a sense of insulation from personal danger, 127–28; as events that liberate and channel chaotic passions that propel the civilizing process, 120; faith in the providential purpose of, 109;

generation of cultural production, 14, 205; laboratories for social reform, 23; may enable survival of corporate society by providing an outlet for modern discontents, 132; middle-class opinion shapers make the case for the emotional benefits of, 119; modern imagination of, 163–68; 1950s marked a significant shift in ways of seeing, 166–67; as objects of popular fantasy, 6; produce widespread "traumatic reactions," 12; promoted popularity of newspapers, 260n59; put pressure on civil liberties, 200; research into the social and psychological dimensions of, 279n111; role in construction of American identities, power relations, economic systems, and environmental practices, 3; role in shaping American beliefs and systems, 32; sensational and sentimental media coverage of, 196; as spectacles, 6–8; thrill response to, 105–6; viewed through visual and emotional language of the blockbuster, 181; view of as material blessings since the nineteenth century, 24, 32, 44–45, 50–53, 75–76, 77–78, 202. *See also* spectacles of chaos
disaster-security state, 23, 25, 180, 204
disaster sermons ("jeremiads"), 63, 79, 235n71
disaster shows, 123–24, 126, 167, 268n145
disaster studies, 163–64
disaster victims: direct grants to, 169; restitution to, 160
distributive justice, politics of, 171
Ditzel, Paul C., 259n57
Dodd, Thomas J., 161
Doll, Bob, 211–12
Donahue, Phil, 200
Donne, John, "A Valediction: Forbidding Mourning," 34
Doughton, Russell, 189
Dow Jones industrial average, after Hurricane Katrina, 212

innovating and expanding American economy, 76, 99–100, 253n100
Greider, William, 76
Grid, The, 288n76
Griffith, D. W., 187–88
Ground Zero, health risks, 203
Grutzner, Charles, 159, 160
Gulf War coverage, 290n95
Guthrie, Woody, 218

Hagen, Harold C., 150–51, 152
Hall, David D., 46
Hall, G. Stanley, 125, 265n108
Halliburton, 217
Ham and Eggs fire, 69–70
Harper's Weekly, 119
Harriman, Carter H., 261n64
Hartt, Rollin Lynde, 125–26, 127
Harvey, David, 3, 75, 85, 204, 221n25; technical analysis of "creative destruction," 249n54
Harvey, George, 75–76, 79, 94, 248n43; welcomed the San Francisco earthquake as an investment opportunity, 86
Haussmann, Baron, 89–90, 91, 92–93; admission to the Académie des Beaux Arts, 249n55; determination to save Paris from an urban crisis, 89; gentrification of Paris, 89; harnessed creative destruction for the purposes of the imperial state, 89; rebuilding of Paris, 92–93; reforms promoted capital accumulation and economic productivity in imperial Paris, 250n67
Hawgood, Mary, 121
Hegel, G. W. F., "slaughterbench" of history, 3
Hepburn Act, 256n23
Hicks, Chief Charles, 59
Hiroshima, mushroom cloud produced by the atomic bombing of, 138, 139
Hirsch, Marianne, 206
History of Plymouth Plantation (Bradford), 37
Hollywood film industry, treats wars and natural disasters alike, 180. *See also* disaster films

Hone, Philip, 62, 81, 82, 84, 246n28, 247n32
Honoré, Russel, 216
Hoover, Herbert: coordinated rescue and relief operations after flood of 1927, 146–47; *Memoirs*, 147
Hubbard, William, 45–46, 51
Hume, David, 38, 229n27
Hurricane Andrew, 172, 271n171
Hurricane Betsy, 170
hurricane control, 279n109
Hurricane Diane, 142, 170; "Naugatuck, August 19, 1955," after the floods following, 156
Hurricane Donna, 171
Hurricane Hazel, 274n23
Hurricane Hugo, 99, 172
Hurricane Katrina: attention brought by to issues of class, race, and poverty, 25, 205, 215–17; called into question the efficacy of National Response Plan, 212; and corporations "profiting from disaster," 217; current affairs magazine coverage, 212; effect on oil production, 294n21; focused attention on the environmental and social costs of modern development, 214–15; focused demands for restoration of social contract between government and the people, 215; and the "murder" of New Orleans, 209–18
hurricane research, 163
hurricanes: early descriptions of, 226n12; summer of 1955, 135–36
Hussein, Saddam, 184
hyperreal apocalypse, 185–92
hyperreal imagination, 178, 181, 282n8

imagination of disaster: contribution to modern culture, 256n25; multiple rather than singular, 181–82; role in formation of American individualism, 40
"Imagination of Disaster, The" (Sontag), 166
immigration, 57, 240n139
indentured servants, 57
Independence Day, 6

303

Mather, Cotton (*continued*)
for dirty chimney, 50; suspected
that American Wilderness had
been Satan's realm before arrival
of English Protestants, 229n26;
suspicion that witches were
responsible for earthquakes, 38;
worry about absence of calamities, 40
Mather, Increase, 33, 54; calamity
offered corrective to the materialism
of the age, 50–51; *The Day of Trouble
is Near*, 47; disaster as unique
burden of chosen people, 41; on
fires that swept through Boston
over the seventeenth century,
51–52; jeremiads, 63; justification
of his exclusive authority as an
interpreter of disasters, 48; King
Philip's War "intensified" the
politics of calamity, 46; on need
for moral and spiritual reformation
to forestall future punishments,
46–49; personal authority and
influence, 47; preoccupation with
calamities as wonders that inspired
scientific inquiry, 48–49; *Remarkable
Providences*, 49, 109; response to
Boston fire, 47–48, 78, 235n76
Maus (Spiegelman), 206
May, Lary, 268n145
McCarthy, Joe, 141
McChesney, Robert, 199
McEwan, Ian, 29
McLuhan, Marshall, 4
Meat Act, 256n23
media coverage of disasters:
9/11, 193, 199, 194–96, 182–83;
erosion of deliberative democracy,
197; formation of imagined
communities, 130, 141; nation-
building role, 130; politics of disaster,
140; presents an activist federal
government in a favorable light,
141; sensational and sentimental and
lacking in historical or geopolitical
understanding, 196; tends to present
politics and morality in black-and-
white terms, 200. *See also* news
coverage; newspapers; television

Meiji Restoration, Japan, 20
mercantile (protocapitalist) economy,
17
Merrill Lynch Investment Managers,
211
middle- and upper-class Americans,
tendency to regard disasters as
"blessings," 76
Midwestern floods of 1993, 281n144
Mill, John Stuart, 80
Millbank, John, 291n102
millennialism: beliefs of broad sectors
of American public, 186; disasters as
portents of the apocalypse, 43, 44;
and natural calamities in the 1810s,
241n143
Miller, Perry, 225n2, 228n22; "The End
of the World," 165
Mills, C. Wright, 168
Mississippi flood of 1927, 24, 27, 142;
caused by modern disaster policy,
145–46; led to modern system of
disaster management, 146–50;
local policies and practices favored
whites at the expense of the black
population, 147–48; and the politics
of flood control, 143; "refugee camp
on the levee," 146; a typical highway
scene, 145
Mississippi River Commission, 144–45
Missouri River, 170
"Model of Christian Charity, A"
(Winthrop), 55
modernity: and American ways of
imagining and managing disasters,
181; born of engagement with the
perils and ordeals of everyday life,
13; catastrophic logic of, 9–20, 26,
256n25; defined, 12–13; as a dynamic
system of spatial reorganization
and capital accumulation (creative
destruction), 10, 14, 84; established
conditions for future calamities,
18; extreme, 19; "love" of disasters,
103; as a plural rather than singular
condition, 13, 221n26; as a project
originating in the social and cultural
conditions of seventeenth- and
eighteenth-century Europe, 13;

Whewell, William, 242n153
Whitefield, George, 15, 43, 221n33, 233n53
White Noise (DeLillo), 1–2, 4–5, 8, 9, 10, 19, 166, 177, 188, 210
Whitman, Christie, 292n114
Wiebe, Robert, 104
"wild-cat" banks, 81
Wilentz, Sean, 247n32
Wilkerson, David, 185–86
Wilson, Woodrow, 158
Wiltz, Teresa, 291n99
Winthrop, John, 39, 40–41, 55, 228n20, 232n42
Winthrop, John (great-great grandson), 22
Witt, James Lee, 281n144

Wolfowitz, Paul, 201, 202
Woodruff, Judy, 193
Wordsworth, William, 110, 258n47
WorldCom, 203
World Trade Center, destruction of, 6–7, 25, 175–79. *See also* 9/11
Wormeley, Katharine, 261n72
Worner, Ruth, 101
WPIX, 193

X-Files: Fight the Future, 172–73

yellow fever, 223n45
Youth's Companion, 102

Žižek, Slavoj, 6, 185
Zubly, John Joachim, 44